The Crisis in Social Security

Duke Press Policy Studies

Population and Development in Rural Egypt
Allen C. Kelley, Atef M. Khalifa, *and* M. Nabil El-Khorazaty

U.S. Immigration Policy
Edited by Richard R. Hofstetter; *Foreword by* William French Smith

Alcohol in the USSR
A Statistical Study
Vladimir G. Treml; *Foreword by* Murray Feshbach

The Crisis in Social Security

Economic and Political Origins

Carolyn L. Weaver

Duke Press Policy Studies

Durham, N.C.   1982

The research for this study was partially supported by the National
Science Foundation under Grant SOC 79-08561, The Liberty Fund
and the Center for Libertarian Studies, and The Fiscal Policy Council.

Library of Congress Cataloging in Publication Data

Weaver, Carolyn L.
  The crisis in social security

  (Duke Press policy studies)
  Includes bibliographical references and
index.
  1. Social security—United States—History.
I. Title. II. Series.
HD7125.W397   1982   368.4'3'00973   82-9623
ISBN 0-8223-0474-0

Contents

Tables and Figures

Tables

Figures

Preface

By any reasonable system of accounting, the Social Security system is going broke. Collecting taxes at a rate of $16 billion a month, the system is officially projected to be unable to continue paying full benefits beyond the next eighteen to twenty-four months. Some $200–$400 billion may be required—over and above the more than $3 trillion that will be collected—just to keep the system afloat until 1992. If the program were to simply stop collecting payroll tax contributions, less than three months would elapse before the last dollar in benefits was paid to any of the system's 36 million beneficiaries.

However significant this "short-term" problem is judged to be, it pales by comparison to the long-term financial condition of Social Security. According to Social Security actuaries, in excess of 40 percent of the benefit obligations we expect to incur in any year after 2025 can not be met with the current tax structure. The tax rate that would be necessary to finance benefits when the college students of today begin to retire is on the order of 25–30 percent (employee and employer, combined), and could be as high as 40–50 percent. The system, as Haeworth Robertson has described it, is a slumbering giant awakening.

How is Congress dealing with this reality? Congress has been effectively paralyzed by the politics of Social Security. Nowhere is this more evident than in the current round of negotiations over the Federal budget deficit. As Congress and the Administration struggle to control the largest Federal budget in history, scrutinizing programs ranging from national defense to adoption assistance for needy children, Social Security—the largest single item in that budget—has been removed from consideration. The program that spends $1 for every $4 spent by the entire Federal Government has been deemed "off limits"—at least, as they say, until the President's National Commission on Social Security Reform makes its report later this year.

This book is about how Social Security got where it is today. From the perspective of a political economist, this book offers an explanation for Social Security's emergence, growth and evolving crisis that is rooted in the economic approach to the study of government and the rich body of research that now exists on the economics of bureaucracy, political participation, and information and agenda control. It is my hope that this book will jointly illustrate the power of these models in explaining real political phenomena as well as the power of Social Security—as an important democratic institution—in influencing political decisions. The book concludes with my thoughts on the direction that a reform must take if Social Security is to prevail as a politically and economically viable system in the decades ahead.

I am indebted to many people and institutions for their assistance in the completion of this book. For valuable comments at various stages in the preparation of the book, I would like to thank: Richard Wagner of Florida State University, Robert Mackay of the University of Maryland, James Buchanan and Gordon Tullock of Virginia Polytechnic Institute and State University, Ed West of Carleton University, Robert Staaf of the University of Miami, William Mitchell of the University of Oregon, Jonathan Hughes of Northwestern University, Gary Libecap of Texas A & M, Gary Freeman of the University of Texas, Edgar Browning of the University of Virginia, Laurence Kotlikoff of Yale University, Joseph Reid of Virginia Polytechnic Institute and State University, Ed Berkowitz of Brandeis University, and Robert Myers and Robert Ball of National Commission on Social Security Reform. For their expert technical assistance throughout the preparation of the manuscript, Margaret Weaver, Brenda Madison, and Robert Wright each deserve a special note of thanks. Finally, I am grateful for the financial assistance provided by the National Science Foundation, the Liberty Fund, the Center for Libertarian Studies, and the Fiscal Policy Council.

I should note in closing that the research for this book was completed in 1980. The exceptionally valuable experience I have gained since that time, while on Capitol Hill, has not prompted me to alter the manuscript. Instead, it has underscored the seriousness of Social Security as a potent political and economic force yet to be reckoned with.

The views expressed here and any errors remaining are mine alone, of course, and should not be ascribed to any member of the Senate Finance Committee, the National Commission on Social Security Reform, the intstitutions that have supported my research, or to any of those who commented on the manuscript.

The Crisis in Social Security

Chapter 1. The Political Economy of Government Growth

What is clear from the proliferation of bureaucracy is that government programs grow in ways that are often unforeseen and with results that are often unpredictable. The federal agency that assists more Americans than any other—the Social Security Administration—is a perfect case in point. Founded during the Depression, the almost universally praised institution now sends a monthly check to one in every seven Americans.[1]

In the mid-1970s it was announced that the Social Security program had "unexpectedly" accrued a deficit of \$4.3 trillion, triggering the widely held belief that there was a "crisis" in Social Security.[2] Elimination of this deficit would, it was suggested, require massive tax increases. Payroll tax rates projected in 1972 to peak at 11.9 percent (employee and employer combined) early in the twenty-first century were projected only three years later to reach nearly 30 percent by the year 2050. To this state of affairs past Secretary of Treasury William Simon was prompted to say, "The future prospects of the system as we know it are grim."[3]

According to the official perspective, which saw the crisis as essentially financial, the 1977 amendments put the claims of impending bankruptcy to rest and marked the passing of the crisis. Indexing provisions that overresponded to inflation were modified, and tax-rate and taxable earnings schedules were adjusted upward so that projected deficits were "slashed" by 80 percent. In the words of the acting commissioner of social security, the system was, once again, "sound" and would "remain so."[4] For President Carter, these "tremendous achievements" represented the most important amendments to the law since the program's inception in 1935.[5]

From an actuarial perspective, however, the deficit that remained was still quite substantial. Even with the 1977 amendments, which entailed the largest peacetime tax increase in United States history, the Social Security Board of Trustees now reports that the old-age and survivors' insurance program will be unable to pay full benefits beyond June 1983—and even this will require a transfusion from the disability and hospital insurance trust funds. Under forseeable circumstances, the combined reserves of the entire Social Security system are then projected to be depleted within the following eighteen months.[6] Over the long term the system's deficit—the amount by which benefit promises are expected to exceed scheduled tax income over the next seventy-five years—is projected to reach \$6 trillion. By 2030 expenditures are projected to equal 26 percent of taxable payroll in the economy, outstripping revenues by roughly 72 percent.

Stated somewhat differently, when the college students of today retire, all three trust funds are projected to be exhausted and people who are working at that time—numbering only two per beneficiary—will be expected to impose a 26 percent tax rate on themselves to finance Social Security alone. Evidently, it cannot reasonably be said that the financial crisis in Social Security is behind us.

But is the Social Security crisis simply financial in nature? Do the fundamental sources of this crisis lie in such recent and "unexpected" problems as double-indexing, cyclical recessions, and declining fertility rates? Long before any of these problems materialized, the size and cost of Social Security grew at unprecedented rates. From a limited objective, old-age insurance program designed to distribute monthly benefits to retired workers, Social Security grew in just forty-six years to encompass old-age, survivors, disability, and hospital insurance, distributing monthly cash benefits on a pay-as-you-go basis to retired and disabled workers, to their spouses, ex-spouses, children, grandchildren, parents, and grandparents, and, in the event of death, to their survivors as well. Between 1940 and 1980 the number of beneficiaries thus grew from 222,000 to 35 million, and they now, on average, receive a monthly benefit in excess of $340. While this expansion took place, the combined employee-employer tax rate was increased from 2 percent paid by 35 million people to 12.26 percent paid by more than 115 million people, and the maximum tax payment (employee and employer combined) rose from $60 to $3,175, more than ten-fold in real terms. Having spent a half trillion dollars in the thirty-nine years between 1937 and 1975, the largest domestic government program in the United States spent another half trillion dollars by the end of 1980 and will have spent another half trillion dollars by the end of 1983.[7]

That we are now faced with an enormous program that few can fully comprehend and that this program poses serious economic, political, and social challenges that go well beyond restoring actuarial "balance" seems unquestionable. Furthermore, how we choose in the decades ahead to deal with these challenges will be determined in large part by our understanding of the political and economic forces that shaped the system to date. In the words of Friedrich A. Hayek, Nobel Laureate, "Political opinion and views about historical events ever have been and always must be closely connected. Past experience is the foundation on which our beliefs about the desirability of different policies and institutions are mainly based. . . . Yet we can hardly profit from past experience unless the facts from which we draw our conclusions are correct."[8] Misunderstandings about the nature and historical evolution of the crisis in Social Security can produce, at best, little more than legislative patchwork which holds the system together until the next "crisis" inevitably develops.

Drawing on the insights of the economic approach to the study of government, the central purpose of this study is to critically reexamine the emergence, redirection, and growth of Social Security so as to provide new perspective on the current-day crisis. To date, there have been no attempts to explain the evolution of Social Security within a consistent framework that incorporates both the demand for public-sector activity and the legislative-bureaucratic supply.[9] The history and institutional evolution of the program are recast and reviewed in this way so that the size, growth, and emergent crisis in Social Security need not be viewed as entirely "unforeseen" or "with results that are often unpredictable."

While it may be difficult to generalize from the findings of a study of the life of a single government program, even one as significant as Social Security, it is nevertheless hoped that these findings will contribute to our understanding of the process by which government grows. The weight of the empirical evidence of a number of such studies, taken together, may allow us to reject existing theories of politics and government or suggest new refinements. A better awareness and deeper understanding of political processes in the United States—the forces that have led to the pronounced centralization of government, the dramatic increase in government's share of the economy, and the acceleration in the growth of nonmarket controls—are much-needed steps toward reform.[10]

Alternative Frameworks for Explaining Nonmarket Institutional Change

A general framework for explaining nonmarket institutional change or, more specifically, the emergence and development of government institutions, requires the integration and extension of two distinct views within the economic approach to the study of politics. Referred to as the "demand side" and the "supply side", these two views constitute conflicting explanations of the determination of political outcomes.[11] According to the demand-side view, the government is composed of public-spirited or competitively constrained politicians and bureaucrats who respond passively and automatically to satisfy the demands of citizen-voters. According to the supply-side view, the government is comprised of self-interested politicians and bureaucrats who participate actively in the collective choice process, possess significant discretionary power, and affect political outcomes to advance their own ends. A brief look at these two views reveals their strengths and weaknesses for explaining the development of Social Security and makes evident the need for integration.

The Demand-Side View and Implications for Social Security

In its pure form the demand-side view of the collective choice process embodies a democratic conception of government in which political outcomes reflect the demands of citizen-voters as transmitted and aggregated by the political process. The observed growth and development of government institutions are traced directly to changes in citizens' demands for more public goods and services or more government activity in general, and to their acquiescence in paying additional taxes.[12] The demands may be many and varied but, according to the demand-side view, they generally result from the inefficiencies and inequities created by market failures.

More specifically, the state and the various programs it undertakes are seen to emerge as if by complex agreements among the members of society to capture the efficiency gains from collective action.[13] That is, since the provision of public goods, the internalization of external economies and diseconomies, the regulation of natural monopolies and imperfect competition, the redistribution of income, and the protection of individually incompetent decision-makers can potentially make everyone better off, government intervention results from citizens' demands to bring about these individually and collectively preferred outcomes. Whether because of the benevolent nature of "public servants," the existence of fierce political competition, or constitutional constraints on political outcomes, demand-side models make the critical assumption that government is staffed by a body of bureaucratic and political representatives—political "agents"—who automatically respond to broad-based citizen demands to secure for their "principals" these efficiency gains.[14]

From this perspective, there are two explanations of the emergence in 1935 of a compulsory federal old-age insurance program. Both are based on the premise that marked changes in economic conditions adversely affected the material status of the elderly and private institutions were unable to efficiently accommodate these changes. According to one explanation, industrialization, urbanization, and lengthening lifespans increased poverty among the elderly, and generated demands for an institutional means of enforcing upon the individual the obligation to insure against the financial hazards of old age. Whether it represented a decision on the part of the members of society to enforce this obligation upon themselves, or a decision on the part of a broadly based majority to enforce this obligation on other less long-sighted people, or simply a decision on the part of taxpayers to offset the disincentive effects of public-welfare institutions, a compulsory system of old-age insurance was a direct means of sharing and ultimately reducing the real cost of public welfare.[15]

Another demand-side view of Social Security's emergence is that the onset of the Great Depression in 1929 made voters painfully aware of the fallibility of, and the risks inherent in, the free-market process and, in particular, private savings and insurance institutions. Given the plight of the elderly, it was necessary to supersede the normal market process to make old-age insurance available on a broad-scale and safe basis.[16]

Despite the apparent plausibility of these arguments, two fundamental questions about the nature and evolution of Social Security are left unresolved. In particular, if the myopia or disincentive argument is accepted, then how can we explain why the program involves provision by a single public producer rather than simply involving compulsory purchase of insurance (through, say, a law to save)? Or, if the market-failure argument is accepted, then how can we explain why the program involves compulsory participation rather than simply involving, say, federal regulation or even federal production? In either case why does Social Security contain such significant redistributive elements?

Even if Social Security is viewed as an institutional means of resolving more than one problem simultaneously, the rapid growth of the program must remain perplexing to proponents of the pure demand-side approach.[17] When real personal income rose three-fold between 1950 and 1977, can the forty-fold increase in real expenditures, the 150 percent increase in real benefit levels, and the near quadrupling of the tax rate during the same period be explained as simply an increasing proclivity to "save," an increasing proclivity to care for the elderly (and their spouses, former spouses, parents, grandchildren, and children), or an increasing preference for income equality? Is there, in fact, no "fiscal crisis" as people have been fully conscious of implied changes in future tax rates necessary to finance an actuarial deficit that exceeds a trillion dollars? Indeed, are pure demand-side models, based as they are on market-failure notions, any longer relevant in explaining the evolution of a program in which 35 million Americans are direct recipients of public funds in their capacity as beneficiaries, and 75,000 are recipients in their capacity as Social Security employees?

The Supply-Side View and Implications for Social Security

The supply-side view of the collective choice process, most appropriately described as a non-"democratic" conception of government, incorporates an explicit theory of bureaucracy.[18] The passive or perfectly constrained political "agents" which characterize demand-side models are replaced by an array of self-interested bureaucrats who not only participate actively in the collective choice process, but also have a measurable impact on political outcomes. From this perspective, supply-side agents "are not helpless, passive pawns in the game of politics as it affects their lives; they are active, energetic persistent participants. The motives of their leaders and members to preserve the organization to which they belong are very strong. The techniques they can use are abundant, and their experience in using them is extensive."[19]

Essential to this approach is a recognition that the institutional environments within which private firms and public bureaus operate are qualitatively different. The production, price, and output decisions of the public bureau are therefore different from those of its private counterpart. By its nature the bureau is generally immunized from the efficiency generating forces of the competitive market process.[20] Not only is the bureau's output financed by a compulsory tax rather than sold in the market at a per unit price, but also the bureau may have legal sanction as the sole producer. In this setting the public bureau attains a type of monopoly power surpassing that available in the private sector, since the private monopolist is without the means to compel purchase.

A natural outgrowth of this environment is that the bureau develops primary control over the production of information relevant to decision-making by citizens and their representatives. Since individuals no longer face a group of firms freely competing for customers and differentially profiting on the basis of their success in meeting customer demands, they lose the automatic and reliable price and profit signals generated by the competitive market process as a means for evaluating the bureau's performance. Instead, in the presence of costly and imperfect information, citizens and legislators find themselves in the position of making decisions on the basis of the most readily available information. The bureau, funded to generate information on its own performance, often becomes the dominant source of information on the effectiveness and cost of both existing and alternative programs.[21] Because of the typically wide sharing of tax costs and the dispersed "ownership" of the bureau, the incentive of the taxpayer or his representative to actively monitor the bureau's activities is reduced as well.[22]

What motivates public suppliers who possess this discretion is seen to vary, in some cases widely. Supply-side models allow not only for individuals who are narrowly self-interested and solely concerned with their own advancement, but also for zealots and advocates looking to cure society's ills.[23] The interests of bureaucrats are seen to vary, that is, from the desire for income, power, prestige, and professional respect to the desire to realize their own conception of a "good society." It is a central premise of this approach, however, that each of these interests is positively related to the derivative interest of maximizing the bureau's budget or enhancing the scope of its activities.

The bureaucracy is seen to have a variety of methods for increasing the size and scope of its activities and thereby redistributing the benefits from public sector activity. It may provide biased information to citizens and legislators, draft legislation which ties popular changes to a complex array of "technical" changes that enhance their monopoly power, use all-or-nothing offers to ensure passage of favorable legislation, or even shirk on the job or engage in other inefficient uses of resources.[24]

Evidently, the supply-side approach envisions public-sector institutions and changes in them as vehicles for isolating the bureau and its beneficiaries from the market process and reducing their exposure to political competition. The growth and proliferation of government then become the by-products of a largely unconstrained endeavor by supply-side agents to maximize their own "wealth."[25]

The implication of these models for Social Security is a view of the program's institutional evolution as one of gradual monopolization in the provision of old-age insurance.[26] Federal production and compulsory purchase from a single supplier were the initial means by which program advocates secured monopoly power and isolated themselves from the market process. The expansion of compulsory coverage and increases in the ceiling on taxable earnings served to shelter this monopoly, and the introduction of a redistributive benefit formula and the movement toward a pay-as-you-go system were means of differentiating the product from that attainable privately. In essence, each of these was a direct means of reducing the efficiency-generating forces of competition and thus reducing the monitorability of the bureau's output.

With this perspective, however, unanswered questions arise once more. Foremost, what accounts for the delay in creating Social Security? The United States was the thirtieth country in the world to enact compulsory old-age insurance—more than forty-five years after social insurance emerged in Europe and, importantly, six years after the onset of the Great Depression in the United States. How can the historically sustained popularity and relatively broad-based support for Social Security be reconciled with this view? Finally, is it conceivable that a society with traditionally strong reliance on individual responsibility within this sphere of economic activity would tolerate the creation of government institutions that would intervene increasingly in the private sector and thus permit massive wealth transfers within and between generations?

Limitations and the Need for Integration

Evidently, the demand-side and the supply-side approaches generate two quite different views of the emergence of government and its evolution over time. These differences result largely from the assumptions made about the constraints on the collectivity and the meaning of private ownership claims.[27] Demand-side models, on the one hand, implicitly assume that the rights of the collectivity are clearly defined and the scope of its activities constrained so as to ensure an increase in the expected benefits from collective action, both across projects and over time. Political institutions are thus assumed to be structured in such a way that it is unprofitable for groups to devote their energies to using the political process for restructuring property rights so as to redistribute wealth and income in their favor. Supply-side models, on the other hand, conjure a collectivity that is largely unconstrained in the scope and extent of its activities, with rights that are not clearly delineated. Within such a framework, the notion of private ownership claims takes on an entirely different meaning as government becomes a powerful vehicle for coalitions of demanders and suppliers alike to use for redistribution. Rather than being a positive sum game, government reduces to a zero- or negative-sum game.[28]

In their pure or extreme forms neither the demand- nor the supply-side view provides a generally applicable framework for understanding nonmarket institutional change. In reality governments fail to provide efficiently and automatically those "public goods" demanded and, although government and its associated bureaucracy may appear to grow in an ineluctable manner, the process is certainly not without constraint. These facts have fostered the more recent development of less idealized models of government.

The Special-Interest Demand-Side View of Government

The failure of the pure demand-side view to explain the actual pattern of government intervention in the economy—evidenced by the lack of coincidence between government intervention and serious market failure—has led both economists and political scientists to develop theories of political failure that explain why the political process does not generally respond to broad-based demands derived from public-goods or market-failure considerations. These theories maintain that these demands are not likely to be made effective because of the costly nature of participation in the political process. The "universalistic" nature or publicness of benefits leads to a free-rider problem that often allows these demands to be overwhelmed by the more narrowly based demands of special-interest groups for "particularistic" or private benefits.[29]

In this new view the relevant demands for government action—those that signal political action—are those of interest groups attempting to influence government policy so as to redistribute wealth or income in their favor or to prevent the passage of policies that would adversely affect the group's interests. In the more rigorously developed presentations dealing with economic regulation, legislators are modeled as brokers who strike bargains with politically effective coalitions of voters to arrange wealth transfers.[30] The administrative agency and the staff of regulators born of this political bargain are modeled as the faithful agents of the legislature in enforcing and carrying out the terms of the bargain.[31]

The interest-group view is certainly an improvement over the pure demand-side view of government, allowing as it does for special-interest groups and politicians to play active roles in determining political outcomes. For a complete understanding of government, however, it remains inadequate since it either assumes an identity between politician and bureaucrat as "public supplier," or it assumes effective political control over the bureaucracy so that any bureaucratic failure stems singly from lack of knowledge or skill.[32] Characteristic of the pure demand-side view, the bureaucracy possesses no discretionary power and has no independent impact on political outcomes.

Evidently a means of bridging the gap between the demand- and supply-side views is still needed, particularly if we are to bridge the gap in our understanding between the emergence of a relatively well-constrained Social Security program in 1935 and the existence today of what Hayek has described as a "play-ball for vote-catching demagogues" that defies comprehensibility.[33] The following section offers an alternative view of the process whereby government programs evolve—from demand-side origins to supply-side control.

Institutional Evolution: From Demand-Side Origins to Supply-Side Control

Institutions evolve, but those that prosper and survive need not be those which are "best," as evaluated by the men who live under them. Institutional evolution may place men increasingly in situations described by the [Prisoner's] dilemma made familiar in modern game theory.[34]

The view of nonmarket institutional change presented here is employed throughout the remaining discussion as a conceptual framework with which to view the emergence, redirection, and growth of Social Security. The key elements of this framework are first presented as a sequence of stages intended to characterize the process of emergence and growth for a legislative program and its associated bureaucracy. Explanation and further elaboration then follow.

Stages in the Emergence and Growth of a Bureau[35]

Stage 1: An individual reformer-zealot or group of reformer-zealots first identifies and then begins to focus on a "social problem." Initial investigations are made, the nature of the problem is defined, and their conception of "the" solution is put forth. Through publications, an attempt is made to popularize their conception of the problem and its required solution.[36] Public opinion is influenced, although legislative investigation does not necessarily result.

Stage 2: Some significant economic, political, or social change, perhaps a "crisis," focuses broad-based attention on an aspect of the "problem" and provides the catalyst required to set off the legislative reaction.[37]

Stage 3: Official legislative or possibly executive inquiry results. The investigating committee or executive commission is dominated by advocates who draw on their fellow reformer-zealots, now viewed as "experts," for testimony. The findings of the committee and its proposed remedies reflect, for the most part, the views of this group.

Stage 4: With evidence on the "need" for public action substantiated and a "solution" involving the public sector crystallized, legislative debate ensues.

Stage 5: Legislation is passed, the timing of emergence and the *major* objectives of the program being consistent with the vaguely articulated demands of a relatively broad-based group of citizens and legislators. These demands, of course, have been highly conditioned by the information provided by advocates.

The specific institutional features which characterize the original legislation or program, however, are strongly influenced and, for the most part, shaped by public suppliers—reformer-advocates, existing bureaucrats, and candidates for the new bureaucracy. With sufficient support from the executive or from particularly powerful legislators for either the major objectives or else some central element of the proposed legislation, in fact, advocates drafting the legislation may tie features (or even programs) that lack any political support to other parts of the total package.

Stage 6: The administrative bureaucracy is established with program advocates and sympathetic bureaucrats from other programs installed at the policy-making level.

Stage 7: The new bureau, initially vulnerable to opposition attacks, attempts to consolidate its position. It searches out and encourages the formation of special-interest constituencies or lobby groups whose interests coincide with its own desire to expand the scope and size of the bureau, and whose demands politicians find "profitable" to satisfy. At the same time the bureau becomes the key source of information on its own activities and performance and works diligently to disseminate this "information."

Stage 8: The bureau then seeks to advance its position by drafting new legislation. Designed to improve "effectiveness," proposals initially involve an expansion of the existing program. Over time, and as the problem which formed the basis for the initial program withers, the bureau discloses new "problems" requiring further legislation to expand the initial mandate. Becoming more complex over time, legislative proposals fundamentally involve attempts to eliminate competition.

Stage 9: As the number of program objectives proliferates, as the variety of methods for achieving the objectives increases, and as the public sector in general grows, demand-side control over the program becomes more costly.[38] As competing sources of supply are foreclosed, citizens and politicians lose the comparative information necessary for effectively monitoring the performance of the bureau and controlling its activities. For special-interest groups, their representatives, and the bureaucracy, the political costs of redirecting and expanding the program to increase its redistributive potential thus decline over time.[39] The demands satisfied by the bureau become less the broadly based demands for the government to solve some social "problem" and more the special-interest demands for wealth redistribution. The majority of citizens acquiesce to this transition, placated by the bureau's publicity on the "public benefits" resulting from its activities.

Stage 10: Supply-side pressures ultimately dominate—if not create—demand-side pressures for changing the initial institutional arrangements. Over time supply-side explanations become increasingly descriptive of the observed evolution and growth of the program.

As summarized, this view of a bureau's life contains a paradox: new programs and their bureaucratic apparatus emerge in response to broadly based changes in citizen demands, but the detailed institutional features of programs—which are critical to the bureau's survival, growth, and redirection—are deduced mainly from the interests of the new bureaucracy and only in part from citizen demands. This mixture of demand- and supply-side views warrants elaboration.

Since wealth or income redistribution is a by-product of all government activity, a "demand" for more government naturally always exists. These typically narrowly based demands, however, are often those of special-interest groups or even those of existing and potential public suppliers. In most cases they are not sufficient to call forth political action and legislative response. Something more is necessary to generate the broad-based demands or, at a minimum, the voter acquiescence necessary for the creation of new government programs.

It is argued here that the catalyst is generally some significant market change, possibly a "crisis," whether of the traditional market-failure type or simply one involving pecuniary externalities—that is, costs that are incurred by the individual or firm over which they have no direct control. Such externalities could result, for example, from the sudden entry of new suppliers or from adverse shifts in relative prices due to, say, unexpected and exceptionally large shifts in demand or supply.

In discussing the history of nonmarket controls in the United States, Jonathan Hughes advances a similar argument about the timing of a program's emergence: "The American distrusts the free market and accepts its decisions willingly only when they suit his needs. When the market creates shortages of goods and services in response to the expressed desires of consumers, the consequences are resented and the call goes out for government to intervene. And it has, over time, case by case."[40] In effect, the "crisis" provides the impetus for politically isolating and reexamining a particular market and opens it to political attack. This reexamination, however, takes place in the soil already carefully prepared by the earlier studies of reformer-zealots.

Conducive to the emergence of government intervention, a crisis provides a political-economic environment that is unique in that citizens are motivated to make their demands known. The individual's generally low incentive to acquire the costly information necessary for articulating and communicating his political demands[41] is overcome to a significant extent by several factors. The news media, for example, provides public focus on the crisis and a relatively cheap source of information. Legislators, bureaucrats, and advocates, clamoring to gain political support for their own proposals, generate information on alternative proposals. The potential bureau and objectives of the new program are visible and relatively well defined. The availability of this information and the knowledge that new programs bestow uncompensated losses and gains raises the likelihood that citizens will take an active part in the decision-making process. In short, by the time proposals for new government programs reach the stage of active debate in Congress, the cost to the voter of obtaining at least general information on proposals is relatively low, while the incentive to participate may be quite high.

The existence of a relatively broad-based demand for the government to "do something" about a problem that has already been identified will, of course, call forth a speedy legislative response. Program advocates and existing and potential bureaucrats are motivated to articulate demands, and legislators are motivated to respond to these demands by providing the legislation sought by active participants.[42] Because bureaucrats and government advocates are ever in the business of proposing legislation, and politicians are ever in the business of legislating, strong elements of demand control are evident at the time of emergence capable of constraining the timing and determining the general objectives of new government programs.

While political competition helps to ensure that a new program emerges in response to broadly based (even if only vaguely articulated) demands, and that its initial design is roughly consistent with achieving the objectives demanded, the fiscal institutions that characterize the original legislation are better explained by supply-side factors. That is, with respect to specific institutional features, information and therefore control are on the supply side. Any number of taxes applied differentially to various voter groups can be chosen to raise revenues; the program can be financed by earmarking or by general revenues; the distribution of benefits and the organizational pattern of the new bureau can take on many forms. Most frequently this sort of legislation reaches Congress in "packages," inclusive of tax, expenditure, and administrative plans, to be voted upon together. The dominant role in formulating these packages of institutional features is played by the relatively small group of "experts"—those advocates, zealots, legislators, and potential bureaucrats who have an expected income or utility flow associated with support, passage, and future growth of the program.

Not excluding significant ideological motivations, then, supply-side agents have strong incentive to participate actively in the collective choice process. Not only is it from the ranks of the overlapping group of advocates, bureaucrats, and legislators that persons are drawn to create and sponsor new government programs, but also it is generally from this group of "experts" that newly created bureaus are staffed and to whom research funds typically flow. Indeed, it was the reliance of Congress on advocate-experts in 1935 that led one opponent of compulsory old-age insurance to say:

> No careful and intelligent observer in these unhappy times can have failed to observe that this has ceased to be a government in which legislation is by congressional action and vote, but has become a government by experts. . . . A man who feels himself qualified to participate in the formulation of legislation, to have any voice in its formulation, should not offer himself for election to the Senate or the House of Representatives, but he should procure for himself a position as a member of some commission, or as an employee of some commission, or as an employee or agent of some bureau of the Government.[43]

Given the reliance on advocate-experts for drafting legislation and staffing new bureaus, it is not difficult to explain the apparent paradox whereby a new program can emerge in response to changes in citizen demands while its institutional features may be deduced only in part from these demands. In public discussion advocates rationally promote concepts rather than arrays of specific institutional features and advance notions that the new program is needed to inject "safety," "security," or "stability" into an otherwise imperfect market economy.[44] These emotionally and politically appealing but ill-defined concepts can thus be met by the broad objectives of the new program while being tied to less appealing institutional features in a complex package. Even at the time of emergence the extent to which most citizens register their preferences at all is unlikely to exceed an expression of approval or disapproval of the major objectives of the new program. Unless they expect to incur major losses or gains by enactment, this will be the type of information most readily available and easiest to convey.

As program advocates are nonetheless aware, the institutional "details" of the new program and its administration are of utmost importance to the bureau's survival and growth, since the ability of the bureaucracy to affect fiscal outcomes depends critically on the degree to which it becomes isolated from the competitive process. In most cases government programs are financed by a compulsory tax or set of taxes so that purchase of the government output becomes compulsory. In other cases the consumption of the output is compulsory as well. The introduction of a program that compels purchase from a single supplier necessarily reduces the efficiency-generating forces of competition from both private and local public sectors. By narrowing the range of alternative sources of supply and, in some cases, eliminating voluntary patronage flows between private and public producers as an indicator of social value, comparative information on existing and alternative prices and outputs is sacrificed.

The question arises, of course, why opponents are generally ineffective in offering competing proposals that would improve the institutional design of the program. The answer lies in the costs and rewards of lobbying activities.[45] Specifically, economic theories of lobbying predict an underinvestment of resources devoted to lobbying for or against government programs for which the benefits are shared collectively. While the direct costs of lobbying by opponents include the time and effort involved in such activities as accumulating and disseminating information and drafting legislation, there may be no direct benefits to the opponent that are not shared equally with all other opponents. Effectively blocking the new government program or improving its design secures benefits for all opponents, whether or not they participate in sharing the costs. When the number of opponents is large, the free-rider problem can be expected to arise so that an underinvestment in lobbying against the proposed government program is then predictable. This effect is enhanced since the research and lobby activities of opponents of government intervention are, by their very nature, appeals for inaction rather than proposals for concrete legislative action.

On the other hand, while advocates incur direct costs and derive benefits that are also shared collectively, they can expect to enjoy large private benefits from their lobbying. Unlike an opponent, an advocate may individually reap benefits that are contingent upon his "lobbying" or actively supporting the new program: a job in the newly created bureau or the Administration, a staff position in Congress, an expanded realm for an existing agency, jobs for students and colleagues, consulting and research possibilities, to name a few. In addition, advocates of government are not infrequently employed in those occupations that facilitate, if not fund, research supporting government (government agencies, social work, labor unions, universities) thus reducing the direct costs to the individual. Because of the differential rewards to opponents and advocates, therefore, advocates have a very clear incentive not only to gather information, but also to take an active role in disseminating it. Not surprisingly, we observe the advocate investing in organizing and rallying support for new government programs, sometimes years before they are politically feasible from the demand side. In a very real sense advocates embody early supply-side pressures for government action.

Because of legislatively created elements of monopoly in the supply of an activity, program advocates—once installed in the new bureaucracy—are bestowed control over the primary source of information about that activity. Whereas advocates may have been in the position of footing their own time and money costs of lobbying prior to the creation of the program, advocates within the bureau are now federally funded to undertake research, disseminate information, initiate and draft legislation, and even evaluate their own performance. They can determine not only what is studied and proposed or what research is funded and disseminated, but also what is not. Stated most succinctly: "Freely available information naturally doesn't afford those who possess it any advantage. Therefore, influence is maximized by obtaining exclusive access to sources of information and by securing the position of exclusive supplier of it to those who make policy."[46]

Possessing this type of influence, public suppliers generally find it to their advantage to selectively bias the information made available to decision-makers, thereby placing disproportionate weight on the benefits of their program while obscuring the true tax cost. At a minimum, this results from the cost-reward structure of the public bureau whereby the current position and future prospects of the employee are tied inextricably to program survival and budget growth rather than to cost minimization or profit maximization.[47] The provision of selectively biased information and, more fundamentally, the certainty of internal supply-side pressures for expansion therefore result from the nature of bureaucracy, combining as it does expansionists of two types: those who, based on personal values, seek government control over a particular sphere of activity or an extensive public sector per se, and those who find their future incomes tied to the program's growth.

An intense internal desire to prosper, coupled with elements of monopoly in supply, does not, of course, assure the existence of a market over time. Whether it is a private firm or a public bureau in a noncompetitive setting, the process of eliminating competitive forces and securing a market is a gradual and imperfect one. For this reason, and because the functions of new programs are relatively limited (still unobscured), the early years in the life of the bureau are particularly critical. These are the years still marked by threats to survival by the market alternative.[48]

On the other hand, time is on the side of public suppliers. As voter-taxpayers discount the losses associated with government intervention, incentive is reduced to lobby against costly program changes that have only a marginal effect on the taxpayer's total taxes. Moreover, as the program becomes just one more in an array of government programs with multiple finance and expenditure schemes, the cost increases for the voter and his representative to obtain accurate information.[49] The political costs of redirecting and extending the program thus decline so that suppliers are in a position to effect institutional changes that facilitate growth.

The policy recommendations emanating from the new bureau will likely be designed to expand the realm and complexity of the bureaucracy's activities. Discretion is thus enhanced since complex programs and complex changes place politicians with limited time in the position of voting on "key" issues— generally expansionary—leaving it to the experts to decipher the array of technical changes to which they have been tied. Then, too, the politician directly benefits from the development of complex redistributive programs, for such programs are generally financed in a way that provides taxpayers with little incentive to invest resources in opposition. The broad distribution of taxes and the frequent reliance on general revenue financing makes the individual's tax change small and virtually impossible to isolate from those resulting from other policy changes. Benefits, on the other hand, since they are clearly focused and relatively narrowly distributed, make lobbying for expansion a good "investment" for special-interest–beneficiary groups. Simply stated, the legislator finds himself in a better political position after having worked to improve the lot of a coalition of actively participating beneficiaries than to have made marginal improvements in the lots of a vast majority of taxpayers. Precisely for this reason, congressional review committees tend to be staffed disproportionately by representatives of high-demand, special-interest groups, resulting in a lack of effective constraints on the expansionary demands of the bureau.[50]

In effect, a complex program, the details of which can only be mastered by "experts," increasingly removes the bureau from direct voter control and, at the same time, tends to disguise the program's typically narrow distribution of benefits and generally dispersed tax costs.[51] By making the program susceptible to political demands for income redistribution, the bureaucracy's expansionary stance is legitimized as the demands of beneficiary groups become increasingly coincidental with the recommendations of the bureau. While the bureau (using public funds) actively publicizes the inherent "publicness" of or "social gains" to its program and still maintains discretion over institutional redesign, massive wealth transfers can be effected by simply permitting the political process, now dominated by the demands of special interests, to run its course. "Technical changes" in the distribution of benefits that bestow special treatment to "deserving" beneficiaries effectively generate demands for expansion to eliminate the apparent "inequity." Rules and regulations made applicable to only one market, in a complex interrelationship with other markets, are generally ineffective and generate demands for the proliferation of rules into yet other markets so that original objectives are achieved. Ultimately, even the lobby groups most powerful in influencing legislation and the representatives who "broker" for them find their demands conditioned by the actions of the bureaucracy.[52]

To summarize, the life of a bureau is governed by two developments that bias political outcomes toward survival and growth: (1) the isolation of the bureau from the competitive market process and the consequent loss of comparative information, and (2) the disproportionate representation of special-interest beneficiary groups made possible by imperfect tax institutions. Once these biases dominate, supply-side explanations become most descriptive of the observed growth and evolution of government programs.

Optimistically, of course, the possibility exists for a cycle of demand-side control over the life of the bureau so that the process of increasing bureaucratic control need not be continual and unchecked. Just as a "crisis" was likely to play a key role in the emergence of the program, so might a "crisis" once again focus attention on the performance of the bureau. From the voter-taxpayer's perspective, however, a majority of net losers is not sufficient to evoke institutional change. Not until a majority of citizens perceives net losses and organizes for change can meaningful demand-side reform be effected. Competing sources of information must then surely have reemerged—with marginal increments in tax bills becoming discrete changes—to reinstill the elements of and incentives for demand-side control.

More realistically, public suppliers can be expected to achieve control that is enhanced over time. Not only do they play the key role in assessing the "viability" of reform measures, but they also have a strong vested interest in opposing proposals involving a reduction in their discretionary power. Government institutions therefore are predicted to evolve from demand-side origins to supply-side dominance.[53]

Drawing on the conceptual framework developed above, the remainder of this book is devoted to an examination of the emergence, growth, and redirection of Social Security. By recasting and reexamining traditional views of the evolution of

Social Security, it is hoped that insight may be gained into not only the prospects for reforming the Social Security system but also the more general phenomenon of government growth. To begin, the economic and political environment in the pre–Great Depression years is first examined as it sets the stage for a consideration of the emergence of compulsory old-age insurance in the 1930s.

Part I. The Pre–Great Depression Years: The Origins of Compulsory Old-Age Insurance?

Chapter 2. Poverty Relief Before 1900: A Brief Historical Overview

> The vast expansion of public assistance functions and expenditures beginning in the 1930's was superimposed upon a long tradition of disdain totally incongruous with the political and economic power assumed by the public welfare sector.[1]

Before the advent of Social Security the public sector had only a limited role and the federal government had essentially no role in alleviating poverty. Of the 4,207 benevolent institutions in the United States in 1904, only 485 were public and they housed less than a third of all inmates.[2] As late as 1927, when private philanthropy was estimated to exceed $1 billion, welfare expenditures by all levels of government amounted to only $161 million, 94 percent of which was at the state and local level. There were no federal grants for this purpose.[3] Town- and county-controlled almshouses were still used in virtually all states, and cash assistance represented less than half of all welfare expenditures.[4]

The role of the public sector in preventing poverty through the provision of insurance was even more modest. In the late 1920s annual premium income of private life-insurance companies exceeded $3 billion, and nearly $1.7 billion was being paid out in benefits to policyholders.[5] In the public sector, by contrast, the revenues accruing to all forms of public insurance were less than $240 million in 1927, with just $140 million paid out to beneficiaries.[6] Less than a fifth of all persons covered by retirement pension schemes were covered publicly, and all of them were public employees.[7]

These demarcations between the role of the private and public sectors and the various levels of government, as well as demarcations between the activities of poverty alleviation and prevention[8] were the product of political choices which, though evolving, had persisted over decades and even centuries.

Between 1935 and 1940 all of this changed. In 1936 Social Security's first year in effect, public-welfare expenditures by all levels of government reached $1 billion, three-fourths of which was cash assistance. Federal public assistance grants in that year alone amounted to $28 million, and they rose in the following two years to more than $200 million, or in real terms, to 150 percent of what had been spent on welfare activities by all levels of government a decade earlier.[9] Two years later, in 1940, a quarter of a million people were receiving cash benefits under the insurance titles of the new act, financed by a compulsory tax on more than thirty million workers.[10] To what extent these profound changes in the type, magnitude, and mix of government activities were simply political responses to fundamental changes in citizen demands and to what extent these demands were a by-product of the disruptions created by the Great Depression are vitally important to understanding the emergence of Social Security.

As a preliminary step to explaining the emergence of Social Security, Chapter 2 traces the historical evolution of public assistance. The purpose is to provide needed perspective into the customs, attitudes, and experiences that conditioned responses of citizens and politicians to proposals for aiding the elderly with public funds. In exploring the prevailing methods of assistance and how they evolved— from the early days of the colonial period to the beginning of this century—the following types of questions are addressed. In the absence of direct cash transfers, for instance, what were the various means by which communities dealt with poverty? What was the general attitude concerning a collective responsibility for the poor as reflected in the design of public institutions? What factors influenced the trend away from private cooperative schemes to aid the poor and, within the public sector, the trend away from local provision? Who were the groups emerging to shape the public-welfare system and what were their rewards for doing so? And, what were the likely consequences for both government and private charity activities of the professionalization of previously volunteer social workers and reformers at the turn of the century?

The Origins of Government Action

When the first villages were settled in New England, there were no laws for the public provision of assistance to the poor. The population was low and typically concentrated in communities where the ill, the disabled, and the destitute could be cared for by families, friends, and churches. Voluntary mutual assistance was a natural response to the hardships of the New World at a time when the bonds of family and friends were direct and survival made it a necessity.

Without means of regulating entry into communities, the viability of mutual assistance, as a method of caring for the poor, was easily threatened. The first public efforts to deal with poverty, therefore, involved legal restrictions on its entry and growth. In Boston and Plymouth, for example, restrictions on the sale of property and visitation by strangers were imposed in the 1630s to control the influx of the poor, the criminal, and those of incompatible religions, some of whom were deliberately imported by English Poor Law officials.[12]

In the following forty years, as population and dependency grew, more formal laws emerged in the colonies to provide tax-supported poor relief. Fashioned after the English Poor Law of 1601, colonial poor laws acknowledged—through compulsory taxation—a public responsibility to the destitute.[13] Simultaneously, this responsibility was declared to extend no further than the community's own poor, those for whom the causes and merits of individual cases were well understood.

Towns were made financially responsible for the poor within their limits, but only those who had remained quietly settled in the town for some period and gained the status of "inhabitants" were eligible as town charges.[14]

For nearly a century, there were no public institutions for the sick and poor, and no categorical conditions for eligibility. Individual cases were separately heard and considered, and those deemed in need by town authorities were placed in private homes to be cared for at public expense.[15] For the temporily needy, some outdoor relief was granted along with concessions such as free medical attention and the abatement of taxes or parish dues. Those who were poor by way of spending their time "idly or unproductively" could expect to be bound over to compulsory labor as indentured servants, whipped and run out of town, put in jail, or otherwise inflicted with harsh punishment.[16]

Eighteenth Century Accommodations to Changes in Poverty

Over time the increased density, heterogeneity, and mobility of the population threatened this individualized form of relief. The information required by town authorities became more costly to obtain and their ability to scrutinize individual cases was hindered. The community bonds necessary to care for the indigent, particularly the insane, the epileptic, and other "defectives," were naturally loosened. New institutional arrangements were thus sought to deal with the larger scale and changing nature of the poverty problem. There emerged: state participation in the financing of poor relief on a very limited basis,[17] the practice of auctioning off the care of individuals to the lowest bidder, and the creation of public almshouses and workhouses.[18]

It is interesting to note that as these quite significant developments took place, there remained a basic continuity in the character of poor relief. It resulted from the clear distinction made between the "poor" and the "pauper."[19] A person who found himself temporarily dependent could be "grudgingly tolerated," as poverty reflected an "inability through ignorance, improvidence, or other bad habits to triumph over the economic struggle."[20] This form of dependency was considered surmountable. Temporary exposure to the conditions of public relief, just as the conditions of poverty itself, was thought to stimulate the individual to greater effort. Paupers, on the other hand, were the idle, the lazy, the "drones" of society.

This prevailing distinction influenced institutions through the eighteenth and into the nineteenth centuries. Poor relief was designed to discourage the pauperization of individuals and hasten the restoration of the poor to the status of self-supporting. As in England, the work provided and the remuneration in almshouses were intended to be less desirable than attainable outside.[21] Upon receipt of relief funds recipients could lose their personal property, the right to vote and, in some cases, the right to move. In some larger towns and cities of the 1800s relief recipients were actually required to wear the pauper's badge, the letter "P" on the right shoulder.[22] Relief was generally restricted to those with no surviving legally responsible relatives.[23]

The Movement Toward Outdoor Relief

Despite these precautions, relief expenditures—already the largest item in town and city budgets—rose sharply in the post-Revolutionary War years.[24] Over the course of the next century localities were prompted once more to experiment with new methods of provision. To deal with the high cost and crowded conditions of public institutions, there was, first, an increasing reliance on outdoor relief. Orders or payments for groceries and other goods, employment and medical services, and outright cash transfers were not atypical. Second, public subsidies to private charitable institutions were introduced to foster new sources of supply. Finally, as efforts were made to differentiate between classes of the poor, specialized public institutions emerged to deal with their varied problems.[25]

A Reversal of Trends

Controlling the cost and effectiveness of these new forms of poverty assistance proved to be a difficult political task. Difficulties monitoring the needs of individuals in their own homes, monitoring the use of public subsidies (which were normally unencumbered grants), and monitoring elected officials in distributing outdoor relief were all soon manifested. Rising relief expenditures in the mid- to late 1800s were then accompanied by examples of political abuse in the distribution of outdoor relief in larger cities,[26] and a proliferation of private charities, particularly religious ones, seeking larger public subsidies.[27]

Fuelled by the demands of special-interest groups, these developments had major ramifications for poverty relief during the post–Civil War years. Public outdoor relief, once introduced, was restricted in amount and kind, limited to the relief of the temporarily needy and, in some cases, abandoned altogether.[28] Whereas by 1900 outdoor relief was legally authorized in twenty-four states, it was utilized in only a few. As late as 1928 major cities such as San Francisco and New York were still legally prohibited from dispensing outdoor relief.[29] In addition, there was a substitution of investigated for uninvestigated relief, the introduction of investigation and supervision over overseers of the poor, and a movement away from public subsidies to private charitable institutions.[30] Investigation, supervision, and coordination of charitable sources, donors, recipients, and methods became the latest trends in poor relief. In effect, there was a questioning of the efficacy of the poor laws that led to, and in part had been created by, an emerging class of social workers.[31]

The Drive for Control of Relief Monies

While poor relief expenditures increased steadily and public institutions for the care of certain needy groups proliferated during the post–Civil War years, the last decades of the nineteenth century are noted for the flourishing of private charity. This rapid growth in private charitable contributions, coupled with growth in the public sector, created an environment conducive to demands by reformers for the coordination, supervision, and control of both public and private monies.[32]

In the public sector state charity boards emerged in several northern and midwestern states between 1863 and 1873. While their functions varied from direct administrative control to supervisory roles, their primary function was to investigate charities within the state, providing information on the source and use of funds and the characteristics of recipients.[33]

In the private sector there was a parallel movement to coordinate and investigate private charities. Along the lines of London's Charity Organization Society, the first American charity organization society was established in Buffalo in 1877.[34] Concerned primarily with the duplicity and thus lack of control over public and private charities, the declared motive of these societies was to centralize and improve charity provision by "scientific organization." Their efforts were attributed to the "prodigality and inefficiency of public relief" and the profuse yet "chaotic state of private charity."[35] Investigation of individual cases and the maintenance of complete records on recipients and donors, they argued, were paramount to improved efficiency.

Reformers of the period argued for the creation of specialized public institutions for the poor and for the elimination of public outdoor relief to the able-bodied. The able-bodied poor, they said, were being pauperized by public relief and should be released to private charity where they could be carefully screened and made subject to undesirable work.[36] In this way, they argued, the impersonal and indiscriminate giving of alms could be replaced by personal, friendly, but discriminating visits by charity workers.

Most frequently attracting women from the middle and upper-middle classes, charity work represented a means of transferring and inculcating common values.[37] At this early date charity workers were without political force, having not yet attained the status of paid professionals, and their organizations lacked coercive elements. To a large extent, therefore, political responses to their demands must have reflected a broader based demand for changes in poverty relief arising out of basic economic, political, and social changes of the period. Such changes were abundant.

A depression in the 1870s, for example, brought to focus an inability to mobilize resources during an emergency. Bread lines and soup kitchens formed and free lodging was made available, yet rioting reached the point that many states had to send in militias and even federal troops.[38] During calmer days the problems of coordination remained. By the turn of the century there were cities with more than a thousand charitable organizations, each providing specialized services to particular classes of dependents. The problem of matching the poor with the proper agencies was thus vital.[39]

Then, too, well-known examples of the "pauperizing" effect of outdoor relief, of political corruption, and of pure politics led reformers and taxpayers alike to question the viability of public relief. During the aftermath of the Civil War recipients collected relief under several names, sold the goods they were given, and became seasonal visitors to almshouses during the winter months.[40] Describing the politics of tax-supported relief, the mayor of Brooklyn said in 1870, "The general demoralization which set in after the Civil War placed a corrupt man in charge of the poor funds . . . first preference went to families with voters and particularly those who were known to be friends with politicians."[41] In one year alone during the 1880s, liberalized and retroactive eligibility requirements for Civil War pensions were instituted which doubled federal pension expenditures the following year. Within the next decade expenditures tripled and the number of recipients doubled.[42]

Finally, as the economy prospered during the early stages of industrialization, Social Darwinism became a prevailing philosophy.[43] This view of "survival of the fittest," connoting as it did a minimal role for the state in poverty relief, was fostered by a continuously improving standard of living in the United States. Not only were individuals placed in ever better positions from which to care for themselves and their families, but also there was an intensified influx of immigrants, not all of whom native-born taxpayers wished to subsidize.[44]

The Professionalization of Social Work

Just as quickly as these economic and demographic changes were taking place, the ranks, methods, and objectives of charity workers and scientific reformers were undergoing dramatic changes as well. A second major economic downturn in 1893, heightened immigration, industrialization, and urbanization all threatened the traditional friendly society of the late nineteenth century. Door-to-door efforts to instill the elements of the neighborhood and to imbue the poor in major cities with such values as the work ethic were rendered infeasible by differences in language and culture, the mobility of urban populations, and the extent and nature of poverty (more frequently resulting from large-scale unemployment and industrial accident).

Evidently, as one noted student of the period states, "a new relationship had to justify interference" in the lives of the poor; "the answer seemed to lie in the establishment of a professional relationship in which the social worker's authority rested upon superior expertise."[45] Emphasizing supervision, investigation, and casework, charity workers sought to create a new field of professional social work over which they would possess a skill monopoly.[46] In 1898 the first school of social work was opened, and by 1900 paid professional caseworkers were replacing the volunteer worker of the nineteenth century. By 1920 there were associations of social workers, standards of quality were imposed by the associations and schools, and these standards were influencing the hiring decisions for public social service programs.[47] Ironically,

> The charity organization societies of the late nineteenth century, which had revolted against the "officialdom" of existing relief agencies and imbued voluntary service with a semireligious sanctity, were among the leading architects of welfare bureaucracy and professionalization. . . . The paid social worker's claim to expertise, the emergence of a professional identity nurtured by schools and associations, and the development of a formal organization of bureaucracy as a characteristic feature of administration were crucial in the devaluation of voluntarism.[48]

By the time the Great Depression was well underway, there existed a professional apparatus and a political coalition between social workers and social scientists[49] that actively sought and was prepared to administer an expansion of the "welfare state." By then, social workers had come to recognize the profitability of the government as a key avenue for their employment.[50]

Social Welfare Before Social Security

Several important developments in the early history of poverty relief would have major ramifications in the early twentieth century on the coming of Social Security. State participation in the funding and administration of poor relief;[51] differentiation of classes of dependents in almshouses and their subsequent removal to specialized state and local institutions; supervision and control of charities; and bureaucratization of social work were among these. Already evidenced were the political difficulties of monitoring and controlling the nature of income transfer programs when recipients included not only the poor but also caseworkers, administrators, politicians distributing the funds, and recipients of contracts awarded.[52]

Understanding the state of affairs in the pre–Social Security years, however, requires more than a knowledge of trends. What were the important elements in the nature and magnitude of poor relief as it existed in the early 1900s, particularly as they contrast with those of today? First, there was still a predominant role for the private sector in the pre–Social Security years. In 1915, for example, public funds covered only approximately 20-25 percent of all expenditures on outdoor relief.[53] As late as 1928 total charity expenditures (institutional and noninstitutional) by states and cities amounted to only $75 million, having experienced a rate of growth considerably less than total government expenditures.[54] Second, within the public sector there was a very modest role for cash relief. In spite of the emergence of categorical public assistance programs during the 1920s, as late as 1929 only 3 percent of state welfare budgets were devoted to noninstitutional relief.[55] Finally, there was considerable geographic variation in the causes and magnitude of the "poverty problem," considerable variation in local attitudes toward the care of the poor and, because of the federal system of government and the maintenance of local control, there were highly varied institutional accommodations to the problem.

In comparison with the present, and despite precedents and trends to the contrary, the fabric of social welfare in the pre–Great Depression years was private voluntary care, supplemented by local public relief and guided by a philosophy of self-reliance. Only with this perspective can one appreciate the radical differences between the role of the public sector in the United States and in other countries at the turn of the century, and how truly radical were the demands of social insurance advocate-zealots who sought compulsory, federal schemes of income redistribution.

The history of public welfare clearly suggests that radical changes in the economic, political, and social environment of the early 1900s would be necessary to produce federal social legislation by the 1930s. Both the amount, type, conditions of eligibility, and the highly decentralized nature of relief at the turn of the century revealed a limited and cautious acceptance of government in a realm of activity most noted for "voluntarism."[56]

Admittedly, long-term forces were at work leading to a decline of voluntarism. The drive for an expanded role of the public sector and for higher levels of provision were fostered, on the one hand, by the increasing heterogeneity and mobility of the population and continued industrialization. On the other hand, there were the political effects of reduced competition in the public sector coupled with an ability to use government to geographically redistribute tax costs. Then, too, a catalyst was emerging—a new profession of social workers who would find their livelihoods increasingly tied to the control of charitable monies and to an expansion of the "welfare state."

As of the 1920s, however, a great deal of centralization was still required before the state would dominate the localities in the care of the poor. As for the organization of social workers and reformers, the formal schools, professional associations, and public-welfare departments that would produce a commonality of interests necessary for affecting policy were only beginning to come of age.

Chapter 3. The Elderly and the State: 1900–1929

> Compulsory social insurance is in its essence undemocratic.
>
> Samuel Gompers, 1917[1]

Although public poverty relief first emerged in the colonial period, by the first decades of the twentieth century there were still no special provisions for the elderly beyond locally administered poor laws. As late as 1920, in fact, the only form of permanent public assistance for the elderly in most states was the town- or county-controlled almshouse, still used in some localities to house petty criminals, the insane, and the "feeble-minded." Designed to provide institutional care for the destitute, these public institutions often did not segregate the elderly from other inmates or, as a rule, segregate inmates on the basis of sex, senility, or overall health. In 1923 some 42,000 inmates, or more than half of the total almshouse population, were aged.[2]

During the 1920s, the elderly experienced a sharp rise to prominence, becoming one of the leading social issues of the decade. State legislatures created commissions to study their financial condition and report on the advisability of state action, and proposals to make cash transfers to the elderly were debated in most state legislatures. By 1929 ten states had programs to provide cash assistance to the elderly poor, and six years later the Social Security Act was passed. Contained within it were provisions for federal matching funds for assistance to the elderly poor as well as provisions for a federal program of compulsory old-age insurance. Within five years more public funds were being spent on cash transfers to the elderly than had been spent by all levels of government on all public-welfare activities less than a decade earlier.[3] With the momentum for public action having begun early in the 1920s and with social insurance having already emerged throughout the world by 1929, it would thus appear that Social Security and, in particular, compulsory old-age insurance, were responses—both long-awaited and inevitable—to conditions existing prior to the Great Depression. Determining whether this is so is the concern of Chapter 3.

More specifically, Chapter 3 will determine if, at any time before the Great Depression there were significant and broad-based demands for compulsory, federal old-age insurance—the heart of the Social Security Act. Alternatively, were there clearly discernible trends that would have likely culminated in the enactment of such a program in the 1930s?

To provide adequate answers to these questions, several other questions must be addressed. For instance, what were the conditions underlying the elderly's rise to prominence in the 1920s? Was it the result of an existing or expected deterioration in their financial position or the ability of private markets to provide financial

protection? How extensive was poverty among the elderly, to what was it attributable, and how was it likely to be affected over time? Was there a lack of institutional
outlets for saving and insurance among workers or other failures on the supply side
of private markets? Or, were workers unwilling to make advance provision for
themselves or were there other failures on the demand side of private markets? If
not, what were the motives for compulsory old-age insurance schemes involving
federal production and for what were they a remedy? Indeed, who advocated compulsory insurance and on the basis of what arguments? Finally, what was the political response to social insurance advocates' proposals for federal action and how
was it effected, on the one hand, by a much-advanced social insurance movement
in Europe and, on the other hand, by a much-advanced private insurance industry
and an emerging system of state and local relief to the elderly poor in the United
States?

To address these questions, this chapter undertakes a detailed examination of
the economic, political, and social changes that affected the elderly (or the workforce vis-à-vis the elderly), changed the demand or supply of policy proposals, and
ultimately influenced public policy. The period of interest spans 1900-1929, the
years during which the elderly were escalated from a nonexistent to a live political
issue.

The Sources of Emergent Interest in the Elderly

Whereas American social policy had long been directed toward the care of "the
poor" by 1900 and was recently turning to the care of such groups as the insane,
widowed mothers, and dependent children, interest in the needs of the elderly poor
as a class was strictly a twentieth-century phenomenon.[4] The first public inquiry
into the extent of old-age poverty was not authorized until 1907. Yet within the
following twenty-two years, eleven other states conducted such studies, and
special cash-assistance programs were beginning to emerge. The emergent political
interest in the problems of the elderly which set the stage for proposals for compulsory insurance, can be explained in part by previously described trends in American poor relief, in part by economic and demographic changes in the population
and, in part, by trends in European social policy as they influenced the demand for
and supply of alternative policy proposals. These trends are examined in turn.

The Almshouse and the Aged

By 1929 the county-controlled almshouse was still the only form of permanent
assistance to the elderly poor in virtually all states.[5] In most states, moreover,
caring for the elderly had become the primary use for the almshouse. Rather than
reflecting conscious political and social decisions, the increasing use of the almshouse for the care of the aged was primarily a result of the late nineteenth-century
trend toward the removal of children, the blind, the insane, and others with special

Table 3.1. Number and age distribution of paupers in United States almshouses, 1880-1923

Age group	Number of paupers			Age distribution of paupers			Age distribution of U.S. population, 1920
	1880	1904	1923	1880	1904	1923	
All ages[a]	66,203	81,764	78,090	100.0%	100.0%	100.0%	100.0%
Through 19 yrs.	10,718	3,891	2,584	16.2	4.8	3.4	40.7
20-49 yrs.	25,089	20,978	12,148	37.8	25.7	15.6	43.9
50-64 yrs.	13,493	22,205	20,508	20.4	27.2	26.3	10.7
65 and older	16,903	33,141	41,980	25.6	40.6	53.8	4.7

Source: U.S. Department of Commerce, Bureau of the Census, *Paupers in Almshouses: 1923* (Washington, D.C.: U.S. Government Printing Office, 1925), pp. 9-10.
a. Includes persons with unknown ages.

problems to institutions specifically designed for their care. The consequence, as illustrated in Table 3.1, was a continuous historical decline between 1880 and 1923 in the proportion of paupers in almshouses under age fifty. By 1923, 53.8 percent of the almshouse population was over sixty-five, and in some states, particularly those in the west, the aged made up nearly two-thirds of the almshouse population. As further illustrated, a decline in the almshouse population beginning in 1910 was met by a continuous rise in the number of elderly paupers. By 1923 there were approximately 42,000 paupers in United States almshouses over the age of sixty-five, or nearly 1 percent of the aged population.

Needless to say, except in their capacity to provide institutional care and some degree of medical attention, almshouses were decidedly not designed to care for the elderly. Since as early as the colonial days, and before the days of asylums, hospitals, and reformatories, the almshouse had been designed as an institution to house all classes of "defectives" unable to care for themselves. Most almshouses were very old, many lacked modern sanitation or electricity, and some were still contracted out to the lowest bidder. Whereas in some states almshouses had effectively become free hospitals for the poor and there had been some effort to segregate the elderly from others, most almshouses did not segregate inmates on the basis of senility, sex, or general health.[6] The overall rise in the nation's well-being in the late nineteenth and early twentieth centuries naturally led to a reexamination of all forms of poverty relief. The fact that many counties were left with an institution not designed for what had become its primary use certainly hastened this development and brought attention to the problems of the elderly.

The Private Sector Benchmark

The increasing attention accorded the elderly poor was also a natural outgrowth of developments in private care for the elderly. As social policy had been directed toward the poverty problems of other social groups, private homes for the care of the poor and other elderly sprouted up throughout the country. In 1929 the Bureau of Labor Statistics located more than 1,200 such homes, housing 63,000 elderly persons and having capacity for 17,000 more. Some of these houses were run by religious (408) and fraternal organizations (101), others by nationality groups (34) and trade unions (5), and some were simply privately run (350). Private or semiprivate rooms, recreation, amusement, medical attention, and even small allowances or burial expenses were provided commonly.[7] Public almshouses, of course, paled by comparison to these homes that had been specially designed to meet the needs of the elderly and to provide charity to the elderly poor.[8]

Special Provisions for Veterans and Other Government Employees

Then, too, there existed in the public sector differentially favorable treatment for special classes of the elderly. Dating to the colonial and American revolutionary periods, there were homes, pensions, and other special privileges for veterans, military personnel, and other government employees that proliferated in the early decades of the twentieth century.[9] Veterans, for example, were accorded institutional care outside the almshouse, outdoor relief and other exemptions from poor laws, and pensions for service. By the 1920s, and although not confined to the elderly, the federal pension system for veterans and soldiers had become the "largest pension system in America and probably the most expensive one in the world," spending more than $260 ($996)[10] million a year. Liberalized by nearly every Congress, the average pension for war veterans rose three- to four-fold between 1910 and 1932 alone. State and city expenditures on relief, pensions, and gratuities to soldiers and sailors exceeded $80 ($297) million in 1925.[11]

Though a more recent development, there was also a proliferation of retirement systems for public employees in the first decades of the 1900s. There first emerged state and local systems for police, firemen, and teachers in the 1890s, statewide and citywide systems for public employees during the period 1911-15, and finally, a federal system for federal civil-service employees in 1920.[12] These systems, many of which were notoriously unsound, implied significant wealth transfers to retired public employees. In 1927, only seven years after its creation, the federal retirement system paid an average annual annuity to retirees of $721 ($2,711), more than half of the average annual compensation of these employees during their working years.[13] In these few years, during which time disability benefits were introduced and the ceiling on pensions payable was increased and then eliminated, real expenditures rose four-fold, reaching nearly $10 million. In states and cities more than $55 ($209) million was being spent on former employees in 1928.

As most of these systems involved at least partial public financing, income transfers were not simply between working and retiring government employees; they involved direct transfers from taxpayers as well.[14] Gratuitous transfers made to special classes of elderly at public expense naturally evoked interest on the part of other elderly persons seeking similar treatment as well as social reformers who sought an equitable solution to the problems of the elderly poor.

Table 3.2. Population and labor-force trends among the elderly, 1880-1930[a]

Year	Aged population (in thous.)	Aged population as percent of:			Median age of total population	Male workers age twenty	
		Total population	Labor force[b]	Gainfully occupied		Probability of living to age sixty-five	Expected no. of retirement yrs.[c]
1880	1,723	3.4%	—	—	20.9	—	—
1890	2,417	3.9	4.3%	4.30%	22.0	.41	1.42
1900	3,080	4.1	4.0	4.10	22.9	.51	1.85
1910	3,950	4.3	3.9	3.85	24.1	.52	2.41
1920	4,933	4.7	4.3	3.98	25.3	.60	2.89
1930	6,634	5.4	4.0	4.50	26.5	.60	2.91

Sources: U.S. Bureau of the Census, *The Statistical History of the United States from Colonial Times to 1970* (New York: Basic Books, 1970), pp. 15, 19, 131-32, 134; Michael R. Darby, *The Effects of Social Security on Income and the Capital Stock*, Studies in Social Security and Retirement Policy, No. 227 (Washington D.C.: American Enterprise Institute for Public Policy Research, 1979), p. 23.

a. Aged sixty-five and older.

b. The proportion of elderly males in the labor force fell from 68.3 percent in 1890 to 54 percent in 1930, whereas the proportion of elderly gainfully occupied fell from 41.7 percent to 33.2 percent during the same period.

c. Retirement is defined as nonparticipation in the labor force by a person sixty-five or older.

Demographic Changes

Important demographic changes, recognized by the 1920s to be long-run trends, were also taking place at the turn of the century that increased the voice of the elderly in the policy arena. With each decade that passed, for example, there were simply more old people in relation to the total population. As illustrated in Table 3.2, the number of people over sixty-five doubled in the first three decades of the twentieth century, reaching 6.6 million by 1930. The rate of increase in the number of elderly thereby exceeded the rate for the entire population in each decade between 1880 and 1930. Between 1920 and 1930 alone the number of elderly persons increased at twice the rate of the overall population, and the proportion of elderly persons rose consistently to reach 5.4 percent of the total population.

These population trends raised the median age of the population, increased the probability that a young worker would survive to age sixty-five and, taking account of labor market trends, increased the number of years he could expect to spend in retirement. As further shown in Table 3.2, the median age rose from twenty-two to more than twenty-six between 1890 and 1930, and the probability of a twenty-year-old living to age sixty-five rose from 41 percent to 60 percent, the odds exceeding fifty-fifty for the first time at the turn of the century.[15] In the labor market the elderly represented a relatively stable 4.1 percent of the labor force and of the gainfully occupied, although a declining proportion of the elderly were in the labor force. These population and labor-force trends interacted to more than double the young worker's expected retirement years, from roughly one and a half to nearly three years between 1890 and 1930. In effect, "old age"—in the sense of living beyond one's work life—was a new phenomenon to be reckoned with.

Taken together, these demographic changes suggested that the elderly would ultimately emerge as both a political force in their own right, and also a new political issue among the working-age population. Post-retirement income policies would interest an increasing proportion of workers not only because the probability of attaining "old age" was now more significant, but also because they could be utilized to encourage the elderly to leave the labor market, particularly during periods of high unemployment. At the present, however, there were any number of reasons the elderly, especially the elderly poor, were without political strength. Their numbers were yet few, they lacked organization, they lacked a common cause, and they lacked leadership. The spark to interest was a quite active old-age pension and social insurance movement throughout the world.

The Elderly in Europe and the Transport of Ideas

During the forty-year period between 1889 and 1929 public financial aid for the elderly emerged, in the words of social insurance advocates, in most countries of the "civilized world." By 1929 thirty-five countries had enacted programs for the elderly and they were of three general types.[16] At one extreme was the compulsory "contributory" old-age insurance program (social insurance) inaugurated in Germany in 1889. Characteristic of the American Social Security program that would be adopted in 1935, social insurance coerced certain segments of the working population, generally the lower paid, to make tax payments during their working years so as to finance and become eligible for benefits upon retirement. These tax payments were typically supplemented by a tax on employers and a general revenue contribution, financing benefits that were either earnings-related, tax-payment-related or, in some cases, the same for all workers. Social insurance thereby redistributed income from covered workers to retirees, from general taxpayers to retirees, and among retirees. As shown in Table 3.3, this type of program became prevalent in the second and third decades of this century.

At the other extreme were voluntary, subsidized insurance schemes. The first such program emerged in Belgium in 1891, and similar experiments were undertaken by 1895 in Italy and France. These programs typically involved retirement funds that were subsidized with public monies so as to provide insurance on a voluntary basis at less than competitive rates. The programs, claimed to have been too costly for the results obtained, were superseded by compulsory programs and never came into general use.[17]

Finally, there were "noncontributory" old-age pension programs of the sort initiated in Denmark in 1891. Similar to the old-age assistance program that would be adopted in the United States in 1935, these programs simply provided government supported, means-tested, poverty relief to the elderly poor. Reputable citizens of long residence were granted benefits (regardless of prior occupation and

Table 3.3. Compulsory old-age insurance and pension programs abroad, 1933[a]

Year passed	Compulsory old-age insurance		Noncontributory old-age pensions
	General coverage[b]	Limited coverage[c]	
Before 1900			
1889	Germany		
1891			Denmark
1898			New Zealand
1900-1910			
1905			France
1908			Australia
			Ireland
			Great Britain
1909			Iceland
1910	France		
1911-20			
1911	Luxemburg		Newfoundland
1912	Rumania		
1913	Netherlands		
	Sweden		
1916		Switzerland	
1919	Italy	Uruguay	Uruguay
	Portugal		
	Spain		
1921-33			
1921		Argentina	
1922	Greece		
	Russia		
	Yugoslavia		
1923		Brazil	Norway
1924	Belgium		
	Bulgaria		
	Chile		
	Czechoslovakia		
1925	Great Britain		
1926			Greenland
1927	Austria	Cuba	Canada
1928	Hungary	Ecuador	South Africa
1933	Poland		

Sources: Barbara N. Armstrong, *Insuring the Essentials: Minimum Wage Plus Social Insurance—A Living Wage Program* (New York: Macmillan, 1932), pp. 399-412; U.S. Committee on Economic Security, *Report to the President of the U. S. Committee on Economic Secutity* (Washington, D.C.: U.S. Government Printing Office, 1935), pp. 69-70.
a. Programs in existance in 1933.

b. Generally involved the coverage of wage earners in industry and commerce.

c. Generally involved the coverage of only, say, employees of public utilities, banks, or railways. The first programs of this type were established in Austria (1854), Belgium (1868), France (1894), and Italy (1909), each of which was superseded by general programs.

earnings) if they were destitute in old age. Whereas before World War I countries experimented with each of these forms of public provision, there was a general trend in the postwar years toward compulsory insurance.

In an important sense, European developments provided the basis for the transport of ideas to the United States by an emerging class of social reformers and social insurance advocates. The success of the movement on all fronts—workmen's compensation, health insurance, unemployment insurance, and old-age insurance—formed the basis for a great number of books written by advocates of "social justice" and "worker security" at the turn of the century and provided the model for legislative proposals in this country.[18] Social workers, social reformers, intellectuals, socialists, and other progressives became the core of advocacy in the United States.[19] For their purposes the elderly had been identified as a new social class, they were a class with problems meriting special attention, and these problems now had a resolution with an established tradition in the public sector.

To an important extent the first two decades of this century involved a process of: (1) defining a "problem" of old age; (2) crystalizing a public resolution to the problem; (3) attracting the attention of and informing potential advocates; and (4) developing a core of "experts." These were all necessary predecessors as well as the spark to public inquiry and legislative action.

Origins of the American Social Insurance Movement

The American Association for Labor Legislation (AALL), established in 1906 as a branch of the German-created International Association for Labor Legislation, was the point of origin for the social insurance movement in America. Bringing together a group of labor-union officials and social workers under the leadership of social scientists from major universities, the AALL linked the study of social problems, the initiation of policy, and the advocacy of "social justice" and "worker security" to the "intellectual." Leaders of the AALL included John R. Commons and Richary Ely (Wisconsin), Henry Farnam (Yale), J. W. Jenks (Cornell), Samuel McCune Lindsay and Henry Seager (Columbia). Among its nonacademic economists were John B. Andrews, Adna F. Weber, and Isaac Rubinow, of whom the latter certainly became the most prolific.[20]

Partly because the AALL was the point of origin the early social insurance movement here, as abroad, was not focused on the needs of the elderly. Instead, the focus was on the condition of the "wage-earning" classes.[21] The AALL carried out investigations on the conditions of workers, disseminated information, and drafted model legislation which led to a rash of state workmen's compensation laws after 1911, to a series of state health-insurance bills between 1916 and 1920, and raised social insurance to an issue of live political debate by the second decade of the 1900s.

As articulated by proponents, social insurance was a policy designed to reduce economic insecurity and thereby promote and foster the gains of a "more secure working class."[22] The movement sought a substitution of income certainty and security through government action for the insecurity and uncertainty inherent in the private sector—whether in labor markets or ultimately in the family, church, private charity, and financial institutions. Involving a transfer of activities and responsibilities from the individual and voluntary groups to the government, the social insurance movement aspired toward the centralization, collectivization, and coercion necessary to reap the gains of a "more secure working class." Rather than sharing the optimism brought about by the economic progress of the twenties, advocates found the United States and the conditions of workers "pitifully behind the rest of the civilized world."[23]

From the early days of the movement there was a fundamental conflict—at the level of both fact and rhetoric—over the purpose of social insurance. Was social insurance fundamentally designed to prevent worker insecurity through the principles of insurance and incentive schemes or was it designed to maintain security in old age through income redistribution? Andrews and Commons professed a conception of social insurance for the prevention of worker insecurity. In their words, "In all the work we've done together we have thought first of prevention and second of relief in dealing with each form of social insurance in this country."[24] Universal, compulsory coverage would force all employers, especially the less progressive, to contribute to the well-being of the working class. By making resources available should the worker's income be interrupted by illness, disability, unemployment, or old age, employers would be helping to alleviate a problem which they, it was claimed, had helped create.

Rubinow, by contrast, advocated the use of social insurance for the maintenance of a decent living standard for all workers. The government had the resources and the responsibility to make workers more secure, he argued, and social insurance was the vehicle through which social justice—income redistribution toward wage earners—could be attained.

Isaac Rubinow, a Russian who emigrated to the United States in 1893, epitomized the challenge to voluntarism inherent in the social insurance movement.[25] His conception of social insurance drew heated debate, bringing attention to the role of the state envisioned by social insurance advocate-zealots, and exposing the function of compulsory old-age insurance as it would come to be designed in this country. Rubinow's views and those of certain of his outspoken colleagues attacked the core of what had come to be known as traditional American values: thrift, self-reliance, and the market system as a means of organizing society. Their views revealed most starkly the development of a new prevention-insurance rhetoric for what were inherently redistributive programs.

Worker insecurity, it was argued, was the outgrowth of an economic system that distributed rewards on the basis of work. Since nearly everyone worked, worked for someone else, and earned a livelihood in wages, advocates said, nearly everyone faced economic insecurity. In the words of Abraham Epstein, an avid follower of Rubinow and leading proponent of social insurance,

Ever since Adam and Eve were driven from the sheltered Garden of Eden, insecurity has been the bane of mankind. The challenge confronting us in the twentieth century is that of economic insecurity, which weighs down our lives, subverts our liberty, and frustrates our pursuit of happiness. The establishment of economic security has become a paramount issue because our modern system of industrial production has rendered our lives insecure to the point of despair. The wage system has made economic security depend entirely on the stability of our jobs. Such utter dependence upon a wage for the necessities of life has never before been known in any society.[26]

In the absence of government intervention the worker's command over goods and services was seen to be tied singly to his current flow of wage income such that "the slightest interruption or reduction in wages or any increase in expenditures" would "immediately condemn (him) to defenseless poverty."[27] Private savings and insurance against future contingencies were not the answer, it was argued, because they were simply out of the reach of the vast majority of low-income wage earners. Throughout the world the standard of wages was simply insufficient to produce a surplus over and above current expenditures.

What was it about social insurance that, according to spokesmen, could deal with this problem? According to Epstein, social insurance aimed at "the maximum application of the principle of insurance. . . . By the spread of risk to its logical maximum, by the inherent low overhead and by distribution of the costs upon all elements, social insurance not only brings protection within the reach of those who need it most, but also makes possible the assurance of a minimum standard of living for all."[28] For Rubinow, social insurance was "the policy of organized society to furnish that protection to one part of the population which some other part may need less, or if needing, is able to purchase voluntarily through private insurance."[29] A reputable scholar in actuarial science, Rubinow admitted that social insurance would be subject to severe criticism if judged by the "true scientific principles of insurance."[30]

Evidently, social insurance had two functions: compensating workers for interruptions in earnings and raising their standard of living. While the insurance function could certainly have been met through alternative (private and voluntary) means, the redistributive function required coercive state action. By requiring universal coverage and universal tax support, a "more equitable" distribution of income could be attained. The policies were admitted to be "true class legislation."[31]

Social Insurance and The Elderly: The "Problem" of Old Age and Its "Solution"

Contained within the writings and legislative proposals of early proponents was a quite novel vision of the elderly, one they were instrumental in defining and popularizing. For essentially the first time in history the elderly were identified as a distinct social class, as a class with problems meriting special attention, and these problems were seen to have a resolution with a now-established tradition in the public sector. The problem was said to be old age in an economic and social system possessing an inherent conflict between the interests of the elderly and the new industrial state.[32]

Variously described as the "tragedy," the "universal problem," the "economic hazard," and the "haunting fear in the winter of life," the problem of the elderly was said to be poverty in old age resulting in dependency on others—whether on friends, families, private or public charitable organizations, or ultimately the public almshouse.[33] The source of the problem, it was claimed, was the modern industrial society. According to social insurance advocates and others concerned with social ills, the movement from farm to city and the change in employment from agricultural to industrial rendered the elderly worker obsolete. On the farm the elderly could continue working by scaling down work effort or hours worked, or by finding new tasks to perform as the physical and mental deterioration of age set in. When work ceased, they had the specialized knowledge and experience that increased in value with age. They were, it was said, a vital part of the work unit—the family—and they maintained income or at least dignity and self-respect in their declining years.

In industrial employment, on the other hand, the elderly worker was said to be an unknown party to an impersonal and, by nature, insecure wage contract. He was becoming less and less useful in an increasingly specialized and mechanized world. The physical stamina required to meet the pace set by the youngest, most vigorous workers, along with maximum hiring ages, compulsory retirement, and inflexibility in hours and tasks, hastened the aging process, denied the importance of their accumulated knowledge, and made employment, once lost, difficult to find. With a livelihood tied to the flow of wage income the loss of employment then cast them "helplessly into utter despair."

Why were the elderly unable to turn to their own financial resources in old age or to those of their families? Because of the low wages paid in industrial employment, high premium costs for insurance, and restrictive eligibility conditions for pensions, "thrifty savings [became] a practical impossibility."[34] Any savings accrued, moreover, however modest, were quickly wiped out by sickness or accident, both likely to be more severe among the elderly. As revealed by the oft-repeated phrase, "saving presumes a surplus, and a surplus presumes a living wage,"[35] old-age poverty was viewed as the result of factors beyond the individual's control, rooted in the modern industrial state.

The ultimate choice for the elderly then became one of private charity, said to be meager, unpredictable, and demoralizing, or the almshouse, the shocking conditions of which were well known. In the absence of government action the only resolution of the problem of old age, said Barbara Armstrong, leading figure in the compulsory old-age insurance movement, was "to leave this world early, before the period of superannuation set in."[36]

For the future, industrialization, an ongoing phenomenon, and well-known demographic trends would, advocates argued, combine to produce the "iron-law" of increasing old-age dependency.[37] As industry was weeding out the worker at an earlier age, average life expectancy and thus the period of insecurity and dependency were rising as well.

According to social insurance advocates, there were two means for dealing with these problems, both of which were governmental and both of which were being adopted throughout Europe. As a temporary expedient, states or the federal government should provide old-age pensions—means-tested, general revenue financed, cash payments to the elderly poor. Designed as pure poverty relief, pensions would do no more than hold "body and soul" together, while allowing the elderly to live in their own homes or in the homes of their children. They were an immediate solution to the already existing and, in their view, unsatisfactory means of dealing with the elderly poor.

The only real solution to the problem of old age, advocates went on to argue, was a federal system of compulsory old-age insurance. Designed to distribute low-cost retirement benefits to the working classes, the public system would reduce premium costs by eliminating advertising and sales expenditures and profit. The cost of insurance to the low-income worker would be further reduced since the need for discrimination on the basis of higher mortality rates and higher forfeiture and nonpayment rates among industrial workers would be eliminated as well.[38] As the problem of old age was principally the result of low wages in working years, they said, the program should be financed either by federal general revenues or by a payroll tax levied predominately on employers.

Among advocates the superiority of compulsory insurance was clear. It could improve the lot of working men in their old age without the stigma of a means-test and, as a right rather than a privilege, distribute benefits that were large enough to provide a minimum standard of living rather than simply subsistence. In short, the amount of income redistribution to the wage earner would be more significant.[39]

The Failure of the Social Insurance Movement

A very poor greeting was accorded proposals for social insurance and other collective welfare schemes in the United States. At a time when poverty relief was predominately a county, city, and town activity and private insurance was thriving, proposals for compulsory state and federal activity were denounced as socialistic, communistic, or at least paternalistic. To opponents, social insurance was an "alien" system based on compulsion and imported from Germany.[40]

Reflecting the opposition of business interests, the Pennsylvania Chamber of Commerce in 1924 responded to compulsory public schemes to aid the elderly (notably welfare) as "un-American and socialistic and unmistakably earmarked as an entering wedge of communist propaganda."[41] For Samuel Gompers of the American Federation of Labor (AFL), whose opposition was a major detriment to the movement, social insurance was "in its essence undemocratic."[42] Compulsory schemes threatened the viability (and member attracting features) of trade-union pensions, and, like other collective welfare schemes, Gompers argued, they were advanced by job-seeking intellectuals who criticized the industrial society and thereby denied the success of trade unions in meeting the needs of working men.[43] In 1916 he vowed to assist in the "inauguration of a revolution against compulsory insurance."[44] Finally, reflecting the views of all those who rallied around the banner of self-reliance and other nongovernmental solutions to the problems of the elderly, an insurance representative argued that to adopt public insurance or pensions would be to "concede that the social and economic development of the nation [had] been in the wrong direction, that the education in thrift [had] been defective, and that the virtues of intelligent self-denial and self-sacrifice [had] been replaced by considerations of selfish indulgence and indifference to the welfare of others."[45]

During a period spanning less than thirty years the elderly had risen from a position of political nonexistence at the turn of the century to prominence as the leading social issue, and compulsory old-age insurance grew from an idea in the minds of social reformers to a topic of live political debate—only to recede once more.[46] State legislatures created commissions to study the financial condition of the elderly and report on the advisability of state action, several such studies were conducted, and proposals to make cash transfers to the elderly were debated in most legislatures. Yet from the twenty-one reports that were ultimately commissioned by state legislatures by 1929, there came only one endorsement of compulsory insurance as the solution to the needs of the elderly.[47] At the federal level no bills for compulsory old-age insurance were even introduced into Congress. Expressing most pointedly the views of opponents and foreshadowing responses to follow, the Massachusetts Commission on Old-Age Pensions concluded that to adopt a pension program would be to admit that the "whole economic and social system [had been] a failure"; compulsory insurance was "unthinkable and distasteful."[48]

With evidently great ideological overtones, the defeat of social insurance in the post–World War I years was decisive.[49] Denounced by representatives of business and organized labor alike, compulsory insurance was neither endorsed by major lobby groups nor popularly endorsed. National health insurance was bitterly defeated in 1920, after a series of legislative proposals reached state legislatures. That movement was not to be revitalized in any serious manner for another thirty-five years. By 1929, and before any legislative proposals for compulsory old-age insurance were even introduced into Congress, moreover, the level of interest in compulsory insurance had declined to the point that it was simply no longer an issue of serious political debate. The social insurance movement in the United States, an acknowledged defeat by the 1920s, was described by Leifur Magnusson of the International Labor Office as "practically untouched, irrelevant and meaningless . . . a mirage in a sunlight sea of prosperity."[50]

The Sources of Failure: From Rhetoric to Reality

While focusing attention on the condition of the elderly and helping to prompt public inquiry, the claims of advocates were unable to withstand public scrutiny. Beginning with the first state to commission a study, in 1907, and continuing through the eleven states that followed suit by 1929, there was general agreement that social insurance was not "the solution" to the problems of the elderly.[51]

The first commission to study old-age dependency and the possibility of state action was established by the Massachusetts General Court in 1907. Said to "mark the first significant entry of the aged into American social politics,"[52] the Massachusetts Commission on Old-Age Pensions reported findings that were by no means supportive of the movement for public action. Making its final report in 1910, the commission estimated that out of 177,000 elderly persons in the state, nearly 80 percent were self-supporting. Only 2 percent of the elderly were found to reside in almshouses, 3 percent were supported by organized private or public charity, and the remainder were supported by family and friends. As such, the commission found the extent of old-age dependency insufficient to warrant state action in the area of insurance or pensions, arguing that such policies would tend to depress wages, attract pension-seekers from other states, and, most importantly in their view, weaken family solidarity and individual initiative—the final buttresses to old-age dependency.[53]

Evidently, understanding the failure of the compulsory insurance movement lies in unraveling the poverty-insecurity-insurance rhetoric of advocates. The ex-post problem of poverty among the elderly and prevailing methods for alleviating it were quite distinct from the ex-ante problem of preventing poverty and the methods available for individuals and groups to voluntarily redistribute income over their lifetimes. A careful examination of then-current studies of the elderly along with other known facts about financial institutions provide valuable insights into the nature of the problem of old age and political sentiments toward its resolution.[54] The following major conclusions can be drawn from such an examination.

1. *Even among the most industrial states, the vast majority of the elderly were dependent on neither organized private or public charity or the almshouse. Instead, they were self-supporting or supported by families and friends.*

The information contained in Table 3.4, based on survey results in New York and Massachusetts, helps substantiate this point. According to the findings of the New York Commission on Old-Age Security, for example, out of the estimated 603,700 persons over sixty-five residing in the state in 1929, nearly 90 percent were either self-supporting or voluntarily provided for by friends and families. Of these, 43 percent were supported by their own earnings, pensions, or other income, and 50 percent (*including all wives* without their own sources of income) were supported by other family members or friends.[55] Less than 4 percent of the state's

Table 3.4. Survey findings on support of aged population in New York, 1929

Class	Persons sixty-five and older		Persons seventy and older	
	Number	Percent	Number	Percent
Estimated total	603,700	100.0	350,400	100.0
Self-dependent:	263,507	43.6	126,535	36.0
Public pensions[a]	50,390	8.3	38,478	11.0
Private pensions	10,937	1.8	10,557	3.0
Current earnings				
(Excluding housewives)	172,000	28.5	60,000	17.0
Income	30,180	5.0	17,500	5.0
Dependent on friends and relatives (including housewives):	303,753	50.4	199,802	57.1
Dependent on organized charity:				
Public	12,924	2.1	9,095	2.6
Private	8,421	1.4	6,740	1.9
Confined by Government[b]	15,104	2.5	8,228	2.4

Source: State of New York, *Old-Age Security: Report of the New York State Commission on Old-Age Security,* Legislative Document No. 67 (Albany, N.Y.: J. B. Lyons, 1930), p. 39.

a. Federal civil and military retirement pensions, state and local retirement pensions, and military homes.

b. Includes inmates of mental institutions and prisions. Those in almshouses placed under "dependent on organized public charity."

elderly were found to be dependent on organized private charity or public assistance, and this figure did not appear to rise significantly with age, as the decline in the proportion of self-supporting over age seventy, for example, was found to be roughly offset by the rise in the proportion aided by friends and families. The major findings of the New York study were borne out by a more extensive, though earlier, study by the Massachusetts Commission.[56]

For a broader view focusing on the extent of institutional care for the elderly, it should be noted that in most states dependence on the almshouse was minimal. In only six states did the number of elderly paupers exceed 2,000 in 1923, whereas there were twelve states with less than 150 elderly paupers. For the United States as a whole, less than 1 in 115 elderly persons resided in almshouses. Proponents of government action often misinterpreted statistics on almshouse trends in an effort to influence policy, yet the proportion of the aged residing in almshouses was actually stable to declining throughout the period 1880-1923.[57] None of these figures, of course, suggest the absence of a serious poverty problem among the elderly.

Table 3.5 Findings of five surveys on financial condition of the elderly, 1925-29[a]

Wealth, income, and need	Otsego	Canton	Selected cities	NCF	Mass.
Owning property of $5,000 or more:	21.9%	52.1%	36.5%	47.6%	40.8%
Annual income of those owning less than $5,000 property:					
$100–$400	31.0	10.5	9.7	6.0	9.2
Less than $100	27.8	16.5	27.2	18.2	23.2
Property less than $5,000 and income less than $400:	45.9	12.9	23.4	12.7	19.2
Proportion in need of assistance:[b]	22.1	10.9	11.4	—	11.4

a. Calculated on the basis of information contained in State of New York, *Old-Age Security: Report of the New York State Commission on Old-Age Security*, pp. 53-54, 56-57, 61, 74-76. In each of these studies both members of married couples, if sixty-five or older, were counted and placed in same financial group.

b. Proportion of elderly with property valued at less than $3,000, incomes of less than $400, and no children to support them. Because of residency requirements and the like, this figure exceeds the proportion eligible for proposed assistance.

2. *There certainly did exist poverty among the elderly, as there did among all age groups, but it was for reasons not clearly discernible from those for other age groups. It was not at all clear, moreover, that the magnitude of the problem would increase over time, as industrialization was intertwined with economic growth.*

To illustrate, the results of five then-current surveys of the financial condition of the elderly with varying economic and social backgrounds are presented in Table 3.5. Included are the results of an Otsego study of a small rural county in New York, the only strictly rural study made in the United States; the Canton study of a representative village in New York; a study of selected cities in New York; the National Civic Federation study of selected cities in New York (excluding New York City); and a Massachusetts Commission study of its own entire state. As detailed in the table, the proportion of elderly people with property valued in excess of $5,000 ($23,800), considered adequate, was as low as 22 percent in Otsego, the most rural area, and averaged 40 to 50 percent in other areas.[58] Using their own standards for evaluating adequacy, the proportion of the elderly with critically low incomes—less than $400 ($1,904) annually—and low property holdings averaged 20 percent. On the basis of these figures, and taking into account family status and property holdings, it was estimated that roughly 10 to 20 percent of the elderly were in need of assistance.[59]

To the extent that there existed a common cause of this poverty, evidence was lacking to suggest that it derived from either the failure of short-sighted workers to make financial provisions for their old age or the failure of insurance institutions to meet the demands of long-sighted workers. Instead, poverty seemed to result from low earnings during working years and the consequent inability to weather the inevitable reduction or discontinuation of earnings that resulted from illness, disability, or loss of spouse.[60] In New York, for example, it was estimated that roughly three-quarters of the dependent elderly men had been unskilled farm or general laborers. In California most had been farm laborers, miners, or lumbermen. In both states the vast majority of women had been either housewives or domestic servants. Within the almshouse population surveyed in New York, moreover, 80 percent of the aged had never owned a home, 37 percent were illiterate or without formal education, 90 percent were widowed or single, and 73 percent were without living children. One-third had no living relatives at all. In California 70 percent of the needy aged were widowed or single, two-thirds had no living children, and more than two-fifths had neither living children nor other relatives.[61]

As for the cause of impaired earnings in old age, the studies conducted by the National Civic Federation and the Massachusetts Commission along with evidence from Pennsylvania suggested that physical impairment was critical.[62] To the extent that physical infirmities were more detrimental to continued employment in industry than agriculture, this fact in isolation thus suggested that the process of industrialization would lead to an increase in unemployment and poverty among the elderly. Then, too, industrialization and urbanization could be expected to harm the elderly by increasing worker mobility and reducing family solidarity.[63]

That these facts implied a net deterioration in the financial prospects of the elderly over time, however, was uncertain at best.[64] Industrialization, associated as it was with economic growth, improved the ability of workers to make advance financial provision. Increased job insecurity simply made this task more urgent.[65] To wit, the growth of real incomes in the late nineteenth and early twentieth centuries coincided with a rapid growth of savings, a reallocation of saving toward more illiquid retirement saving forms, and a rapid growth and development in private insurance and pension institutions, each of which are discussed below.

3. *Regardless of the measure employed, aggregate saving rates showed no downward trend in the predepression years.*

Whether the household's saving decision is assumed interdependent with the saving decision of corporations or with the government as well, each of several key saving rates for the period reveal what has since been noted in the long run. Households and corporations tended to save one-eighth to one-ninth of their incomes, and including the actions of government, approximately one-fifth.[66]

4. *The components of total saving, however, were undergoing a major realignment toward relatively illiquid saving forms more clearly suited for providing financial security in old age: life insurance, annuities, and retirement pensions.*

As illustrated in Table 3.6, the share of total personal saving accounted for by these saving forms rose from less than 7 1/2 percent in the period 1900-1908 to more than 12 percent in the period 1922-29.[67] Between 1900 and 1929 there was a doubling of their share in the assets of the nation's balance sheet. By 1929 $1.1 ($5.3) billion of total personal saving was in the form of life-insurance reserves and $390 ($1,875) million was in the form of pension and retirement funds.

5. *There was rapid growth and innovation in both private life insurance and*

Table 3.6 Personal saving and its pension and insurance components in selected years, 1900–1929

Year or period[a]	Total personal savings[b]	Pension & retirement funds			Life insurance reserves
		U.S. Gov't.	State & local	Private	
Amounts (in millions)					
1900	$ 1,270	—	—	—	$ 110
1908	2,000	—	—	—	180
1914	2,550	—	—	—	200
1920	6,570	20	20	—	520
1929	11,490	160	70	160	1,120
Shares					
1900-1908	100		.0	.0	7.3
1909-1914	100		.0	.0	7.1
1922-1929	100		1.6	.5	10.0

Sources: U.S. Department of Commerce, Bureau of the Census, *Historical Statistics of the United States from Colonial Times to 1970,* Bicentennial Edition (2 vols; Washington, D.C.: U. S. Government Printing Office, 1975), 1: 266-67; Alicia H. Munnell, *The Effect of Social Security on Pesonal Saving* (Cambridge, Mass.: Ballinger, 1974), pp. 39, 107.
a. Normal periods exclude war years and recessions.
b. Including consumer durables.

pensions in the predepression years establishing long-run trends that would clearly persist.

There were marked improvements for buyers in the terms and nature of contractual relations, the net cost of acquiring insurance, and in the financial condition of insurers that increased the attractiveness of these saving and insurance forms, especially in ways that benefited low-income workers. Much of this was a quite recent development.

Life Insurance

In the area of life insurance, for example, during the mid-1800s there were only five thousand life-insurance policies in force, averaging $1,000 or more. Overall economic expansion, advances in financial markets, science and medicine, and actuarial science, however, all fostered unprecedented growth in the industry during the post–Civil War years.[68] Between 1860 and 1912 annual premium payments increased from $5 million to $670 million, or from 1 percent to 2 percent of personal income.[69] The process of competition within an emerging legal structure, moreover, made life insurance an ever-improving outlet for the middle- and lower-income family. Profit-sharing arrangements, grace periods, and surrender values became prevalent, nonforfeiture laws emerged, and warranties were abandoned as representations of the truth became acceptable and contracts became ultimately incontestible. By 1920 most states regulated the activities, investments, and reserve positions of insurance companies and controlled essential features of their contracts.[70] Between 1880 and 1920, moreover, deferred dividend plans were developed and industrial and group insurance emerged to compete with fraternals in meeting the requirements of wage earners.

Fraternal societies provided the dominant source of insurance protection for wage earners before 1900. Designed for the mutual aid of their members and operated along the lines of mutual life-insurance companies, American fraternals were an attractive means of voluntary organization which, through the local lodge system, maintained the personality of clubs and provided low-cost insurance. Since lodge members were voluntary solicitors, there were no middlemen, and the lodge system permitted a significant reduction in the costs associated with field work and administration.[71]

Fraternals expanded rapidly with the overall insurance industry in the late 1800s. Between 1890 and 1900 fraternal membership climbed from 3.7 million to 5.3 million, and coverage was estimated at $6 ($59) billion. By 1900 there were six hundred societies, 60 percent of which had emerged in the previous decade.[72] Although fraternals, like so many other insurance organizations, underwent a "painful process" over the course of the next twenty to thirty years of buttressing their often unsound reserve positions, most fraternals were operating on the same reserve basis as commercial companies by the 1920s.[73] By this time the assets of fraternal life insurance exceeded a half billion dollars, their relative postion having been eroded by the development of group and industrial policies.[74]

For workers without the friendly society option, industrial insurance provided a viable form of insurance.[75] In both size of premium, frequency of payment, and method of collection and servicing, industrial insurance was specifically designed for industrial workers and their families. Premiums were as low as 5 cents a week, collected on a weekly or biweekly basis at the home of the insured. Requiring no medical examination, these policies, which averaged $190 ($913) in 1929, could be (and often were) taken out on the lives of all family members, including wives and children, whether as young as one year or older than sixty.[76] Because of high forfeiture rates and relatively high mortality rates among industrial workers, and high collection costs, these policies were, of course, relatively expensive per dollar of face value. Being a key vehicle for the low-income worker to cover funeral and medical expenses at the time of death, however, they were nevertheless rapidly adopted. The number and amount of policies in force doubled every decade between 1875, when first introduced, and 1930. By 1930 there were 82.9 million industrial life-insurance policies in force.[77]

Finally, group life insurance, which emerged in 1911, was yet another form of insurance providing advantages to workers. Offering blanket protection for all employees in a firm, such policies avoided problems of adverse selection and precluded the need for medical exams and age-graded premiums. From the time these policies were introduced and continuing through to the Great Depression, the amount of group life insurance in force grew at approximately twice the rate of ordinary life insurance.[78]

By the time social insurance proposals were being advanced in the 1920s, the

Table 3.7 Life insurance policies in force, 1900-1929

Year	Number (in millions)	Value (in billions)				Average size of policy		
		Total	Ordinary	Group	Industrial	Ordinary	Group	Industrial
1900	14	$ 7.6	$ 6.1	—ᵃ	$ 1.5	$2,160	—	$130
1915	41	21.0	16.7	$0.1	4.3	1,800	$ 830	130
1920	65	40.5	32.0	1.6	6.9	1,990	960	150
1925	97	69.4	52.9	4.2	12.3	2,270	1,340	170
1929	123	102.1	75.7	9.0	17.4	2,470	1,590	190

Source: U.S. Department of Commerce, Bureau of the Census, *Historical Statistics of the United States from Colonial Times to 1970,* 2:1056.

a. Less than $500,000

insurance industry was entering a "golden age" in which "all conditions affecting the life-insurance business were good and kept getting better."[79] Rising interest rates and declining mortality rates raised dividends and reduced the net cost of insurance to an all-time low. Double indemnity and disability benefits were popular innovations, while inheritance taxes and $10,000 policies issued by the federal government during World War I elevated interest in larger policies. Between 1919 and 1929 the total amount of life insurance in force tripled, reaching $100 ($481) billion, and both the annual amount of new insurance paid for and admitted assets doubled.[80] As illustrated in Table 3.7, there were 123 million life-insurance policies in force in 1929 and, in that one year alone, approximately $2 ($9.6) billion was paid out to policyholders.[81] The progress of the industry surpassed that in any other country of the world.

Importantly, by the 1930s, there were already in existence each of the major insurance forms we know today, each having different saving and insurance components, and each providing financial protection for the elderly in different ways. There was term life insurance, both convertible and renewable; there was whole life insurance, both ordinary and limited payment; there were endowment policies and annuities, both immediate and deferred; and there were individual and group policies for both life insurance and annuities. Policies could be purchased to provide income singly for the policyholder in old age, or for the policyholder during old age and his survivors after his death, or simply for his survivors. Interestingly, the ratio of annuity premiums to life insurance premiums was at the start of a sharp historical rise: from less than 1 percent in 1915, to 2.8 percent in 1929, reaching 15 percent in 1935.[82]

Private Pensions

Although a significantly later development, private pensions emerged within the first twenty to thirty years of the 1900s and showed growth comparable to that of life insurance. Since pensions protected against the risk of living beyond one's work life, a viable market for these plans had awaited economic and demographic changes that lengthened life spans, shortened work lives, and increased rates of

Table 3.8. Pension systems in the United States, 1928

Classes	Number covered	Number of beneficiaries
Government employees		
a. Federal executive civil service	568,715	14,119
b. State employees	34,500[a]	1,397
c. Municipal employees	93,374[b]	4,619
Teachers		
a. State	317,835	13,094
b. City	54,776	3,949
c. Carnegie fund, including teachers' widows	—	922
Policemen and firemen	67,765	20,327
U.S. war pensioners	—	491,194
Industrial pensions, including railroads	4,000,000	80,000
Trade union benefits		
a. Pensions	640,000	11,509
b. Disability for old age	352,000	—
c. Superannuation benefits	143,000	—
YMCA and YWCA secretaries	4,707	312
Ministers	—	28,319

Source: National Industrial Conference Board, *The Support of the Aged: A Review of Conditions and Proposals* (New York: National Industrial Conference Board, 1931), p. 25; and "Care of Aged Persons in the U.S.," *Bulletin of the U.S. Bureau of Labor Statistics* No. 489 (Oct. 1929): 3.
a. Figures for Connecticut, Massachusetts, New Jersey, and New York. Maine and Pennsylvania also granted pensions to state employees.
b. Figures for Baltimore, Boston, Chicago, Detroit, Minneapolis, New York City, Pittsburgh, and San Francisco. Philadelphia also had a municipal employee pension system, but figures not available.

return above those attainable on ordinary savings accounts, for example, or standard deferred annuities. As these preconditions were met, the direct involvement of firms or unions on behalf of workers reduced the relatively high administrative costs of processing smaller, more frequent premium payment policies, and the market for private pension plans expanded rapidly. Between 1920 and 1929 the assets of private self-insured pension funds alone rose from $50 million to $500 million, more than eleven-fold in real terms.[83]

For the low-income wage-earner, the most important developments along these lines were in industrial pensions, popular because of their modest and regular premium payment provisions.[84] Premiums were small, say 1 percent of wages, and monthly pensions averaged $40 to $50 ($190 to $237) in 1927.[85] Whereas in 1900 there were fewer than 15 industrial pension plans in existence, there were 168 by 1915 and 440 as of June 1929.[86] As illustrated in Table 3.8, four million workers, or two-thirds of all persons covered by major public and private pension plans in 1928 were covered by industrial pension plans. Excluding fraternal membership, there were nearly 6.4 million persons or 14 percent of the labor force covered by some major pension plan.

None of this is intended to suggest that private pension programs or life insurance were ideal, of course. There were a number of important problems, some created by tax incentives (under the 1928 Revenue Act, for example, pension plans lent themselves to tax-avoidance schemes), others by the courts' enforcement of the terms of contracts, and still others by the fact that these industries were still maturing. The key point is that evidence was lacking to establish that imperfections in these markets were either permanent, an inevitable part of private supply, or correctable by public production.[87]

Each of these points on poverty, saving, and insurance in the predepression years clearly suggest that evidence was lacking to indicate that poverty among the elderly was due to a significant problem of myopia among workers or to a problem of lack of available institutional outlets for saving. That is, evidence was lacking to establish the need for the two central features of social insurance—coercion and public production. From the perspective of demand-side models of government, it should not be surprising therefore that social insurance did not emerge.

Advocates failed to define a problem of old age that could withstand careful investigation and failed to define a resolution that, except through rhetoric, bore some relation to the sources of the problem. This failure ultimately killed the compulsory old-age insurance movement. After all, how could social insurance possibly reverse the process of urbanization and industrialization, raise wages, improve family solidarity, or be subject to less financial difficulties than previously tried state and local retirement systems?[88]

In Search of an Interest Group

Less idealized models of government would suggest that it may well be necessary to look beyond demands based on considerations of "market failure," however, to understand the presence or absence of government. Such demands may be unlikely to survive the filtering of the political process, being overwhelmed instead by the more intense and narrowly based demands of special-interest groups.

Concentrating on the activities of interest groups, that is, even the complete absence of efficiency arguments for compulsory old-age insurance need be sufficient to have precluded enactment. As a tax-transfer scheme, social insurance constituted a direct means of utilizing the coercive powers of the state so as to redistribute income. In this regard the failure of compulsory insurance can also be traced to its failure to amass active support from a well-organized would-be beneficiary group such as the elderly or organized labor.

The Elderly, Organized Labor, and the Politics of a Pay-As-You-Go System

Those who were already elderly or near-elderly could clearly expect to receive net transfers of income under social insurance, at least under most reasonable distributions of taxes and benefits. Throughout the world and even in most private systems unearned benefits were typical of the start-up phase of retirement programs. In the first decades of this century, however, the elderly (nonveterans) were without political strength. Their numbers were yet few, they lacked organization, they lacked a common cause, and, to a large extent, they still lacked leadership. While the 1920s were formative in the development of a political coalition of the elderly, it was not until the early 1930s (when a plan was introduced into Congress promising transfers many times as large as those implied by Social Security) that the elderly emerged as a political force in their own right.

For younger workers organized representation existed through labor unions, and an intergenerational transfer scheme was potentially profitable. Since social insurance programs were not typically fully funded, for many years, retirees would not "purchase," in an actuarial sense, the benefits to which they became entitled. Instead they could earn some extra-normal return on tax payments as income was transferred intergenerationally.[89] Social insurance offered another profit potential, moreover—one that could prevail over time—in that expected returns for similarly situated workers in any particular generation were not constrained by market forces to be equal. Instead, they were politically determined such that depending upon income class, family or marital status, and the like, the return to particular classes of retirees could be even higher than that earned on average.

These benefits, however, were potential and contingent upon the initially agreed-upon institutional design actually coming to pass at the time of retirement. A decision some time in the future to lower taxes could well result in lower benefits and rates of return for current retirees and lower benefits for all workers when they retired. The same would hold true for any decline in the growth of tax revenues (such as those due to economic and demographic changes), only these would have permanent effects on returns. In the absence of constitutional or legal guarantee, assurance of an extranormal or even positive return required the assurance of political control over time—the ability to raise taxes to buttress returns as retirement neared.

The experience workers had with such underfunded schemes—including public retirement systems for state and municipal employees, some company and trade union pensions, and many of the life insurance companies that failed in the late 1800s—all clearly revealed a high degree of risk in this regard.[90] Overexpansion of benefits in the early years when assessment rates were deceptively low produced too high a structure of future tax rates and an unwillingness on the part of younger workers to continue benefits. Benefit reductions and outright default in such plans were commonplace. In trade-union plans themselves, there were ongoing struggles between retirees over benefit levels and workers over assessment rates, with no clear pattern of resolution.[91] While compulsory participation at the federal level could add permanence to such an intergenerational transfer scheme by preventing voluntary exit by the young, this would only be true to the extent that younger workers lacked political control.

From the perspective of organized labor, therefore, social insurance involved a relatively certain tax on its members in exchange for uncertain future benefits, and it involved the likely termination of their own pension plans, over which they had direct administration and control, in exchange for shared political control. As of 1928 some 1.6 million workers or 41 percent of all trade unionists belonged to unions providing old-age benefits, and at least during the predepression years, these benefit plans were perceived as both member-attracting and member-sustaining features.[92]

The Social Worker

What about social workers? Were they a cohesive interest group capable of affecting policy, who could also profit from the enactment of compulsory insurance? Certainly these questions are worthy of investigation since, in a direct financial sense, an enlargement of the welfare functions of the government—as implied by social security—provided a potentially profitable method of increasing the demand for their services.

In the 1920s, however, social workers were still suffering the consequences of their transition to professional status.[93] As a result they were neither a well-organized front nor active proponents of social insurance. Numbering just forty thousand, social workers were a community fragmented on issues as diverse as "skill" versus "sentiment," traditional versus psychiatric casework, private versus public poverty relief, and, among proponents of government action, fragmented over relief versus social insurance. While many of these issues were in the process of being resolved and others would be resolved with the onset of the Great Depression, social insurance would still have a difficult time mustering the active support of social workers. At least in part, this must have been due to the fact that the employment opportunities offered by social insurance for administrative and field workers with their skills were dwarfed by those offered by the many public-welfare programs yet to be enacted.[94]

With this overall lack of concerted support from either the elderly, organized labor or social workers, it should not be surprising that concerted opposition by interest groups such as the insurance industry and the medical profession could have prevented compulsory insurance from being considered in Congress.

The Emergence of Public Assistance for the Elderly

As the compulsory insurance movement was suffering defeat, momentum was gaining for old-age pensions—cash assistance for the elderly poor.[95] All of the evidence of the twenties reiterated what surely was already known: there were poor among the elderly and almshouses were not suited for their needs. The political questions that then attracted attention were, first, which institutional alternatives might be superior to existing methods of caring for the elderly and, second, at what level of government might they be best administered and financed.

Of the states investigating the problems of the elderly, three-quarters of them endorsed old-age pensions.[96] Most state legislatures debated the issue of old-age

Table 3.9. Principal features of old-age pension laws in the United States, 1935

State	Date enacted[a]	Pension-able age	Maximum annual pension	Residence requirements in yrs.	Property limit	Annual income limit	Administration	Source of funds (state, county, town
Optional local participation								
Mont.	1923	70	$300	15	—[b]	300	County	C
Nevada	1925	65	365	10	$3,000	390	County	C
Wisc.	1925	70	365[c]	15	3,000	365	County	S-C-T
Ky.	1926	70	250	10	2,500	400	County	C
Colo.	1927	70	365	15	2,000	365	County	C
Md.	1927	65	365	15	—[b]	365	Circt. court judge	C
Utah	1929	65[d]	300	15	—[b]	300	County	C
Wyo.	1929	65	360	15	—[e]	360	County	C
Minn.	1929	70	365[c]	15	3,000	365	County	C
W. Va.	1931	65	360	10	0	0	County	C
Hawaii	1933	65	180	30	—[b]	300	Local	C-T
Mandatory participation								
Calif.	1929	70	365	15	3,000	365	County or City	S-C or T
N.Y.	1930	70	—[f]	10	—[g]	—[g]	County	S[i]
Mass.	1930	70	—[f]	20	—[h]	—[h]	Public welfare svc.	S-C or T
Del.	1931	65	300	5	—[b]	300	State	S
Idaho	1931	65	300	10	—[b]	300	State	C
N.H.	1931	70	390	15	2,000	300	County	C-T
N.J.	1931	70	360	15	3,000	—[g]	State & county	S-C
Ariz.	1933	70	360	35	—[e]	300	County	S-C
Ind.	1933	70	180	15	1,000	180	County	S-C
Maine	1933	65	360	15	300[j]	365	State & local	S-C-T
Mich	1933	70	360	15	3,500	365	State & local	S
Neb.	1933	65	240	15	—[b]	300	County	C
N.D.	1933	68	150	20	—[b]	150	State & county	S

State	Date[a]	Age						Administered by	
Ohio	1933	65	300	15	3,000	300		State & local	S
Oregon	1933	75	360	15	3,000	360		County	C
Wash.	1933	65	360	15	—b	360		County	C
Pa.	1934	70	360	15	—b	Indigent		State	S
Iowa	1934	65	300	10		365		State	S
Alaska	1915	65 M / 60 F	420 M / 540 F	0		Insufficient means of support		State	S

a. Date of first effective law.
b. Annual income of property computed at 5 percent of its value.
c. Pension plus income.
d. And unable to work.
e. Annual income of property computed at 3 percent of its value.
f. Adequate
g. Unable to support oneself.
h. Not specified.
i. And public welfare district.
j. House not considered property.

Sources: U.S. Committee on Economic Security, *Report to the President of the Committee on Economic Security* (Washington, D.C.: U.S. Government Printing Office, 1935), Table 15; Abraham Epstein, *Insecurity: A Challenge to America* (New York: Random House, 1938), pp. 534-35; National Industrial Conference Board, *The Support of the Aged: A Review of Conditions and Proposals* (New York: National Industrial Conference Board, 1931), pp. 58-60.

pensions during the 1920s, and by 1929 social insurance advocates had been joined by representatives of organized labor and fraternal societies, two long-time opponents of such measures, in their advocacy of means-tested relief for the elderly poor.[97]

The first old-age pension law was enacted in Arizona in 1914.[98] Soon declared unconstitutional, there was no further action until 1923, when similar programs emerged in Montana, Nevada, and Pennsylvania. Within the following six years pension programs were created in Wisconsin (in 1925), Kentucky and Washington (in 1926), Colorado and Maryland (in 1927), and California, Utah, Minnesota, and Wyoming (in 1929).

As revealed in Table 3.9, there was a great deal of similarity in the design of these laws, and their objectives were clear: to provide the elderly who were destitute and without family care a subsistence level of income. The typical law stipulated a maximum monthly pension of $25-30 ($119-$143) for people seventy years of age or older who had resided within the state for a long period of time, generally fifteen years.[99] The recipient was prohibited from earning more than $300 ($1,429) a year or possessing more than $3,000 ($14,286) of wealth, and was required to have the value of all pensions deducted from his estate upon death. Reminiscent of the poor laws, an elderly person could generally be denied a monthly pension if he: (1) had financially responsible relatives; (2) failed to work according to his ability; (3) had deserted his family; (4) was a tramp or beggar; (5) disposed of property to qualify for the pension; (6) was a recipient of another government pension; or (7) was an inmate.[100]

Though referred to as "state" old-age pensions, these early laws were neither state financed, state administered, statewide, nor mandatory. Instead, they were county-optional laws whereby the state determined the maximum pension payable and broad conditions on eligibility, while funding, administration, and even the decision to participate were county controlled. In effect, the state simply empowered localities to collect and dispense public funds for this purpose.

Seemingly modest in objective and method, the adoption of these programs marked a major liberalization in the treatment of the elderly poor that was not yet without political opposition.[101] As partly illustrated in Table 3.10, the early pension movement was fraught with constitutional, financial, and other political difficulties during the prosperous decade of the 1920s. Laws were vetoed, found unconstitutional, repealed, and amended; and among the states with laws that were operative by 1929 the rate of county participation and the number of pensioners were extremely low.[102] At the federal level, there were no old-age pension bills involving federal financing even reported out of congressional committee.

On the Eve of the Great Depression

As the 1920s drew to a close, the financial problems of the elderly poor had clearly emerged as a political problem to be reckoned with, and political sentiments

Table 3.10. State action on old-age pensions

1915: Alaska enacted first old-age pension law.

Arizona passed law abolishing almshouses and establishing old-age pensions. The law was shortly thereafter declared unconstitutional.

1923: Old-age pension laws passed in Nevada, Montana, and Pennsylvania.

Residents of Ohio defeated by referendum vote of 2-1, a proposal to institute old-age pensions.

1924: Pennsylvania pension law of 1923 found unconstitutional.

1925: Old-age pension law passed in Wisconsin. In California, pension law passed by the state legislature but vetoed by the governor.

Nevada law of 1923 repealed, modified, then reenacted.

Efforts to repeal the Montana law of 1923 unsuccessful.

1926: Old-age pension law enacted in Kentucky. Governer of Washington vetoed recently enacted pension law.

1927: Old-age pension laws passed in Maryland and Colorado.

1929: Old-age pension laws enacted in California and Wyoming—the first statewide, mandatory laws—and in Utah. During legislative year 1928-29, bills failed to attain approval in either house of thirteen state legislatures.

1930: Old-age pension laws enacted in Massachusetts and New York.

1931: Old-age pension bills pending in thirty-eight states. Laws passed in Deleware, Idaho, New Hampshire, New Jersey, and West Virginia.

Previously passed laws amended in Wisconsin, Colorado, Wyoming, Minnesota, and Maryland.

Nine years after Pennsylvania passed first law (found unconstitutional) it passed a constitutional amendment permitting enactment of old-age pension law.

1933: More old-age pension laws passed than in any other year: Arizona, Indiana, Maine, Michigan, Nebraska, North Dakota, Ohio, Oregon, Pennsylvania, Washington, and Hawaii.

Law also passed in Arkansas, but found unconstitutional.

1934: Iowa passed old-age pension law, and earlier laws which had been optional in Maryland, Washington, and Minnesota made mandatory.

By end of year, twenty-eight states and 2 territories had established old-age pension laws.

Source: "Congress Faces the Question of Old-Age Pensions," *The Congressional Digest* 14 (March 1935): 76.

toward a resolution were crystalizing. On the one hand, proposals to alleviate poverty via the public sector without resorting to the almshouse were beginning to gain broad-based support. As the elderly became an increasingly important part of the overall population, as immigration rates declined,[103] as states shared the burden of finance,[104] as constitutions were amended to permit the distribution of public monies for benevolent purposes, and as almshouses were further out-dated, the remaining opposition to cash assistance would decline and state and local participation would rise. The Great Depression would certainly hasten this process since the institutional form of relief still prevailing in most states was incapable of dealing with a serious or prolonged economic downturn. Only with outdoor relief could public assistance be made available on a broad-scale basis in a relatively short period.

On the other hand, the 1920s witnessed a clear failure on the part of social insurance advocates to muster political support for their proposals. According to one disgruntled advocate, "the leadership of the movement was silenced and interest waned."[105] The level of interest in compulsory insurance schemes fell from the point of attracting open opposition from major lobby groups to the point that they were simply no longer an issue of serious political debate.

As the likely success of a social insurance movement with income redistribution at base relied heavily on the existence of unattended poverty, the favorable response to old-age pensions and the spread of this legislation during the 1920s seriously weakened the underpinnings of a political market for advocates' proposals.[106] Their market was further weakened by continued economic expansion and marked progress in private pensions and insurance, since their schemes, involving as they did coercion and federal production, were also predicated upon an increasing poverty problem and serious failures in insurance markets. As long as private markets functioned relatively smoothly, the doomsday pictures painted by social insurance advocates were simply without political force. The prospects for a revival of interest in their proposals would deteriorate over time.

The findings of this chapter clearly suggest the absence of broad-based demands for compulsory old-age insurance in the predepression years. Denounced by representatives of business and organized labor alike, compulsory insurance was neither endorsed by major lobby groups nor popularly endorsed. As a consequence, only one of the state commissions reporting by 1929 endorsed compulsory old-age insurance and no such bill was even introduced into Congress for consideration. By the close of the decade the social insurance movement was an acknowledged failure, with advocates having failed to gain any political momentum for their proposals.

A stronger, more significant conclusion can also be drawn. In all probability the basis for compulsory insurance, as envisioned by early advocates, would have been weakened over time had it not been for the Great Depression and Franklin Roosevelt. The emergence and growth of life insurance, pensions, and homes for the aged in the private sector, the proliferation of poverty assistance programs for the elderly at the state and local level, and overall economic expansion all tended to undermine the arguments for and the profitability of social insurance. In effect, while the private sector was responding to demands for financial protection in old age, the local public sector was responding to demands for a new means of alleviating poverty among the elderly and a viable political "market" for compulsory insurance was being foreclosed. This was what set the United States apart from the remainder of the world and constrained the expansion of the federal government in the pre–Social Security years—a strong reliance on markets and, within the public sector, a strong reliance on local control.

Part II. Emergence

Chapter 4. Preludes to Social Security: The Great Depression, President Roosevelt, and the Report of the CES

When in 1929 the United States entered into the most prolonged economic depression in history, banks failed, individuals' savings were destroyed, jobs were lost—and millions of people resorted to public assistance. By 1933 some fifteen million persons were on emergency relief from all levels of government.[1] Two years later President Roosevelt signed into law the Social Security Act—a comprehensive system of compulsory federal old-age insurance, coupled with a tax-offset system of unemployment compensation and grants to states for old-age poverty relief, maternal and child welfare, public health, aid to dependent children, and assistance for the blind. This pervasive and unprecedented federal action was undertaken with great speed: only two years had elapsed since Congress first seriously considered federal programs to aid the elderly poor and, more importantly perhaps, the first bill ever introduced into Congress for compulsory old-age insurance was the one passed eight months later as the Social Security Act.

Given the findings earlier in this book which indicated a lack of broad-based demands for compulsory old-age insurance, Chapters 4 and 5 explore the underlying economic and political changes that led a majority of elected representatives to support such a program in 1935. The questions addressed in this chapter include the following. How did private saving and insurance markets and the local public relief sector perform during the depression, and how did this influence demands for federal government action? What was the political significance of President Roosevelt's appointment of a Committee on Economic Security (CES) which was independent of Congress in drafting the proposed legislation? What was the impact on the ultimate design of the new law of staffing this committee with existing bureaucrats and social insurance advocates, and what inherent advantages did they possess in controlling the legislative agenda? What were the alternatives to the Administration's bill, and what were the strategic advantages for the Administration and other social insurance advocates of bundling the compulsory old-age insurance program with a series of politically popular relief programs into a single legislative package that was presented to Congress as an all-or-nothing offer?

The Great Depression and the Demand for Government Action

The Great Depression, a poorly understood economic phenomenon thought to be widespread "market failure," destroyed the reliance on the private sector that was characteristic of the predepression years and created an environment conducive to government action. The economic rewards and incentives produced by the market seemingly failed to provide protection or security. The collapse of private banking and savings institutions and sustained high rates of unemployment, particularly acute among the elderly, threatened two vital means of financial support for persons of all ages. Between 1929 and 1933 one-fifth of all commercial banks failed and unemployment reached a quarter of the labor force.[2] During the three and one-half years between September 1929 and June 1932 the real value of all stocks listed on the New York Stock Exchange fell nearly 80 percent, and by 1934 real personal savings had fallen $33 billion.[3] As late as November 1934 some nineteen million persons, or 15 percent of the population, were receiving emergency direct or work relief from the various levels of government.[4]

It was in the midst of this economic environment, in which the "survival of American capitalism seemed almost a matter of touch-and-go,"[5] that advocates of social insurance, social reformers, and New Dealers realigned to amass political support for programs they had advanced unsuccessfully for nearly thirty years. Whereas the prosperous decade of the 1920s all but paralyzed the social insurance movement, the depression provided a political climate conducive to demands for the federalization of many activities, only one of which was old-age insurance. Fueling the notion that the depression was the failure of a "wage-based" economy, or in the words of President Roosevelt, the product of a "disintegrating system of production and exchange," advocates urged that the depression provided final evidence that reliance on a market economy was the reliance on an unstable, insecure, and unjust economic system.[6] To opponents of government action the fact that governmental failure may have provided the underpinnings for the economic debacle must have been little consolation.

State Pension Movement Intensified

The severity and type of poverty created by the Great Depression, which cut across economic and social groups, eroded much of the opposition that remained to cash assistance for the elderly poor.[7] Old-age pension programs (means-tested welfare) sprouted up throughout the country in response to broad-based demands to aid the elderly. Whereas before the depression old-age pension programs had been created in only six states, in each case funded and administered at the county level on an optional basis, by the end of 1934 there were old-age pension laws in twenty-eight states, plus Hawaii and Alaska, twenty-two of which were county-mandatory. It was typically the case that administrative authority was granted to the state rather than the locality, and states contributed partially if not entirely to financing.

The operation of old-age pension programs was profoundly affected by the depression.[8] Not only did the number of pensioners and annual pension expenditures rise dramatically, but also average benefits fell and the differences between state payment levels became more pronounced. As illustrated in Tables 4.1 and 4.2, between 1930 and 1934 the number of pensioners increased from 10,648 to 235,265

Table 4.1. Trends in old-age pension laws, 1928-35

Year	Total	Percent of counties w/ operative laws	No. of pensioners	Average pension	Yearly pension expenditure	Total	Mandatory
		States with operative laws				States w/ laws	
1928	6	16.92%	1,514	$16.42	$ 284,509	7	3
1930	9	34.08	10,648	16.73	2,138,441	13	7
1931	15	39.56	76,663	19.01	16,251,794	18	11
1932	16	50.34	102,894	20.78	25,048,227	18	11
1933	17	52.39	115,549	19.25	26,167,117	29	23
1934	27	73.94	235,265	14.53	32,394,993	30	22
1935	32	75.65	408,502	15.57	65,001,665	41	30

Sources: "Experience Under State Old-Age Pension Acts in 1935," Monthly Labor Review 34 (Oct. 1936): 830-36; and "Congress Faces the Question of Old-Age Pensions," The Congressional Digest 14 (March 1935): 72.

and the yearly cost rose from $2 ($10) million[9] to $32 ($198) million. Monthly benefits, which averaged $19 ($121) in 1933, averaged less than $16 ($102) in 1935. While benefits ranged from $6 in Indiana to $30 in Maryland in 1933, they ranged from $1 in North Dakota to $27 in Nevada by 1935.[10]

As the depression worsened, and the material status of the elderly deteriorated, so too did the ability of states and localities to finance their new relief programs. The rate of county participation increased quite substantially, but there was a tendency among states to restrict their fields of operation. By 1933 "sharply curtailed benefits and a refusal to take on new pensioners, even the discontinuance of the system altogether until times improved" were all measures employed in states with limited or declining appropriations, particularly those where funding was by county alone.[11] In a number of states there were waiting lists (including cases that had been approved but not granted plus other applicants) that equaled and even exceeded the number of individuals receiving pensions.[12]

Given these developments, congressional attention turned to the possibility of federal participation in the provision of old-age pensions. Federal funding was now tempting to states and localities in several ways: it could provide much-needed financial assistance for meeting benefit obligations in the face of shrinking tax bases, it could provide financial incentives for remaining states to enact pension laws, and it could serve to geographically redistribute the tax burden of welfare.[13]

For each of these reasons demands for federal participation in state and local assistance programs clearly emerged during the depression. Whereas before the depression only a handful of bills for federal aid were introduced into Congress, none of which were reported out of committee, in 1934 a bill calling for federal grants to states with pension laws would be reported with unanimous approval from both committees in the House and Senate.

Table 4.2. Operation of state old-age pension laws, 1933

State	Year enacted	Pension age	No. of pensioners	Percent of pensioners to persons of eligible age	Average pension	Yearly cost
State-wide mandatory						
Alas.	1915	65	446	11.1%	$20.82	$ 95,705
Ariz.	1933	70	1,974	21.6	9.01	200,927
Calif.	1929	70	19,300	9.2	21.16	3,502,000
Col.	1933	65	8,705	14.1	8.59	172,481
Del.	1931	65	1,610	9.7	9.79	188,740
Hawaii	1933	65	(a)	(a)	(a)	(a)
Idaho	1931	65	1,275	5.7	8.85	114,521
Ind.	1933	70	23,418	16.9	6.13	1,254,169
Iowa	1934	65	3,000^c	1.6	13.50	475,500
Maine	1933	65	(b)	(b)	(b)	(b)
Mass.	1930	70	20,023	12.8	24.35	5,411,723
Mich.	1933	70	2,660	1.8	9.59	306,096
Minn.	1929	70	2,655	2.8	13.20	420,536
Nebr.	1933	65	(c)	(c)	(c)	(c)
N.H.	1931	70	1,423	5.5	19.06	298,722
N.J.	1931	70	10,560	9.4	12.72	1,375,693
N.Y.	1930	70	51,228	13.7	22.16	13,592,080
N.Dak.	1933	68	0^d	0.0	0.00	0
Ohio	1933	65	24,000	5.8	13.99	3,000,000
Ore.	1933	70	(a)	(a)	(a)	(a)
Penn.	1933	70	0^d	0.0	0.00	0
Wash.	1933	65	2,239	2.2	(a)	(a)
Wyom.	1929	65	643	7.4	10.79	83,231
County optional						
Ky.	1926	70	0^d	0.0	0.00	0
Md.	1927	65	141	.2	29.90	50,217
Mont.	1923	70	1,781	12.4	7.28	155,525
Nev.	1925	65	23	.5	15.00	3,320
Utah	1929	65	930	4.1	8.56	95,599
West Va.	1931	65	0^d	0.0	0.00	0
Wisc.	1925	70	1,969	1.8	16.75	395,707

Sources: U.S. Committee on Economic Security, *Supplement to Report of the CES*, Hearings before the Senate Finance Committee on S. 1130, 74th Cong., 1st Sess., 22 Jan.-20 Feb., 1935 (Washington, D.C.: U.S. Government Printing Office, 1935), pp. 50-51.

"Congress Faces the Question of Old-Age Pensions," *The Congressional Digest* 14 (1935): 72.

a. Information not available.
b. Not yet in effect.
c. Lack of funds.
d. No pensions being paid.
e. Law just put into effect.

Renewed Interest In Social Insurance

Alongside the escalation of interest in relieving poverty among the elderly, there was renewed interest in social insurance.[14] Quieted by the prosperity of the twenties and the success of the more moderate pension movement, social insurance advocates were now ready—in an atmosphere of crisis—to articulate citizen demands for "security."

By the time the social insurance movement reemerged, important changes in leadership and direction had taken place.[15] Isaac Rubinow and John Andrews of the American Association for Labor Legislation (AALL), were superseded by Abraham Epstein of the American Association for Old-Age Security (AAOAS), Paul Douglas, and Eveline Burns, the prominent spokesmen during the depression. In addition, philosophical and tactical differences which surfaced by the 1920s now split the ranks of advocates.

Rubinow, Epstein, and other more ardent proponents of social insurance viewed the pension movement as a serious threat to the viability of more comprehensive redistributive programs.[16] They sought mandatory pension legislation and a full-scale social insurance movement that drew heavily on its European counterpart. More moderate proponents, including Andrews and Commons, urged that social insurance be designed for the purposes of preventive insurance, not redistribution, and that the movement's identification with Europe be downplayed, especially in light of the bitter defeat of health insurance in 1921.[17] These differences were not resolved.

The Performance of Industrial Pensions

As the movement for compulsory old-age insurance came to life again, competitors for social insurance naturally became the subject of renewed criticism. Industrial pensions drew particularly sharp criticism because they provided the largest source of voluntary coverage in the United States, embracing approximately four million workers or 15 percent of all workers in industry and commerce.[18] Advocates criticized these plans for having excessively long service requirements, for lacking pension guarantees or contracts, for being risky in the face of economic downturn, and for paying "inadequate" benefits.[19] As critics were quick to point out, there were service requirements of up to twenty to twenty-five years that created a residual group of workers not entitled to annuities; the courts had established that workers were without contractual claims to annuities for which they had made no direct contributions; and the depression had resulted in a higher rate of discontinuance of pension plans than in any preceding period.[20] The forthcoming social security legislation was thus marketed as being similar to private insurance, only with the added features of "safety," "adequacy" and "guaranteed" benefits.

Were there merits in these claims? Did the depression nullify early progress in private pensions so as to lay the groundwork for federal retirement insurance? No market was immune to the ravages of the depression, of course. Having been less than thirty years in the making when the depression hit, moreover, the pension industry was particularly vulnerable. The relevant issues for understanding the demand (or lack of demand) for public action, however, seem to be whether there were features of industrial pensions deemed undesirable in the 1920s that persisted over time and whether this industry was less able to withstand economic downturn than others.

Developments during the depression years suggest that this was not the case. Industrial pension plans not only grew steadily during the depression but also proved quite resilient, with certain features improving markedly. At the same time that the real value of saving and income was falling dramatically, for example, the early depression years "witnessed an almost unprecedented activity in the establishment of industrial pension systems."[21] Between mid-1929 and the spring of 1932 the rate of establishment of these plans was, with the exception of the World War I years, higher than in any other period in history, and by 1935 there were some 750 plans as compared to the 420 that existed in 1930.[22]

The rate of failure for existing plans, moreover, was relatively modest.[23] Of the systems operating in 1929, those that were discontinued, closed to new employees, or suspended by 1932 involved less than 3 percent of all covered employees. The large majority of these plans continued benefit payments to current pensioners. Eighty-five to ninety percent of the plans in existence in 1932 were operating normally. Even from a historical perspective, it was not unusual for employers to rotate the layoff of workers in order not to break their service requirements during periods of prolonged unemployment. And, while the courts did deny workers contractual rights to noncontributory pensions, in practice even failing firms continued to make benefit payments as a matter of course.[24] Trade-union pension plans, by contrast, proved to be considerably less resilient.[25]

Despite the dislocations of the depression, pension plans created after 1929 differed in several important respects from those created earlier.[26] In contrast to most early pension plans, most of the new plans were contributory and reinsured by private insurance companies. Few established service requirements or compulsory retirement. As contributory plans, workers accrued rights to future annuities with regular vesting of the employee's premiums. In some cases the employer's contributions were vested as well. In effect, workers could leave the plan at any time with a paid-up annuity.

In many ways, then, private pension plans were adapting to changing economic conditions as they affected demands for income "security." They proved to be a "safer" investment than common stocks and bank deposits, and, compared to benefits forthcoming in the original Social Security Act, which ranged from $10 to $85, industrial pensions were more "adequate" as well. The average monthly pension in the private sector was $60 ($324) in 1931.[27] The advantages were clear of a contributory pension plan which could provide contractual claims for workers and beneficiaries over a compulsory federal program which would not.

If there was a proper role for the federal government in the provision of retirement income, it may well have been in promoting the more rapid development of pension plans or in hastening the formation of contractual relations for these plans. Changes in the tax status of pension funds and premium payments or changes in the legal status of the worker vis-à-vis the pensioning firm vis-à-vis the government, for example, could have been utilized to stimulate these new developments. Such changes, however, were not a part of social security proposals.

At least in part these facts help explain why some five years after the onset of the depression, a bill had not yet been introduced into Congress for compulsory old-age insurance; there were simply no significant demands for such a program. As late as 1934 a leading proponent of social insurance conceded that the majority of the working population did not "clamor" for social insurance and that "in practically all of Europe, it was governmental authority that was behind social insurance measures."[28]

Congressional and Presidential Initiatives

With local relief costs escalating, assistance for the elderly poor became a major election-year issue in 1934, and serious attention was given to proposals for federal participation in the funding of old-age pension programs. In that year a bill drafted by the AAOAS was introduced into Congress by Senator Clarence Dill (D.-Wash.) and Representative William Connery (D.-Mass.) which called for federal aid to states enacting old-age pension laws. "The first time in history that a Congressional measure for old-age pension legislation was favorably reported on," the Dill-Connery bill gained unanimous support in both the House Labor Committee and the Senate Finance Committee.[29]

By mid-1934, the movement for old-age poverty relief on a federal-state matching basis had thus gained widespread support. Organized labor, social reformers, and the Democratic party had been joined by the Chamber of Commerce and the Republican National Committee in endorsing federal government action for the elderly poor.[30] Despite the widespread support for the Dill-Connery bill, however, congressional supporters were unable to muster President Roosevelt's sanction for their bill. The 72nd session of Congress ended before the bill came to vote. Paul Douglas, an active proponent of social insurance in the 1930s, explained Roosevelt's delay. In his view, "There was an undercurrent of feeling among the progressive members of Congress that the President wanted to delay congressional action in order that he might make the program his own. . . . The President's desire to combine old-age pensions with a general program of social security and his belief that a unified program should be worked out were, therefore, powerful factors in preventing Congress from passing the Dill-Connery bill."[31] Broad-based support for federal assistance for the elderly poor could be used as political "leverage" for less attractive features of a comprehensive bill.

On June 8 1934, shortly after the demise of the Dill-Connery bill and only two days after the Republican National Committee endorsed government action for the elderly and unemployed, President Roosevelt addressed Congress on the issue of social security. In order to provide "security" to the nation, Roosevelt called for reconstruction measures to create adequate housing, jobs, and "some safeguards against the misfortunes which cannot be wholly eliminated in this man-made world of ours."[32]

Endeavoring to take the momentum gained in the last legislative session to propel his own program of social security prior to the general election, Roosevelt chose not to encourage Congress to hasten its consideration of pending legislation for the poor, the aged, and the unemployed. Instead, he announced his intention to undertake the studies necessary for formulating a comprehensive plan "to provide at once security against several of the disturbing factors in life—especially those which relate to unemployment and old age."[33]

The Committee on Economic Security

Three weeks later, by executive order, Roosevelt created the Committee on Economic Security (CES). Delegated with the responsibility to fully explore the question of social security during the remainder of the year, the CES was instructed to report to Congress with a definite program of action in January. CES members and staff were selected soon thereafter.

At the top of the policy group were five cabinet members who constituted the committee: Frances Perkins, secretary of labor and first woman cabinet member; Harry Hopkins, Federal Emergency Relief administrator; Henry Morgenthau, secretary of the treasury; Homer Cummings, attorney general; and Henry Wallace, secretary of agriculture—with Perkins named chairman. Subordinate to the committee were three other agents created by the executive order: a technical board to be selected by the CES and comprised exclusively of individuals within existing federal departments and agencies, an executive director selected by the CES, and an advisory council selected by the President.[34]

Arthur Altmeyer, second assistant secretary of labor, was appointed head of the technical board to oversee the design of a program of studies and to review alternative proposals emanating from the executive director and his lower level of staff experts. Dr. Edwin Witte, member of the Economics Department at the University of Wisconsin and acting director of the Wisconsin Unemployment Compensation Law, was selected as the executive director to oversee the research staff and act as liaison between the various experts and the CES.[35] Under the chairmanship of Dr. Frank Graham (president, University of North Carolina), the advisory council, comprised of "distinguished private citizens," was established to represent "the public" at large. Social reformers, progressives, and other advocates of social insurance—who in any real sense constituted early supply-side pressure for social insurance—were well represented at all levels in this administrative organ of the President.[36]

The combined efforts of the CES, its staff, and its various advisory boards culminated with the Report of the CES, transmitted to Congress by the President on 17 January 1935. In a covering letter to the report President Roosevelt said, "We pay now for the fearful consequences of economic insecurity and dearly. This plan presents a more equitable and infinitely less expensive means of meeting the costs. We cannot afford to neglect the plain duty before us . . . I strongly recommend action to obtain the objectives sought in this report."[37]

As embodied in the CES Report, the President's proposals for the elderly included three distinct programs. First, a program of federal subsidies (matching grants) to states enacting approved old-age pension laws was proposed, similar in most respects to the Dill-Connery bill. Second, a proposal was detailed for a compulsory federal old-age insurance program to be applicable to virtually all workers. The proposed program was similar to the German social insurance program enacted in 1889 and to the types of programs advanced for many years by social insurance advocates. Third, a program of voluntary annuities was proposed to provide old-age insurance for people not covered by the compulsory program and for those who wished to supplement their government benefits. According to the President, the assistance program of old-age pensions was intended to provide relief to the elderly poor who would not have had an opportunity to contribute to the insurance program. The old-age assistance program would therefore be temporary; in the President's words, "ultimately to be supplanted by self-supporting annuities."[38]

Since the comprehensive array of proposals included in the CES Report would vitally influence the design of the Social Security Act, those proposals relating to the elderly are described in some detail below.[39]

Noncontributory Old-Age Pensions

In order to encourage the twenty states without pension laws to adopt legislation and to encourage the other states to liberalize their laws, the CES recommended a system of federal subsidies (matching grants) for states with federally approved pension programs (means-tested welfare for elderly poor). The proposed subsidy was 50 percent of state expenditures, up to a maximum federal payment of $15 ($93) per month per recipient, plus 5 percent of the state's administrative costs.

The following requirements on state laws were recommended:

1. The law had to be statewide and mandatory.

2. A state welfare authority had to be designated which would be responsible to the federal government.

3. There had to be established a minimum pension that would provide the pensioner with a "reasonable subsistence."

4. Every person satisfying the following conditions had to be eligible for a state pension: (a) sixty-five years of age; (b) United States citizen; (c) state resident for at least five years out of the preceding ten years; (d) not an inmate of an institution; (e) owned property valued at less than $5,000 ($30,864).

5. The federal pension would constitute a lien on the pensioner's estate which, upon death, would be collected by the state and refunded to the federal government.

Finally, the CES urged that it was "essential that as soon as possible these persons be brought into the compulsory system of contributory annuities, else the annual government contributions will be so high as to constitute an impossible charge on the taxpayer."[40]

Compulsory Contributory Annuities

To supplement and eventually supplant the noncontributory pension system, a compulsory contributory annuities (old-age insurance) program was recommended. The outline of the plan was as follows.

Coverage. Every manual and nonmanual worker, excluding government employees and persons covered by the Railroad Retirement Act, earning less than $250 ($1,497) per month would be covered by the program.

Taxes. The program would be financed by a payroll tax imposed equally on the employee and his employer, beginning 1 January 1937. To keep the reserve within "manageable limits," the CES suggested a combined tax rate (employer plus employee) of 1 percent for the first five years, rising to a maximum of 5 percent in 1957. The tax was to apply to incomes up to $150 ($898) per month.

Benefits. Benefits would not be paid until the program had been in operation (collecting taxes) for five years. Individuals would qualify for benefits at age sixty-five if they had fully retired from gainful employment and had paid taxes for at least two hundred weeks. If the worker died before attaining the age of sixty-five or before receiving in benefits the amount he had contributed, his survivors were to be entitled to the difference between his contributions and what he received, plus 3 percent interest. Individuals covered who did not become eligible for benefits were to have their own contributions refunded plus 3 percent interest. "In all cases," said the CES, "members shall not receive less than the actuarial equivalent of their own contributions."[41]

Actual monthly benefits were to be calculated on the basis of two different benefit formulas, depending upon when the worker first entered the system. As illustrated in Table 4.3, "early" entrants, those who would begin paying taxes between 1937 and 1941, would be subject to a more generous formula than applied to later generations.[42] According to the CES, the payment of these "unearned" benefits (benefits well in excess of the actuarial equivalent of tax payments) to individuals who at that time were middle-aged and older would be desirable because they said, "annuities build up only very slowly."[43] The separate benefit formula for younger workers was designed to provide actuarially fair benefits for future generations who, it was said, would fully pay for their own benefits.[44]

The CES estimated that the cost of unearned benefits would total approximately a half billion dollars a year. They recommended that this expense be incurred by the federal government out of general revenues, but the payment of this debt would

Table 4.3. Comparison of monthly old-age benefits proposed by the CES to those "actuarially earned"

Age in 1937	Date benefits payable	Actuarially earned on avg. annual earnings of:			CES, for early entrants,[a] on avg. annual earnings of:			CES, for late entrants,[a] on avg. annual earnings of:		
		$600	$1200	$3000	$600	$1200	$3000	$600	$1200	$3000
60	1942	$ .24	.48	.72	$ 8	$15	$23	$ 5	$10	$15
50	1952	1.68	3.35	5.03	15	30	45	10	20	30
40	1962	4.88	9.75	14.63	20[b]	40[b]	60[b]	15	30	45
30	1972	9.79	19.57	29.36	20	40	60	20	40	60
20	1982	16.69	33.37	50.06	20	40	60	25	50	75

Sources: Hearings before the Ways and Means Committee on HR.4120, U.S. House of Representatives, 74th Cong., 1st Sess., pp. 90–93; and Douglas, *Social Security in the United States* (New York: McGraw-Hill Book Co., 1939), p. 59.

a. "Early entrants" were those who would enter the system 1937–41. "Late" entrants were those who would enter anytime thereafter.

b. Benefits were at a maximum for people age forty-five and younger.

be postponed. In particular they proposed that the federal government make no contribution until 1965 on the grounds that it would prevent the accumulation of an excessively large reserve (about $75 billion) and remove the "unfair" burden on the younger generation who would not only have to pay for their own annuities but also for the unearned annuities to older entrants.[45] The CES recognized that the "creation of this debt will impose a burden on future generations."[46]

Voluntary Old-Age Annuities

Finally, to supplement the compulsory old-age insurance program, a system of voluntary old-age annuities was recommended to provide persons not covered by the compulsory program the opportunity to purchase "annuities similar to those issued by commercial insurance companies" in a "systematic and safe" way.[47] These annuities, guaranteed in terms of future income, also would have been available to supplement the compulsory program. The following recommendations were made:

1. The plan would be self-supporting, and administered by the Social Insurance Board, part of the Department of Labor.

2. The terms of the plan would be simple, with only a few types of standard annuities offered.

3. Premiums and annuities would be kept small, say, $1 ($6) monthly premiums with a maximum monthly pension of $50 ($309).

Since the voluntary program was designed "primarily for the same economic groups as those covered by the compulsory system," the CES also recommended that a means be found to partially finance, with federal revenues, the annuities purchased by older and lower income workers.[48]

These three programs for the elderly were included with proposals for a tax-offset system of unemployment compensation and federal grants to states for mothers' pensions, care for dependent and crippled children, and public-health programs in the report, which was introduced into Congress two days later as the "economic security bill."

Alternatives to the Administration's Report

In its entirety the Report of the CES represented a comprehensive and quite radical plan to alleviate poverty in the near-term and to set up permanent programs to benefit the aged and unemployed in the long-term. As the recommendations implied an unprecedented role for the federal government in traditionally state and private domains, heated debates naturally ensued between conservatives, who believed the federal government was proposing to overstep its proper bounds, and liberals, who advocated more extensive federal programs. Interestingly, the economic security bill would make its way through Congress largely unscathed in just eight months.

With regard to the provisions dealing with the elderly, the eventual success of a temporary subsidy program designed to improve relief provision at the state and local level was all but inevitable. The depression left elderly persons throughout the country without support and some localities without the funds to continue or extend pension payments to the elderly poor. The widespread support for the Dill-Connery bill, moreover, was support for just the type of subsidy program outlined in the report.

The eventual success of a permanent, compulsory old-age insurance program, however, was most unlikely. Advocates of the federal program argued the merits of the potentially lower administrative costs in the public sector, the possibility of unearned benefits to the near-elderly, and "guaranteed" benefits to all persons under the system. But subsidies to one group could only be afforded by taxes on another. Independent of the current economic debacle and seriously considered alternatives, these arguments were without force.

Importantly, the depression was at best poorly understood and proposed remedies were diverse. Like so many other New Deal programs, the economic security program was thus hailed as a remedy for the effects of the depression and a means of preventing another. To quote Roosevelt, "No one can guarantee this country against the dangers of future depressions, but we can reduce these dangers. We can eliminate many of the factors that cause economic depressions, and we can provide the means of mitigating their results. This plan for economic security is at once a measure of prevention and a method of alleviation."[49]

And what were the alternatives to the Administration's proposals for the elderly? For a number of reasons to be discussed, the only real alternatives to the economic security bill were more radical. Of the various proposals for more radical action, the two that really gained attention were Senator Huey Long's (D.-La.) proposal to "Share-Our-Wealth" and Dr. Francis Townsend's plan to provide noncontributory pensions to everyone over sixty.[50]

The "Share-Our-Wealth" Society

In the spring of 1933 Senator Long proposed a federal tax of 100 percent on annual incomes in excess of $5 ($32) million, and property valued at more than $50 ($320) million. According to Long, the bill would put into action what Roosevelt had demanded at the presidential convention in June of 1932 when he announced his intention to give the American people the opportunity to "share in the redistribution of wealth."[51] On 12 March 1933 the Senate rejected Long's plan to "Share-Our-Wealth" by a vote of 54-18.

By the time the social security movement sprang to life again in 1934-35 Senator Long's scheme to share the wealth had taken new form. The proceeds of the federal tax on incomes, inheritances, and property were now to be distributed as $30 ($185) monthly pensions to everyone over sixty who had annual incomes less than $1,000 ($6,173) and property valued at less than $10,000 ($61,728). Strength was added to the "Share-Our-Wealth" Society on 5 March 1934 when Roosevelt announced his plans to undertake measures "by lawful, constitutional processes to reorganize a disintegrating system of production and exchange. . . . The reorganization must be permanent for all the rest of our lives in that never again will we permit the social condition in which we allowed the vast section of our population to exist in an un-American way, which allowed a maldistribution of wealth and power."[52]

In June of 1935 Roosevelt addressed Congress with a proposed tax plan which included increased taxes on inheritances, gifts, large personal incomes, and net corporate income. It was generally believed that this plan, in conjunction with the economic security bill, was a defensive political move on Roosevelt's part to capture the developing left-wing support behind Senator Long and Dr. Townsend prior to the 1936 election.[53]

The Townsend Movement

The Townsend movement was larger and better organized than Long's society, but no less radical. Dr. Townsend, a retired physician from Los Angeles, gained attention in 1933 when he circulated a petition to Congress proposing monthly pension payments of $200 ($1,274) to all persons older than sixty, whether married or single, rich or poor, to be financed by a transactions tax.[54]

Within two years, his movement, described as having "many attributes of a religious cause," mustered nearly 3.5 million paid supporters. Townsend Clubs sprang up at the rate of 100 per week, reaching seven thousand in 1935, and the *Townsend National Weekly* reached a peak circulation of two million. As one opponent said, "No proposal put before the American people in recent years has had so widespread an emotional appeal nor has so quickly enlisted vast multitudes of devoted followers as has the Townsend plan."[55]

Townsend's first bill was introduced by Representative McGroarty the day after the CES made its report. The bill proposed the payment of a $200 ($1,235) monthly pension to everyone over sixty, the only stipulation being that the recipient quit work and spend the entire check within the month received. The plan was to be financed by a 2 percent tax on the gross value of all transactions.

In response to criticism that the program was underfinanced a second bill was introduced by McGroarty in April as a substitute to the old-age provisions of the economic security bill. The "Old-Age Revolving Pension Plan" proposed a 2 percent tax on transactions, a 2 percent tax on all inherited property, and a 2 percent tax on all gifts larger than $500 ($2,994). In this version benefits were to be payable only to persons with annual incomes less than $2,400 ($14,371), the level of which would be set to meet revenues. Townsend figured that his plan would release four million jobs previously held by the elderly.[56]

Regardless of possible economic critiques of the workings of the Townsend plan or political critiques of its radical nature, the movement gained national attention, and it is this latter fact that merits attention. The fact that the movement gained such avid popular support among the elderly helps put the Great Depression and the success of the New Deal in perspective. As recently as 1933 no bills for old-age pensions had ever been reported out of committee. From the "individualistic" environment of the predepression period, opposed to federal government intervention in the realm of social welfare measures, the environment had changed to one in which Congress was not only considering proposals to dramatically expand the role of the federal government but also entertaining more radical proposals.

Did the emerging support for radical redistribution programs represent a fundamental change in values whereby individualism was being abandoned for collectivism?[57] In all probability, the answer is no. More likely, the success of the Townsend movement, at least in part, was "some measure of the desperation felt by the old people."[58] Also, its success must represent some measure of the extent to which the New Deal government made clear the inherently redistributive nature of the political process. As the redistributive potential of the federal government became widely recognized, the elderly emerged as a prominent special-interest group no longer content with earned benefits when there existed the potential for much more.

Then too, the success of the Townsend movement may well have been more apparent than real, for a great deal of the literature on the movement was written by affiliates of the CES and other social insurance advocates. The incentive was strong to overstate the popularity of radical plans so as to pose false alternatives to the economic security bill.[59] Indeed, the immediate effect of both the Townsend and the Long movements was to smooth the way for the Social Security Act, which by contrast could only appear moderate.

The Politics of the Legislative Agenda

Neither proponents of these more radical plans, nor opponents of social insurance were able to exert effective opposition to the economic security bill and the bill was passed largely in its entirety. Can this fact, along with the fact that the only serious alternatives were more radical, be taken as evidence that a reasonably broad-based majority had come to support compulsory old-age insurance, unemployment compensation, and a whole series of federal-state welfare programs?

To deduce the distribution of voter demands from the skewed distribution of policy alternatives in 1935 or, similarly, to deduce the support for any particular title in the economic security bill from the support received by the entire bill (as expressed by the final vote) is to implicitly make very strong assumptions about the responsiveness of political institutions to citizen demands. Characteristic of demand-side models of government, such deductions would presume, for example, that there was effective political competition between existing and would-be legislators to satisfy the demands of constituents. Also, monopoly elements would be presumed absent in the creation and presentation of policy alternatives and in the production of information that conditioned how voters and their representatives valued these alternatives. In short, full citizen control of agendas and ultimately political outcomes would be presumed whereby individuals, groups of individuals, or their representatives freely competed in supplying the proposals among which they later freely chose.

It is quite possible, however, that an entirely different political environment was descriptive—one in which failures in the agenda formation process prevented the array of proposals from reflecting the demands of a broad-based majority. If, for example, only certain participants in the collective choice process such as program zealots, bureaucrats, or legislative committee members were willing and/or able to put forth alternatives to be voted upon, access to the agenda was restricted. Alternatively, if only certain general features of the public programs were subject to a vote rather than the technical and institutional composition of each program, then the scope of the agenda was restricted as well. In the presence of such restrictions—whether legally, institutionally, financially, or incentive induced—the outcome of what appears to be a democratic voting process may reflect little more than citizen demands among a narrow array of predetermined alternatives.[60]

The evidence presented in both this chapter and the following one, in which the journey of the economic security bill through Congress is documented, suggests that this latter scenario is more descriptive of the political environment in 1935. Existing and potential public suppliers including Roosevelt, the CES, and other social insurance advocates played disproportionate roles in the timing and form of the Social Security Act.

Information Control

Social insurance advocates secured a measure of control over the outcome of the political process in 1935 by simply dominating the information presented Congress and the public on such issues as the "failure" of private savings and insurance institutions, the extent and causes of poverty among the elderly, and "viable" institutional alternatives. This was, in part, the outgrowth of their having stronger incentives than opponents to invest in acquiring information on alternative social policies and to take an active role in disseminating it.[61]

The rewards to the advocate who exhibited active support for social security and helped see it through to enactment went beyond the shared benefit of having improved the world for all advocates. A job in the newly created bureaucracy, a staff position in Congress, an expanded realm for an existing agency, jobs for students and colleagues, as well as expanded research and consulting possibilities were but a few of the spillovers that accrued to the individual for his "expertise" and for his having advanced "the cause." At the same time many advocates were employed in the types of employment (such as government agencies, social work, or universities) that facilitated, if not funded, research in support of government programs. The costs to the individual of engaging in these types of lobbying activities were thereby reduced. For both benevolent and selfish reasons, therefore, it is not surprising that for years before the depression, social insurance advocates studied the early European social insurance schemes. As advocates and high demanders of "social justice," their endeavors rarely included studies of the functioning and relative advantages of American savings and insurance institutions.

In contrast, a number of factors inhibited opponents of social insurance such as political conservatives, business interests, and, in particular, the insurance industry from being equally effective in offering competing sources of information and competing policy proposals. On the one hand, since proposals for compulsory old-age insurance were not seriously entertained before the time of the economic security bill, there was little incentive for opponents to invest in acquiring and disseminating counterinformation and in drafting counterproposals. For the same reason, there were no well established congressional committees or subcommittees to oversee such studies. On the basis of time alone once the CES had been appointed and its staff of experts organized, opponents simply could not compete in turning out more than twelve volumes of documentary support for their proposals in less than five months—an accomplishment of the CES.

On the other hand, an inability to individualize the benefits of costly research and lobbying activites would discourage efforts to block the new government program. Since effectively blocking compulsory old-age insurance would secure benefits, for example, for all insurance companies whether or not they had participated in sharing the costs, each opponent was motivated to free-ride on the others' activities. Finally, to represent "selfish capitalist" interests during an era referred to as the "highwater mark of radicalism" exposed insurance companies to the risk of possibly retaliatory scrutiny and regulation. For each of these reasons, an underinvestment in opposition to Social Security was predictable.

In essence, even if the CES had not been created to supersede Congress, and had not presented Congress with a complex tied package of institutions, competing sources of information were likely to be outweighed by the information made available by proponents of social insurance in particular and government activity in general. They had the time, the funds, and the expertise as well as the ability to individualize the rewards of their activities. The consequent bias in proposals and in the information utilized by policy makers was an important incentive-induced failure in the political decision-making process.

Agenda Control, Tie-In Sales, and All-Or-Nothing Offers

Given this environment, President Roosevelt then superseded Congress to establish a committee and staff that would draft its own legislation. Staffed by an array of carefully selected cabinet members, bureaucrats, and other social insurance advocate-"experts," the CES had a vested interest in expanding the role of the federal government and in advancing programs with specific institutional features. The CES responded to the emerging demands for old-age "security" not with proposals for changes in legal, tax, or direct financial incentives for pensioning firms, for example, but by advancing a compulsory federal old-age insurance program much like the early German program, along with an entire array of federal-state welfare programs.

Of what significance was the appointment, staffing, and ultimate policy recommendations of such a nonlegislative committee? If the CES had simply been one of many freely competing suppliers of proposals, there would have been little significance as to who drafted the bill and the particulars of the bill. But by creating, staffing, and funding the CES with the purpose of formulating a social security program outside of Congress, elements of monopoly were created in the agenda formation process. The CES was federally subsidized to produce a bill and to produce a bill of a certian type—one which satisfied Roosevelt's expressed demands for a comprehensive, unified, and permanent program of social security, and one which was consistent with the objectives of its members. With the aid of President Roosevelt and direct federal funds, moreover, the dissemination of information and publicity for their proposals was federally subsidized as well.[62]

These subsidies produced a type of power for the CES and other advocates that could not be eroded by competing suppliers. Once the CES Report was on the agenda, reasonable counterproposals were costly to submit in both time and dollar outlays. In many cases these costs would have been borne directly by participants rather than diffused through taxpayer support. And, as suggested earlier, the creation of a counterproposal to the CES Report would have been analogous to the production of a public good. The benefits to opponents of having a counterproposal placed on the agenda would have been shared while the costs need not have been. The CES's power via subsidized information was thereby compounded by the pervasive problem of an undersupply of proposals to yield important restrictions or biases in the agenda.

If the influence of the CES and other advocates over the final outcome had not exceeded that which has been described to this point, there still would have been a strong possibility that compulsory old-age insurance would not have emerged from Congress. As documented in the next chapter, opposition to these titles of the bill was intense in the committees and on the floor of both houses, at many times threatening to lead to the bill's demise. The decisive factor would be the ability of the Administration and the CES to employ standard monopoly practices, including the tie-in sale and all-or-nothing offer, to exploit their discretionary power.

The tie-in sale, in this context, was the exchange of a congressman's vote for a bundle of programs whereby the right to "purchase" one activity over which the government maintained a monopoly (such as emergency relief funds) was then tied to the purchase of some other activity.[63] The report tied, for example, the creation of an old-age assistance program to the adoption of a federal system of old-age insurance. Rather than being able to register opposition to old-age insurance by voting against it, congressmen had to weigh the losses associated with its enactment against the losses that would be incurred by voting down the entire bundle and, with it, federal relief funds. The political support for old-age welfare could thus be employed to offset opposition to old-age insurance.[64] By increasing the number of politically appealing welfare programs (aid to mothers, the blind, and orphans) bundled with old-age insurance, the President and the CES simply increased the likelihood of swinging opposition votes.

As the tie-in sale was an effort on the part of the Administration to restrict the scope of the legislative agenda, the ultimate check on this practice would have been an amendment to separate the titles of the bill and have a separate legislative vote on each. The ability of the CES to effectively utilize the tie-in sale thus required the additional control over the agenda provided by the all-or-nothing offer.[65] An all-or-nothing offer, in this context, was the implicit exchange of a congressman's vote for all items in the bundle or none at all. The congressman was thereby placed in the position of supporting the entire bundle as long as he assessed his position to be better than with none of the programs at all.

The source of this power lay in Roosevelt's clearly stated position (or threat) that the economic security bill was to be considered as a "unified," "comprehensive" bill and that the extension of welfare to the needy aged would have been unacceptable without the creation of a permanent annuity program.[66] At a minimum, federal welfare funds would have been slow to materialize. As Epstein, one of the leaders of the social insurance movement, assessed the situation in Congress:

> There was an insistence from the beginning that the bill be jammed through Congress in its omnibus shape. This presented a real dilemma to earnest members of Congress genuinely interested in bringing about social security. They could not physically find the time to master the details of the many subjects involved in the bill. Nor could they place themselves in the same category with the anti-social members of Congress in opposing the entire bill. As a result, although many Congressmen were fully conscious that the bill embodied economic fallacies, many social dangers, and constitutional difficulties in many phases, there was a general conviction that the subsidies set up for old-age pensions, mothers aid, the blind, etc., for which the AASS [American Association for Social Security] had prepared the ground for many years, were sound and socially

desirable. Since their choice was "*all-or-none*" [italics mine] they voted for all and left it to the Supreme Court to separate the good from the bad. This was the tenor of debates in both houses.[67]

The evidence presented in this chapter suggests that given the Great Depression, President Roosevelt and social insurance advocates were in unique positions to affect the timing, acceptance, and form of the original Social Security Act, especially the provisions dealing with compulsory old-age insurance. On the demand side the perceived failure of private savings and insurance institutions and the dramatic increase in unemployment led to a positive reevaluation of the benefits of federal government action. The environment was conducive to the emergence of new government institutions to deal with the problems of the elderly. Importantly, however, there were many ways that demands for old-age "security" could have been satisfied.

Any one of a number of programs ranging from federal-state relief programs to subsidized or insured private insurance plans might have satisfied citizens' demands for old-age "security," yet social insurance advocates stood ready to articulate specific institutional packages to satisfy citizens' yet unarticulated demands for federal action. Advocate-"experts" controlled the information made available to citizens and representatives, and Roosevelt worked diligently to control the choices they were presented. The President, the CES, and social insurance advocates used this control to their advantage as the social security bill made its journey through Congress.

Chapter 5. The Journey of Compulsory Old-Age Insurance Through Congress

> I doubt whether any part of the social security program other than the old-age assistance title would have been enacted into law but for the fact that the President throughout insisted that the entire program must be kept together. Had the measure been presented in separate bills, it is quite possible that the old-age assistance title might have become law much earlier. I doubt whether anything else would have gone through at all.[1]
>
> Edwin Witte, Executive Director
> Committee on Economic Security

As enacted on 14 August 1935 the Social Security Act constituted an unprecedented expansion in the role of the federal government. In just twenty-nine pages, the act was divided into ten titles that created a compulsory federal program of old-age insurance; a federal-state tax-offset program for unemployment compensation; three federal-state categorical grant programs, old-age assistance, aid to dependent children, and aid to the blind; and two federal-state nonuniform grant programs for maternal and child welfare and public health. In most important respects the act differed little from the CES Report embodied in the Administration's bill submitted to Congress on 17 January.

The rapid enactment of Social Security raises several important questions. In particular, do the marked similarities between the Administration's comprehensive bill and the final act provide evidence that the CES and its fourteen advisory councils actually anticipated and hastened the process of crystalizing policies to satisfy citizen demands? Alternatively, in light of the ongoing depression and the all-or-none nature of the legislation, did Congress simply acquiesce to the Administration's power in determining the final outcome? If not, what were the ways in which Congress endeavored to reinstate its control over the bill? In essence, were there any real threats to the survival of compulsory old-age insurance and, if so, what were the strategies employed by the Administration to deal with these threats?

To address these questions, this chapter opens with an examination of the major issues of debate surrounding the old-age insurance titles of the "economic security bill." Given a sampling of these issues, the journey of the bill through Congress is then relayed and the major amendments affecting the provisions for the elderly are examined. In an important sense, the chapter provides substantiating evidence for the theories presented in Chapter 4. It concludes with an assessment of the institutional "details" of the original Social Security Act as they would set the stage for the growth and evolution the program has since experienced.

From a historical perspective, Congress moved quickly on the CES Report. Immediately after President Roosevelt presented the report to Congress on 17 January 1935 a bill capturing most of its elements was introduced by Representatives David Lewis (D.-Md.) and R.L. Doughton (D.-N.C.), and Senator Wagner (D.-N.Y.). Because of the importance Roosevelt attached to speed, hearings were held in the two committees simultaneously, commencing 21 January in the House Ways and Means Committee and 22 January in the Senate Finance Committee. They were concluded in less than a month.[2] During this relatively short period each committee heard testimony from nearly one hundred government witnesses and other interested parties and together produced more than 2,500 pages of hearings on the economic security bill.

Because the hearings were concluded only a month after the CES unveiled its report, the hearings were naturally dominated by proponents who had a great deal of knowledge about the legislation and had been actively involved in its preparation. Beginning with several days of testimony from Edwin Witte, executive director of the CES, a series of government witnesses then appeared on behalf of the bill, the vast majority of whom had official connections with the CES. Other advocates heard included Eveline Burns, Paul Douglas, Abraham Epstein, and President Green of the AFL. The only real opposition was voiced by those who advocated more radical action, such as Dr. Townsend and supporters of the Lundeen bill. While testimony was heard from some opponents of the bill, such as representatives of manufacturers' associations, they lacked the detailed knowledge of the bill and a concrete legislative alternative necessary to be effective.[3]

Major Issues of Debate

Of the three programs designed to prevent and alleviate poverty among the elderly, the program to provide noncontributory pensions (public assistance) to the elderly poor generated the least serious controversy. It was widely believed that the elderly poor were not being adequately provided for at the state and local level.[4] In the short run the depression had left many states with swollen caseloads and seriously depleted revenue sources. In the longer run, it was believed, the mobility of the poor from other states could force more "progressive" states into prohibitively (politically) costly programs or into enforcing very long residency requirements. Federal participation on a matching grant basis would provide all states needed assistance and less progressive states the financial incentive to create their own programs.

As this portion of the bill made its way through Congress a series of changes were made to reduce the federal government's control over eligibility and benefit levels. By and large, however, the debates were of a technical nature and the final version of the bill was reported with little modification of the federal-state relationship or the nature of the subsidy.

In contrast, the contributory old-age insurance programs—both compulsory and voluntary—were very controversial, perhaps more so than any other features of the bill. Opposition to these titles led to serious attempts to limit the scope of the compulsory program, culminating in fairly significant changes in the compulsory program and an elimination of the voluntary program. Certain of the key issues of debate are relayed below as they provide useful insight into political sentiments of the day and reveal the extent to which critics understood the potential pitfalls of social insurance.[5]

The Bill's Complexity

Aside from those who were actively involved in drafting the CES Report and testifying on its behalf, virtually everyone was in some way concerned with the bill's complexity. In particular, why were temporary relief measures combined with permanent insurance programs in a single legislative bill? And why was such an assortment of fiscal and administrative institutions (block grants, matching grants, and tax-offsets, for example, as well as federal provision, federal authority, and federal-state participation) combined, when each required careful scrutiny?

The recognition that the Administration was endeavoring to maneuver Congress into adopting an entire package of programs, radical ones tied to noncontroversial ones in an all-or-none fashion, met with opposition from congressmen across party lines. Not only did the package of programs inhibit flexibility and scrutiny, but also it put congressmen in the position of voting for everything or being labeled as opposed to "social security."[6] According to Paul Douglas's account of the legislative history of the act, "Many Congressmen were opposed to the omnibus character of the measure and resented the Administration's attitude that it must be all-or-nothing. There were many who did not like to be forced to adopt a vast series of untried measures in the original drafting of which they had had no part."[7]

Social insurance advocates certainly recognized the dilemma for opponents posed by the tied programs. The federal-state welfare movement had gained such widespread popular support in Congress during the previous legislative session that efforts to block the old-age insurance titles were made very costly. This was especially true since Roosevelt had made his position on this issue so clear: an expansion of poverty programs for the elderly was unacceptable without the creation of a longer run social insurance program.[8]

Opponents of compulsory insurance or any other item in the bill ran the very real danger of further delaying federal relief funds—already delayed some five years after the onset of the depression—with efforts to "unbundle" the President's package. The legislation was, according to Roosevelt, a unified package of recovery and reconstruction measures not to be considered as a series of separate programs.[9] It was clear, moreover, that to ensure the passage of the heart of the bill—old-age insurance—Roosevelt must stand firm on the package; to ensure passage of the entire bill, he had strong incentives to use whatever strategies were necessary to move the bill through Congress quickly. Economic recovery would not serve his purposes well. As some indication of the intensity of opposition to compulsory old-age insurance, efforts to unbundle the President's package were nevertheless made and other serious challenges surfaced as well.

Individualism and Voluntarism vs. Centralization and Coercion

Because of the widely differing views held on the development of the private insurance industry and its role in providing old-age "security," there naturally arose fundamental debates over the advantages and disadvantages of compulsory, federal "insurance." Throughout the hearings and in public debate, questions of individualism and voluntarism were contrasted by demands for centralization and compulsion.

Opponents of social insurance, such as Senators Hasting (R.-Dela.) and Gore (D.-Ok.) of the Senate Finance Committee, warned that the comprehensive federal program would, by its very nature, threaten individual property rights. It was a coercive program that lacked effective constraints on growth. Attacking the legitimacy of the private insurance analogy and the use of the terms "contractual rights" and "earned benefits," Senator Hastings pointed out that the term "contract" connoted voluntary agreement between the parties involved and a legal right to the terms of the contract.[10] A government program made binding on future workers was not voluntary and the nature of the political process could not guarantee benefits. In the words of Senator Gore, "Congress has found this bill on its doorsteps. What guarantee is there? Has the citizen got any constitutional guarantee? Has the citizen got any moral guarantee under this plan that some man might not come into power who would take more than he ought to take from one and give to another?"[11]

Further, opponents argued, the federal program would require extensive new public institutions—bureaucratic, coercive, and, in some cases, inefficient institutions. Once established, the program would be subject to increasing political demands of the sort that plagued public retirement systems for police, firemen, and government employees.[12] Benefits would be increased and coverage and eligibility would be liberalized, while the cost of the program and the size of the bureaucracy would be difficult to limit. Opponents already foresaw the possibility that as special-interest groups formed, each trying to pass their share of the cost on to other groups, there might eventually arise the need for the federal government to take over financing. At that time there would be no doubt remaining about whether the program was truly insurance.

These concerns led to pressure to strike the compulsory old-age insurance program altogether, or else to instill into the federal program provisions for competition from the private sector. Opponents recognized that only by making compulsory old-age insurance available through competing producers—whether private or public—could citizens retain the choice necessary to control and monitor the public program and thus to protect their noncontractual rights to future benefits.[13]

From quite the opposite perspective social insurance advocates argued that there was a whole host of reasons why the federal government was the preferred vehicle for insuring the masses against losses of income. It was said that only the government could insure poor people and old people who would find insurance prohibitively costly in the private sector where firms "worked for a profit." Through the taxing power of the state, moreover, benefits could be "guaranteed" and through coercion risks could be pooled over a large section of the population to provide higher rates of return. Others, in particular the CES, argued that as the proportion of elderly in the population rose, welfare to the needy aged would become prohibitively costly and that a longer run insurance program that coerced participation was needed to prevent the problem of dependency before it occurred. Collective foresight, it was said, would thus replace the need for individual foresight.[14]

As the debates revealed, the term social "insurance" was used to the advantage of social insurance advocates rather than to connote descriptive reality. Social "assurance" would surely have been more descriptive. Armed with studies revealing the "maldistribution" of income in the United States, advocates believed that all individuals inherently deserved to be protected from the losses of income due to old age, unemployment, sickness, and disability.[15] Universal protection could not be provided without compulsion. Adequacy could not be provided without centralization.

Advocates of the program generally neglected to address the question of how the government could provide "adequate" benefits to the poor and elderly without subsidizing them at the expense of young and higher income workers. Indeed, they ignored "the basic truism that insurance is not a means of lowering aggregate costs" but rather a means of redistributing those costs.[16] In addition, arguments like that of the CES failed to address why a law which simply required people to save would not have been sufficient to deal with short-sighted workers and why the production of insurance could not have been left in the hands of private industry. These fundamental issues were never resolved, of course, as views of opponents and advocates stood juxtaposed to one another.

The Payroll Tax and Tax Splitting

The Administration's choice of a payroll tax, nominally shared by employees and employers, was also the subject of a great deal of congressional debate. First employed to finance the early German social insurance program, the tax was defended on two grounds: (1) this type of wage tax most aptly conjured the private insurance analogy, and (2) the employee and employer together had an obligation to provide for the worker's financial future. In the private sector individuals who were covered by industrial insurance, for example, were accustomed to paying premiums on a weekly or monthly basis. Proponents recognized that the tax would be viewed similarly by covered workers as the payment of regular premiums in return for "earned contractual rights" to future annuities. On a more practical level the tax would focus the cost of the program on those who would be beneficiaries and encourage women, children, and persons over sixty-five to leave the labor market at a time when unemployment was particularly high.

The employers' share of the tax was defended on the grounds that employers were in part responsible for poverty among the elderly—by not setting up adequate pension plans, by not feeling a moral obligation for their support, by forcing early retirement, or even by not paying adequate wages—and therefore had part financial responsibility. The tax provided, in their words, a simple, automatic method of, "meeting depreciation charges on human factors cooperating in production similar to the usual accounting charges for depreciation of plant and equipment."[17]

As was this defense of the employer's tax, the debates that raged over the appropriate employee and employer shares of the tax were seriously confused by uncertainty over the incidence of the payroll tax.[18] Some argued that the employer's tax would tend to be shifted back to workers by depressing wages. Others argued the tax would be shifted forward to consumers by raising product prices. In either case the burden of the regressive tax on workers would be enhanced. As yet another possibility business representatives suggested that the tax would, by raising costs and depressing dividends, be borne by owners of firms.

Each lobby group sought a shifting of the tax burden, but it was nevertheless apparent that the private insurance analogy—and benefits restricted to those who had paid for them—were crucial to attaining political support for an old-age "insurance" program. General-revenue financing would destroy this analogy by eliminating the tax-benefit link along with an important difference between the funding source of the old-age assistance and annuity titles. Then too an employer's share of the tax made good sense from the advocates' perspective because its uncertain incidence would likely lead workers to understate the true cost of the program. It was a source of revenues to which individuals would accrue no "rights."[19]

Once the program was established and collecting taxes the payroll tax would give workers a vested interest in the long-run continuation of the program. In the words of President Roosevelt, "I guess you are right on the economics, but those taxes were never a problem of economics. They are political all the way through. . . . With those taxes there, no damn politician can ever scrap my program."[20] The earmarked payroll tax would provide the new Social Security bureaucracy with annual appropriations immune from direct competition from other governmental bureaus.[21]

The choice of the payroll tax and the tax-splitting feature of the old-age insurance program were not modified as the bill made its way through Congress.

Federal Contributions and the Size of the Fund

Just as is the case today the degree of funding for the compulsory old-age insurance program was a primary source of controversy in Congress in 1935. The CES and other income redistributionists endorsed the accumulation of a small fund in excess of benefit payments and relatively low tax rates, as included in the Administration's bill. Such a funding scheme would necessitate future federal contributions and allow a postponement of costs onto future workers and noncontributors.[22] The secretary of treasury and certain opponents of the federal system, by contrast, endorsed a large self-sustaining program on the grounds that it made good actuarial sense and would tend to concentrate the burden of finance onto those directly benefiting from the program.[23]

Advocates of the Administration's proposal defended the limited fund and government share with now-familiar arguments: (1) it was the taxing power of the federal government that would "buttress the guarantee of security" in old-age benefits, not the existence of a fund; (2) if unearned benefits were to be provided to older workers, the federal government should logically cover this portion of the costs; (3) contributions from more progressive tax sources could offset the regressivity of the payroll tax; and (4) federal contributions would allow tax rates and the size of the fund to be kept low—deemed "economically" desirable during the depression. The federal contributions they believed were necessitated by this logic, however, would not have been made for another thirty years.

Social insurance proponents certainly recognized that a self-supporting program with substantial funding requirements would have focused the cost of benefits for any particular generation on that same generation. It would significantly limit the program's ability to effect income transfers, both between and within generations. Because this would have been a difficult case to make against funding—politically that is, with the private insurance analogy so important—the "right" size fund was discussed almost exclusively in terms of economics. If economic rationalizations could be made to keep the fund low, political rationalizations for relatively low tax rates and federal contributions would be superfluous. This is not to say that economic considerations were not important. Indeed, the depression and a fear of intensifying the depression were of great concern. In actuality, though, the economic arguments advanced against the accumulation of a large fund were misdirected and in many ways simply begged the issue.

According to critics of funding, the imposition of the payroll tax would lead to an immediate withdrawal of purchasing power not offset by benefit payments until 1942. This withdrawal would reduce the demand for consumption goods and increase unemployment. If the sums so collected were then immediately invested, the increase in unemployment could be offset. But if businessmen were hesitant to build new factories or buy new machinery, it was argued, there was no guarantee that the reserves could be invested. In this event there would be a reduction in and "sterilization" of purchasing power that might worsen the depression.[24]

Alternatively, critics went on to argue, the government might find it necessary to create new government debt obligations in order to invest the fund. If this were the case, other government expenditures could be bond-financed rather than tax-financed, creating a paradox whereby revenues from a regressive payroll tax on workers would be used to relieve the tax burden on the rich.[25]

Despite these arguments social insurance opponents and advocates of the private insurance analogy were successful in amending the bill on the grounds that the merits of a self-supporting program requiring a substantial fund outweighed other considerations. Since the payroll taxes necessary to finance the system would be paid by workers in return for future benefits, these taxes did not represent pure money losses. To the extent that the imposition of the tax decreased the purchasing power of workers, the purchasing power among those individuals (whether private individuals, banks, or the federal government) who sold securities to the fund consequently would be made higher. And a situation where the government, unable to bid for outstanding government bonds, found it necessary to issue new government debt, could only result if the size of the fund exceeded the national debt. Congress, in this event, could always consider alternative investment policies allowing the federal government to invest, for example, in the national debt of other countries or in private debt. Finally, if the central issue was that of economic stabilization, there were other monetary and fiscal instruments that could be called to task.

If, instead, the program was an insurance program, there seemed to be no persuasive argument for transferring the burden of finance onto future generations and, possibly, onto noncontributors. Not only would a funded system tend to focus the burden of finance onto those who would receive the benefits but also the ability to retire public debt and make productive investments with the fund would, by lightening the burden on future generations, help ensure that benefits were payable in the distant future.[26]

By the time the bill made its way through Congress scheduled tax rates were increased and the old-age insurance program was modified to be funded on a self-supporting basis, the need for federal contributions having been eliminated.

Given this sampling of the key issues of debate, the journey of the Administration's bill through Congress is relayed below and the major changes affecting provisions for the elderly are examined. Successful amendments to the Administration's bill as well as certain key amendments which were ultimately defeated offer perspective for evaluating the importance of President Roosevelt and the CES in determining the final outcome. Revealed most clearly, even at this early date, was the existence of quite broadly based opposition to the old-age insurance titles of the bill. Just as clearly evidenced, however, was the important role played by the Administration in shielding the essence of its bill from attack.

The Bill in the House

Compulsory old-age insurance faced its first serious challenge in the Ways and Means Committee, thought by some to be "Administration controlled."[27] According to Edwin Witte, in the week before the committee made its report, "it seemed probable that the old-age insurance titles would be completely stricken from the bill."[28] With opposition to the old-age insurance titles found to be so intense, Arthur Altmeyer recounted, "Leading members of the Ways and Means Committee approached the President to ascertain whether he wanted the omnibus character of the bill kept intact and to tell him that it would not be possible to get a favorable vote on this feature of the bill. The President informed them that he wanted the whole bill passed and that old-age insurance must stay in the bill."[29] As the bill was ultimately reported, several fundamental changes had been made in the financing of the system and the voluntary annuities program had been eliminated altogether.

In compulsory old-age insurance, the most significant change to emanate from the House was the one made by the Ways and Means Committee to put the

Table 5.1. Size of accumulated fund under alternative tax and benefit schedules (dollars in millions)

Year	Proposed by CES	Proposed by Morgenthau
1937	$ 302	$ 622
1950	7,674	18,683
1965	15,267 (max.)	42,123
1980	15,267	50,094 (max.)

Source: Hearings before the Committee on Ways and Means on HR. 4120, U.S. House of Representatives, 74th Cong., 1st Sess., p. 903.

annuities program on a self-supporting basis. Under the Administration's bill, the payroll tax would not have been sufficient to cover the cost of the program in the long term and deficits were scheduled to be alleviated by federal contributions. In order to keep the program on a strictly self-financing basis, Treasury Secretary Morgenthau, member of the CES, proposed fairly extensive changes in the tax and benefit provisions of the bill.

Morgenthau recommended a tax rate that was higher initially and rose more quickly than that proposed by the CES, and annuities that were lower in the first forty years but substantially higher thereafter.[30] Under the Administration's bill the combined tax rate (employee and employer) would have been 1 percent in 1937, rising by a percentage point each five years until it reached a maximum of 5 percent in 1957. Under Morgenthau's proposal, by contrast, the tax was 2 percent initially, rising a percentage point each three years until it reached a maximum of 6 percent in 1949.

The impact of these changes on the reserve fund would have been significant. As shown in Table 5.1, the tax increases and benefit reductions would have allowed the accumulation of a reserve fund on the order of $50 billion by 1980, or more than ten times annual benefit payments.[31] Morgenthau argued for this redistribution of costs toward present generations by saying,

> There are some who believe that we can meet this problem as we go by borrowing from the future to pay the costs . . . They would place all confidence in the taxing power of the future to meet the needs as they arose. We do not share this view. We have already cited the fact that the aggregate benefit payments under our proposal, as under that of the economic security bill, will eventually exceed $4 billion a year. We cannot safely expect future generations to continue to divert such large sums to the support of the aged unless we lighten the burdens upon the future in other directions. . . . We desire to establish this system on such sound foundations that it can be continued indefinitely in the future.[32]

Even before the CES Report had gone to the President, Morgenthau argued for sounder actuarial principles underlying the financing of the old-age insurance program.[33] The CES rejected his recommendation to put the program on a self-supporting basis, although his proposal was widely supported in Congress and was said to be supported by the President as well.

The Ways and Means Committee accepted the essence of his proposal.[34] Tax rates were increased and the benefit formula was modified to put the system on a self-sustaining basis. The particular benefit schedule chosen by the committee consolidated the two benefit formulas (for early and late entrants) proposed by the Administration by more heavily weighting benefits in favor of people with low incomes and few contributing years. Rather than basing benefits on average covered earnings and the length of time in covered employment, moreover, they proposed that benefits be paid on the basis of total covered wages.

Finally, and quite distinct from the proposals of Secretary Morgenthau, the Ways and Means Committee significantly reduced the extent of compulsory coverage under the old-age insurance program. Agricultural labor, domestic servants, casual labor, seamen, employees of nonprofit organizations, and persons over sixty-five were all removed from coverage.[35] The exclusion for the first three groups was based on administrative infeasibility: it would simply cost too much to set up payment and coverage schemes. The exclusion of employees of nonprofit organizations, on the other hand, was a response to pressures by representatives of church and private charity funds. They argued, as did so many other groups, that compulsory coverage would force the abandonment of their own pension funds. According to Director Witte, the exemption was granted because neither the CES nor the Ways and Means Committee "could afford to incur the enmity of any church group."[36]

Regarding voluntary annuities, the Ways and Means Committee simply struck this proposal from the bill. On the grounds that the government would have been placed in direct competition with the private insurance industry, the elimination of the program was a concession to critics of federal intervention to the end of maintaining the heart of the President's bill—the compulsory program.

Committee action on the assistance program for the elderly reduced federal standards and increased state control over benefit levels and eligibility criteria. The "conditions of the state" were to be taken into account in the determination of benefit levels and the list of federal conditions on eligibility was collapsed into a single citizenship requirement. The latter change allowed states more flexibility in denying benefits for other reasons. These changes were responses to the demands of representatives concerned with states' rights and representatives of southern and western states (with relatively large minority populations and/or low per capita incomes) who stood to fare poorly in a system where the federal government could use standards of uniformity to compel them to pay higher benefits than state residents desired.

Overall, the Report of the House Ways and Means Committee, as it pertained to the elderly, resulted in the following major changes in the Administration's bill:

1. The compulsory old-age insurance program was made self-sustaining with the building up of substantial trust funds.

2. Compulsory coverage was restricted.

3. The benefit formula was liberalized in favor of lower-income workers and those with shorter periods of covered employment.

4. States' control over eligibility requirements under the assistance program was increased.

5. The voluntary annuities program was eliminated.

Some important changes in administration were also made. Against the opposition of Labor Secretary Perkins, the committee made the Social Security Board an independent agency, not under the auspices of the Labor Department. Against the opposition of Harry Hopkins, the board rather than FERA was given control over the old-age pension program. Finally, the federal authority to set minimum standards on state personnel was abolished.[37]

A minority report was issued, signed by all the Republicans on the Ways and Means Committee, that revealed significant opposition to the compulsory titles of the bill. In their view the federal government was without authority to impose the system on private industry. The creation of such a program, they argued, in competition with private insurance, was likely to retard the development of private plans. Such plans typically provided more generous benefits than would the public program. To deal with poverty among the elderly, they favored a substantial increase in the funds for old-age poverty relief.[38]

The Ways and Means Committee bill was debated for a week on the floor of the House. A series of amendments and two more radical substitute bills were considered, but no significant changes were made. The bill went on to be passed on 19 April by a vote of 372-33.

Because of the all-or-none nature of the legislation, of course, the overwhelming support for the entire Social Security bill, inclusive of welfare and unemployment compensation titles, was an imperfect measure of the support for opposition to compulsory old-age insurance. With a 3:1 majority of Democrats in the House, an amendment to strike the old-age insurance titles entirely from the bill actually mustered a third (65-128) of the votes cast[39]—a substantial vote in light of the pressure to consider the bill as a package.

The Bill in the Senate

Having made it through the House, the provisions of the bill dealing with the elderly were not yet prepared for smooth sailing. The survival of the insurance features, as envisioned by the Administration, was threatened many times in the Senate. While only limited changes were ultimately made in the Finance Committee, the bill's first stop in the Senate, the "question of whether a compulsory old-age insurance provision should remain in the bill" was, according to Edwin Witte, "one on which the outcome was most uncertain."[40]

As the bill was finally reported by the committee, just two relatively small policy changes in compulsory old-age insurance had been made—one creating a "retirement-earnings test" and one altering the administration of the program.[41] The Committee amended the bill so that the entire amount of old-age insurance benefits would be forfeited if the individual remained in "regular employment" beyond age sixty-five. The change, endorsed by President Roosevelt and the CES, was made on the grounds that it would encourage older workers to leave the labor market and, in their words, eliminate the "anomaly that employees over sixty-five may draw old-age benefits while earning adequate wages in full-time employment."[42] Also, because the proposed functions of the Social Security Board were thought to be so similar to those of the Labor Department, the Committee placed the board within the Department of Labor rather than designating it an independent agency.

Reversing the House action, the Finance Committee also reinstated the voluntary annuities program. Individuals could purchase "United States Annuity Bonds" from the federal government on a tax-exempt, contractual basis at a maximum yield of 3 percent. The program was to be placed under the auspices of the Department of Treasury, however, rather than the Social Security Board.

In response to pressure by conservatives to reduce the discretion of the federal government in the assistance program, moreover, all reference to "reasonable subsistence" was removed from the definition of allowable benefit levels.

Action on the Senate floor soon revealed that the Finance Committee Report did not well represent the desires of the Senate as a whole in areas affecting the elderly. When the report reached the floor in mid-June, changes were approved that put extensive limitations on the power of the federal government. The most important of these involved a fundamental restructuring of the compulsory old-age insurance program that introduced voluntary choice, further liberalization of the conditions for federal aid under the pension program, and an elimination of the voluntary annuities program altogether.[43]

Beginning with the old-age assistance program, an amendment was offered by Senator Russell of Georgia to make the federal grants payable to states for up to two years even in cases where they had not yet enacted pension laws.[44] Senator Russell argued that the elderly poor should not be deprived of federal assistance while states sought constitutional amendments required to enact and finance such legislation (twelve of the fifteen states without laws were southern states). The amendment passed with little opposition.

In response to a movement led by Senator Lonergan of Connecticut, moreover, the voluntary annuities program was eliminated from the Senate bill. Representing the state of Connecticut, headquarters of many private insurance companies, Lonergan successfully argued that, without according it serious attention, the Finance Committee had permitted the passage of a proposal that would place the government in competition with the private annuity industry and thereby hamper its development.[45] In his view when the committee passed the proposal for voluntary annuities by a margin of only two votes—with as many as twelve members out of twenty-one absent—it did so under the mistaken belief that private insurance companies did not even sell annuity bonds, especially those in small sums.

Senator Lonergan informed the Senate that monthly annuities were available in most any denomination, even $10 or less, and that the private insurance industry had proved remarkably strong during the depression. In his words,

> The insurance companies of this nation have been our last wall of defense in our depressing times. When our banks crumbled and finance was chaotic our insurance companies stood like the rock of Gibraltar. . . . Is the Senate going to enact into law a provision in this bill which will injure these companies? Is the United States Senate going to discourage sound development of the annuity insurance business along a much broader front than the government could possibly undertake?[46]

By Senator Harrison's own admission the Finance Committee had viewed the voluntary annuities program as a "minor" provision in the entire Social Security bill and had simply voted to place it in the bill on the basis of the recommendations of the CES.[47] The program was thus stricken from the Senate bill.

The Clark Amendment: The Threat of Competition

Along similar lines, but by far the most substantial change to emanate from the Senate, was an amendment to allow employers who had set up their own annuity programs for their employees the right to "contract out" of the compulsory old-age program. Comprising less than ten sentences, the amendment offered by Senator Clark from Missouri cut through the insurance rhetoric of the debates and threatened the redistributive underpinnings of Social Security. The effect was to place the federal government in the position of regulating and competing with private plans providing old-age insurance rather than monopolizing its own. Leading to more serious controversy in the Finance Committee, on the Senate floor, and ultimately in conference than did any other, the Clark Amendment was killed in committee by a tie-vote and went on to be passed on the Senate floor by a substantial margin.[48]

The basics of the Clark Amendment were as follows.[49] A private employer who had in operation an annuity program for his employees that required combined premiums at least equivalent to the federal payroll tax and that could provide benefits at least as great as those granted under the government plan was to be given the option to "contract out" of the compulsory program. The only other stipulations were that: (1) the annuity program had to be available to all employees, regardless of age; (2) premiums had to be deposited with an ordinary insurance company or other approved trustee; (3) if an employee's job was terminated, the employer had to refund to the government the equivalent of his combined premiums plus interest; (4) in the event the employee died, the estate had to receive at least the amount it would have been entitled to under the federal program; and, finally, (5) the employer's records and accounts were to be subject to federal scrutiny. At any time, employees of firms that had contracted out would have had their choice of plans— federal or private.

Clark argued that the compulsory program would force the discontinuance of many private pension plans, possibly even ones that could provide more generous benefits, as firms would find it unprofitable to continue financing private pension plans in addition to the compulsory contributions to the federal plan. The private alternative, he argued, would provide flexibility and freedom of choice not possible under a compulsory federal program.[50]

It was difficult for critics to devise a convincing case against the Clark Amendment if the compulsory annuities program was, as advocates asserted, an "insurance" program. Since private plans would have been regulated to comply by the provisions of the old-age insurance law, they would necessarily have been as "safe" and "actuarially sound" as the federal program. Since benefits paid by private plans would have had to be as generous as those in the federal plan, they would therefore have been "adequate." If a compulsory program was deemed desirable to coerce short-sighted persons to save over their working lives, the private option would pose no problem. And, since workers would have had a free choice between the private and public plan, they could not have been "exploited" by private, profit-making insurance companies.

As such, the Clark Amendment posed a very serious threat to the viability of the federal old-age insurance program. By subjecting the federal plan to competition, the government would have been forced, if only by default, to maintain a sound old-age insurance program. The voluntary flow of participants between competing suppliers would have dramatically reduced the potential monopolization of the old-age insurance industry. At the least, the amendment, like the private alternative, made the redistributive nature of the federal "insurance" program very clear. It was this fact that led the amendment to attract more heated (yet carefully worded) debate in the Senate and conference committee than any other.

Opponents of the Clark Amendment included sponsors of the Social Security bill and social insurance advocates, including Senators Wagner, LaFollette and Harrison, as well as organized labor and the Administration. Critics argued, erroneously, that the introduction of Social Security would not eliminate or discourage the creation of new private pension plans. Others argued that the private alternative would create an "inequity" whereby, depending upon the timing of a worker's privately and publicly covered employment, a worker who spent his early years in public coverage, then chose the private alternative would receive an "inequitably" larger retirement income than would a worker who timed his coverage in reverse.[51] Organized labor opposed the provision, arguing that a compulsory federal old-age insurance program might well improve labor's bargaining position with industry.[52]

The key argument advanced against the Clark Amendment, however, was that contracting out would lead to an "adverse selection of risk" to the disadvantage of the public program. The downward weighted benefit formula would attract the near-elderly, those who were relatively costly to "insure," and thus make the government program prohibitively costly. In the words of Senator Wagner, sponsor of the Social Security bill, "I am firmly convinced that if this amendment were adopted we should find the Government holding the bag for older men . . . while industries would take care only of the younger men who earned every bit of annuity they received."[53]

This argument was undoubtedly correct, of course. A private plan simply could not provide the relatively large benefits to early retirees required by the bill without charging them significantly higher premiums. Likewise, the government could not finance unearned benefits to the elderly and near-elderly without imposing the cost on younger workers. In a competitive setting and in the absence of coercion, neither the private company nor the federal government could provide unearned benefits to one group at the expense of another. This was the fundamental issue. Stated most succinctly by Senator LaFollette, ardent opponent of the amendment, "If we shall adopt this amendment the Government having determined to set up a federal system of old-age [insurance], will provide in its own bill creating that system, for competition, which in the end may destroy the Federal system. . . It would be inviting and encouraging competition with its own plan which ultimately would undermine and destroy it."[54]

Given Roosevelt's desire to see forms of compulsory social insurance enacted that went well beyond the pending legislation, the President "wanted desperately to see it [the Clark Amendment] stopped."[55] Drawing upon now-familiar political strategies of using "experts" to control information and all-or-nothing offers to control political outcomes, Roosevelt assigned several expert advisors to each of several key senators in order to influence the vote on the Clark Amendment, then threatened to veto the entire Social Security bill if the amendment were passed.[56]

These efforts were not effective. If private pension plans were required to provide the same "good" as the government program, there was no persuasive reason to permit a government monopoly. As one opponent of the Clark Amendment admitted, "In view of all the safeguards, it seemed to the majority of the Senate and to a goodly section of the public that there was really no legitimate objection against granting such an exemption."[57]

On 19 June 1935 the Senate—with a Democratic majority of more than 2:1—passed the Clark Amendment by a vote of 51-35. Shortly thereafter the Senate bill was voted upon and passed easily in the Senate by a vote of 76-6. Action by the Senate Finance Committee and the Senate floor had led to the following amendments to the House bill:

1. Qualified private retirement plans could contract out of the compulsory old-age insurance program.

2. Persons working beyond the age of sixty-five had to continue to pay old-age insurance taxes, plus they would lose the full monthly benefit for each month of employment.

3. The voluntary annuities program was eliminated.

4. The determination of "adequate" pensions was left up to the states.

5. States without pension laws could receive federal aid for up to two years.

The House-Senate Conference

By mid-July the joint House and Senate conference committee had, for the most part, reached agreement on the differences between the House and Senate versions of the Social Security bill.[58] The Russell Amendment to the old-age pension program, for example, was modified so that local governments had to be making contributions in order for states to receive federal aid. Also, the voluntary annuities program was finally struck from the bill and the Social Security Board was designated an independent agency.

Importantly, however, no agreement could be reached on the Clark Amendment. The House strongly opposed the amendment on the grounds that it would ruin the federal insurance program. Also, there were concerns that the amendment could render the old-age program unconstitutional by leading to the differential taxation of employers who had and had not contracted out of the federal program. The Senate refused to budge. After nearly a month of deliberations, conferees returned their reports to their respective houses, receiving approval on all issues of compromise except the Clark Amendment.

To deal with the problem of the Clark Amendment, conferees appointed a special committee to draft an amendment which preserved the private annuity option while avoiding the constitutional complications of a tax exemption and the consequent dangers to the federal system. On 8 August the committee reported that it could achieve these ends through a series of grants to employers with annuity plans. The details of a workable amendment, however, would require up to an additional two weeks' study.[59]

Conferees concluded that a further delay in enacting the Social Security bill over a single amendment to a single program could not be warranted. They decided to delete the Clark Amendment from the bill and appoint a special joint legislative committee that would study the matter more thoroughly and report to Congress the following year. A major victory for advocates of social insurance had been scored. The Clark Amendment was never reconsidered.[60] The Social Security Act was then quickly passed by both houses of Congress and signed by the President on 14 August 1935.

The Social Security Act: August 1935

The original Social Security Act, enacted 14 August 1935, constituted an unprecedented expansion in the role of the federal government. In only twenty-nine pages the act was divided into ten titles which created one federal compulsory program, the old-age insurance program (Titles II and VIII); a federal-state tax-offset program for unemployment compensation (Titles III and IX); and three federal-state categorical grant programs (old-age assistance, Title I; aid to dependent children, Title IV; and aid to the blind, Title X). Two other programs were created with nonuniform federal grants to states for maternal and child welfare (Title V) and public health (Title VI).[61] The provisions of the original old-age insurance and old-age assistance programs are outlined in an appendix to this chapter.

Attributes

One cannot help noticing the simplicity of the original Social Security Act. As enacted in 1935, Social Security consisted of only one compulsory federal program, old-age insurance, and it was simple, relatively narrow in scope, and possessed some of the attributes of private insurance. There was only one beneficiary, for example, the fully retired worker who was eligible for monthly benefits ranging from $10 to $85 ($60 to $509). Coverage was limited to 60 percent of the workforce, generally concentrated in lower-paid occupations, and tax rates were modest. The initial payroll tax (employee and employer combined) was just 2 percent on the first $3,000 ($17,964) of earned income, scheduled to rise to a maximum of 6 percent in 1949. By this time it was anticipated that a large fund would have accumulated which together with interest earnings and tax revenues could support the system indefinitely.

Benefit tables similar to those of private insurance had been designed to ensure that each worker received back at least what he had paid in taxes (employee's share only) plus interest, and, importantly, that everyone with the same earnings history was entitled to the same monthly benefit. Benefits were related singly to total earnings in covered employment, and thus to total tax payments, and there were no benefit increments for additional family members. While the benefit formula tended to favor workers with lower incomes, the program was primarily designed, in the wake of the Great Depression, to supplement private sources of retirement income in some systematic and safe way, while relegating the relief of old-age poverty to a separate, general-revenue financed old-age assistance (means-tested) program. Individual equity was the benchmark for treatment.

The objectives of the original program were clear: (1) benefits should be directly related to earnings and payable only to those who had contributed toward their cost; (2) coverage should be limited; and (3) the system should accumulate substantial reserves and remain self-financing.

Constraints on Expansion and Redirection

The central features of the original program provided a set of potentially effective institutional constraints on the size of the program and its redistributive potential. Foremost, the program was simple—a most direct source of voter control. There was one requirement, a single benefit formula with only three tiers, no benefit increment or benefit reduction provisions, a permanent tax structure and a tax ceiling not designed to be altered as a method of finance. There was little ability to finance expansion by postponing tax costs to future generations, moreover, because reserve funding would require workers to currently meet the tax obligations implied by future benefit promises. Finally, by having restricted compulsory tax and benefit coverage to lower-paid workers, by placing a ceiling on taxable earnings, and by restricting benefits to worker-taxpayers only, the ability to employ the program as a means of redistributing income within generations was limited as well.[62] Each of these important features served to define a range of acceptable political outcomes.

Political Reality

These means of constraining the growth and redirection of the program, which were essential to the program's marketability, were at once political expedients from the point of view of program advocates. Opponents of the new program were certainly aware of the inability of institutional constraints, when unbuttressed by contractual agreement, to limit the growth and scope of the new government program. The Social Security law did no more than bestow statutory rights to individuals, protected by statutory guarantees. Unlike private insurance, public "insurance" could, as asserted by advocates, buttress its promises with the police and taxing powers of the state. But, unlike private contracts, the rights or claims chosen to be protected would be politically determined. The Social Security program thus created an apparatus through which coalitions could vote for transfers to themselves to be made good by claims on other workers' income.[63] In an important sense the insurance terminology was little more than a "stroke of promotional genius" that would allow advocates to "capitalize on the goodwill of private insurance."[64]

The likelihood that demands for income redistribution would arise was enhanced by the method of benefit computation. By having just one benefit formula which was progressively weighted, the near-elderly, lower income workers, and workers with short periods of covered employment were effectively granted unearned benefits, in an actuarial sense, as a "right" under the earnings-related insurance program, even though they had not fully contributed to their cost. The distinction between the objectives of old-age insurance and old-age assistance was already confounded. With the distribution of retirement income removed from the market process, political pressure was certain to mount for larger unearned benefits as a matter of "right," "social adequacy," or "social justice"—all to the neglect of tax payments. This development could have been constrained, "only if, from the outset, the distinction [had been] clearly made between benefits for which the recipient has fully paid, to which he has therefore a moral as well as a legal right and those based on need and therefore dependent on proof."[65]

Another crucial flaw was that the original act removed broad-scale, old-age insurance from the realm of voluntary, private-sector activity and, in so doing, took an important step toward monopolizing the provision of old-age insurance. The introduction of compulsory old-age insurance compelled the purchase of insurance from a single supplier, the federal government. In one fell swoop a government bureau became the single largest producer of retirement income in the country, and as long as the act survived, its market was guaranteed. By eliminating voluntary flows of customers between competing insurance carriers as an indicator of social value, this step sharply curtailed the information and efficiency generating forces of competition, thus buttressing the power of social insurance advocates in the new bureaucracy.

Initial Response to the Act

The Social Security program was met with varied reactions, intense at both extremes. To opponents the creation of a large federal bureaucracy and the redirection of the program to permeate yet other realms of private-sector activity were right around the corner. For advocates, old-age insurance was just one part of a landmark in the history of social legislation. In the words of Abraham Epstein, Social Security was "the most outstanding and courageous program that has ever been attempted in the history of the world. . . . No man, not even Bismarck or Lloyd George, ever dared to present as comprehensive, as thorough-going, as vital a program in all its all-embracing aspects."[66] Destined to mark a permanent change in the relation between the federal government and social welfare, the Social Security program was, in President Roosevelt's words, a "a cornerstone in a structure being built."[67]

From the outset advocates disagreed over whether the old-age insurance program could adequately redistribute income and achieve the desired "social objectives." Coverage was not universal, benefits were tied to earnings, and there appeared to be a preoccupation with individual equity. Also, benefits were restricted to the elderly. There was no health insurance, disability insurance, medical insurance, or "cradle-to-grave" protection as initially sought by President Roosevelt.[68]

An expansion of the program was only a matter of time. The Social Security Board would have great latitude in appointing its own "experts" to fill staff positions and they would be entrusted to initiate policy. Special-interest groups could be counted on to rally for special benefit increases and a transference of costs.

An examination of the debates, the major changes in the bill that were approved, as well as key amendments which were defeated, provide important insights into political sentiments in 1935 and offer perspective for evaluating the vital role played by President Roosevelt and the CES in determining the timing and form of the original Social Security Act. What is evidenced most clearly is both a significant understanding of the difficulties that would eventually come to plague compulsory insurance as well as, once again, the existence of quite broadly based opposition to the old-age insurance titles of the bill.

The legislative history reveals nearly continuous efforts on the part of opponents to instill elements of competition into the provision of old-age "security." In the presence of the largest Democratic majority in history opponents in Congress managed to reduce the federal government's discretion over state old-age pension laws, eliminate the voluntary annuities program, and modify the compulsory old-age insurance program so as to finance it on a funded, self-supporting basis. From the time the bill entered the House Ways and Means Committee until the time it emerged from the Senate, the compulsory old-age insurance program was a primary source of controversy and faced serious threats to survival.

Just as clearly evidenced, however, is the importance of the Administration in shielding the essence of its bill—compulsory old-age insurance—from attack at key points in its progression through Congress. As the bill finally emerged from the conference committee, for example, the last and most serious threat to the viability of the compulsory federal program had been eliminated under the threat of presidential veto of the entire Social Security bill. The control over information maintained by advocate-"experts" and the ability of proponents to tie a series of seemingly unrelated titles into a single legislative bill facilitated the passage of a compulsory, federal old-age insurance program that alone clearly would not have gained passage during the 1930s. Rather than marking a "new awareness" on the part of Americans to the needs of the poor and elderly, or the institutionalization of broad-based demands for social insurance, the emergence of compulsory old-age insurance marked the culmination of the combined efforts of public suppliers.[69]

It is indeed a reflection of the times that, by today's standards, the original compulsory old-age insurance program was simple, relatively narrow in scope, and had some attributes of private insurance. There was only one beneficiary category, the eligible retired worker, and the objectives of the program were clear: (1) benefits directly related to earnings, payable to worker-taxpayers only, (2) limited coverage, and (3) a self-financing program. Together, these objectives defined a set of potentially important constraints on the ability of special-interest groups to exploit the program for their own purposes.

Despite the apparent simplicity of the new law, however, within it lay the seeds of redirection and growth. Any "rights" implied by Social Security were noncontractual. As such the institutional constraints embedded in the new law which might have limited the future course of the program were merely statutory and therefore subject to change. Given this crucial flaw, the choice of a split payroll tax as a means of finance, a progressive benefit formula as the means of benefit distribution, and the federal government as the means of production were all certain to buttress the discretionary power of social insurance advocates within the bureaucracy in relaxing these constraints.

To summarize, the evidence presented in the past three chapters is consistent with each of the following hypotheses. First, "social security," broadly defined and in some general sense, did emerge out of the Great Depression in response to broad-based citizen demands for government action. These demands, however, were vaguely articulated and may have been satisfied with any of a number of government policies. Second, the compulsory old-age insurance titles of the act lacked broad-based political support. Without the ability of proponents to bundle the program into an entire legislative package of "security" and, moreover, into one that was presented to Congress as an all-or-none offer, compulsory federal old-age insurance would most likely not have emerged from Congress in the 1930s. Finally, the institutional "details" of the new program were controlled by public suppliers and would enhance the discretion of suppliers over program expansion in years to come.

Appendix: *Titles Pertaining to the Elderly in the Original Social Security Act*

Title II: The Old-Age Benefit Program

Coverage. Every employee in the United States was covered (had to pay the payroll tax and was potentially eligible for old-age benefits) except: agricultural labor,

Table 5.2. Illustration of monthly benefits payable under original social security program[a] (current dollars)

Age in 1937	Date benefits payable	On avg. annual earnings of[b]		
		$600	$1200	$3000
60	1942	$15	$18	$25
50	1952	20	27	50
40	1962	25	37	62
30	1972	30	47	75
20	1982	35	54	85 (max.)

Sources: Calculated on the basis of the benefit formula contained in the Social Security Act of 14 Aug. 1935, Sec. 202. See also Paul Douglas, *Social Security in the United States* (New York: Macmillan Publishing Company, 1939), p. 164.

a. The Social Security Act was amended before this benefit schedule was employed.

b. For comparison, the median age in the population was twenty-eight in 1935, and median annual earnings among covered workers were $761 in 1937. See U.S. Bureau of Census, *Statistical History of the United States: From Colonial Times to the Present* (New York: Basic Books, Inc. , 1976), and *Social Security Bulletin: Annual Statistical Supplement, 1975* (Washington, D.C.: U.S. Government Printing Office, 1976).

domestic service in private homes, casual labor, seamen, employees of the United States government or any of its instrumentalities, or state and local governments, and employees of any nonprofit organizations, including educational, religious, and scientific organizations.

Benefits. Beginning 1 January 1942, old-age benefits were to be payable to qualified individuals at the age of sixty-five, in the form of equal monthly payments until death. A function of total covered wages (TCW), these annuities would range from $10 ($60) to $85 ($509) per month.[70] As illustrated in Table 5.2, the benefit formula generated benefits that were even higher than proposed by the CES and more favorable to persons who would retire with low earnings early in the life of the program.

Earnings Test. An individual who continued to work in regular employment beyond the retirement age of sixty-five would lose the full monthly benefit payment for each month of employment.

Qualified Individual. An individual whose total income during the period 31 December 1936 through the attainment of the age of sixty-five did not exceed $2,000 or who did not receive wages from covered employment on at least one day out of five different calendar years would not qualify for monthly benefits.

Payments Upon Death. Everyone who paid Social Security taxes was assured of receiving benefits equal to at least 3 1/2 percent of TCW. If the individual died before reaching age sixty-five, his estate would be credited with this amount, a lump sum payment comprised of 1/2 percent interest on the maximum employee tax of 3 percent. If the individual died during retirement but before receiving the full 3 1/2 percent, his estate would be credited with the balance.

Payments to Individuals not Qualified for Benefits. If, at sixty-five, the individual was not qualified for benefits, he would be entitled to receive a lump sum payment of 3 1/2 percent of TCW.

Financing

Because the constitutionality of the old-age benefit program was seriously in doubt, the law was written so that it would be financed by appropriations from general revenues. In a completely separate title, the payroll tax was described. No link was made between Title II benefits and Title VIII taxes since it was thought that the federal insurance program could be unconstitutional (discussed in Chapter 6). It was taken for granted, of course, that the Title VIII taxes would provide the source of revenue from which the secretary of treasury would make annual appropriations.

Each fiscal year beginning 20 June 1937 funds were to be appropriated by the secretary of treasury to the "Old-Age Reserve Account," a newly created account in the Department of Treasury. Amounts appropriated were to be calculated "on a reserve basis in accordance with accepted actuarial principles." The treasurer would be responsible for estimating the amounts required for benefit payments, given tables of mortality and a 3 percent rate of interest, and amounts credited to the account in excess of current withdrawals were to be invested by the treasurer in United States interest-bearing obligations with at least a 3 percent annual yield. Accrued interest and the proceeds of sales were simply to be credited to the account.

Title VIII: Payroll Taxes

Beginning in 1937 a payroll tax (referred to as an "income" tax on employees and an "excise" tax on employers) would be levied on the earnings of all covered workers, up to a maximum amount of taxable earnings of $3,000 ($17,964) per year. An equal tax would be levied on employers. As shown in Table 5.3, the combined rate of taxation would be 2 percent in 1937, rising by one percentage point each three years, reaching a maximum of 6 percent in 1949. The tax on employees would be deducted by the employer from each paycheck and would not be permitted as a deduction for the employee in calculating net income.

Title I: Old-Age Assistance

Through a system of matching grants, states were encouraged to provide for the needy aged within their boundaries. Any state with an old-age assistance program

Table 5.3. Scheduled tax rates under the original Social Security Act

Years	Combined employee and employer tax rate
1937-39	2%
1940-42	3%
1943-45	4%
1946-48	5%
1949 and thereafter	6%

Source: Social Security Act of 14 Aug. 1935, Secs. 801-11.

that was satisfactory to the Social Security Board would qualify for federal revenues equal to half of all assistance payments to the elderly up to a maximum federal payment of $15 ($90) per person per month. An additional 5 percent of this amount was payable for administrative costs.

In order to qualify for federal grants, state programs had to satisfy the following federal requirements:

1. The program had to be statewide and mandatory.

2. The state had to participate financially.

3. A single state administrative agency had to be created with "efficient administration."

4. One-half of any property collected by the state from the recipient's estate had to be turned over to the federal government.

5. After 1 January 1940, no age requirements exceeding sixty-five could be imposed.

6. No residency requirement which would exclude individuals who had lived in the state for five out of the previous nine years, with one continuous year preceding assistance, could be imposed.

7. No citizenship requirement which would exclude a United State citizen could be imposed.

Title VII: The Social Security Board

The Social Security Act authorized the establishment of a Social Security Board, a three person committee appointed by the President with the advice and consent of the Senate. Appointments were to be made for a period of six years, with one of the members designated chairman. The responsibilities of the board included studying economic security and making recommendations for legislation and administrative policy. The board was empowered to appoint and determine the pay of officers and employees deemed necessary to execute the Social Security program. "Experts" could be appointed without regard to civil-service laws.

Part III. Redirection and Growth

Chapter 6. The Institutionalization of Expansionary Forces and Program Redirection: 1935–39

> Passing the laws is only, as it were, a "curtain-raiser" in the evolution of such a program.[1]
>
> Arthur Altmeyer, Chairman
> Social Security Board

Only months after the Social Security Act was passed President Roosevelt appointed the three-member Social Security Board, and its staff was being organized. The staff nucleus of the new agency drew largely from the ranks of social insurance advocates affiliated with the Committee on Economic Security, the committee that formulated the Social Security program. Expansionary forces were thereby internalized into the bureaucracy in its earliest stages of development.

Four years later the most radical redirection in the history of Social Security was accomplished, with two of the primary objectives of the original program being abandoned—individual equity and reserve funding. Enacted before any monthly benefits were paid under the old-age insurance program, the 1939 amendments marked the first redirection and expansion of the program that had been "recommended" by Social Security officials, endorsed by the Advisory Council on Social Security, and made possible by the institutional weaknesses of the 1935 Act. During the following twenty years the metamorphosis of Social Security from a limited objective, old-age insurance program to a broad-scale and complex redistributive scheme was virtually completed.

Given the apparently limited nature of old-age insurance and the lack of broad-based political support for the program in 1935, how can this evolution to a highly complex, redistributive program be explained? This question is the major concern of Chapters 6 and 7. Several other questions are also addressed since they provide economic and political insight into this broader phenomenon. For example, recognizing the importance of supply-side control over the original institutional features of the program, can this later course of events be explained by supply-side models? If the bureaucracy did dominate the program's evolution, what were its sources of power and how was it able to overcome the initially intense opposition to compulsory old-age insurance? How was the bureau able to shield itself from competitive pressures from the local public sector and private sector? What was the impact of eliminating the accumulation of a large fund in 1939, for example, and expanding coverage during the 1950s on the monopoly position of the bureau and the ability to employ the program to redistribute income? Indeed, can the evolution of the program from 1935 to 1960 be explained as the outcome of an active bureaucracy influencing the political forces that generate income redistribution?

To address these questions, this chapter focuses on the period 1935-39, a period capturing three vitally important stages in the life of the new bureaucracy: the creation and staffing of the new bureau, its survival through serious political and legal attack, and finally, the enactment in 1939 of the first, most important amendments to the Social Security Act.

Staffing the Board: The Institutionalization of Expansionary Forces

The Social Security Board came into operation as a permanent, independent agency in the fall of 1935, with three operating bureaus subordinate to it: the Bureau of Old-Age Benefits, designed to administer the new old-age insurance program, the Bureau of Public Assistance, and the Bureau of Unemployment Compensation.[2] Appointed to the board were John Winant (chairman), Arthur Altmeyer, and Vincent Miles, who set out almost immediately to undertake the most crucial task of staffing the new bureaus. Canvassing, interviewing, and selecting staff and other personnel would consume the largest proportion of the board's time in its first two years of existence.

The extent of the board's involvement in staffing, which necessarily derived from an intense desire to control the loyalties of new appointees in a not-too-hospitable environment, was facilitated by several factors. First, an "expert clause" in the Social Security Act permitted the appointment of experts and lawyers without regard to civil service laws. Second, a resolution adopted by the board limited all appointments made by the lower-level bureau heads and the executive director to ranks below the second lowest professional grade. Its control over salaries and promotions, moreover, "embraced the entire organization."[3]

Predictably, the board made every effort to utilize these powers so as to staff key positions with friends of the social insurance movement. The staff nucleus of the newly created agency was drawn heavily from the overlapping group of CES staff and advisory council and other advocates who played the major role in formulating the Social Security program. As two close observers described it: "The Social Security Board was in a double sense a continuation of the CES: not only were its activities an application of the new functions envisaged by that investigating committee, but the staff nucleus with which the board began was carried over from the committee."[4] This close relationship between the board and the CES is reflected in

The board's interest in making its own staffing decisions extended from the appointment of high-level officials down to the selection of regional and field-office staff, and they used the "expert" clause skillfully. By February 1937, for example, the vitally important Bureau of Research and Statistics had more than fifty experts on its staff and, in total, some 20 percent of the board's employees were "experts."[5]

The board's efforts to control the selection of its staff were ambitious and led to

Table 6.1. Members and staff of the Social Security Board and prior positions

Name and position	Prior positions
John Winant, chairman, 1935-36	Governor, N.H.; Director, International Labor Org.; member, CES Advisory Board
Arthur Altmeyer, member, (Chairman, 1936-53)	Second assistant secretary of labor; secretary, Wisc. Industrial Comm.; chairman, CES Technical Board
Vincent Miles, member	Lawyer, member of Democratic National Committee
Frank Bane, executive director	Director, American Public Welfare Association; Chief, Tenn. Welfare Department
Thomas Eliot, general counsel	Associate solicitor, Department of Labor; Member, CES Technical Board; Chief draftsman of Social Security Act
Murray Latimer, director, Bureau of Old-Age Benefits, 1935-37	Economist, Industrial Relations Counselors Member, CES Technical Board
Henry Seidemann, director, Bureau of Old-Age Benefits	Member, Brookings Institute
Jane Hoey, director, Bureau of Public Assistance	Professional social worker; associate director, New York Welfare Council
William Williamson, chief actuary, Bureau of Old-Age Benefits	Actuary, Travelers Insurance; actuary on Unemployment Compensation Staff, CES
Robert Myers, assistant to chief actuary, Bureau of Old-Age Benefits	Actuarial asssitant, CES
Walton Hamilton, director, Bureau of Research and Statistics	Director of the Graduate School, Brookings Institute; chairman, NRA Advisory Council
Ewan Clague, ass't director Bureau of Research and Statistics	Faculty, Univ. of Wisc.; consultant to Employment Opportunitites Staff, CES
Wilbur Cohen, staff member, Bureau of Unemployment Compensation	research assistant to Executive Director Witte, CES; Aid in drafting the Social Security Act

Sources: Charles McKinley and Robert Frase, *Launching Social Security, A Capture and Record Account: 1935-37* (Madison: Univ. of Wisc. Press, 1970): 495-503.

Edwin Witte, *The Development of the Social Security Act* (Madison: Univ. of Wisc. Press, 1963), pp. 7-55.

two years of continuous conflict with the Civil Service Commission. According to the commission, the board was using a biased selection process to make its staffing decisions; no one was being hired from the private insurance industry, for example, to staff the bureau administering the old-age insurance program, the new Bureau of Old-Age Benefits (BOAB). According to board members, however, a perfectly natural selection process was being utilized; new selections required exhibited interest in and knowledge of the program and its administration. The board, they said, hired only the "best."[6]

In the fall of 1937, after the principal staff positions had been filled, the board finally gave up the expert clause. As board members had come to learn, the clause gave them wide latitude in hiring, but it gave congressmen similar latitude in demanding political patronage appointments.[7]

As suggested by these early years, the creation and staffing of the new bureaus were vitally important, and were perceived to be so by those most directly affected. Monopolizing and bureaucratizing research, information, and legislative agendas were the sources of control over political outcomes, and it would be growth-oriented advocates in possession of this control that could further the ends of the new social insurance bureaucracy. The initial staffing-screening process, coupled with civil-service laws that shielded certain appointments from political competition, ensured that expansionary forces were institutionalized into the Social Security bureaucracy. Individuals who, based on personal values, sought an extensive social insurance system or public sector per se were combined with those who simply found their future incomes tied to the program's growth.[8]

Advocates within the new bureaucracy were now federally funded to undertake research, disseminate information, initiate and draft legislation. They were in the position of determining not only which issues would be studied internally and which results would be communicated, but also which ones would not be.[9]

Whether for ideological or self-interested reasons, the bureaucracy could not have been expected to use this unique position to provide balanced information on the costs and benefits of their program relative to those actually or potentially available in the private sector, or to advance proposals to limit the growth of their program. Instead, it had every incentive to use its influence to expand the scope and complexity of Social Security. According to Robert Myers, past deputy commissioner of social security, "Over the years most of the American staff engaged in program planning and policy development have had the philosophy—carried out with religious zeal—that what counts above all else is the expansion of the program."[10]

The ability of the bureaucracy to have an independent effect on political outcomes and profit from the position, of course, depended critically on the degree to which it became isolated from competitive forces. Working to secure the bureaucracy a measure of monopoly power were the compulsory participation features of the program and their consequences for private competitors. Compulsory participation would erode, at least initially, the position of private insurance and pension companies by reducing their pool of customers and perhaps increasing their relative administrative costs, and, given the progressive benefit formula, would erode the ability of private firms to provide insurance to lower-income workers and the near-elderly.[11]

On the other hand, more than 40 percent of the working population were not covered by the original old-age insurance program, and that portion of workers' incomes above the ceiling on taxable earnings could still be used to freely purchase private insurance. Moreover, there were a number of related forms of insurance that individuals would turn to private markets to purchase, such as disability and health insurance, supplementary annuities for dependents, and life insurance for survivors. Indeed, because of the program's concentration on retirement benefits for worker-taxpayers only the public "product" was not yet significantly differentiated from that which was privately produced—a necessary ingredient for monopolization.

The process of eliminating competitive constraints on growth and redirection must be gradual and imperfect for any bureau, but this was particularly true for the BOAB. Compulsory old-age insurance emerged from Congress without broad-based political support, and the operation, administration, and political support associated with each of the new programs were no longer inextricably tied to one another. The new bureau was in an independent position from which it had to derive its own sources of power and influence. Yet the payroll tax would not be collected for two years, so that the bureau was in the position of having to compete for funding with other government agencies. And benefits were not payable for seven years, so that there were yet few direct beneficiaries of the program whose support could be employed by the bureaucracy to offset the early opposition. Given these circumstances, the new program was particularly vulnerable to the forces of political competition, and the next general election was only months away.

Early Threats to the Board's Survival: Long, Landon, Townsend, and the Supreme Court

At the same time that the Social Security staff was embarking on a huge administrative undertaking, and to the alarm of officials who recognized the crucial importance of political-financial support in the early years, external political and legal problems were developing. Almost immediately the board was faced with problems of funding, attacks during the 1936 election, continued pressure from the Townsend movement, and, most importantly, serious constitutional questions. These problems severely constrained the board's early staffing efforts as well as the bureaucracy's ability to market and attempt to expand the old-age insurance program. From 1935 to 1937 the board was effectively engaged in a struggle for survival.

The Social Security Board's activities were inhibited initially when funds failed to be appropriated by Congress for its first fiscal year. Since the payroll tax was not yet being collected, the board was in the position of having to rely on congressional appropriations from general revenues. At the outset, however, no funds were made available as a filibuster by Senator Long prevented the passage of a deficiency bill before Congress adjourned in 1935. The board was forced to rely entirely on $112,000 from the Department of Labor, initially intended for the Works Project Administration, and a staff borrowed from the "demobilizing National Recovery Administration and other sympathetic agencies."[12] By June of 1936 the board was funded for the 1937 fiscal year, but with 20 percent less money than requested.[13]

Then, still just months after Social Security was passed, the old-age insurance titles of the act became a major election issue in 1936. According to the Republican party platform, New Deal policies endangered rather than provided social security. Calling for an abandonment of the current system, they argued, in effect, for a greatly expanded old-age assistance program. Social Security should be universal, they argued, so as to provide all elderly persons with a pension in accordance with need, and the program should be currently financed on a federal-state matching basis, with the use of a broadly based tax.[14]

Led by Republican presidential nominee Alf Landon, conservatives attacked New Deal legislation as communistic and singled out Social Security as a key issue. Governor Landon described the old-age insurance program as "unjust and unworkable.... And to call it "social security" is a fraud on the working man.... The savings forced on our workers is a cruel hoax. ... To get a workable old-age pension plan, we must repeal the present compulsory insurance plan."[15]

Landon's remarks had an immediate impact on the Social Security Board and its role in "public relations."

> Chairman Winant replied with a dramatic resignation that permitted him to rush to the open political defense of the system. . . . The Board broke loose from the inhibitions that had largely paralyzed the work of the Informational Services since the AAA [Agricultural Adjustment Act] court decision. Leaflets and moving picture films intended to educate the people for the post-election registration effort were brought out of hiding and given to the public with a free hand. The Board and its staff, in the last weeks before the election, vigorously cooperated with the Democratic party and the labor unions in getting out publicity in defense of the system.[16]

"We The People and Social Security," a movie seen by some four million people, was released by the board and aired on Times Square prior to the election. Eight million copies of an Information Service circular entitled "Social Security in Your Old-Age" were printed, of which three million were distributed to AFL unions across the country. Social Security officials and key staff members were flown to the New York Democratic National Committee headquarters to write speeches for Democratic campaigners.[17]

Not surprisingly, the campaign waged against Social Security, as a campaign against an incumbent President and a now-incumbent bureaucracy, proved to be a difficult undertaking, particularly in light of the many other popular relief and employment programs created by Roosevelt. Roosevelt won the 1936 election with 60.7 percent of the popular vote,[18] and it was believed by some that the Republican attack had actually been a "blessing in disguise" for board members: "It awakened the American public to the fact that there was a Social Security Act and . . . it made it possible to run a quick and effective campaign for registration."[19]

Alongside conservative opposition to old-age insurance the Social Security Board faced continued pressure from the Townsend movement. On 11 December 1935 Edwin Witte, executive director of the CES, wrote Merrill Murray, associate director of the Bureau of Unemployment Compensation, of his concern:

> In the last three months I have become more concerned than ever with the Townsend plan. There is no doubt that this movement has made tremendous headway. The battle against the Townsend plan has been lost, I think, in pretty nearly every state west of the Mississippi, and the entire Middle Western area is likewise badly infected. At this time, the Republican party organization is at least flirting with the Townsendites, and I think it is mighty significant that not one of the major business organizations of the country has attacked the plan.[20]

As late as 1938 the Townsend movement was still strong. In a letter written to Abraham Epstein, Witte reiterated his concern over the threat of the Townsend movement when he said, "More and more it is becoming clear that the next major election issue in relation to Social Security is whether we want the Townsend plan or not. . . . The real issue is between the Social Security Act and the Townsend Plan."[21] In that year more than ninety Republicans who had "indicated some commitment" to the Townsend plan were elected to Congress, more than half of the total number of Republicans.[22]

While the Townsend movement was not effective, changes in the program were nevertheless forthcoming.

In the midst of these not inconsequential problems the board was also faced with growing concern over the constitutionality of the Social Security Act. Between 1935 and early 1936 seven out of nine New Deal acts had been found unconstitutional,[23] one of which had particular bearing on the Social Security Act—the Supreme Court's invalidation of the legal and financial power of the federal government to maintain crop restrictions in the Agricultural Adjustment Act. The adverse ruling was based on the premise that Congress had invaded states' rights by using its taxing and spending powers to purchase compliance of an end that it was not constitutionally permitted to achieve directly. As a result it was feared that although Congress could appropriate funds for all types of general welfare purposes, as in the welfare titles of the Social Security Act, the restrictions imposed on the matching grants (such as the restriction that a state law must be compulsory in all political subdivisions) might be found unconstitutional as attempts to coerce states into an action and thus regulate state affairs.[24] According to Witte, the welfare titles of the act had been "rendered very doubtful" by the AAA decision.[25]

With regard to the federal old-age insurance program and the taxes imposed to finance it, constitutionality rested on whether the Supreme Court chose to test the validity of the spending and taxing provisions separately or in combination. If judged separately, as hoped by legal draftsmen, the old-age benefit title could be upheld as a federal spending program to improve general welfare, and the taxes could be upheld as simply another appropriation or levy to support the activities of the federal government. The bill had been carefully drafted so that the old-age insurance benefit and tax titles (Titles II and VIII) were entirely independent, without any reference to one another. Even among those arguing the best case for the validity of the act, however, it was said that "the AAA decision [had] shaken the foundation of the hope" that the validity of the tax would be determined without regard to the intended use of its revenues.[26]

If interpreted in conjunction with one another, it was generally agreed that the titles could not be found constitutional. First, the Court had already invalidated efforts to "expropriate from one group for the benefit of another," so that the legality of taxing employers for the benefit of employees had been rendered doubtful. Second, the titles in combination might be interpreted as producing, for example, a compulsory savings program, establishing conditions of employment, and regulating relations of employees and employers—none of which were constitutional through direct federal action. Viewed together, that is, the tax might be viewed not as a true tax levy at all but as a contribution toward implied future benefits and thus a part of a regulatory insurance scheme.[27] In short, it was said: "The only hope for these titles (II and VIII) is that the Court will find that they do not, in fact, establish an old-age insurance system. Again the question will be whether this is a genuine tax levy or part of an unconstitutional plan to establish a federal insurance program."[28]

Possibly the most important side effect of these constitutional doubts was that they effectively paralyzed the ability of the board and the BOAB to market their output. After the AAA decision was handed down, and on the advice of General Counsel Thomas Eliot, the Information Service was instructed to "play down the use of such terms as 'insurance' and not to allow, in any official reports or publicity material, the coupling of the tax titles with the two insurance titles lest the Court take judicial notice when considering constitutionality of the Act. Supercaution had to be exercised, and every public statement relating to these titles was checked and double-checked to see that the language used was sufficiently opaque."[29] Social Security executives and staff were thus placed in an uncomfortable position since political acceptance of the program relied (and would continue to rely) so heavily on the program's private insurance analogy.

A series of fortuitous events were taking place, quite outside the control of the Social Security Board, that much improved the act's chances of being upheld. Shortly before Roosevelt was inaugurated for his second term in 1937 he announced that "means must be found to adapt our legal forms and our judicial interpretation to the actual present national needs of the largest progressive democracy in the modern world."[30] On 5 February the President then proposed a reorganization of the federal judiciary which would have empowered him to appoint an additional Supreme Court justice to assist any justice who was seventy years of age or older. With six out of nine Justices already over seventy, the proposal would have empowered the President to increase the size of the Court to fifteen Justices.

Despite the largest Democratic congressional majorities in history, bitter battles ensued over whether Roosevelt's plan was "packing" or "unpacking" the Supreme Court. Liberals joined with conservatives in opposing the President's plan.[31]

Threats of Supreme Court reorganization laid constitutional questions open to the political arena, and it was during the resulting flurry of activity that all the titles of the Social Security Act were upheld. In 1937 conservative Justice Willis Van Devanter announced his plans to retire, and Senator Joseph Robinson, court-reorganization leader in the Senate, died. Between 29 March and 24 May 1937 the Supreme Court sustained the constitutionality of the second Frazier-Lemke farm-mortgage law, a 1936 act conferring collective bargaining rights to railway employees, a minimum-wage law in Washington, the National Labor Relations Board, as well as the old-age benefit provisions and unemployment compensation titles of the Social Security Act.[32]

Delivering the opinion of the Court on 24 May 1937, Justice Cordoza referred to the payroll tax imposed in Title VIII (designated "income taxes on employees" and "excise taxes on employers"), saying "the proceeds of both taxes are to be paid into the Treasury like internal revenue taxes generally, and are not earmarked in any way. This title creates an account in the United States Treasury to be known as the "Old-Age Reserve Account." No present appropriation, however, is made to that account. . . . Not a dollar goes into the Account by force of the challenged act alone."[33] On the subject of the old-age benefits in Title II, which would seemingly be financed out of appropriations from general revenues, Cordoza went on to say that the investigations of the CES and others revealing the number and proportion of elderly persons and the extent of poverty among the elderly made clear that the payments under the program furthered the "general welfare." Likening the benefits to gratuitous transfers,[34] the problem of old-age dependency and its alleviation were, he said, "plainly national in area and dimension. . . . Needs that were narrow or parochial a century ago may be interwoven in our day with the well-being of our nation."

Since, in the original act, there was no written provision for financing the program from the Title VIII payroll taxes and there was no reference to the term "insurance"—reference was rather to the "old-age benefit program"—the Court was able to simply "leave open" a decision concerning the validity of the titles when interpreted in conjunction with one another.[35] The Court's judgment, of course, was based on an interpretation of the act that was contrary to the most fundamental understanding as expressed in the CES Report, presidential statements, congressional hearings, and the popular press.

Remarkably, the insurance terminology was introduced into the bureaucracy's vocabulary immediately after the Court's decision was handed down.

Pressures for Change

Despite the 1935-37 interlude in which the Social Security bureaucracy struggled for survival, mid-1937 marked the beginning of a brighter future. The act had been validated, President Roosevelt had been reelected, and Democratic majorities in Congress had swollen. The Democrats held 331 out of 435 seats in the House and 76 seats in the Senate as compared to the 16 held by Republicans.[36] Then too the collection of the payroll tax had begun. In the future the BOAB would automatically receive appropriations, and taxpayers, accumulating entitlements to future benefits, would soon have vested interests in the continuation of the program. In short, the board was in a more secure position from which to amass political support for expansion.

Supply-side pressure for expansion soon surfaced. The day after the Supreme Court handed down its decision, Altmeyer, who had become chairman of the Social Security Board, addressed a group of social workers and announced:

Passing the law is only, as it were, the "curtain-raiser" in the evolution of such a program. It is already possible to distinguish at least three phases of this evolution, each with its distinctive emphasis—first, the double barrelled job of setting up administrative machinery and of getting it into operation; second, the development and integration of administration and services within the present framework; and third, further expansion to liberalize existing provisions.[37]

The first formal step toward amending the Social Security Act came in 1937 when Congress faced its first appropriation to the old-age reserve account—an appropriation on the order of a half billion dollars. According to Senator Vandenberg (R.-Mich.) of the Senate Finance Committee, this appropriation made imperative a reexamination of the whole method of financing the system. The prospect of accumulating a $47 billion reserve fund in the decades ahead was, in his words, "the most fantastic and the most indefensible objective imaginable. It is scarcely conceivable that rational men should propose such an unmanageable accumulation of funds in one place in a democracy."[38]

At the initiative of Senator Vandenberg, the Finance Committee created a Special Subcommittee on Social Security (Senators Harrison, Byrd, and Vandenberg) to join with the Social Security Board in appointing a "detached advisory council of experts." The council was to be delegated with responsibility to study the size and disposition of the reserve fund, and to "assist in studying the advisability of amending old-age insurance" in the following ways: (1) expanding compulsory coverage; (2) commencing benefit payments before January 1942; (3) increasing benefits payable to early retirees; (4) extending benefit coverage to survivors; (5) increasing tax rates less rapidly than scheduled; and (6) providing disability benefits.[39]

In May the first Advisory Council on Social Security was appointed to consider these liberalizations, and shortly thereafter the Social Security Board was requested by Roosevelt to do the same.[40]

In January of 1939 President Roosevelt addressed Congress to transmit the board's recommendations. Before any monthly benefits had been paid under the old-age insurance program, the President said, "We would be derelict of our responsibility if we did not take advantage of the experience we have accumulated to strengthen and extend its [the Social Security Act's] provisions."[41]

The proposals of the Board and the "citizens'" advisory council—constituting radical changes in the nature of Social Security—virtually mirrored one another. On the benefit side their major recommendations included making monthly benefit payments beginning in 1940 rather than 1942, increasing benefits for early retirees, establishing new beneficiary categories for wives, children, widows, and widows with children, expanding the program to disability insurance, eliminating the "money-back guarantees," and reducing benefits for single retirees. Regarding coverage, they recommended extending tax and benefit coverage to persons older than sixty-five, agricultural labor, maritime employees, domestic servants, and employees of nonprofit organizations and instrumentalities of the federal government. On the tax side they endorsed supplemental financing through nonpayroll taxes. Additional recommendations of the Advisory Council included the establishment of a contingency fund, the designation of a "trust fund," the appointment of a board of trustees, and the automatic appropriation of payroll tax receipts to the fund.[42]

By design the tax rates and ceiling on taxable earnings set in 1935 were not to be altered, while benefits were to be extended dramatically in the early years—the goal of accumulating a large reserve was to be abandoned. Benefit formulas were to be more heavily weighted toward lower-income people, those with shorter periods of covered employment, and those with families to enhance the redistributive impact of the program. Finally, individual worker equity was to be largely set aside for the attainment of such "social goals" as family protection and adequacy in benefits. The effects of these changes were clear: they would speed up the creation of vested interests in the program, create coalitions of beneficiaries whose interests were coincidental with those of the bureaucracy, and eliminate the potential discipline of a funded system.[43]

That the recommendations of the administration, the bureaucracy, and the advisory council all coincided and that they foreshadowed the forthcoming policy outcome was not too surprising since in several important respects, a wide range of policy choices was precluded from consideration even before hearings commenced in Congress. First, the legislative agenda, inherent in the list of areas to be investigated, was predetermined to include only expansionary changes within the current monopolistic institutional framework. Second, it was agreed before the advisory council was appointed that the Social Security Board's monopoly on information would not be violated ("it is understood that the Social Security Board will make all necessary studies and furnish all necessary technical assistance," and that all topics will be "jointly considered with the Social Security Board"). Finally, the Board retained the power to help select the "nonpartisan" council of experts.[44]

As an outgrowth of the selection process, "employees" were represented on the council by six officials from organized labor, by then an important ally of the bureaucracy. Among the twelve members representing the "public" were Edwin Witte, past executive director of the CES and now consultant to the board; Alvin Hansen, past member of the technical board and executive committee to the CES; and Douglas Brown and Paul Douglas, past consultants or affiliates of the CES and now consultant and staff member to the board. Finally, "employers" were represented by six top-level officers in private industry, two of whom were CES advisory-council members and well known for being "progressive": Gerald Swope, president of General Electric, and Marion Folsom, Treasurer of Kodak (who would later become secretary of the Department of Health, Education, and Welfare).[45]

The first Advisory Council on Social Security was thus no exception to what would become historical rules. Despite the apparent balance of interests between employees, employers, and citizens, advisory councils were dominated by social insurance expansionists; with only recent exceptions (since 1975), councils included influential members of the CES, some of whom went on to become part of the Social Security bureaucracy; and the information upon which council members based their decisions on highly complex policy issues was provided exclusively by Social Security staff.[46] Acting as a vehicle for legitimatizing and transmitting the board's policy proposals, the 1938 advisory council was thus no exception in failing to inject competing views and failing to operate as a demand-side monitor of the bureau. It was said of Altmeyer that, as chairman of the board, he "utilized skillfully the advisory council and the reformers and interest groups represented in it to further the movement."[47]

When the hearings on amending Social Security opened in the House Ways and Means Committee in February of 1939, the issues of debate ranged widely, as they did in 1935, from philosophical questions of economic security versus individual liberty, to political questions of welfare versus insurance, to the apparently practical question of how to fund the program.[48] The sources and types of policy recommendations, the stands of key lobby groups, and the issues of political debate in 1939 were the same as they are today. How should benefits be distributed? Who should bear the cost of the program? How should the program be financed?

Critics, such as fiscal conservatives who opposed compulsory insurance, argued on economic and political grounds for a reliance on voluntary organizations for the provision of retirement income, supplemented by the expansion of an old-age assistance type program, or else a dramatic reduction in the resources devoted to the federal insurance program. Liberals, who sought a more extensive program meeting more welfare goals, criticized the fiscal conservatism inherent in financing the program upon actuarial principles. Appearing before the Advisory Council on Social Security, Abraham Epstein said:

> The underlying defect of the present system of old-age insurance embodied in the Act lies in the fact that although intended as a social insurance measure, it completely violates what has been known as social insurance for the past 50

years. . . . In social insurance it matters little whether the people bearing the risk pay the contributions themselves. What is of prime concern is that those who suffer most should receive the greatest protection. Since its chief aim is to accomplish socially desirable ends, the premium rates are dictated by social policy, not by the actuary.[49]

Townsend, still calling for guaranteed uniform pensions to all of the elderly population, appeared before the committee and called the existing program "the height of absurdity."[50] Social Security officials, members of the advisory council, and President Roosevelt urged the program was in need of improvement—where improvement was, and for four decades to come would be, synonymous with expansion.

The most important issue, as it truly encompassed all others, involved the appropriate size of the fund. The major issue was whether the program should be financed on an actuarial reserve basis, as contemplated in the original act, or on a more nearly "pay-as-you-go" basis, possibly with federal contributions.

Conservatives, who would have preferred the revenues be diverted to old-age assistance, argued for a pay-as-you-go system as the only means to guard against the misuse of the very large accumulated fund in the years to come.[51] Insurance companies, who would benefit from near-term tax reductions and the consequent expansion of their market, argued for a pay-as-you-go system because, they said, a federal insurance program could remain solvent with its power to tax even without a fund. Organized labor and other social insurance advocates, who sought the supplement from general revenues they believed would ultimately be required under a pay-as-you-go system, argued for an abandonment of reserve funding because, they said, it depressed the economy and improperly focused the cost of the system on current generations.

In the face of these demands only a few argued that the movement toward a pay-as-you-go system would dangerously obscure the true cost of the system and thus lead to an expansion of the program which might be unsustainable in future years.[52] After all, taxes, scheduled to rise from 2 percent to 3 percent the following year, were thought to be "oppressive." Monthly benefits, which were not even being paid for another three years, would be on average less generous than those paid the elderly poor under the old-age assistance program and, of course, were considerably less generous than those offered by Townsend. And there was a tempting $1.7 ($10) billion fund on hand which Social Security officials coyly announced would be sufficient to allow a reduction in taxes over the next twenty years and still allow scheduled benefits to be paid "for a long time to come."[53]

Fundamental weaknesses in the 1935 act gave representatives from right to left a stake in abandoning the fund. The original law lacked protections against the premature disbursement of the fund, rules to define the proper relation between trust-fund assets and outstanding liabilities, and objective standards for defining "adequate" benefits.

What was the board's position? At least for its first three years in operation the Social Security Board consistently upheld the reserve principle. Without a funded system, they argued, "It would be possible for succeeding generations to meet obligations accruing through this early period only by means of a much higher tax rate than the maximum in the present law, or by a large government subsidy."[54] The intent of the original law was clear, they believed, as was their responsibility to (1) provide limited coverage and a close benefit-earnings link, and (2) finance the program on the reserve principle.[55]

By 1939, not alone in their desire to begin paying benefits and to pay benefits larger than scheduled, the board was prompted to reevaluate its position. Altmeyer came to characterize the funding issue as "consisting largely of 'sound and fury, signifying nothing,' " since the method of financing the system would only affect future generations, when "it is impossible to properly assay the conditions."[56] In 1939, Social Security executives effectively rejected the reserve principle.[57]

In an unusual way the weaknesses of the 1935 act allowed the considerable opposition to old-age insurance to combine with supply-side pressure for expansion so as to produce a resolution that would be vitally important to the future growth and proliferation of the program. Moreover, the emergent support for near-term benefit increases and tax cuts would facilitate the enactment of a whole series of very specific but fundamentally important changes in the distribution of benefits that the bureaucracy had chiefly engineered.

The 1939 Amendments and Their Political Implications

The 1939 amendments enacted into law most of the changes in benefits and financing proposed by the Social Security Board and the Advisory Council; and they would have profound consequences on the future of the program.[58]

The Distribution of Benefits

For example, the amendments modified the benefit formula, applying it to average rather than total earnings, and introduced monthly benefits for survivors and dependents of retired workers. The pattern of returns was made more progressive and discrimination was introduced on the basis of family size. The new distribution of benefits, made to differ increasingly from the distribution that would have arisen in a competitive setting, strengthened the monopoly position of the bureau, and eliminated the individual equity benchmark and the requirement of benefits-restricted-to-taxpayers as means of evaluating future changes. What quantitative standards remained to define the notion of equitable or socially adequate benefits, and to constrain the extent of redistribution?[59]

These changes in the distribution of benefits complicated the system in a way that would make individual cost assessment difficult and a reliance on bureau-generated information more likely. In 1935 there was only one beneficiary category, the retired worker, and only one set of eligibility criteria. In 1939 benefits were instituted for elderly wives, elderly widows, widows with children, dependent children, surviving children, and even dependent, surviving parents. The benefit rate for dependents was half that payable to the retired worker; the rate for survivors was three-quarters that payable to the worker. Age and eligibility criteria were diverse.

The net effect of program complexity, as introduced in 1939, would be to enhance the role of beneficiary groups, including the bureaucracy, in the lobbying/legislative process, while dulling the incentive and ability of taxpayers to monitor program growth and redirection. Young taxpayers, faced with a high and possibly prohibitive cost of information about the effect of policy changes would find themselves in the position of abstaining from gathering information at all or else relying on information made available by those inside Social Security—those least motivated to constrain expansion. How, after all, could the young covered worker possibly assess the likely impact of a policy change on benefit payments to be received by him or his family forty years hence, or his share of the future tax payments required to finance them? For the self-interested beneficiary (whether the recipient or the bureaucrat), by contrast, it would only be necessary to observe the effect on the size and duration of benefit payments or on employment opportunities to assess the desirability of policy changes.

With taxpayers underestimating the cost of changes, broadly sharing the cost of changes, and possibly not registering their demands at all, legislators would naturally respond to the complexity of Social Security by voting on the basis of key issues, leaving it to the experts to decipher the "technical details." The key issues would tend to be benefit increases—clearly perceived and lobbied for by beneficiaries bearing only a small proportion of the additional cost—and they would facilitate the passage of a complex array of technical changes to which they would generally be tied.

To help finance the previously described expansion of benefits, the amendments made other changes that actually reduced the expected value of benefits for certain people: the single retiree, the worker who would die without eligible survivors, and the worker who would not eventually become eligible for benefits. In short, the amendments repealed the "money-back guarantees" implicit in the original act.[60] Benefits were also reduced for people who would retire well into the future. By imposing losses on these worker-taxpayers, these institutional changes clearly elevated the redistributive potential of the new program. They revealed that there were, in fact, no minimum or "guaranteed" rates of return; from the individual's perspective, no necessary permanence to the structure of the program. Moreover, they ensured the Social Security Board a source of revenue on which it owed no return.[61]

As illustrated in Table 6.2, the resulting change in the distribution of benefits was pronounced. A married couple who would retire early in the life of the program, regardless of earnings, was "promised" more than double the amount a single annuitant had been previously scheduled to receive. Benefits for married couples who would retire late in the life of the program, however, hardly exceeded the amount a single annuitant had been previously scheduled to receive.[62] As also revealed in the Table 6.2, monthly benefit payments became payable in 1940, two years earlier than scheduled.

Table 6.2. Illustration of monthly old-age benefits under the 1935 act and as amended in 1939[a]

Years of coverage	1935 Act	1939 Amendments Single	1939 Amendments Married
Average annual earnings of $600			
3	-b-	$21	$31
5	$15	21	31
15	20	23	35
25	25	25	38
35	30	27	40
Average annual earnings of $1200			
3	-b-	$26	$39
5	$18	26	39
15	28	29	43
25	38	31	47
35	48	34	51
Average annual earnings of $1800			
3	-b-	$31	$46
5	$20	32	47
15	35	35	51
25	50	38	56
35	57	41	61
Average annual earnings of $3000 (max.)			
3	-b-	$41	$62
5	$25	43	63
15	50	46	69
25	63	50	75
35	75	54	81

Sources: "The 1939 Amendments," *U.S. Statutes at Large*, Vol. 53, Part 2, pp. 1360-1402; John D. Corson, "Explanation of Federal OASI Under the 1939 Amendments to the Social Security Act," Bulletin No. 17, 3 Aug. 1939, "Director's Bulletin of Progress: 1938-40" (unpublished memos by Director of Bureau of OASI, Library, U.S. Department of Health, Education, and Welfare), p. 4; and Paul Douglas, *Social Security in the United States* (New York: McGraw-Hill Book Company, 1939), p. 164.
  a. Below dashed line, 1939 amendments actually reduced benefits for single annuitants.
  b. Benefits not payable until after five years of coverage.

In effect, aggregate benefit expenditures over time were not expected to increase as a consequence of the amendments; instead, they were redistributed forward in time. The extent of this redistribution was partly revealed in a statement prepared by Altmeyer for the Ways and Means Committee, in which he said,

A worker who becomes 65 years old on January 1, 1940, and who has been making, on an average, $100 a month since the old-age insurance plan went into effect on January 1, 1937 [having therefore paid an employee tax of $1 per month for three years], could retire on his birthday in 1940 with benefits amounting to $25.75 every month for the rest of his life instead of a single lump sum of $126 provided under the plan at present. If his wife is also 65, he would receive 50 percent more on her account, or $38.63.[63]

The actuarial equivalent of this individual's tax payments was something less than one dollar a month.

Taxes and Financing

What about taxes and the effect of the amendments on reserve funds? Without altering the tax rate in effect after 1942, the tax increase scheduled to take place in 1940 (from a combined rate of 2 percent to 3 percent) was repealed. With aggregate benefit costs substantially higher in the early years and taxes lower, the projected fund was thus cut by more than half, from nearly $50 billion to less than $20 billion.

By rejecting the intention of building up a large accumulated fund in favor of a pay-as-you-go type system, a decision was made that was clearly anticipated to obscure and defer the cost of an expedient political decision to young workers and future generations. Under the system designed in 1935, the fund was explicitly adopted in order to distribute over time the burden of early, unearned benefits in such a way that tax rates would not become oppressive as the system matured and demographics changed. It was a decision to adopt a public program much like a funded private program in which the fund would be invested and would earn interest income, while allowing for a smoothing of premium rates over time. Conceptually at least, the funded system represented a collective decision to save some minimum proportion of current income for retirement purposes, the rate of return being determined by the productivity of investment in the economy.

Under a pay-as-you-go system, on the other hand, as current benefits are financed by current tax levies, there is no significant asset accumulation over time. Moving toward such a system thus shifts the burden of financing unearned benefits onto future workers and obscures aggregate benefit costs, which necessarily rise as an increasing proportion of the population gains eligibility.[64] In the words of Edwin Witte, " 'pay-as-you-go' does not mean meeting all the costs, but only the current disbursements, which in the early years are very much less than the real costs. It is essentially deficit financing, in which a large part of the costs computed on an actuarial basis are left unprovided for, to be met in the future as best they may."[65] Such a plan, he concluded, was financed in a "very dangerous" way and was "likely to prove very unfair to present younger workers and to future employers and employees."[66]

When coupled with the very wide dispersion and misunderstood incidence of the payroll tax, these changes clearly dulled incentives for monitoring the course of the program.[67] The ability to do so was hampered by the absence of viable competitors with the pay-as-you-go social insurance scheme and the resulting lack of alternative sources of information on such issues as the actuarial status of the system, "premium costs" over time, rates of return payable in the distant future—all vitally important for rational decisions on the continuation of the system.

Concurrently, there was a dramatic change in the incentives for beneficiary groups to lobby for expansion as the implicit return earned on tax payments would now be determined by the aggregate tax-take *after* retirement. The movement toward pay-as-you-go financing and the drawing down of accumulated reserves allowed this, as would the ultimate operation of a pay-as-you-go system. Beneficiaries would actually profit from an increase in the tax rate, an increase in coverage or the number of people subject to the tax, or by an increase in the ceiling on taxable earnings. Since pressures for these types of changes could only intensify as the proportion of the elderly in the voting population increased and as politicians became more responsive to their demands, this shift in the method of finance thus produced a political environment in which the interests of beneficiaries, politicians, and bureaucrats would become increasingly coincidental and an increasingly dominant force in shaping the evolution of the new system.[68]

The ultimate power of these groups to influence the future was (and continues to be) derived from the ability of a pay-as-you-go system to make current decisions binding on future generations. Regardless of how high the tax rate or how large the transfer to current retirees might become, such a system could not be terminated or even curtailed without imposing losses on all those who had paid taxes up until that time. A reduction in the rate of growth of tax income would reduce everyone's return.

In short, when the reserve principle was abandoned, so was an effective political constraint on the size of the old-age insurance program and the ability to transfer the cost of the program onto future generations. Reserve funding had been a rule that defined, in some senses, a range of acceptable fiscal outcomes.

More on Funding vs. Pay-As-You-Go

To appreciate the important differences between the "actuarial reserve" system adopted in 1935 and the "contingency reserve" system sought in 1939, it is useful to consider in some detail the operation of their two conceptual counterparts, the fully funded and the pay-as-you-go systems.[69] The fully funded program is one in which the system has assets sufficient to cover accruing liabilities. For simplicity, it can be assumed that each individual receives in benefits the actuarial equivalent of his tax payments.[70] Under such a system workers would save some minimum proportion of their earnings over their working lives in return for a right to the actuarial equivalent of their tax payments upon retirement.

The system would operate in the following manner. From the first year of operation tax payments would be deposited with the federal government and invested in interest-bearing assets. As persons who had paid taxes over some or all of their working lives retired, the accumulating fund would be drawn down to make benefit payments. Each year, tax payments would grow by the rate of growth of the wage base, and covered workers would accumulate entitlements to their tax contributions plus interest.

Should voters prefer to increase benefits, the tax rate would have to be increased first, and only those persons who had paid the new higher tax rate would become entitled to higher benefits. Since rates of return are determined by market forces, this change would then simply reflect a collective decision to increase the rate of saving in the public program, not the rate of return on one's investment. Alternatively, should voters prefer to abolish the program altogether and, therefore, set the tax rate equal to zero, the accumulated reserve would be just sufficient to pay off outstanding liabilities.

Accordingly, a funded system of the sort described would have the following attributes. First, by guaranteeing each retiree a market rate of return on tax payments, no one could be made worse off than if he had invested the same sums privately.[71] Second, since the program could be terminated without imposing losses on anyone, no decisions would be binding on future generations. Third, since revenues in excess of current benefit payments would be invested, the introduction of the system would have no adverse effect on capital accumulation in the economy. Fourth, the economy could suffer economic recessions and demographic changes without affecting the ability of a generation to meet its benefit obligations. Finally, and perhaps most important, the information requirements of taxpayers would be minimal with a funded system since a decision to increase future benefits would at once represent a decision to increase current taxes rather than alter the distribution of returns between generations. Retirees would have no entitlement to current period benefit increases for which they had not fully contributed.

In essence, the funded program just described would be constrained to generate market-like outcomes, with the exception that the collective rate of savings may exceed that which would have arisen voluntarily. Like the program envisioned in 1935, it would thus meet the needs of two frequently cited social objectives: coercing the myopic to save over their lifetimes, and protecting against the failure of private savings institutions by compelling certain individuals to save some minimum amount in a systematic and safe way. If income redistribution within the retired generation was also a politically desirable goal, as it was in 1935, a distribution of returns could be introduced as long as the average return paid to current beneficiaries equalled the market rate of interest.[72] This type of redistribution would relax a constraint on expansion by politicizing the program to some extent, but it still could not be employed to impose costs on future generations. To remain funded, benefit increases for a generation of retirees must be preceded by tax-rate increases.[73]

What could not be accomplished with a funded program, of course, would be any transfers of resources between generations (intergenerational transfers). Such a system cannot be introduced, begin paying benefits immediately to the currently elderly, and remain funded. If, however, unearned benefits were deemed socially desirable at the outset, they would logically be financed by general revenues.

As described, a funded system would have many attractive features for a fiscal conservative. Yet fiscal conservatives in 1939 helped promote the transition to a pay-as-you-go system. There were two key reasons. Foremost, there is the very serious problem of how to invest the fund. Unless the government's portfolio includes private securities, the return on investments would be less than a market return. But if the government were to invest in private securities, a very large trust fund could lead to a quite significant centralization in the ownership of capital. If the government's portfolio is then limited to government securities, it must be limited to outstanding securities so that private resources can be freed for investment in productive activities, and so investing the fund does not lead to the creation of new government securities, thereby providing relief for general taxpayers. At a more practical level a huge reserve would provide great temptation to increase benefits without raising taxes, possibly producing a ratchet effect of ever higher taxes.

Quite distinct from the funded system just described, a pay-as-you-go system of finance is one in which there is essentially no reserve accumulation; instead there is a tax transfer in which benefits to the currently retired are paid by taxes imposed on the currently productive generations. Such a system has been described as analogous to a "chain-letter" in which young workers transfer income to the elderly for a noncontractual agreement that, at the time of their retirement, future generations will be willing to similarly transfer resources to them.[74]

The significant political advantage of this type of program is that it can immediately begin paying benefits to the elderly and near-elderly. Moreover, everyone who retires early in the life of the program, before paying taxes over their entire working lives, can earn a rate of return on their tax payments above that available privately and certainly above that which the system can afford later generations. This follows since once the system is underway, the maximum return payable on a generation's tax payments is the rate of growth of the covered wage base. This "advantage" was well appreciated by the CES in 1934 and later by the Social Security Board. It was actually anticipated that if the CES Report had been adopted, everyone who retired before the year 2000 would have received unearned benefits.[75]

Who bears the cost of unearned benefits? In a very real sense, the payment of the initial subsidies is made possible by imposing uncompensated losses on worker-taxpayers who are alive if and when the program is terminated.[76] In the unlikely event that the program is terminated everyone who has paid taxes up until that time would lose since there would be no reserves, other than a contingency fund, with which to pay off liabilities.

It should be evident, of course, as it was in the 1930s, that to offset conceptual advantages there were practical disadvantages. From an economic point of view a pay-as-you-go system would be faulted by the uncertainty of benefits and returns payable and by its likely impact on private savings. Economic and demographic changes such as a recession, a reduction in the rate of growth of the population, or a weighting of the age distribution toward the elderly would all reduce the system's flow of revenues relative to expenditures. The return on tax payments would thus fall—unless, of course, tax rates are increased—and they may well fall below that payable privately or with a funded system.

In 1939 recognition of this fact caused a great deal of concern among opponents of a pay-as-you-go system and among proponents of the long-run maintenance of the program. As demographics (and the insurance status of workers) inevitably changed so as to increase the proportion of beneficiaries to workers, it was believed that the increase in tax rates ultimately required to buttress returns may well be politically unsustainable. In large part this explains why virtually all proposals to abandon the fund for a pay-as-you-go system involved future federal contributions from general revenues.

Another practical disadvantage was that the imposition of the tax would not be offset by any fund accumulation and investment in the private or public sector. The introduction of a pay-as-you-go system could thus be expected to depress capital accumulation and economic growth.[77]

Without downplaying the importance of these economic problems, the political problems are the key to understanding the ensuing growth and redirection of Social Security. Just as those persons who are elderly when the system begins can receive gratuitous transfers, so could any generation that is elderly when the tax rate is increased. In effect the larger the tax rate imposed during this period, the higher is the return for the currently retired, the near-elderly, and any other individuals who are not subject to the higher tax for their entire working lives. The incentive for groups representing the elderly and other beneficiaries to lobby for expansion are clear since a decision to increase the tax rate represents a collective decision to alter the distribution of rates of return between generations, rather than simply a decision to "save" more.

Similarly, since benefits payable would vary directly with the number of persons subject to the tax, and since tax rates necessary to finance any given level of benefits would vary inversely with the number of persons subject to the tax, both current beneficiaries and current taxpayers would be motivated to expand compulsory coverage to nonparticipants. In short, because there are no implied minimum rates of return, the introduction of a pay-as-you-go system bestows considerable power to majority coalitions. The only binding constraints on intergenerational transfers are the total resources in the economy and the age distribution. This is ultimately the case because once the system is underway, it cannot be repealed or reduced in size without imposing losses on all those who have already paid taxes—current decisions are made binding on future generations.

At the same time the incentives are established for beneficiaries to lobby actively for program expansion, the ability of voter-taxpayers to monitor the growth and evolution of the program is reduced. Because of the susceptibility of rates of return to political, economic, and demographic changes, that is, and because of the lack of competing suppliers of viable substitutes, the information requirements for voter-taxpayers are more significant than under a funded system, while the information role played by the bureaucracy is consequently larger. Similarly, the cost of obtaining information on the impact of complex program changes on returns payable in the distant future is significantly higher for taxpayer groups than for beneficiary groups.[78] For both these reasons program expansion would be predictably difficult to constrain.

As one's age increased, or as the proportion of elderly persons increased, or as the political power of the elderly in a majority voting context increased, political pressure for expansion would result. It is not unlikely that a tax rate (or benefit level) could ultimately be established that would be politically infeasible were future generations able to vote, or were it voted upon at the inception of the program.

The difficulty of constraining expansion would be even more significant in the type of system adopted in 1939. The 1939 amendments created a political structure in which the return one group (such as married or lower-income workers) could earn was also a function of their ability to exploit other groups within their own generation. Intergenerational income redistribution then becomes a way for minority coalitions to protect their "investments."

An understanding of these problems and, in particular, the political infeasibility of the tax rates that might ultimately be required to maintain the system were well recognized at the inception of the program, even if forgotten in the interim. Even before the politics of expansion unfolded, and as is the case today, there was an unwillingness on the part of Congress in 1939 to legislate the tax rates required to finance the program in the long run, even though, with a pay-as-you-go system, this would simply have involved scheduling rates to be payable thirty to forty years later.

Yet a clear understanding of the long-run problems of a pay-as-you-go system could not deny or offset the short-run political payoff to abandoning the fund. Lacking effective political constraints on "spending" the accumulated fund as would be required to achieve a fund's positive attributes and in the presence of an active bureaucracy fueling demands for current expansion, the rejection of the fund in 1939 was nearly as predictable as would be the forthcoming evolution of the pay-as-you-go system.

Program Marketability

Incredibly, this massive restructuring of incentives and constraints in 1939 was coupled with the formal introduction of insurance terminology into the Social Security law and into the vocabulary of the bureaucracy. To improve the program's marketability, the Old-Age Reserve Account was renamed the Old-Age and Survivors' Insurance Trust Fund, old-age benefit payments were renamed "insurance" benefits, and Title VIII income and excise (payroll) taxes were repealed and replaced by "insurance contributions" in the Federal Insurance Contributions Act (FICA), part of the Internal Revenue Code. Also a three-member "Board of Trustees" (secretary of treasury, secretary of labor, and chairman of the Social Security Board) was created to oversee, safeguard, and make recommendations on the use of the fund. This had the derivative effect of counterbalancing the unilateral power previously granted an outsider, the secretary of treasury. In President Roosevelt's words, the millions of people in covered employment could all be "likened to the policy holders of a private insurance company."[79]

Public vs. Private "Insurance"

The irony, of course, is that the insurance terminology was introduced into the Social Security Act at the same time that the private insurance analogy was rendered no longer applicable. Unlike the private insurance company, which, in a competitive setting, must operate in a manner that ensures individual equity, Social Security no longer restricted benefit payments to individuals who had contributed toward their cost, and began discriminating on the basis of family size. Workers with large families were provided additional coverage at the same "premium rate" as single workers and workers who wished not to purchase the additional protection. Moreover, unlike the benefits provided by a private insurance company, individuals evidently possessed no enforceable contracts. It was established in 1939 that the statutory "rights" under Social Security would not be treated with the same force as contractual rights in the private sector.[80] Finally, unlike private insurance, Social Security would not, by design, accrue a substantial reserve fund.

Describing most succinctly the new system and the differences between public "insurance" and private insurance, Eveline Burns, proponent of social insurance, said,

> It is no longer a matter of offering each individual a choice as to how much protection he will buy at the range of premiums yielded by the calculations of the actuary. Unlike the private insurer the government is not restricted by the fear of competition, and can safely offer differential benefits for uniform contributions, or discriminate against certain insured groups. . . . In private insurance, the purpose is to make a profit out of selling people something they want. The essential criterion governing every decision as to terms and conditions is its effect upon the continuing existence of the company. Obviously, if the company is to continue operating in a competitive world, it must offer services that people think are worthwhile to pay for and run its affairs in such a way that the guarantees offered will be honoured when due. . . . In social insurance, the purpose is different.[81]

The years 1935-39 were vitally important for Social Security. It was during these few years that the new administrative-bureaucratic machinery was set in place with a growth-oriented staff committed to social insurance. It was during these years that, with the help of President Roosevelt, Social Security emerged the victor from a series of financial, political, and constitutional challenges. By the end of the period, pressure to cut taxes, increase benefits, and thereby radically change the nature of the system resulted in the amendments of 1939. The importance of the 1939 amendments cannot be overstated as they liberalized the program and redirected it from its initial insurance function. By doing so, and by introducing at the same time misleading insurance terminology, the stage had been set for the growth and liberalization the program has since experienced. Once the concept of individual equity was dismissed as the guiding principle of the program, almost any future change, whether demanded by special-interest groups or recommended by public suppliers, could be rationalized on the grounds of social justice or welfare arguments.[82] When the reserve principle was abandoned, there remained few effective constraints on transferring the cost of the program onto future generations. And, when the complexity of the program was increased, the ability of taxpayers to assess true tax costs and monitor the course of the program was reduced dramatically. Each of these changes thus buttressed the monopoly power of the bureaucracy and the power of the special-interest–beneficiary groups that would come to be allied with the bureaucracy in shaping the evolution of the program.

Chapter 7. Coverage Expansion and Program Proliferation: 1940–60

> After seven years of experience we all know that the program doesn't go far enough. Our steps toward social security in this country have been sound steps but they have not yet led into all our homes nor all the situations that breed hazards and insecurity.... We believe the time has come to extend our present program to fill in the gaps.[1]
>
> Ellen Woodward, Member, Social Security Board

Greatly expanded in scope and just beginning its first year paying monthly insurance benefits, in 1940, Social Security was subjected to a new round of policy recommendations. Neither Social Security officials nor key expansionist lobby groups were content with their achievements in 1939. Predating congressional action by fifteen to twenty years, lobby groups such as the American Federation of Labor and the National Consumers' League called for the expansion of the program to include disability and health insurance, as well as the extension of compulsory coverage.[2] Three years later, in the midst of World War II, the Social Security Board echoed these demands, calling for a "single, comprehensive system of social insurance with provisions for unemployment, sickness and disability, old age, and death, and a considerable part of the expenses of hospital and medical services."[3] For the existing old-age and survivors insurance program (OASI) the bureaucracy's detailed legislative agenda for the future involved universal coverage, increases in benefit rates, and reductions in age and eligibility requirements.[4]

During the following fifteen years virtually all of these recommendations became legislative achievements. Between 1950 and 1960 coverage was expanded from six out of ten to nine out of ten workers (including the self-employed), monthly cash benefits were made payable to the disabled (at age fifty) and their dependents, age requirements were liberalized for five beneficiary groups, seven new beneficiary groups were created, and benefits were increased on four occasions. Significantly, the resulting nine-fold increase in real expenditures was made possible with only a three-fold increase in real tax revenues.

The purpose of this chapter is to examine the political and institutional process by which coverage expansion and program proliferation were achieved during the period 1940-60. Of necessity the chapter is devoted in some detail to the legislative history of these program changes. The ultimate goal is to offer an explanation of the strategic advantage and political popularity of coverage expansion and to examine the roles of the bureaucracy and the institutions themselves, as defined in 1939, in either accommodating or creating political demands for program growth and proliferation.

Despite the large direct gains to beneficiaries from the expansion of a pay-as-you-go Social Security system, program expansion was effectively blocked during the early 1940s by the still hesitant support for the program, the very small number of beneficiaries, and the onset of World War II. In 1940 there were just 222,000 people, or less than 1 percent of the elderly population, receiving Social Security benefits. The average monthly amount was roughly $20, less than the means-tested old-age assistance payment made to the elderly poor. In the first year Social Security benefits were paid, just a half-million elderly people met the insured status requirements necessary to be eligible for monthly benefits.[5] Faced with this not-too-impressive army of beneficiaries, President Truman took office in 1945 to meet a conservative postwar Congress captured by the Republicans in 1946—a Congress that was not inclined to enact costly program changes.

The political outlook for Social Security was very different by the end of the decade. On the tax and revenue side, the economy prospered during the postwar years and so did the trust funds. With no expansion of coverage or increases in taxes, revenues to the system increased from $300 million to $3 billion, or more than 300 percent in real terms. Assets reached $14 billion.[6] Congress found itself in the position of being able to defer any tax increases at all during the entire decade.

On the benefit side the passing of a decade permitted millions of people the time required to gain insured status. Between 1940 and 1950 the number of elderly persons eligible for benefits quadrupled and, as illustrated in Table 7.1, the number of program beneficiaries reached 3.5 million.

When Truman was returned to office in 1948, it was on a platform of social insurance expansion. Democrats had recaptured Congress, and momentum reemerged for program expansion. Beginning in 1950, Social Security was elevated to a key political issue, with some form of benefit increase or benefit liberalization enacted in every election year of the decade.

Of the many changes enacted during the period, the two most notable were coverage expansion and disability insurance. Twenty-two million workers were brought into the system between 1949 and 1960, and in 1956 monthly cash benefits were made payable at age fifty to the insured worker who "retired early" because of disability.[7] Whereas coverage expansion constituted a vitally important change in the nature of the program that would help finance unprecedented expansion, disability insurance was one of several ways found by bureaucrat-advocates to utilize the rapidly expanding tax base so as to expand their sphere of operations and create additional claims on the system, ensuring that Social Security was not, as initially conceived, a limited objective, old-age insurance program.

The Politics of Coverage Expansion

Rather than simply defining an "objective" of Social Security, the extent of the program's compulsory coverage was a vital determinant of competition for the pro-

Table 7.1. Beneficiary and taxpayer data, 1940-80 (numbers of people in millions)

	No. of taxpayers	Median annual tax (employee only)	No. of beneficiaries	Average annual retirement benefit (worker only)	Proportion of elderly receiving benefits
1940	35.4	$ 7.6	.2	$ 240	0.7%
1950	48.3	28.9	3.5	506	16.4
1960	72.5	86.8	14.8	840	61.6
1970	93.1	210.0	26.2	1,370	85.5
1980	114.3	424.0	35.6	4,097	94.0

Source: Social Security Administration, *Social Security Bulletin: Annual Statistical Supplement, 1977-79* (Washington, D.C.: U.S. Government Printing Office, 1980), pp. 74, 87, 104-05.

gram and revenues to finance its operations. Quite predictably, therefore, after two of the three major objectives of the original program had been eliminated in 1939—reserve funding and benefits restricted to worker-taxpayers[8]—the bureaucracy persistently advocated universal coverage as the next step in "perfecting" the program.

Fortunately for program bureaucrat-advocates, coverage expansion was the finance scheme of least resistance during the 1950s. Coverage expansion was not only politically appealing to covered workers and beneficiaries but also was sought by many uncovered groups of workers. It was a direct means through which each of these groups could exploit the redistributive potential of the pay-as-you-go system.

From the point of view of uncovered workers, particularly lower income and older persons, Social Security provided an unusually attractive "investment" during the 1950s. In its first years in operation individuals were retiring with benefit payments well in excess of their actuarial equivalent. As illustrated in Table 7.1, the average annual retirement benefit in 1950, for example, was $506, payable until death. Individuals retiring in that year, eligible for 50 percent larger benefits if married, could have paid no more than $30 a year in taxes (employee only) since 1937. (The worker with median earnings would never have paid more than $19 a year.)

As estimated by Robert Myers, chief actuary of the Social Security Administration between 1947 and 1970, "The proportion of OASDI benefits that [were] 'actuarially purchased' by those retiring in the early decades of operation [was] from less than 1 percent in some instances to at most about 10 percent."[9]

From the point of view of currently covered worker-taxpayers and current beneficiaries, coverage expansion—especially to higher income workers—was also clearly desirable. Because of the nature of a pay-as-you-go system, the tax rate necessary to finance any given level of benefits would vary inversely with the number of people subject to the tax. Since higher-income workers were relatively cheap to "insure" (i.e., they received a relatively low return on their tax payments), moreover, the net long-term financial position of the system could be improved by their coverage. Alternatively, holding the tax rate constant, benefit levels could be in-

Table 7.2. Financing social security, 1937-59[a]

Years effective	Maximum taxable earnings	Employee and employer combined			
		Tax rate		Maximum tax payment[a]	
		OASI	DI	Nominal	Real (1980 dollars)
1937	$3,000	2%		$60	345
1938	3,000	2		60	351
1939	3,000	2		60	355
1940	3,000	2		60	353
1941	3,000	2		60	335
1942	3,000	2		60	303
1943	3,000	2		60	286
1944	3,000	2		60	280
1945	3,000	2		60	275
1946	3,000	2		60	253
1947	3,000	2		60	221
1948	3,000	2		60	205
1949	3,000	2		60	208
1950	3,000	3		90	308
1951	3,600	3		108	343
1952	3,600	3		108	335
1953	3,600	3		108	332
1954	3,600	4		144	442
1955	4,200	4		168	517
1956	4,200	4		168	509
1957	4,200	4	.5%	189	553
1958	4,200	4	.5	189	539
1959	4,800	4.5	.5	240	678

Source: Social Security Administration, *Social Security Bulletin: Annual Statistical Supplement, 1975* (Washington, D.C.: U.S. Government Printing Office, 1976), pp. 32-33.

a. See continuation in Chapter 8.

creased with an expansion in the number of people subject to the tax. In light of this, the persistence of lobby-group demands for universal coverage as well as Congress's proclivity to ulitize the resulting revenues to help finance program expansion were certainly understandable. As illustrated in Tables 7.2 and 7.3, coverage expansion helped finance a twelve-fold increase in real expenditures between 1949 and 1959, with only a three-fold increase in the maximum individual tax payment.

Finally, from the point of view of Social Security officials and other advocates, coverage expansion represented an important and, at that time, noncontroversial means of reducing competition and further securing the market for social insurance. The existence of large uncovered groups who relied on private savings and insurance institutions permitted the growth of competing sources of supply, and limited the possible range of redistributive outcomes.[10] This concern would be clearly expressed by proponents in the debates preceding the 1950 amendments. Then too, in later years, uncovered groups with their own retirement plans could pose a serious threat to worker-taxpayers' acquiescence to compulsory coverage by revealing the inevitable deterioration in the "deal" offered by the system.

Table 7.3. OASDI trust funds, 1937-60 (in millions)[a]

	Revenues		Expenditures		Assets		Assets/
Year	Nominal	Real	Nominal	Real	Nominal	Real	Exp.
1937	$ 767	$ 4,408	$ 1	$ 5.8	$ 766	$ 4,402	766:1
1940	368	2,165	62	365	2,031	11,947	33:1
1945	1,420	6,514	304	1,395	7,121	32,665	23:1
1950	2,928	10,027	1,022	3,500	13,721	46,990	13:1
1955	6,167	18,975	5,079	15,628	21,663	66,655	4:1
1960	12,445	34,666	11,798	32,864	22,613	62,989	2:1

Source: Social Security Administration, *Social Security Bulletin: Annual Statistical Supplement, 1975,* pp. 66, 67.
a. Real values are in 1980 dollars. See continuation in Chapter 8.

On what grounds did the Social Security Board and early advisory councils justify abandoning their earlier position of limited coverage to defend universal compulsory coverage? "Ten years experience with incomplete coverage," they said, "revealed the many inequities and anomalies which arise" when workers move between covered and uncovered employment.[11] Since the system was designed to benefit people with relatively short periods of covered employment (by weighting the benefit formula toward low average earnings), these same people were very costly to provide with benefits. Rather than question the true source of the "anomaly"—the benefit formula—the bureaucracy was content to discredit people who were able to profit from its construction, arguing program expansion as the "solution."[12] With great ingenuity the bureaucracy developed a new political rhetoric that labeled the existence of uncovered individuals outside the system as "inequitable" and inconsistent with the "objectives" of the program. An effective means of generating demands by covered workers for compulsory coverage of other groups had thus been found.

While coverage expansion was certainly opposed by groups who anticipated faring poorly (for example, those with higher incomes or later retirement ages such as doctors, federal government employees, and farmers), coverage expansion had bipartisan support. Support from certain of the more conservative Republicans and employer groups, however, was prompted by quite different motives. Throughout the period they sought a revamping of Social Security that involved universal coverage, strict adherence to current financing, and a uniform pension for all elderly persons.[13] Universal coverage would serve as a stepping stone toward a universal pension program for the elderly that was simply designed and clearly understood to redistribute income from workers to retirees and across retirees as well.

With relatively little controversy coverage was expanded to nine out of ten workers, as illustrated in Table 7.4, and billions of dollars of additional revenues were generated during the 1950s. Rather than being invested, as would have been the case with a funded program, these revenues translated into benefit increases for current beneficiaries and gratuitous transfers to new beneficiary groups. And

Table 7.4. OASDI coverage, 1937-80

Date enacted	Employment covered		
	Compulsory	Elective by employer	Elective by employee and employer
1935	All workers in commerce and industry (except railroads) under age sixty-five in continental United States, Alaska and Hawaii, and on American vessels.		
1939	Age restriction eliminated.		
1950	Regularly employed farm and domestic workers. Nonfarm, self-employed (except professional groups). Federal civilian employees not under retirement system. Americans employed outside United States by American employer—Puerto Rico and Virgin Islands.	State and local government employees not under retirement system.	Employees (other than ministers) of nonprofit organizations employees voting against coverage are not covered, new employees are covered).
1951	Railroad workers with less than ten years of service.		
1954[a]	Farm self-employed. Professional self-employed except lawyers, dentists, doctors, and other medical groups. Additional regularly employed farm and domestic workers. Homeworkers.	Americans employed outside United States by foreign subsidiary of American employer.	State and local government employees (except firemen and policemen) under retirement system.
1956	Members of the uniformed services. Remainder of professional self-employed except doctors. Farm landlords who materially participate in farm operations.		Firemen and policemen in designated states. State and local government employees under retirement system in designated states may be divided into two systems, one excluding employees not desiring coverage (new employees covered).
1965	Interns. Self-employed doctors.		
1967	Ministers and members of religious orders under vow of poverty.		Firemen under retirement system.
1972		Members of religious orders.	

Source: Social Security Administration, *Social Security Bulletin: Annual Statistical Supplement, 1977-79*, pp. 15-16.
a. In 1954 coverage was extended to ministers on an "elective by individual" basis.

rather than taking full advantage of the tax reductions made possible by an expansion of coverage, Congress legislated changes that would generate more and larger benefit claims in the future. Contributing to this seemingly "no-cost" expansion of the program was the fact that excess reserve accumulation, created by economic and labor force growth, could be "spent" as the system transitioned to a pay-as-you-go state. As illustrated in the Table 7.3, the ratio of trust fund assets to current expenditures fell continuously from 33:1 in 1940 to 2:1 in 1960.

The Truman Years: "Cradle-to-Grave" Social Insurance Advocated

As World War II wound down in the mid-1940s and political attention returned to domestic policy, there was no immediate resurgence of interest in Social Security. In fact, at the time President Truman began endorsing the expansion of Social Security to yet other "common risks," Congress twice overrode presidential vetoes to reduce compulsory coverage by a half million workers. Also an advisory council was appointed in 1947 that was, to expansionists, noticeably short of organized labor representatives—important allies of the Social Security Board.[14]

The delay in expanding Social Security and the emerging conservative sentiments were of considerable concern to the bureaucracy and other advocates as they threatened the underpinnings of the existing OASI program and cast doubt on the ability to expand it to, say, disability and health insurance.[15] Each year, as Social Security maintained its size and scope, competing state pension programs and private insurance programs continued to expand. By 1949, for example, the number of persons receiving old-age assistance had risen continuously to reach twice the number receiving retirement benefits under Social Security. The average means-tested payment for the elderly poor was $42 a month as compared to an average retirement benefit of just $25 per month.[16] At the same time the private insurance industry was thriving as well. Between 1940 and 1950 the proportion of the labor force covered by industrial pension plans, for example, more than doubled, and by 1950 the proportion of all nonfarm employees covered by these plans reached 25 percent.[17]

As advocates recognized, a healthy rather than "withering" old-age assistance program and a successful insurance industry could provide needed momentum behind conservative efforts to eliminate the prevailing system of social insurance. As aptly conveyed by Edwin Witte, only months before major coverage expansion was enacted, "At this time we appear to be at a crossroads as regards social security. Growth of social assistance, the spread of private pension plans, and the rapid development of forms of public medical care, doom social insurance in this country unless it is soon made more extensive."[18]

The election of President Truman on a party platform endorsing extensive liberalization of Social Security, the return of a Democratic Congress, and the report of a strongly expansionary but Republican-appointed advisory council, marked the year 1948 as an important turning point for the program.

The Amendments of 1950: Expansion Renewed

Believing that his election represented a "mandate" by the people for Social Security, President Truman addressed Congress early in January of 1949. In his State of the Union message, he said the program's coverage was "altogether inadequate," benefits were "too low," and the system lacked sickness and disability insurance.[19] Within a week he addressed Congress again, with a set of more specific proposals to extend coverage to "nearly all" workers, "sharply" increase benefits, make benefits payable to women at an earlier age, liberalize the retirement test, and introduce disability insurance.[20] Espoused by Truman and endorsed by the Social Security Board for years, these proposals were also embodied in the Report of the 1948 Advisory Council as presented to Congress a month earlier.[21]

Early in 1949 comprehensive hearings were held on the Administration's bill in the Ways and Means Committee.[22] Supported by "cradle-to-grave" social insurance advocates, drafted and explained by Social Security officials, the bill involved a significant liberalization of the program, with benefit increases of up to 100 percent and the inclusion of a compulsory federal disability insurance program.

On 22 August 1949 the Ways and Means Committee reported a clean bill calling for extensive revisions of the act, although moderate when compared to the Administration's proposals.[23] The committee bill expanded coverage by nine million persons (rather than the twenty million as recommended by the Administration), created a disability insurance program to provide retirement benefits to the totally and permanently disabled, and increased the federal public assistance matching rate. By contrast, the committee bill maintained rather than liberalized benefit computation periods and eligibility requirements, increased tax rates and lowered the tax ceiling relative to that proposed by the Administration, and eliminated the Administration's proposal to extend public assistance to the temporarily disabled.

A minority report was issued that was signed by ten Republicans. Aptly reflecting the conservative stand on Social Security, they endorsed the expansion of coverage but expressed concern that the bill was "inconsistent with the fundamental purposes of compulsory social insurance . . . to provide a basic floor of economic protection for the individual and his family and in so doing to encourage and stimulate voluntary savings through personal initiative and ambition. It should not invade the field historically belonging to the individual."[24] Increased federal matching under the public assistance titles, they argued, was transferring too much responsibility to the federal government. Indicating the extent to which Social Security expansion, with its low current cost, was becoming an issue that politicians from left to right had a stake in, the Republicans' arguments were philosophically based, but their votes were with the majority. Seven of the ten members signing the minority report voted with the majority.

The House bill, considered under a "closed rule" which prohibited amendments from the floor or from dissenting members of the committee, was shortly thereafter passed without amendment. As the bill emerged from the Senate Finance Committee the following year, however, it had been modified in some important respects. Most notably, the OASI program and its coverage were vastly liberalized, while the provisions for disability insurance were eliminated altogether.

As finally enacted in August, the 1950 amendments included thirty major changes in the Social Security Act. Compulsory coverage was extended to the nonfarm, nonprofessional self-employed, agricultural workers, domestic servants, federal employees not covered by the federal retirement system, and persons in the Virgin Islands and Puerto Rico—nearly eight million persons—and voluntary coverage was extended to the two and a half million employees of nonprofit organizations and to state and local government employees not covered by their own systems. Among the major expansions in benefits, dependents benefits were made payable to husbands and young wives with children, survivors benefits were made payable to widowers, benefit rates were increased for surviving children and parents, benefit formulas and eligibility requirements were liberalized, and, finally, benefit payments were increased 77.5 percent for current recipients. To partially finance additional expenditures, the ceiling on taxable earnings was increased to $3,600 ($11,429)[25] and future tax rates were increased.[26]

Concerning the public assistance titles of the Social Security Act, the federal matching rate was increased once more, and a new type of categorical assistance was introduced: Aid to the Totally and Permanently Disabled (ATPD). This emerged as a compromise measure, as both in the Senate and, in conference, the Administration's proposal for disability insurance had been rejected.

The net impact of the program changes was to significantly increase the scope of the program and its redistributive impact. Changes such as the introduction of new beneficiary categories, reduced benefit eligibility requirements, and shortened periods for the calculation of average earnings automatically made thousands of people eligible to draw monthly benefits or to draw higher benefits without paying any additional taxes. As in 1939 returns were weighted toward people with low average earnings, married retirees, and people retiring early in the life of the system. In effect, the array of changes moved the program further from the concept of insurance based on individual equity, further obscured the tax-benefit link, and created millions more people who would have a stake in expanding the program.

The expansion of compulsory coverage and the increase in benefits made prospects for the program's survival and growth more certain, dampening fears that the growth of competing sources of supply would limit future expansion. Largely because of the liberalizations in eligibility requirements, the number of recipients of OASI exceeded the number of old-age assistance recipients for the first time in history in 1951. As Social Security assumed a larger share of the welfare functions of old-age assistance, nearly 100,000 recipients of old-age assistance became eligible for OASI benefits immediately upon the enactment of the 1950 amendments.[27]

Finally, because of the way the 1950 amendments were financed, Congress reaffirmed the choice made in 1939 to move toward a pay-as-you-go system. Despite a significant increase in the current and future cost of the system, the payroll tax schedule was actually reduced in the near-term and not increased for the long-term until 1960. With no obligation to maintain a relationship between trust-fund assets and system liabilities, Congress had little incentive to finance expansion through tax increases as long as there were trust-fund assets still exceeding expenditures thirteen-fold.

Only months after the 1950 amendments were signed into law the Federal Security Administration (FSA) issued its annual report praising the advances made but seeking further expansion of the program. They recommended (1) the complete coverage of all gainful workers; (2) the provision of insurance benefits for sickness, disability, and medical care; and (3) public assistance for all "residual needs." In its report the following year the FSA reiterated its demands for expanding the scope of Social Security, describing the lack of medical and disability insurance as "major deficiencies" in the existing program.[28] The first headway toward disability insurance was made two years later.

The Amendments of 1952: The First Real Increase in Benefits

The 1952 Amendments to the Social Security Act were introduced into Congress in May of 1952 and passed just two months later. Contained in the amendments were a 12.5 percent increase in monthly benefits (designed to keep benefits "in pace with the rate of inflation"), a highly controversial "disability freeze," and an increase in federal grants to states for public assistance.[29] While the unprecedented speed with which the amendments were enacted has been attributed to a number of factors, it was clear that as an election year, 1952 was a good year for a benefit increase when not accompanied by a tax increase.[30]

Portending future developments, the most controversy was generated by a proposal to implement a disability freeze. The provision would have allowed covered individuals to have their average earnings and accrued insurance status "frozen" during periods of disability rather than eroded as would normally result during periods of unemployment. The power to determine disability would have resided exclusively with the Federal Security administrator.

While seemingly a modest proposal, it was clear to opponents of expansion that the freeze would have major ramifications for the system. A definition of disability would have to be established, disability would have to be determined on a case-by-case basis, and once this was accomplished, the payment of cash benefits would be but a small step away. The American Medical Association (AMA), backed by congressional conservatives, ardently opposed the provision on the grounds that it bestowed too much power to the administrator, a well-known social insurance advocate, and on the grounds that it would lead to demands for disability insurance. The latter development, they believed, would threaten the financial status of the OASI program and perhaps lead to "socialized medicine."

The House-Senate conference committee resolved the conflict in a bizarre way, indeed. The disability freeze was included in the amendments, but in such a manner that no one could qualify! As enacted, the 1952 amendments allowed disabled persons to apply to preserve their insurance rights beginning 1 July 1953, but the provision was not to remain effective after 30 June 1953. The concept of a freeze was thus formally in the law, having been passed along with Social Security's first increase in real benefits (over and above inflation). At a later date a simple "technical change" could be made to institute the freeze in fact.[31]

The Eisenhower Years: The Drive for Universal Coverage

The Eisenhower years, which ushered in the first Republican president in twenty years, clearly attested to the strength of social insurance expansion. The momentum gained in earlier years by active lobby groups, Social Security officials, and a Democratic Congress was only slightly curtailed by the new Republican Congress. Often with the President's endorsement, amendments were enacted in 1954, 1956, and 1958 which increased and liberalized benefits, extended coverage, and increased tax rates and the ceiling on taxable earnings. Additionally monthly insurance benefits were made payable to the disabled at age fifty (1956) and to their dependents (1958), and the retirement age for women was reduced to sixty-two (1956). The 1958 amendments marked the fifth liberalization of the Social Security program in as many election years. In old-age assistance, a system of nonuniform grants to low-income states was introduced (1958).

The Amendments of 1954: Expansionism—A Bipartisan Issue?

It has been said that the 1954 amendments, passed by a Republican congress and enacted by a Republican president, marked the birth of Social Security as a bipartisan political issue. While the vote would certainly indicate this, the hearings surrounding the amendments revealed most clearly that social insurance expansionism was not yet a bipartisan issue.

Preceding the controversy President Eisenhower called for an expansion of coverage, and later endorsed putting the system more nearly on a pay-as-you-go basis.[32] Since the intention to build up a substantial reserve fund had been abandoned fifteen years earlier, these proposals supported by congressional conservatives, were designed to make more apparent the true cost of the program. Additional expenditures financed partly by coverage expansion, tax-rate increases, tax-ceiling increases, and reserve depletion obscured the true burden of the program. The proposals were intended to reveal that, as basically a pay-as-you-go system, Social Security represented a decision on the part of workers to support the elderly, not to make advance provisions for themselves.

Following these presidential initiatives the Ways and Means Committee set up a special subcommittee to investigate thoroughly the many issues of Social Security. Already two hundred bills had been introduced in the first session of the 83rd Congress. The subcommitte, chaired by Representative Carl Curtis (R.-Neb.), began hearings in July of 1953 and appointed a special research staff to report the following year.[33] Partly as a result of these investigations the Social Security program and its administration faced their first serious public attack since 1936.

According to the subcommittee's final report, entitled *Social Security After*

Eighteen Years, the driving force of the investigations was a widespread misunderstanding of the program, particularly with respect to its basic principles.[34] Most striking, they asserted, was the confusion over who was eligible for old-age assistance, and what type of "contracts" the worker accrued under the insurance titles of Social Security. They found that many people mistakenly believed they were entitled to old-age assistance as a matter of right, regardless of need, and that they had "contractual rights" to future insurance benefits as well.

Devoting a good deal of attention to the confusion over "rights," the report carefully explained that there were no contractual rights under Social Security as had been indicated by the bureaucracy and was believed by many. Presenting examples of cases in which benefit claims had either been reduced in value or totally eliminated, they emphasized that the only rights that existed were statutory and that they could be rescinded at the will of Congress.

The report pointed to erroneous and/or misleading statements and documents issued by the social security administration as the source of confusion. According to Representative Curtis, wage earners had been misled for the past eighteen years into believing that they had contractual rights to earned benefits.[35] His remarks led Arthur Altmeyer, recently resigned commissioner of social security, to admit that there were, in fact, no such rights but that future benefits were nevertheless protected by the "full faith and credit" of the government.[36]

Subcommittee efforts to make clear the nature of Social Security led to bitter attacks by House liberals. In Representative Eberharter's (D.-Pa.) words, the studies were "nothing but an attempt to discredit and smash the present social security system."[37] Later Altmeyer told Robert Winn, subcommittee counsel, that he "was doing more to destroy the confidence of the American people in this system than anybody else—except the Chairman of this committee."[38] Proponents and opponents alike recognized that the sustained popularity of Social Security relied heavily on voters' perceptions that it was grounded on private insurance principles.

As believed by Altmeyer, conservative efforts to establish the violable nature of Social Security rights were quite probably part of an endeavor to create a political environment conducive to radical reform (such as providing uniform pensions to all of the aged, currently financed by a universally applied tax, a proposal endorsed by Representative Curtis and the Chamber of Commerce).[39] While each advance in compulsory coverage during the 1950s was an advance toward this end, the subcommittee hearings did not provide, in the end, a noticeable change in the political environment. Politicians had little independent interest in seeking the "truth," the bureaucracy had no interest in revealing it, and threats to expected benefit streams—whether contractual or not—were already becoming politically taboo. By 1954 half of the nation's elderly were receiving monthly assistance or insurance benefits and some sixty million taxpayers were hoping to do so in the future.[40]

When President Eisenhower finally relayed his proposals for Social Security in a special message to Congress in 1954—an election year—therefore they contained few surprises. Accepting the basic "principles" underlying the program, he endorsed coverage expansion, an increase in benefits, liberalizations in the determination of average earnings and the retirement test, and the institution of the disability freeze.[41]

As the bill made its way through Congress, the hearings revealed not only a divergence in attitudes between conservatives and liberals, but also divergence within lobby groups. The Chamber of Commerce called for universal coverage, while the NAM opposed any major action in 1954. The National Grange and National Farmers Union lobbied for extending coverage to farmers, the American Farm Bureau Federation opposed extension of coverage, and the National Milk Producers Federation endorsed voluntary coverage. Organized labor formed not only a strong but also a unified coalition. It opposed Chamber of Commerce proposals for a universal pay-as-you-go system and favored the introduction of disability insurance and a substantial increase in the ceiling on taxable earnings.

The House and Senate versions of the bill were not significantly different from one another. As finally enacted on 1 September, the 1954 amendments extended coverage to nearly ten million additional workers, especially farm operators and the professional self-employed (except lawyers, dentists, and doctors), and voluntary coverage was extended to employees of state and local governments.[42] Also the retirement test was liberalized, an operative disability freeze provision was introduced, and real benefit levels were increased an additional 12.5 percent. To partially finance the changes, the ceiling on taxable earnings was increased to $4,200 ($12,923) and, beginning in 1970, tax rates were increased. In accordance with the demands of Senate liberals, the current matching grant formula for public assistance was maintained for two years.[43]

The Amendments of 1956: OASI Becomes OASDI

In his 1955 State of the Union address President Eisenhower limited his focus on Social Security to public assistance since, in his view, the 1954 amendments had already made significant revisions in the insurance titles. Congress, recaptured by the Democrats, took no action on the President's recommendations and, in 1956, the House went on to pass a bill containing major liberalizations in OASI. The amendments that followed, signed again only months before an election, attested to the strength of social insurance advocates and the success of the Democratic party in carrying out their demands.[44] Against the opposition of the Administration, and with only a two-vote margin in the Senate, the 1956 amendments enacted into law two fundamental changes in Social Security: a compulsory federal program of disability insurance and a reduced age for women's benefits.

As this important bill made its way through Congress, lobbyists aligned on issues in now-familiar ways. Groups such as the AFL-CIO, Americans for Democratic Action, the United Auto Workers, and the National Consumers League strongly endorsed disability insurance, while the AMA and the Chamber of Commerce opposed it. Proponents—endeavoring to downplay the seriousness of the proposal and drawing on the incremental approach to expansion fostered by the bureaucracy—played heavily on the idea that disability benefits were simply payments to individuals who had to "retire early" due to disability.[45] Such benefits would alleviate a "serious deficiency" in the way payments were currently made.

Opponents argued, by contrast, that disability insurance was a major change in Social Security—indeed, a new form of social insurance altogether. With appreciation for the problems that would come to plague the new system, they argued that "disability" would be difficult to define and costly to determine, and that payments to disabled workers would discourage rehabilitation and defy accurate cost estimation. According to a then-recent study issued by the Brookings Institute, the "danger of abuse" would be "great," as "political and psychological factors would play a large part in determining the cost" of the program. The study continued:

> No country that has ever installed such a system accurately predicted in advance anything approaching actual costs. Government agencies which promote its adoption may be suspected of understating costs in their eagerness to get laws on the books, but the difficulty is probably far deeper than over-optimism. The necessity of earning a living and supporting a family makes many a person hold a job despite partial disability, either temporary or permanent. Relieve them of the necessity, and thousands will take the position that having paid the taxes they are entitled to the benefits.[46]

On the issue of reducing the retirement age for women, proponents argued that because women were typically younger than their husbands and tended to live longer, a hardship was imposed on them by the current system. Ignoring the tax-benefit link altogether, they said the problem with the system was that wives were unable to automatically draw benefits at the same time as their husbands during retirement, and they also had to wait until age sixty-five to draw survivors benefits. At a minimum proponents argued the law contained certain forms of discrimination against women that these amendments would help alleviate![47] Opponents of the early retirement provision for women argued, on the basis of testimony by insurance companies, that life expectancy and the average retirement age among women were both increasing. As such it was clearly unreasonable to institute a very costly amendment that would encourage early retirement among women and tend to lead to demands for lowering eligibility ages for other beneficiaries. The Administration questioned the advisability of amending the act in ways that would increase future costs and thus "raise serious uncertainties for the future."[48]

As passed by Congress, the 1956 amendments were similar in most respects to the bill reported by the Ways and Means Committee.[49] Monthly cash benefits were made payable to totally and permanently disabled workers at the age of fifty, and to disabled dependent children at any age who became disabled before eighteen. Disability insurance (DI) benefits were to be financed by a 1/2 percent (employee-employer combined) increase in scheduled tax rates, with revenues diverted to a separate trust fund. Also OASI benefits were made payable to all women beneficiaries at sixty-two with an actuarial reduction applied to benefits drawn before age sixty-five (two exceptions were widows and dependent parents who were made eligible for full benefits at the reduced age). With the excepton of physicians, moreover, coverage was extended to the remaining self-employed professionals, farm landlords, and some government employees. Finally, the federal matching rate for public assistance was increased again.

After nearly twenty years of prodding by social security officials and many more years by advocates, disability insurance was finally "on the books." Monthly cash benefits would now be payable to insured workers age fifty and older who were determined to have a permanent and total disability (one expected to end in death or be of long-continued and indefinite duration). From the perspective of proponents, of course, it was an exceedingly restrictive program. It only applied to older workers, only to permanent disabilities, benefits were only payable after a waiting period had been met, workers had to have established not only a substantial but also a recent attachment to the workforce, and there were no provisions for dependents' benefits.

From a political perspective, however, these were certainly fleeting limitations. Once disability insurance was enacted, and thus accepted as a legitimate and cost-effective activity of the federal government, each of the rules—the age fifty cut-off, the permanent disability requirement, the six-month waiting period, the recent-work test, and the lack of secondary benefits—would appear seemingly arbitrary, without concrete motivation and lacking any effective constraints on their erosion. In the context of the entire complex Social Security system future changes in these institutional "details" would only be a matter of time, and would now be actively sought by a new beneficiary-constituency of disabled workers and families. This would create great strain on the financing of a system which, by construction, already contained strong work disincentives and a costly determination process.

As history would reveal, the DI program would be seriously and chronically underfinanced. Unlike the OASI program in which tax rates were expected to rise over time (once the pay-as-you-go decision had been made), DI was to be financed on a "level premium" basis with a constant tax rate expected to finance the program in the long-term. Yet, just four years after benefits were first paid, a trust-fund deficit appeared amounting to $69 million, and by 1965 the annual deficit exceeded $400 million. The tax rate expected to be sufficient to finance the program in the long-term was exceeded in 1966, it was doubled by 1970, and tripled by 1978. The program would come to be characterized by uncontrolled and unexplained growth in the early 1970s.[50]

For the rest of the Social Security program as well, it would only be a matter of time until the piecemeal distribution of benefit privileges, particularly as embodied in the 1950 and 1956 amendments, led to an expansion of the program. Benefits were now payable to disabled children but not to disabled wives, widows, and parents. Benefits were payable at a reduced age to women but not to men, and among women only certain groups received full benefits. In short, the creation of these special benefits would likely lead to pressures for expansion to provide these same types of benefits to currently ineligible persons, and to reduce the eligibility requirements for other types of benefits.

The Amendments of 1958: Social Security—An Election Year Issue

The 1958 amendments liberalized the Social Security program during the fifth consecutive election year. It was said that revisions could not await the report of the 1959 Advisory Council on Social Security Financing (established by the 1956 amendments) since the Social Security Board of Trustees had revealed that for the first time in history, the OASI trust fund was paying out more in benefits than it was receiving in tax receipts.[51] Yet rather than stabilize benefit growth or simply raise taxes, Congress responded by expanding the program quite significantly. Only two years after the enactment of disability insurance, all OASI monthly cash benefits were made payable to dependents of disabled workers, the recent-work test for disabled workers was dropped, and cash benefits were increased 7 percent. To partially finance these changes, tax rates were increased, the ceiling on taxable earnings was increased, and coverage was further expanded.

At the initiative of President Eisenhower major changes were also made in public assistance. However, whereas the President endorsed a reduction in the role of the federal government in public assistance, the bill that emerged from the Ways and Means Committee provided for an increased rate of federal matching and an increase in the total amount of state expenditures matched.

Arthur Flemming, recently appointed secretary of HEW, made it clear as he testified before the Senate Finance Committee that the Administration would support a cost-of-living increase in Social Security benefits but "strongly opposed" the House committee bill increasing federal public assistance payments. The Administration's opposition to the public assistance features was serious enough, he said, that he would recommend a veto of the bill unless modifications were made.[52]

By the time the amendments were signed into law on 28 August, the 1958 amendments had been moderated by the Senate and in conference. Along with the previously mentioned changes in OASI, the amendments contained, for the first time, provisions for nonuniform grants to states for public assistance. In particular, the rate of federal matching was maintained for states with per capita incomes at least as high as the national average, while the rate was increased from 50 percent to 65 percent for states with per capita incomes below the national average. Against the President's request, the maximum average welfare payment the federal government would match was increased.[53]

Overview of the 1950s

Evidently, the keynote of the 1950s was program expansion and liberalization. Whereas the 1939 amendments served to mark the formal redirection of the social insurance titles of the Social Security Act, the many amendments enacted in the 1950s were devoted to increasing coverage and increasing the number and proportion of people eligible for benefits. In a series of amendments during the period the age requirements for women workers, widows, and wives were reduced. Also, new

Table 7.5. Beneficiaries of the Social Security program in proportion to total population, 1940-80

At end of year	Recipients of OASDI benefits[a] (in millions)	Recipients of OAA benefits[b] (in millions)	As proportion of total population	
			OASDI	OASDI + OAA[c]
1940	.2	2.1	0.1%	1.7%
1945	1.3	2.1	0.9	2.5
1950	3.5	2.8	2.3	4.1
1955	8.0	2.5	4.8	6.4
1960	14.8	2.3	8.2	9.5
1970	26.2	2.1	12.3	13.2
1980	35.9	1.7	15.3	16.0

Source: Social Security Administration, *Social Security Bulletin: Annual Statistical Supplement, 1973* (Washington, D.C.: U.S. Government Printing Office, 1974), pp. 60, 157, and Social Security Administration, *Monthly Benefit Statistics*, Note No. 11 (Washington, D.C.: Department of Health and Human Services, 14 Dec. 1981):1.

U.S. Bureau of Census, *The Statistical History of the U.S.: From Colonial Times to the Present* (New York: Basic Books, 1976), p. 8.

a. See continuation in Chapter 8.

b. Old-age assistance (OAA) is means-tested welfare for the elderly, replaced by a federal program of Supplemental Security Income in 1972 (includes aid for blind and disabled). Figure for 1980 includes only elderly recipients of SSI.

c. Since some persons receive both OASDI and OAA benefits, these figures are slightly overstated.

beneficiary categories were added, including benefits to disabled workers and their dependents, disabled children, and husbands and widowers of women workers. Finally, the benefit computation period (the number of years used for calculating average earnings) was shortened significantly by amendments enacted in 1950, 1954, and 1956; and the retirement test was liberalized by amendments enacted in 1950, 1952, and 1954.[54] As a result of the many liberalizations thousands of persons immediately became eligible to draw benefits, in some cases on a permanent basis, without any additional tax payments, and thousands were removed from the public assistance rolls. Alongside these developments, the state-administered old-age assistance programs were increasingly federalized.[55]

There were three important effects of these liberalizations in the OASI and DI programs. First, real Social Security expenditures increased more rapidly than during any other decade in the program's history. As shown in Tables 7.3 and 7.5, between 1950 and 1960 real expenditures on the insurance titles alone increased more than 800 percent and, by 1960, 14.8 million Americans, or more than 8 percent of the population, were beneficiaries. By this same time more than 70 percent of the elderly had become beneficiaries of monthly assistance or insurance benefits.[56] Social Security beneficiaries, particularly the elderly, were now an important political force.

Second, the many liberalizations enacted in the 1950s created significantly more and larger future benefit claims that ultimately would have to be made good by a less rapidly growing number of covered workers. The average tax payment rose, in

Table 7.6. Dependents and survivors beneficiary categories, benefit rates, and ages payable, 1939-60.

	Benefits as a percent of worker's benefit[a] and age payable				
	Dependents of retired workers:				
Date enacted	Wife	Wife w/child	Husband	Child	Disabled child
1939	50%(65)			50%(18)[d]	
1950		50%[c]	50%(65)		
1956	(62)[b]				50%(18)
1960					

	Survivors						
Date enacted	Widow	Widow w/child	Divorced widow w/child	Widower	Child	Disabled child	Parent
1939	75%(65)	75%[e]			50%(18)[d]		50%(65)
1950			75%[e]	75%(65)			75%
1956	(62)					50%(18)	(62)[e]
1960					75%	75%	

Source: Department of Health, Education, and Welfare; Social Security Administration, *History of the Provisions of OASDHI: 1935-1973* (Washington, D.C.: U.S. Government Printing Office, 1974), pp. 4-5.

a. Monthly benefit for fully retired worker. In 1956 benefits were made payable to disabled workers, and in 1958 to dependents of disabled workers (at the same benefit rates as for the retired workers). See continuation in chapter 8.

b. Benefits actuarially reduced if granted before age sixty-five.

c. Payable at all ages.

d. For each child, 50 percent payable until age eighteen.

e. For women only.

real terms, by 140 percent between 1950 and 1960, and the maximum individual tax payment rose by 160 percent. These were modest increases relative to those forthcoming, since the rapid expansion of coverage and the reduction of trust fund reserves (relative to expenditures) had allowed a spreading of tax costs across tax-payers and over time. Expectations were thus created about rates of return payable under Social Security that could not be fulfilled in the longer run without continu-ally increasing tax rates.

Finally, as shown in Table 7.6, the stage had been set by the introduction of new beneficiary categories and the erosion of eligibility requirements for further expansion of the program. One could easily predict that demands would emerge very quickly to reduce benefit eligibility ages for male beneficiaries, as lower ages for women had created an "inequity." Similarly, if benefits to disabled children of retired workers could be rationalized, so could benefits to disabled wives and hus-bands, widows and widowers. Once age requirements had been reduced to accept-able limits, and once benefits had been extended to most identifiable categories of people, moreover, one could have predicted that demands would emerge for special category benefit increases. The institutional evolution of the program witnessed many times the impact on voter demands of bestowing special benefit increases to "particularly deserving" subsets of voters. Very quickly demands emerged for "uniformity" in treatment or an expansion of the program to eliminate a seeming "inequity." With majority voting and imperfect information, an activist bureaucracy had both the incentive and the ability to encourage this type of program proliferation.

In all, the array of amendments enacted prior to 1960 simply laid the groundwork for what has been experienced since that time—the exploitation of the redistributive potential of the program by special-interest groups, including the bureaucracy, a rapid increase in individual tax costs, and the emergence of a "fiscal crisis" in the 1970s.

The findings of Chapters 6 and 7 suggest that the rapid growth and proliferation of Social Security in its first twenty-five years resulted from three factors: (1) the public monopolization of the provision of old-age insurance which permitted a selective bias in information made available by the bureaucracy to citizens and legislators; (2) the creation of a program with redistributive potential to which millions of Americans had become direct beneficiaries of public funds; and (3) the ability to obscure and defer program costs during the transition to a pay-as-you-go system. Evidenced most clearly was the difficulty of constraining redistribution and expansion when the demands of special-interest beneficiary groups had become increasingly coincidental with the interests of the bureaucracy—a problem that would be even more pronounced in the 1960s and early 1970s.

What helped to make the 1950s and the expansion during this period so completely different from later decades was the ability of Social Security, as a pay-as-you-go system, to be financed in so many politically "costless" ways in the early years. To finance a nine-fold increase in real expenditures over the decade, public suppliers had a choice of nonlegislative revenue sources that showed buoyant growth, and a set of legislative sources that had yet to be exhausted.[57] Because of trust-fund accumulation, moreover, they also were able simply to spend revenues faster than they were generated. Because of the bureaucracy's persistence in painting the program as one with long-run insurance characteristics, the ability to finance expansion in these ways created expectations on the part of an increasing number of taxpayers about rates of return payable that simply could not be met in the longer run without continually increasing tax rates. In an important sense, the exploitation of the redistributive potential of the program got its stronghold in the 1950s as an initial objective of the program—limited coverage—was eroded along with a constraint on growth. In sum, the amendments enacted between 1939 and 1958 laid a firm foundation for what was to follow in the 1960s and early 1970s: the realization of the program's redistributive potential. Most of the elements of a political crisis were already in order.

Chapter 8. The Realization of Social Security's Redistributive Potential: 1960–73

Although there was always continuity in the redirection and growth of Social Security, there was a marked political escalation of the program in the 1960s and early 1970s. This is evidenced first by the creation in 1965 of a new compulsory federal "insurance" program. Medicare, as it was named, was a nonearnings-related program tied to the financing of OASDI that made benefits available to nineteen million elderly people the day it was officially launched.[1] Second, Social Security became an annual political issue during the Kennedy and Johnson administrations, liberalized nearly every year between 1960 and 1973. Third, across-the-board benefit increases were enacted six times between 1960 and 1973, bringing the real increase since 1940 to 140 percent. As illustrated in Table 8.1, there were only four across-the-board increases enacted prior to 1960, for a real cumulative increase of 32 percent. The 260 percent increase in real expenditures during the 1960s and early 1970s translated into large direct gains for current beneficiaries.[2]

The effect of these changes was dramatic for individual tax costs. The rapid increase in the cost of the program was finally reflected in significant increases in individual tax payments. Unlike the 1940s and 1950s, when coverage expansion and economic growth allowed the spreading of tax costs to new individuals and to future generations, the 1960s were marked by cost increases which had to be absorbed by a group of covered workers whose ranks and earnings were growing more slowly. The tax increase for the median earner was 180 percent between 1959 and 1973.[3] Also, as Congress turned to increases in the ceiling on taxable earnings in lieu of tax-rate increases, the rapidly rising cost of the program was borne more heavily by higher-income workers. Between 1940 and 1959 the maximum tax payment (employer-employee combined) increased from $60 to $240, or 93 percent in real terms. As shown in Table 8.2, the maximum tax payment (employee-employer combined) reached $1,264 by 1973, a real increase of more than 240 percent since 1959. Finally, as Congress legislated program expansion in the early 1970s without making the necessary adjustments in future tax rates, a financing "crisis" in Social Security was thus created. In short, Social Security's redistributive potential was realized.

The central purpose of Chapter 8 is to address the questions of what led to the political escalation of Social Security and how this was manifested in the nature and scope of the program. In particular, what economic and political factors help explain the introduction of large increases in real benefits payable under what had come to be known as an earnings-related insurance program? Why were additional expenditures financed increasingly by increases in the ceiling on taxable earnings rather than by tax-rate increases? How did the introduction of compulsory hospital

Table 8.1. History of percentge increases in benefits and prices (in percent)

Effective date	Across-the-board increases in benefits		Increases in CPI[a]	
	Each amendment	Cumulative from 1940 to amendments of	Between effective dates	Cumulative from 1940 to amendments of
January 1940	—	—	—	—
September 1940	77.0	77.0	75.5	75.5
September 1952	12.5	99.1	9.3	91.8
September 1954	13.0	125.0	.5	92.8
January 1959	7.0	140.8	8.0	108.2
January 1965	7.0	157.7	7.9	124.7
February 1968	13.0	191.2	9.2	145.4
January 1970	15.0	234.9	10.8	171.9
January 1971	10.0	268.4	5.2	186.0
September 1972	20.0	342.1	5.9	202.9
June 1974[b]	11.0	390.7	16.4	252.6
June 1975	8.0	430.0	9.3	285.4
June 1976	6.4	463.9	5.9	308.1
June 1977	5.9	497.2	6.9	336.3
June 1978	6.5	536.0	7.4	368.6
June 1979	9.9	599.0	11.1	420.6
June 1980	14.3	699.0	14.2	494.2

Source: Indexation of Federal Programs, prepared by the Congressional Research Service for the Committee on Budget, U.S. Senate, 97th Cong., 1st Sess. (1981), p. 165.
a. The CPI for "urban wage earners and clerical workers" is the one used for social security purposes.
b. Two-step increase enacted in 1973.

insurance affect the nature and future course of Social Security, and what were the political strategies of politicians and bureaucrats in bringing this expansion about? In essence, what were the circumstances that led to a quite different set of political and institutional responses in the 1960s and early 1970s than in the first two and a half decades of the program's history?

Perspectives into the Political Escalation of Social Security

A number of mutually reinforcing factors help explain the political escalation of Social Security, each of which derives from fundamental weaknesses in the system and in the economic and political environment in which it operated. Foremost, by 1960 a complicated program had been created with multiple beneficiary categories and diverse eligibility criteria.

The program had become far too complex to understand in its entirety, and the objectives of the program were no longer clear. Since the appropriate means for attaining an undefined objective were themselves poorly defined, almost any changes were defensible by Social Security bureaucrats and expansionist politicians. Discrimination against working wives and a retirement-earnings test were

Table 8.2. Financing Social Security 1958-81

| Years effective | Taxable earnings | Combined employer and employee | | | | | | |
| | | Tax rate | | | | Maximum tax payment | |
		OASI	DI	HI	Total	Nominal	Real (1980 dollars)
1959	$ 4,800	4.5%	.50%		5.00%	$ 240	$ 678
1960	4,800	5.5	.50		6.00	288	802
1961	4,800	5.5	.50		6.00	288	793
1962	4,800	5.75	.50		6.25	300	817
1963	4,800	6.75	.50		7.25	348	935
1964	4,800	6.75	.50		8.40	348	926
1965	4,800	6.75	.50		8.40	348	909
1966	6,600	7.00	.70	.7%	8.40	554	1,406
1967	6.600	7.10	.70	1.0	8.80	580	1,432
1968	7,800	6.65	.95	1.2	8.80	686	1,626
1969	7,800	7.45	.95	1.2	9.60	749	1,683
1970	7,800	7.30	1.10	1.2	9.60	749	1,590
1971	7,800	8.10	1.10	1.2	10.40	811	1,652
1972	9,000	8.10	1.10	1.2	10.40	936	1,843
1973	10,800	8.60	1.10	2.0	11.70	1,264	2,345
1974	13,200	8.75	1.15	1.8	11.70	1,544	2,582
1975	14,100	8.75	1.15	1.8	11.70	1,650	2,527
1976	15,300	8.75	1.15	1.8	11.70	1,790	2,590
1977	16,500	8.75	1.15	1.8	11.70	1,931	2,627
1978	17,700	8.66	1.50	2.0	12.10	2,142	2,705
1979	22,900	8.66	1.50	2.1	12.26	2,808	3,187
1980	25,900	9.04	1.12	2.1	12.26	3,175	3,175
1981	29,700	9.40	1.30	2.6	13.30	3,950	

Source: Social Security Administration, *Social Security Bulletin: Annual Statistical Supplement, 1975* (Washington D.C.: U.S. Government Printing Office, 1976), pp. 32–33, and *Social Security Bulletin* 41 (March 1978): 24–25.

defended on the grounds that the Social Security program had goals other than that of insurance, while earmarked taxes were defended on the grounds that the program was like insurance. Real increases in the minimum benefit were defended on the grounds that the program lacked "social adequacy" and did not provide a decent standard of living, while a means test was rejected on the grounds that it would conjure a redistributive welfare program and therefore be contrary to the objectives of an insurance program. Changes enacted one year to bestow "deserving" groups with special benefits were offset in later years by demand for "uniformity" and the equalization of treatment. The program was ripe for exploitation, whether demanded by special-interest groups or "recommended" by the bureaucracy.

The resulting erosion of eligibility conditions, extension of benefit rights, and consequent improvement in the position of beneficiaries relative to taxpayers as revealed in Table 8.3 surely resulted not only from the inability of taxpayers to decipher their impact on the cost of the program and from the deceptively low cost

Table 8.3. Expansion in beneficiary categories and benefit rates: Retired workers, disabled workers, and their decendents deceased workers and their survivors[a]

| | Retired workers | | Disabled workers | Their dependents | | | | | | |
	Male	Female		Wife	Wife w/child[f]	Husband	Divorced wife	Child	Disabled child	Divorced husband
Year[b]										
1935	—[c]	—[c]								
1939	100%(65)	100%(65)		50%(65)				50%(<18)		
1946										
1950					50%(any age<65)	50%(65)				50%(≥18)
1956		(62)[d]	100%(50-64)	(62)[e]						
1958										
1960			(any age < 65)							
1961	(62)[d]					(62)[e]				
1965							50%(62)[e]	(<22)[h]		
1967										
1969										
1972	—[i]	—[i]						(≤22)		
1975										
1977	—[p]	—[p]								
1981								(<19)[e]		50%(65)

Table 8.3—Continued

							Survivors of deceased workers					Dependent parent	
Year	Widow	Widow w/child[f]	Divorced wife	Divorced wife w/child[f]	Disabled widow	Divorced disabled widow	Widower	Widower w/child	Disabled widower	Child	Disabled child	Father	Mother
1935													
1939	75%(65)	75%(any age)								50%(<18)		50%(65)	50%(65)
1946													
1950				75%(any age)			75%(65)			50%+[n]		75%	75%
1956	(62)										50%+ (≥18)[n]	(62)	(62)
1958													
1960										75%	75%		
1961	82½%		82½%(60)[g]				82½%(62)					82½%	82½%
1965	(60)[g]									(<22)[h]		(62)	
1967					82½%(50-59)[k]	82½%(50-59)[k]			82½%(50-61)[m]				
1969													
1972	100%[i]		100%[i]		100%[i]	100%[i]	100%(60)[i]		100%(50-59)[i]	(≤22)[i]			
1975								75%(any age)[i]					
1977													
1981										(<19)[o]			

Source: Social Security Administration, *Social Security Bulletin: Annual Statistical Supplement, 1973* (Washington, D.C.: U.S. Government Printing Office, 1974), pp. 19-22.

a.   Since 1939, benefits expressed as percentages of worker's "primary insurance amount"—his basic benefit amount derived by applying benefit formula to worker's average earnings in covered employment. The fully retired worker, for example, is eligible for monthly benefit equal to 100 percent of his PIA; his wife is eligible for benefit of 50 percent of his PIA. These benefits are reduced if drawn early, if the sum of benefits of each family member exceeds maximum family benefit, or if individual earns more than exempt amount of income. Ages shown in parentheses designate the age at which benefits first become payable for all beneficiaries (including disabled children) except the dependent or surviving child. In these cases, age is for termination of benefits.

b.   Date of enactment.

c.   In 1935, benefits were payable to retired workers who were at least sixty-five and fully retired. There were no dependents' benefits; lump sum payments (based on worker's earnings and tax payments in excess of benefits already received) were payable to the deceased worker's estate.

d.   Benefit permanently reduced 5/9 percent for each month before age sixty-five.

e.   Benefit permanently reduced 25/36 percent for each month before age sixty-five.

f.   With child that is eligible for child's benefits. 1965 legislation excludes children over seventeen. 1981 legislation excludes children sixteen and older.

g.   Benefit permanently reduced 5/9 percent for each month before sixty-two.

h.   Benefits terminated at eighteen unless full-time student.

i.   Benefit permanently reduced 19/40 percent for each month before sixty-five. For beneficiaries of all ages whose husbands (or wives) retired before sixty-five, the benefit is limited to what spouse would have received if still alive, but not less than 82½ percent PIA.

j.   Increased 1/12 percent for each month between sixty-five and seventy-two for which no benefits received.

k.   Benefit permanently reduced 13 and 1/3 percent plus 43/198 percent for each month before 60.

l.   Benefit permanently reduced 28½ percent plus 43/240 percent for each month before 60.

m.   Benefit permanently reduced 5/9 percent for each month between 60-62 plus 43/198 percent for each month before 60.

n.   50 percent PIA for each child plus 25 percent PIA divided among the children.

o.   1981 legislation phases out the student benefit for post-secondary students 18 and older; and for other students 19 and older.

p.   Increased 1/4 percent for each month between age sixty-five and seventy-two in which no benefits received.

Table 8.4. Proportion of aged and total population receiving OASDHI or OAA or both, 1940-73[a]

Year	Number of recipients of OASDHI benefits (in millions)	Proportion of total population receiving:		Proportion of aged population receiving:	
		OASDHI	OASDHI or OAA or both	OASDHI	OASDHI or OAA or both
1940	.2	.1%	1.7%	.7%	24.4%
1950	3.5	2.3	4.1	16.4	36.6
1960	14.8	8.1	9.5	61.6	71.6
1965	20.9	10.7	11.7	75.2	81.7
1970	26.2	12.7	13.7	85.5	89.6
1973	29.9	14.2	15.0	86.7	90.0

Sources: Social Security Administration, *Social Security Bulletin* (May 1977): 46, 64; *Social Security Bulletin: Annual Statistical Supplement, 1973*, pp. 50, 60, 157; *Social Security Bulletin: Annual Statistical Supplement, 1975*, pp. 57, 116; Social and Rehabilitative Service, *Trend Report: A Graphic Presentation of Public Assistance and Related Data* (Washington, D.C.: U.S. Government Printing Office, 1969), p. 41; and U.S. Bureau of Census, *Historical Statistics of the U.S. from Colonial Times to 1970*, Bicentennial Edition (2 vols; Washington, D.C.: U.S. Government Printing Office, 1975), 1:10.
  a. See also Table 7.5.

of a pay-as-you-go system in its first decades, but also from the increasing political power of beneficiary groups. A systematic weighting of the age distribution toward elderly persons, and also a startling increase after the 1950s in the proportion of elderly persons who were direct recipients of net transfers from Social Security were important determinants of the latter development. The proportion of elderly people in the overall population, only 5.3 percent in 1935, rose to 8.7 percent in 1955, 9.5 percent in 1965, and 10 percent in 1975.[4] More importantly, perhaps, only 16.4 percent of the elderly were recipients of monthly OASDI cash benefits in 1950. Ten years later, as shown in Table 8.4, 61 percent of the elderly were beneficiaries, and by 1970 this figure reached 85 percent.

The marked increase in the proportion of elderly persons in receipt of government funds was then met by a fairly significant increase in the number of all persons who were beneficiaries. Between 1950 and 1960 the total number of OASDI beneficiaries quadrupled, doubling again in the following ten years. By 1973 there were thirty million recipients of monthly Social Security benefits, accounting for 14 percent of the total population.[5] Taking account of the relatively large incentive for beneficiary groups to participate in the collective choice process, as well as the incentive for politicians to respond to their demands, these figures suggest a dramatic increase by 1960 in the elderly's and other beneficiaries' political power, and in politicians interest in social insurance expansion.

Another factor influencing the development of Social Security was the rapid growth of state welfare expenditures after 1960, particularly with the introduction of disability assistance in 1950 and medical assistance in 1960. Between 1960 and 1973 real state and local welfare expenditures increased 256 percent as compared to only 16 percent in the preceding decade.[6]

A natural outgrowth of this was the emergence of bipartisan support for increasing the OASDI "minimum benefit"—the lowest benefit payable which was in excess of the amount the individual would otherwise be eligible to receive based on the regular benefit formula. Key congressmen with typically conservative voting records emerged as outspoken proponents of an expanded role for social insurance as this represented a very direct means of reducing "oppressive" state welfare costs. The tax cost of welfare was redistributed geographically and shifted to the federal government.[7] Increases in the minimum benefit, financed by a national payroll tax, dispersed tax costs and took hundreds of thousands of elderly persons off state welfare rolls.[8]

Finally, the presence of responsive administrations in the 1960s, during which time Presidents Kennedy and Johnson elevated domestic policy to a national priority, produced an environment conducive to demands by expansionary special-interest groups. Just as the Roosevelt years exposed the redistributive potential of government institutions, income redistribution was an explicit policy goal of both Kennedy and Johnson. Unlike the 1930s, however, key social insurance advocates were now a part of the Social Security bureaucracy, they had a potent ally with organized labor, and possessed one of the largest public information services in the world at their disposal.

A Brief History of the Health Insurance Movement

Until Medicare was enacted in 1965, the health issue dominated all others in Social Security during the early 1960s. The federal medical and hospital insurance program, enacted against the bitter opposition of Republicans, conservative Democrats, and the American Medical Association (AMA), marked the end of a battle that began early in the 1900s.[9]

Dating to the first decade of the twentieth century, the health insurance movement was led by the American Association of Labor Legislation—the same organization that fostered the American social insurance movement at the turn of the century. At that time "health" insurance proposals were modeled after the early German and British programs, generally involving compulsory contributory systems in which all workers were covered for medical and hospital expenses (including physician and surgical fees, drugs, supplies, and hospital care) and were eligible to receive cash benefits as well.[10]

By 1915 health insurance had become one of the most controversial political issues of the time, attracting opposition at least as adamant as to any other form of compulsory insurance. According to critics—who at that time included the medical profession, the private insurance industry, and even organized labor—federal health insurance was contrary to voluntary private-sector reliance and, through government regulation, would tend to stifle initiative and progress in both the medical and insurance industries.[11] As early as 1920 the AMA House of Delegates declared its opposition to the "institution of any plan embodying the system of compulsory contributory insurance against illness," or which "provided for medical service," whether "provided, controlled, or regulated by any state or federal government."[12] Samuel Gompers, president of the AFL, opposed all forms of compulsory social insurance.[13]

Although the onset of the Great Depression marked an important change in the role of the federal government in the provision of old-age insurance, the same was not true for health insurance. When President Roosevelt's Committee on Economic Security made its final report in 1935, the only reference to health insurance was a recommendation that the newly created Social Security Board study the issue. The suggestion drew such heated attack that the reference was deleted altogether from the bill as enacted eight months later.[14]

It was not until 1945 that President Truman reopened the health insurance issue by endorsing the pending Wagner-Murray-Dingell bill for compulsory health insurance. The demands of the Social Security bureaucracy, early advisory councils, and key lobby groups including the AFL-CIO, the American Association of Retired Workers, the National Association of Social Workers, and the Socialist party, however, were not sufficient to arouse the conservative postwar Congress. Backed by the AMA, the American Hospital Association, the Chamber of Commerce, and others, the predominately Republican Congress was no more inclined to support demands for intervention in the health-care industry than it had been to support expansion in the existing titles of Social Security.

In response to the clear inability to muster popular support for health insurance during the 1940s and 1950s, health insurance advocates sought new means of packaging their proposals. Since comprehensive health-insurance proposals had been condemned for being a step toward socialism, and also for failing to distinguish between the deserving and nondeserving poor, more "modest" programs were proposed. Coverage was restricted to elderly OASDI recipients, benefits were limited to hospital and nursing home care (thus excluding, for example, surgeons' fees), and the proposals were renamed, less offensively, "hospital insurance".

No action was taken in the 1950s, but considerable interest was generated. Hospital cost inflation persistently outstripped price and wage inflation, and the number of elderly persons who would be windfall gainers from the tying of hospital insurance to the OASDI program increased by five-fold. Between 1958 and 1965 Congress held hearings on health insurance annually.

By the time health insurance emerged in the late 1950s as an important political issue, organized labor and key officials in HEW were among the most active and influential advocate-lobbyists. Most notable among these were Nelson Cruikshank, head of the AFL-CIO Department of Social Security; Isidore Falk, consultant to the UMW; Wilbur Cohen, appointed assistant secretary of HEW in 1961; and Robert Ball, a career official with the Social Security Administration, appointed commissioner in 1962. These four advocates sought to muster union support for health insurance legislation and to couple it with the congressional support provided by a powerful sponsor. Representative Forand, who sponsored the first major compulsory health-insurance bill in 1957, was the fourth-ranking Democrat on the House Ways and Means Committee.[15] The first headway toward federal health insurance was made in 1960, in the last major amendments under the Eisenhower Administration.

The Amendments of 1960: The First Headway Toward Health Insurance

Health insurance was the major issue of debate during the hearings that led to the 1960 amendments. This was a presidential election year, and both Vice President Richard Nixon and Democratic presidential nominee Senator John F. Kennedy had endorsed widely different proposals.[16] Hearings, which opened in 1959, were held on a wide array of proposals, each with a common goal: "achieving the cost spread for aged medical care through governmental action, that is, through compulsory taxation."[17] Conservatives generally argued for federally subsidized and state-administered medical assistance for the elderly poor or else voluntary schemes to subsidize the purchase of private health insurance. Liberals generally argued for a federal program, whether or not limited to OASDI recipients.

During early hearings in the Ways and Means Committee, the Forand bill was the center of debate, a bill which would have created a federal hospital-insurance program financed by an increase in the payroll tax. The bill had considerable support from congressional liberals and, in fact, was submitted in the Senate in essentially the same form by Kennedy.

Echoing conservative sentiments, Arthur Flemming, secretary of HEW, testified at the hearings against the Forand bill, saying that it would lead to a "virtual halt in the growth of voluntary insurance efforts" and would have "far-reaching and irrevocable consequences."[18] Representative Wilbur Mills, chairman of the Ways and Means Committee and leading opponent of compulsory health insurance, echoed a more moderate stance by opposing any changes in Social Security that would involve tax increases.

When hearings recommenced in March of 1960, Flemming reiterated his opposition, saying "We will oppose any program of compulsory health insurance," preferring instead to develop a plan that would not stifle private initiative.[19] On 30 March the growing health-insurance movement suffered a major setback when President Eisenhower took a formal stand on the issue. Compulsory insurance, he said, was a "very definite step toward socialized medicine," and "I don't want any of it."[20]

A month later Flemming presented to the Ways and Means Committee the Administration's counterproposal. It included two federally subsidized state programs between which the individual could have had a choice: one that reimbursed the elderly poor for certain medical expenses, and one that subsidized the cost of private medical insurance policies for the elderly. Senator Pat McNamara then introduced a bill, cosponsored by Kennedy and eighteen other Democratic senators, that was similar to the Forand bill but which provided benefits to all of the elderly, not just those eligible for Social Security.

In the Ways and Means Committee the McNamara-Forand-type bills were too radical, while the Administration's bill was somewhat too conservative, and the committee voted to have an alternate health-care plan drafted. Submitted by Chairman Mills, the plan proposed establishing a program of federal grants to states paying certain medical costs for the needy aged, but the states were to be given more flexibility than under the Administration's plan. Containing most of the elements of the more modest Mills bill, the committee bill (HR 12580) also included various liberalizations of the OASDI cash benefit programs. By August the Senate Finance Committee had approved HR 12580 with amendments to liberalize the federal-state medical care program and on 13 September the 1960 amendments were signed into law by President Eisenhower.[21]

As enacted, the 1960 amendments provided for a system of federal grants to the states for medical aid to the aged, needy and also the ill-defined "medically needy"—those persons with incomes too high to qualify for old-age assistance but deemed in need of medical assistance. An expansion of the OASDI program was also enacted, but with considerably less controversy. The retirement test and benefit eligibility requirements were liberalized, benefits to surviving children were increased, and coverage was expanded. Only four years after the enactment of disability insurance, moreover, the age fifty requirement was eliminated and monthly cash benefits were made payable to workers (and their families) becoming disabled—or "retiring early"—as early as thirty-one.

Introduced as a defense against a compulsory federal system of health insurance, medical assistance would provide a stronghold for social insurance advocates and for the eventual extension and centralization of the program. Just as had been the case when aid to the disabled poor was provided in 1950, only to be followed by compulsory disability insurance in 1956, the inevitable rise in state welfare costs and the failure to reach the nonneedy aged would generate more general demands for a national health-insurance system.

The Amendments of 1961

On 2 February 1961 newly inaugurated President Kennedy called for an expansion of Social Security. As his proposals were sent to Congress, he remarked that the changes would "give our economic recovery program needed impetus," and "place increased purchasing power in the hands of almost five million people."[22] Four months later the president signed into law the Social Security Amendments of 1961. The amendments included a 20 percent increase in the minimum OASDI benefit, a reduction in the retirement age for men to age sixty-two, an increase in widows' benefits from 75 percent to 82 1/2 percent and a liberalization of benefit eligibility requirements and the retirement test. Also, the payroll-tax schedule was increased, and the federal matching rate for public assistance was increased once again. The first-year cost of these revisions was estimated at $800 million ($2.2 billion).[23]

The Amendments of 1965: Hospital Insurance Enacted

After the defeat of health insurance in 1960 advocates continued their efforts to repackage and sell their programs. Beginning in 1961 with the inauguration of Kennedy and continuing through to the year of enactment under Johnson, proposals for compulsory health insurance were regularly submitted to Congress by the Administration. Each year the bills became somewhat less extensive, but they retained the basic elements of the "King-Anderson" bill first introduced in 1961. Accordingly, they generally sought coverage for hospitalization, nursing home, home health, and outpatient services for OASDI recipients, with the cost being met out of the trust funds by an increase in the ceiling on taxable earnings.[24]

As had been the case historically, health-insurance proposals were unable to find their way out of the Ways and Means Committee. Chairman Mills, considered the leading congressional opponent, explained his opposition by saying, "I have always maintained that at some point there is a limit to the amount of a worker's wages or the earnings of the self-employed person, that can reasonably be expected to finance the Social Security system. . . . One of the difficulties that has actually impeded the reaching of a sound solution (to the medical needs of the elderly) is the insistence by proponents of medical care on proceeding toward a solution through the existing OASDI system."[25] In his view the Administration's proposals failed to reveal their true cost so that, if tied to OASDI financing, they might seriously undermine support for Social Security.[26]

As late as June 1964, and only months before the next presidential election, the Ways and Means Committee once more postponed action on the King-Anderson bill. It was clear that opposition on the floor was still too strong. The committee did manage, however, to report a bill to increase Social Security benefits by 5 percent, expand coverage, and increase the tax rates and tax ceiling.

It was not until the bill reached the Senate floor that it was amended to include a medicare program. Sponsored by Albert Gore the amendment was of little avail, however, as House-Senate conferees were unable to come to a compromise before the 88th Congress ended. It was generally believed that the Senate was unwilling to compromise on its demands for medicare as the enactment of a Social Security benefit and tax increase in 1964 would have reduced the likelihood of passing a costly medicare-benefit hike package in 1965.[25] A legislative defeat for Democratic presidential nominee Lyndon Johnson, this was nevertheless the first time in history that a compulsory health insurance measure had made it out of either house of Congress.

In 1965 recently elected President Johnson turned his energies to domestic policy and the "Great Society." Three days after his State of the Union address Johnson presented a "Health Message," calling once again for a compulsory hospital insurance program for Social Security recipients financed by Social Security taxes (or, in his words, "modest contributions during working years").[28] For those not covered by Social Security, hospital care would have been financed by general revenues. The President's proposal was embodied in the first bill introduced into the 89th Congress (HR1). Its first-year cost was estimated to be $2 ($5.2) billion.

Three major defensive bills emerged, all of a voluntary nature and providing more generous benefits.[29] The AMA plan, introduced by Representatives Sydney Herlong and Thomas Curtis, was a voluntary plan for the needy aged to be integrated into the Kerr-Mills federal-state grants program. The elderly poor who purchased health insurance privately would have had their premiums set according to income and subsidized by federal-state revenues. A similar plan was introduced by Senator Leverett Saltonstall. Finally, Representative John Byrnes, ranking minority member of the House Ways and Means Committee, proposed a more expensive voluntary plan with graduated premiums to be financed by federal and state revenues and individual contributions.

While attracting significant support, these more moderate proposals failed to curtail the momentum behind more comprehensive social insurance proposals. By July 1965, with the support of the largest Democratic majorities in Congress since Roosevelt's days, the active support of the Social Security bureaucracy, and the endorsement of the 1965 Advisory Council on Social Security, "Medicare" was finally enacted. Partly reflecting the vigorous opposition that still existed, the conference report, which coupled the new hospital insurance program with a significant liberalization of the OASDI program, was approved in the House by a vote of 307-116 and in the Senate (with more than a two-to-one Democratic majority) by a vote of 70-24.[30]

The new provisions, incorporated into Title XVIII of the Social Security Act, created two plans: a compulsory hospital insurance plan, Part A; and a supplemental voluntary plan to cover doctor's bills, Part B. With some deductibles and coinsurance terms, hospital insurance covered the cost of a specific number of days of hospital care, posthospital care, outpatient diagnostic services and home-care visits. The program was to be financed by an increase in the ceiling on taxable earnings and an increase in payroll taxes (not to exceed 1.6 percent in 1987 and thereafter). The supplementary program was designed to pay 80 percent of the elderly's cost of doctor and other medical specialist services, home-care visits, and other health and medical services. This program was to be financed by a three-dollar monthly premium matched by a federal government contribution from general revenues. Finally, the federally subsidized, state-administered medical assistance program created in 1960 was extended to all recipients of public assistance—dependent children, blind, and disabled—no longer restricted to the elderly poor.

At the same time, important changes were made in the OASDI program. Benefits were increased 7 percent, children's and widows' benefits were made payable for a longer period of time (by raising the cut-off age for children from eighteen to twenty-one, and by reducing the eligible age for widows from sixty-two to sixty), benefits were extended to divorced wives, and coverage was expanded to physicians. Eligibility requirements for disability insurance were significantly reduced, and special lenient eligibility requirements were instituted for persons at least seventy-two. The tax rate and the ceiling on taxable earnings were both increased. The first-year cost of the bill was estimated to be a modest $6.5 ($17) billion.

HI and OASDI: Similarities and Differences

Attempts by congressional liberals and the Social Security bureaucracy-advocacy to sell Congress on health insurance failed for decades. There was simply no compelling logic for instituting a federal insurance program. Health-care costs were among the fastest rising components in consumer prices; the elderly, as a group, did have relatively low incomes and were heavy users of medical services but nearly 70 percent of them were already covered by health-insurance plans; the wealth position of the elderly, of course, was not inferior to lower age groups; and the rate of chronic ailments among the elderly did not compare poorly with the rate for all other age groups.[31] The stimulation of demand induced by subsidizing medical services could only exacerbate health-care cost inflation.

Just as with old-age insurance in the 1930s, the Administration jointly brought to focus the high cost of private insurance and medical care for the aged and needy, and it also raised as a political issue the possibility of providing millions of elderly persons with an array of medical services at a fraction of their cost. Despite the growth and development of private medical insurance plans, it was indeed difficult to curb the momentum behind a program that would make nineteen million elderly persons eligible for benefits at no cost the day it was officially launched. Similarly, given any number of proposals to stimulate the already rapid expansion of private alternatives, the Administration espoused a comprehensive, federal system. Finally, just as the old-age insurance program was tied to the creation of politically appealing poverty relief programs in the 1930s to ensure passage of the former, the nonearnings-related Medicare program was tied to an expansion of the now politically popular OASDI program.

Unlike the period of the 1930s rationales for the program did not include the safety of government programs from depression-oriented financial failure or myopia arguments that concluded that people needed to be compelled to purchase insurance throughout their working lives to prevent them from becoming a charge on the state at a future date. Instead, the program was supported on the basis of welfare-alleviation arguments and the need to fill a "major deficiency" in the existing program. Rather than stress-preventive insurance for the future, Medicare and its advocates stressed alleviation of "medical poverty" through cost (or income) redistribution.

Also, unlike the other forms of social insurance, Medicare benefits were not intended to be earnings related. Granting that the tax-benefit link had become less direct over time, cash benefits were still positively related to the worker's earnings as the programs had been designed to offset the loss of income associated with old age or disability, losses which are by definition earnings related. This was not at all the case with hospital insurance. Everyone covered by Medicare was eligible for exactly the same benefits, yet the program was financed by an earnings-related tax.

Finally, Medicare was a cost reimbursement program, not a cash benefit program like OASI and DI. This difference alone was crucial in that Medicare would subsidize and thus stimulate the demand for certain medical services. The operation of the program itself would thereby directly affect its cost. Moreover, policymakers would have to interface not simply with growth-oriented beneficiaries and advocates but also with a new and potent constituency of health-care providers and intermediaries.[32]

On 1 July 1966, Medicare began providing benefits. By 1969 the program's cost was double what it was projected to be in 1965 and a tax increase had already been enacted.[33] By 1970 the Medicare trust fund was in critical financial shape,[34] and in 1973 the tax rate expected to be sufficient to finance the system in the long-term was exceeded.

An Amendment to the 1966 Tax Adjustment Act

On 15 March 1966 President Johnson signed into law the Tax Adjustment Act, designed to provide additional funds for the Viet Nam War and impose, in his words, "fiscal restraint to balance our economic expansion."[35] It just happened to be the case that an amendment was attached that introduced a pure welfare benefit into Social Security. Reminiscent of conservative efforts to "blanket in" all of the elderly in the 1950s, the amendment was introduced unexpectedly by Senator Winston Prouty (R.-Vt.), and called for special monthly benefits for all people aged seventy and older who were not currently eligible under Social Security. The proposed amendment led to heated debate, yet when modified and attached to the Tax Adjustment Act during an election year it passed with little difficulty.

As amended, liberalized benefits for persons at least seventy-two (enacted in 1965) were further liberalized so that anyone that age or older was eligible for a $35 monthly payment (plus $17.50 for a spouse) to be financed from the trust funds, effective 1 October, 1966. Beginning in 1968 the special age seventy-two benefits were to be financed from general revenues and payable only to people with some previous covered employment.

It is worthy to note that this was the first time in history that OASDI amendments were tied to pending nongermane legislation to insure their passage. This tactic would be used again in 1969, 1971, 1972, and 1973.

The last major revisions of the Social Security Act during the Johnson Administration were incorporated into the amendments of 1967, which represented a modified, although still expensive version of the proposals made by the President on 23 January 1967. At that time Johnson requested an average increase in Social Security benefits of 20 percent, an increase in the minimum benefit of 59 percent, the payment of Medicare to disabled workers, and other liberalizations of the program.[36]

Hearings on amending the Social Security Act began in March with a thirty-five-page explanation and endorsement of the Administration-backed bill by John Gardner, secretary of HEW. Issues of debate centered around not only the cost of the proposed program, but also its "adequacy." Robert Ball, commissioner of social security, and Wilbur Cohen, undersecretary of HEW, expressed concern over the political desirability of increasing the payroll tax. Conservatives questioned the advisability of significantly increasing the minimum benefit simply to reduce the number of people in poverty. The AFL-CIO, UAW, National Council of Senior Citizens, and the National Association of Social Workers all endorsed the Administration's recommendations, though sought larger benefit increases. Walter Reuther of the UAW and representatives of the National Association of Social Workers actually called for a 50 percent increase in Social Security benefits.[37]

While the Ways and Means Committee reduced significantly the scope and cost of the Administration's bill, the Senate, where Johnson had presided only six years earlier, approved a huge program, the cost of which was estimated at $7 ($17.3) billion during the first year alone.[38] As the bill made its way through the conference committee and was cleared by Congress, the cost of the program had been reduced to $3.6 billion, Social Security benefits were increased across-the-board by 13 percent, special age seventy-two benefits were increased 15 percent, and the retirement test was liberalized. Also dependents' and survivors' benefits were made payable to disabled widow(er)s at age fifty, additional benefits were provided to children, and disability benefits were extended to persons under thirty-one! To partially finance this expansion, scheduled tax rates were increased, but not until four years hence. In addition to these changes ceilings were imposed on federal Medicaid expenses, as costs already far exceeded those estimated by the secretary of HEW.

The Choice Among Fiscal Instruments

The means chosen to finance the immediate increase in expenditures portended future developments. In particular, the ceiling on taxable earnings was increased from $6,600 to $7,800, constituting the first time in the history of the program that the ceiling exceeded the level established in 1935 in real terms.[39] Thereafter Congress would frequently turn to increases in the real tax ceiling to help finance program expansion.

Social Security executives and congressmen bent on expansion showed over the years a strong inclination to utilize the method of finance of "least resistance," or the one that dispersed the burden so as to reduce the incentive for people to lobby against expansion. Their choices were three—tax-rate increases, tax-ceiling increases, and coverage expansion—and they utilized them effectively.

Coverage expansion was the first of these fiscal instruments actively sought by advocates and utilized by legislators. This made good sense since coverage was sought by many uncovered groups endeavoring to capture the high returns payable in the early decades of the program's existence. By the late 1950s coverage had been expanded to nine out of ten workers and Congress turned to tax-rate increases.

Why, then, were tax-rate increases employed exclusively through 1966 rather than increases in the real ceiling? Recognizing that an increase in the ceiling transferred the burden of additional expenditures onto workers earning more than the previously existing ceiling, it was reasonable to expect the use of real-ceiling increases to be delayed until coverage had been expanded to higher paid occupations. By indicating a willingness to concentrate costs on a clearly defined set of higher-income workers, expansionists would have weakened their position with these workers in a fight for universal coverage. Moreover, the potential for redistributing income by simply increasing the ceiling for currently covered workers was considerably more limited than that made possible by expanding coverage to the higher paid.

It was not until 1965 that compulsory coverage was finally extended to most higher-paid, self-employed professionals.[40] Once covered, they provided an attractive and exploitable source of new revenues for redistributionists. Ceiling increases would bestow windfall gains to current beneficiaries and tax breaks for the average taxpayer and for the near-elderly who, as a group, typically had earnings less than the ceiling.

In conjunction with the tactic first employed in 1966 of tying benefit increases to pending, nongermane legislation, the use of a real-ceiling increase in 1967 was yet another development of the 1960s foreshadowing developments to come. Within ten years the ceiling on taxable earnings would be increased 30 percent, in real terms.

The Kennedy-Johnson Years in Review

In all, a Democratic Congress during the Kennedy-Johnson years put few effective constraints on program expansion. Between 1960 and 1968 there was a doubling of the number of beneficiaries to the Social Security program and real expenditures out of the trust funds more than doubled (see Table 8.5).

Alongside the enactment of a new compulsory, federal hospital insurance program during these years, there was a significant increase in the complexity of the existing insurance titles. Special benefit privileges granted in the 1950s in the form of age or eligibility concessions or benefit-rate increases were granted to other beneficiary groups in the 1960s. Existing privileges were enhanced, and new beneficiary categories were introduced. Between 1960 and 1968 age requirements were reduced for male retirees, disabled workers, widows, and widowers, while the age at which children's benefits were still payable was increased. Also benefits were made payable—at no additional cost—to divorced wives, disabled widow(er)s, and to the survivors, dependents, and retired workers in families in which the worker had minimal to no covered earnings. Finally, benefit rates were increased for widow(er)s, parents, and children of retired workers. By 1968 there were twenty different beneficiary categories under the cash benefits programs with an array of seemingly arbitrary benefit and eligibility criteria. In that year Social Security expendi-

Table 8.5. Status of OASDHI trust funds, 1960-80 selected years (in millions)[a]

Year[b]	Revenues		Expenditures		Assets		Assets/Exp.
	Nominal	Real	Nominal	Real	Nominal	Real	
1960	$ 12,445	$ 34,666	$ 11,798	$ 32,864	$ 22,613	$ 62,989	1.92%
1965	17,857	46,624	19,187	50,097	19,841	51,804	1.03
1968	33,780	80,047	30,294	71,787	30,875	73,164	1.02
1970	42,972	91,236	38,389	81,505	41,270	87,622	1.08
1972	52,025	102,411	47,748	93,992	45,710	89,980	.96
1974	74,090	123,896	69,966	117,000	55,005	91,982	.79
1976[b]	84,226	121,890	86,478	125,149	55,786	80,732	.65
1978[b]	108,109	136,501	111,613	140,926	47,146	59,528	.42
1980	145,800	145,800	149,100	149,100	40,200	40,200	.27

Source: Social Security Administration, *Social Security Bulletin: Annual Statistical Supplement, 1975,* pp. 66-67; *Social Security Bulletin* 42 (June 1979): 33-35, and Social Security Administration, Office of Actuary (15 June 1981).
a. Real values are in 1980 dollars.
b. Figures for 1976 and 1978 are fiscal year data, and are somewhat lower than the comparable annual year data.

tures reached $30 ($71) billion and 24 million Americans, or nearly 20 percent of the voting-age population, were direct beneficiaries to the OASDHI system.[41]

The Nixon Years: 1968-73

The momentum gained and the trends begun in the 1950s and 1960s were not to be abated during the Nixon years. The many amendments enacted during these years attested to the strength of an alliance comprised of expansionary lobby groups and Social Security bureaucrats, and to the political savvy of two powerful Democrats—Wilbur Mills, chairman of the House Ways and Means Committee, and Russell Long, chairman of the Senate Finance Committee. Typically against the threat of presidential veto, amendments were enacted in 1969, 1971, 1972, and 1973. In each of these years, politically appealing benefit increases were tied to the enactment of pending nongermane legislation for which passage was all but certain—the tactic first used by Senator Prouty in 1966.

Aside from rapid increases in benefits, particularly the minimum benefit, and the reliance on real-ceiling increases, an important outgrowth of the Nixon years was the implementation in 1972 of an automatic cost-of-living adjustment for Social Security benefits. The "technically flawed" indexing provision would have a profound effect on the future of the system. The year 1972 would also mark the culmination of a forty-year trend toward the federalization of poverty-relief programs. In that year, each of the state-administered programs of aid to the blind, the disabled, and the elderly poor were collapsed into a single federal assistance program, Supplemental Security Income (SSI).

The Automatic Cost-of-Living Adjustment Issue

In response to the demands of the elderly, and in an effort to routinize an ad hoc procedure in Congress, President Nixon proposed automatic cost-of-living increases in benefits and the ceiling on taxable earnings. The indexing proposal was endorsed, in his words, to "depoliticize, to a certain extent, the Social Security system and give a greater stability to what has become a cornerstone of our society's social insurance system."[42] According to Creed Black, assistant secretary of HEW, indexing would lead to a "substitution of economic determinants for biennial politics" in setting benefit increases.[43]

Beneficiary groups such as the elderly advocated indexing for a number of reasons. They argued that congressional benefit increases had tended to keep pace with changes in the price level, but there were lags in adjustment that generated losses for the elderly who were living off low "fixed incomes." An annual adjustment would hasten a restoration of their purchasing power, without prohibiting congressional action. It was, they said, simply a method of assuring an annual cost-of-living adjustment in (the unlikely) case it had not been legislated. From the perspective of beneficiaries, of course, indexing was a way to ensure themselves a new and higher base for future political negotiations. Any political gains over and above the "depoliticized" indexed levels would then be guaranteed to be real. Others advocated indexing because it would prevent persons earning more than the tax ceiling from being systematically benefited as inflation eroded the real value of their tax payments.

Congressional opponents argued against the automatic adjustment on the grounds that legislative action made the provision unnecessary. The President was evidently offering a proposal that would gain his Administration political favor while challenging congressional prerogative to do so. Stated most succinctly by Chairman Mills, "Is Congress going to get any credit for future adjustments in benefits, or are we going to . . . let the Secretary of HEW get all the credit?"[44] Indeed, Social Security benefit increases were particularly popular election issues at a time when one out of eight Americans were benefit recipients, the vast majority of whom were of voting age.

Others opposed an automatic cost-of-living adjustment because of the possible impact on inflation. As recipients' incomes became immunized against inflation, it was believed that less pressure to constrain and control inflationary policies might result. Also, there was some concern that Social Security indexing might have even broader ramifications by leading to demands for automatic adjustments of welfare benefits, negotiated wage agreements, and other such measures.

For those concerned with the rapid growth of Social Security a major concern over indexation should have been its likely impact on legislated benefit increases and the ability of Congress to control spending during periods of chronic inflation. As the major opposition to a cost-of-living adjustment centered on the undesirability from the politician's point of view of taking the credit for benefit hikes away from elected representatives in election years, it was probable that Congress would maintain its discretion and gain political favor by enacting benefit increases before the automatic increase took place in January, or by enacting larger than cost-of-living benefit increases.[45] During periods of high inflation, moreover, Congress would find itself locked into an "uncontrollable" expenditure for the elderly borne by workers alone.

The "technical" problem with the proposed adjustment, popularly referred to as "double-indexing," was not an issue.[46] Double-indexing was a correctable problem whereby inflation would not only lead to higher benefits once recipients were on the benefit rolls but also, through its impact on earnings, would increase the initial benefit for future retirees. This "flaw"—along with the fact that workers' wages (and therefore tax payments) could grow too slowly to support price indexed payments for the elderly—would be the undoing of Social Security financing.

Welfare Reform and OASDHI

Another issue to be dealt with by the Nixon administration was the startling trend in public assistance. Commencing in the late 1960s, these trends elevated welfare reform to a controversial political issue. Thirty years elapsed before expenditures on public assistance by all levels of government, measured in 1980 dollars, reached $15 billion. Yet, in the following five years real expenditures doubled, and two years later exceeded $40 billion. In spite of, and in part because of, the federal government's increasing role in the financing of public assistance, state expenditures showed similarly rapid growth. Between 1960 and 1970 state and local expenditures increased more than 200 percent in real terms, reaching $9.5 ($20) billion in 1970.[47] With each state desiring to transfer part of its tax cost to others, there emerged bipartisan support for increased federal participation, if not a complete federalization of the programs.

Table 8.6 provides insight into why there arose during the 1960s and early 1970s bipartisan demands for increased reliance on Social Security for welfare purposes. Increasing real OASDHI benefits, particularly the minimum benefit, and reducing eligibility requirements provided direct means through which states could redistribute tax costs through a national payroll tax. While these institutional changes were certainly not consistent with the objectives of an earnings-related insurance program, they were most consistent with the objective of improving the fiscal position of states. Expenditures on old-age assistance actually declined continuously after 1950 as Social Security assumed more of its function.

Amendments to the 1969 Tax Reform Act

Major reform of the welfare system was proposed by Nixon in 1969. He advocated the replacement of Aid to Families with Dependent Children (AFDC), the largest and most costly of the four public assistance programs, with a Family

Assistance Plan (FAP). Unlike the prevailing system which limited benefits to families with dependent children, the FAP would have provided a minimum welfare payment to all poor families with the stipulation that parents accepted training or employment.

The following month Nixon proposed automatic cost-of-living indexing for Social Security (benefits and the tax ceiling) along with a 10 percent increase in Social Security benefits. Hearings began on these proposals during October, but because of the controversial nature of the proposals, action appeared unlikely before the close of the session.[48]

On 5 December the House Ways and Means Committee reported a clean bill (HR 15095) that did not address either of the President's major recommendations. Instead, the bill included an across-the-board increase in Social Security benefits of 15 percent, effective 1 January 1970. This 5 percent increase in real-benefit levels and other changes were to be financed under the currently scheduled tax rates and tax ceiling.

To make certain the 15 percent benefit hike would be passed before the end of the year, the Senate accepted an amendment offered by Senator Long, identical to HR 15095, which was attached to Nixon's tax-reform bill. Threatening to veto the tax-reform bill because of the large benefit increases, Nixon signed the package into law on 30 December 1969.[49]

Amendments to the 1971 Debt Ceiling Extension Bill

The bill containing President Nixon's proposals for indexing and welfare reforms died in Congress during 1970 and was reintroduced in 1971 by Representative Mills (HR 1).[50] In addition to indexing, the bill contained provisions for a 10 percent increase in Social Security benefits, various liberalizations of the Social Security program, as well as the Administration's Family Assistance Plan. The controversial nature of the bill made action appear unlikely even in 1971.

During the period in which the Ways and Means Committee was studying this bill, the committee was also working on a bill to extend the federal debt ceiling, which the House went on to pass during March 1971. Not one to miss an opportunity to increase Social Security benefits, Chairman Long offered an amendment to the debt-ceiling bill to increase Social Security benefits by 10 percent. The amendment was accepted and, as enacted, the bill increased the temporary national debt ceiling, increased Social Security benefits by 10 percent (effective 1 January 1971), and increased special age seventy-two benefits by 5 percent. The Social Security revisions were to be financed by an increase in the ceiling on taxable earnings of more than 15 percent, while an increase in scheduled tax rates was postponed until 1976.[51]

Hearings were resumed in the Ways and Means Committee on the Social Security Amendments of 1970 (HR 1) and on 22 June 1971, the 687-page bill was passed

Table 8.6. Trends in selected public assistance programs: recipients and money payments, 1936-73[a]

Program	1936	1940	1950	1960	1970	1973
Recipients (in thous.):						
Total	1,699	3,365.4	5,185.3	5,854.0	12,757	13,991.9
OAA	1,108	2,070.0	2,786.0	2,305.0	2,082	1,831.0
AFDC	546	1,222.0	2,233.0	3,073.0	9,659	10,857.0
AB	45.2	73.4	97.5	107.0	81	77.9
APTD	—	—	68.8	369.0	935	1,226.0
Payments (in mill.):						
Total	$ 81.4	$ 594.4	$2,040.3	$2,885.7	$6,866.4	$10,548.1
OAA	52.9	449.9	1,437.9	1,614.3	1,823.1	1,724.6
AFDC	22.8	123.3	520.3	961.7	4,065.4	7,128.5
AB	5.7	21.2	51.0	84.6	95.0	104.8
APTD	—	—	31.1	225.1	882.9	1,590.2

Sources: U.S. Department of Health, Education, and Welfare, Social and Rehabilitation Service, *Public Assistance Statistics: Aug. 1973* (Washington, D.C.: Department of Health, Education, and Welfare), Table I; Social and Rehabilitation Service, *Trend Report: A Graphic Presentation of Public Assistance and Related Data* (Washington, D.C.: U.S. Government Printing Office, 1971):9.

a. Expenditures on money payments for the four major means-tested programs under Social Security Act; Old-Age Assistance (OAA); Aid to Families with Dependent Children (AFDC); Aid to the Permanently and Totally Disabled (APTD); and Aid to the Blind (AB). Not included in these figures are expenditures on Medical Assistance for the Aged, General Assistance, administration and capital outlay.

by the House.[52] As approved, HR1 included a comprehensive array of changes in OASDI, Medicare, Medicaid, and public assistance. Aside from an additional 5 percent increase in Social Security benefits and a 13 percent increase in the tax ceiling, the bill included Social Security indexing, special minimum benefits for persons with long periods of employment and low average earnings, higher widows' benefits (from 82.5 percent to 100 percent of the deceased worker's benefit), and a liberalized retirement test. The bill also extended Medicare benefits to nonelderly disabled workers and increased Medicare benefits in general. With regard to the public assistance titles of the act, the House bill unified each of the four federal-state programs into a single uniform federal program with 100 percent federal financing.

While the bill contained important changes in the insurance titles, its major purpose, as stated by a 386-page report by the Ways and Means Committee, was to effect a change in the welfare system by encouraging employable adults to seek employment. Proclaimed by President Nixon to be the "most important social legislation in 35 years," the welfare provisions of the bill attracted opposition from both ends of the ideological spectrum.[53] As the 1971 session of Congress closed, action on HR1 was still pending in the Senate Finance Committee. The need for quick action had been diminished, of course, when the Social Security benefit hike was passed with the debt ceiling bill earlier in the year.

Amendments to the 1972 Debt Ceiling Extension Bill: A Turning Point

An amended version of HR1 was tentatively approved by the Senate Finance Committee on 13 June 1972, two and a half years after President Nixon made his initial recommendations and after eleven months in committee. While the welfare provisions of the bill were widely different from those in the House bill, the provisions relating to OASDHI were quite similar.[54] In particular, there was a 10-percent across-the-board increase in monthly benefits along with a quite significant liberalization of the benefits offered to particular beneficiary groups, an increase in the tax ceiling and tax rates, and, for the future, Social Security indexing (for benefits and the tax ceiling).

Remarkably, when the bill made it to the floor, questions were actually raised concerning whether the 10 percent benefit hike was large enough. A 20 percent hike (14 percent in real terms) was favored by Mills, Long, and fifty-nine senators on the floor, and was endorsed by Ribicoff, Harris, and Nelson! The 10 percent provision prevailed only after a 15-percent benefit hike was rejected by a tie-vote.[55]

Once again, the Ways and Means Committee was simultaneously preparing a bill to extend the national debt ceiling beyond the date it was scheduled to be terminated on midnight, 30 June.[56] As a result, when President Nixon announced on 22 June that he would not compromise with Senate liberals on the welfare provisions contained in the House bill, the Senate accepted an amendment by Frank Church to attach to the debt ceiling bill a 20 percent Social Security benefit increase, indexing, and an increase in scheduled tax rates and the taxable ceiling.

The House refused to accept the very large benefit increase and on the afternoon of 30 June sent the debt ceiling bill to conference. On the basis of findings by a 1971 advisory council that Social Security was *over-financed*, Chairman Mills told members of the House, heroically, that if they adopted the 20-percent benefit increase, "I can assure the membership of this House that we will over the forthcoming 75-year period, take in each year more money than we will be paying out."[57] After having legislated real benefit increases of more than 37 percent since 1968, the conference committee accepted the 20 percent benefit hike, and late in the evening of 30 June the House accepted the conference report.

On the morning of 1 July President Nixon signed into law the debt-ceiling extension bill, and with it a 20 percent across-the-board increase in Social Security benefits, an increase in the ceiling on taxable earnings, a reduction in scheduled tax rates, and provisions for automatic cost-of-living adjustments. It was clear to many observers that had it not been the case that the debt-ceiling extension bill was scheduled to revert to $400 billion, more than $25 billion less than the amount of federal debt outstanding, Nixon would have vetoed the very large benefit increase, which he singled out as threatening to escalate inflation.[58] What was not as clear was the significance of indexing and the fact that a huge and improperly financed expansion in social security had just taken place that would, in Representative Byrnes's words, "mark a turning point in the capacity of the system."[59]

The 1972 Amendments

As Senate liberals undoubtedly knew, early passage of the 20 percent benefit increase in June made positive action on comprehensive welfare reform less likely. In fact, as HR1 was passed by the Senate in October, the bill increased Social Security, Medicare, and Medicaid benefits, and effectively rejected any major welfare reform. As such, the House and Senate versions of HR1 were widely different and in conference welfare reform was deleted entirely.

As cleared by the Congress on 17 October 1972, the bill contained many revisions of Social Security.[60] Among the major changes in OASDHI were: (1) an increase in the ceiling on taxable earnings from $9,000 to $10,800 in 1973, and to $12,000 in 1974; (2) an increase in the schedule of tax rates; (3) an increase in widow(er)s' benefits from 82.5 percent to 100 percent of the deceased worker's monthly benefit; (4) the institution of a special minimum benefit for persons who worked for many years in covered employment at low wages; (5) the institution of a benefit increment of 1 percent per year for persons who continue to work beyond the age of sixty-five;[61] (6) the deletion copayment terms for home-health services under the hospital insurance program and the extension of hospital insurance benefits to the disabled. Concerning the public assistance titles of Social Security, the amendments: (1) consolidated the federal-state public assistance programs for the aged, blind, and disabled, into a single federally financed and administered program, Supplemental Security Income (SSI) to provide the poor with a minimum monthly income of $130, effective 1 January 1974; and (2) protected the eligibility of public assistance recipients for their benefits for another year despite the 20 percent increase in Social Security benefits enacted in 1972.

The increase in widow(er) benefits, the institution of special benefits for low-paid workers, and heavy reliance on real taxable ceiling increases all reflected the continued demands for "social adequacy"—growing demands to redistribute income intragenerationally. The liberalization of the hospital insurance program, demanded since the program's inception in 1966 by the National Council of Senior Citizens, was a likely development under such a comprehensive bill. The provision to allow poor OASDI recipients to continue receiving old-age assistance was simply a popular thing to do a month before a national election.

The creation of a federal public assistance program marked the culmination of decades of debate over states' rights vs. "adequacy" and "equality" in the provision for the poor. Beginning in 1939, when the first change in matching formulas was enacted, fiscal conservatives fought the trend toward federalization.[62] At the same time, congressional liberals sought continuously to increase the federal matching share in categorical grants to states. Efforts by President Eisenhower during the

1950s to limit congressional discretion were fruitless and were followed by the implementation of nonuniform grants to states and larger average expenditures. By the 1970s much of the die-hard states' rights opposition to federalization withered as state welfare expenditures mounted rapidly.

Amendments to the 1973 Renegotiation Act Extension Bill

In 1973 the Ways and Means Committee was again preparing a bill to extend the temporary national debt ceiling. When the bill reached the Senate Finance Committee, nongermane amendments were attached which included an increase in Social Security benefits of 5.9 percent, effective in January, and an increase in the SSI payment level, effective the following year.[63] Only three days before the debt ceiling was scheduled to fall to its permanent level the Senate thus added amendments to the bill that on their own stood little chance of presidential approval.

The House was unwilling to accept these revisions and, in conference, a compromise was reached to postpone the benefit increase until April and, further, to increase the ceiling on taxable earnings to help finance the added expenditures. On 29 June, to the surprise of Representative Mills and other House conferees, the House rejected the conference report, objecting to Senate tactics in adding the amendment to the debt-ceiling bill and to the large spending increase. Gerald Ford, House minority leader, objected that neither the House nor the Senate committees had held hearings during 1973 on amending Social Security.[64]

Not yet stumped, on 30 June the Senate attached the Social Security amendment to a pending Renegotiation Act extension bill which also required passage that day. In a second meeting conferees reached agreement on the Renegotiation Act bill and further postponed the Social Security benefit increase to June 1974.

As enacted, the Renegotiation Act Extension bill raised Social Security benefits 5.9 percent (effective June 1974), liberalized the retirement-earnings test, extended benefits to adopted grandchildren, and increased the ceiling on taxable earnings to $12,600 (January 1974).[65] Also, payments scheduled to be paid to Supplemental Security Income recipients were increased to $140 (June 1974), and a temporary extension was granted to Medicaid recipients so they could continue to maintain their eligibility for assistance despite the previous 20 percent increase in Social Security benefits.

Further Amendments in 1973

Due to the rapid rate of inflation Congress superseded these amendments before they went into effect. As enacted six months later, Social Security benefits were increased 11 percent in two stages: 7 percent in March 1974 and 4 percent in June 1974.[66] Without any change in tax rates, the ceiling on taxable earnings was further increased to $13,200 (January 1974). Also, the previous increase in SSI payments

Table 8.7. Benefits payable to selected beneficiaries, 1940-81

Year	Minimum benefit[a]	Average benefits paid				
		Retired worker		Disabled worker		
		Worker	Wife	Worker	Wife	Child
1940	$ 10	$ 23	$ 12	—	—	—
1950	20	44	24	—	—	—
1960	33	74	39	$ 90	$ 34	$ 30
1965	44	84	44	98	35	31
1970	64	120	61	131	43	37
1975	101	207	105	226	67	59
1981	170	385	194	413	122	123

Source: Social Security Administration, *Social Security Bulletin: Annual Statistical Supplement, 1977-79* (Washington, D.C.: U.S. Government Printing Office, 1980), pp. 142, 153; and Social Security Administration, *Monthly Benefit Statistic*, Note No. 4 (Washington, D.C.: Department of Health and Human Services, 14 Dec. 1981):1.
a. Eliminated for new recipients, beginning January 1981, under PL97-123.

was moved to January 1974, and a second increase was legislated for July 1974 ($146 for individual recipients, $219 for couples). Finally, the method of computing automatic cost-of-living adjustments was changed in order to reduce the time lag between the measurement of the rate of inflation and its reflection in monthly payments.

Visions of Crisis

Although there was almost no opposition expressed to these benefit increases during floor debate on the bill, concern over the future course of the program was finally beginning to surface. According to Representative Broyhill (R.-Va.), for example, as concern for the aged and disabled had mounted, benefits had been increased without regard for the long-range financial status of the trust funds. In his words, the trust funds were only "marginally sound," and payroll taxes had reached "acceptable limits."[67]

In a similar statement Representative Conable (R.-N.Y.) admitted that while he intended to vote for the benefit increase, his vote would probably be different if he really knew how repeated benefit increases were affecting the financial integrity of the system and the program's equity. "Frankly," he said, "nobody is worrying about where we are headed with Social Security. We would better not put off a careful review much longer if we are to face the next generation with as much sympathy as we are here showing to the last generation."[68] As revealed in Table 8.7, at a time when the retired worker's monthly tax payment could never have exceeded $60-$70 (having been less than $30 through 1970), he and his wife could retire with a monthly benefit in excess of $600 ($900).

The Damage That Had Been Done

Few citizens or politicians knew the damage that had been done to Social Security in 1972. In one fell swoop the new indexing provisions converted a system characterized by ad hoc growth to one of automatic and uncontrolled growth; converted the system from one in which economic growth and reserve accumulation preceded legislated expansion into one in which expansion, if properly financed, would necessitate economic growth; and converted a system that was—for a pay-as-you-go system—financed in a relatively conservative way into one that would be chronically underfinanced.

As crafted within the Social Security Administration, the 1972 indexing amendment did not index the system at all, where indexing implies immunizing a system to the effects of inflation. Instead, it provided an automatic benefit adjustment that would, during inflationary periods, lead to benefits that would tend to replace an increasing proportion of workers' preretirement earnings.

Immunizing the benefit side of the system from inflation would have required the worker's earnings history and the dollar amounts in the benefit formula—the nominal values relevant for determining the individual's benefit—to be indexed for changes in the price level. The 1972 amendments did nothing to index earnings, leaving them to be measured in nominal terms, and effectively tied the percentage benefit rates in the benefit formula to changes in the price level. This properly adjusted benefits for people already on the benefit rolls but seriously erred in the treatment of people coming onto the rolls in the future.

Such a system was, in fact, "double-indexed" and overadjusted for inflation.[69] First, the benefit formula would rise during periods of inflation so that any given earnings history would convert into a higher benefit. Second, because of the effect of inflation on nominal earnings, workers would be boosted into higher earnings and benefit brackets. The worker who simply earned his income during periods of more rapid inflation, for example, would have higher average earnings and thus would be entitled to a higher monthly benefit. Given the downward weighted benefit formula, the worker with low average earnings, earned during periods of rapid inflation (for example, the young disabled worker), could actually earn a monthly benefit from Social Security upon retirement higher than his income prior to retirement. Similarly, young workers with inflated nominal earnings could become eligible for benefits in excess of what older workers were eligible to receive based on a lifetime of taxes paid on the same or even higher real earnings.

The effect of the system on replacement rates—the worker's benefit relative to gross preretirement earnings—is illustrated below. As shown in Table 8.8, replacement rates were stable historically at approximately 30 to 40 percent, depending upon income class. Double-indexing, along with the 20 percent benefit hike enacted in 1972, would lead to the continuous rise in replacement rates among middle- and low-wage earners, to the point that the average worker retiring in 1981 would find 50 percent more of his preretirement earnings replaced by Social Security than did a similarly situated worker in 1972.

Table 8.8. Historical replacement rates
for workers retiring at age sixty-five[a]

	Earnings		
Year	Low	Average	High
1952	46%	31%	28%
1960	45	33	30
1970	42	34	29
1972	51	38	36
1974	64	41	33
1976	58	44	32
1978	63	47	35
1980	64	51	33
1981	69	55	33

Source: Office of Actuary, Social Security Administration.
a. Worker's benefit relative to gross preretirement
earnings. Worker and wife would be eligible for 50
percent larger benefit and would, therefore, have 50
percent higher replacement rate than shown.

How could such a system have been properly financed without continually
rising tax rates? After all, the only tax-side adjustment was the indexing of the
ceiling on taxable earnings. Crucially, real wages had to grow, and they had to
grow by nearly twice the rate of inflation. Financing the system on such an assumption not only took great confidence in the future of the economy (in order to make
seventy-five-year projections), but also necessitated a change in the Social Security
Administration's actuarial methodology. As recommended by a subcommittee of
actuaries and economists to the 1971 Advisory Council on Social Security, Social
Security actuaries abandoned the "level-wage" assumption previously used for estimating program costs, adopting instead the assumption of rising average covered
wages.[70] The old method, by consistently producing surpluses, lent itself to program expansion, but at least this expansion occurred after wage growth and surpluses materalized.

The bottom line, of course, is that not since 1972 has Social Security been
soundly financed. The year was followed immediately by two years in which real
wages actually fell. Over the decade real wage growth averaged just .2–.3 percent.
Within three years the trust funds faced insolvency in the near-term, and the system's deficit was in the trillion dollar range in the long-term. It would take Congress five years to "correct" the "technically flawed" indexing provision.

The detailed examination of the legislative history of Social Security between
1960 and 1973 provided in this chapter reveals the importance of an increasingly
complex program, a rising proportion of elderly and other beneficiaries in the
voting population, and the rapid growth of state welfare expenditures in reducing
effective taxpayer opposition to program redirection and growth and in conse-

quently increasing the political power of beneficiaries. Given these political developments, and independent of the interests of current and future taxpayers, a new and powerful alliance was formed between the bureaucracy and special-interest–beneficiary groups, on the one hand, and increasingly activist politicians, on the other hand, that found social insurance expansionism a mutually beneficial goal.

Part IV: Crisis in Social Security

Chapter 9. The Nature and Dimensions of Crisis

There are some who believe that we can meet this problem as we go by borrowing from the future to pay the costs. . . . They would place all confidence in the taxing power of the future to meet the needs as they arise. We do not share this view. We cannot safely expect future generations to continue to divert such large sums to the support of the aged unless we lighten the burdens upon the future in other directions. . . . We desire to establish this system on such sound foundations that it can be continued indefinitely in the future.

H. Morgenthau, secretary of the treasury, 1935[1]

As chief financial officer of the U.S. government, I am required to assess the soundness of the Social Security System. My assessment covers both the system's current financial position, and its ongoing viability. I have been shocked by what I have learned. . . the future prospects of the system as we know it are grim.

W. Simon, secretary of the treasury, 1976[2]

There is one stark and dramatic fact: old-age and survivors insurance will be bankrupt in October 1982.

D. Stockman, director, Office of Management and Budget, 1981[3]

Even the most casual observer of public affairs is aware that nothing about Social Security has been quite the same since 1972. The expansionism and legislative frenzy of election-year politics have been replaced by caution and legislative inaction. Unrestrained confidence and popularity have given way to concern and skepticism. Social Security has entered into a new phase, characterized most aptly by the word "crisis." Though described by program advocates as basically financial in nature, the crisis is—as indicated by the entire history of Social Security—much more significant than this, with sources that go well beyond unexpected and adverse economic and demographic trends. The crisis is political at base and will likely have profound consequences for the future of the system. Perhaps never again will people have the confidence in Social Security that it can, will, or even should be the system that prevails when today's youth retire. It is the purpose of this final chapter to examine the nature and dimensions of the crisis in Social Security—the natural conclusion of the evolution of the program.[4]

Financial Crisis in Social Security

An enormous deficit is surely the most visible manifestation of the crisis in Social Security. Estimated at $1.6 trillion for the cash benefit programs (old-age and survivors insurance and disability insurance) and nearly $6 trillion, inclusive of Medicare, the deficit is the amount by which legislated benefit promises are projected to exceed tax income.[5] Reflecting the inability of Social Security to perform satisfactorily as a pay-as-you-go system, the chronic deficits that have come to plague Social Security represent a deep-seated problem.

To continue operating as a self-sustaining, pay-as-you-go system, Social Security requires two elements: annual tax income sufficient to meet annual benefit payments (and administrative expenses) and a reserve fund capable of buffering unanticipated changes in revenues or expenditures. Should the fund fall below, say, 9-13 percent of annual expenditures, monthly benefits cannot be paid on time, even if annual revenues cover annual expenditures.[6] Should the fund be depleted entirely, any deficit resulting for that year is then the amount of benefits that cannot be paid at all. In this event the system would be insolvent.

The near-term financial condition of Social Security is summarized in Table 9.1 below. Based on the most recent projections of the Social Security Board of Trustees, the table presents the board's "best guess" of trust-fund operations during the next five years. As shown, revenues to the OASI trust fund, the largest of the three, are expected to be insufficient to cover expenditures this year (1981) and in each of the next four years. In 1985 alone the deficit, or the amount of benefits that cannot be paid, is expected to exceed $20 billion. Such substantial near-term deficits would cause assets to be depleted to critically low levels (below 9 percent) some time in late 1982, and within the following year the program would be insolvent. Without an infusion of additional tax revenues, a marked improvement in the economy, or else immediate cuts in benefits, that is, the OASI program would be unable to meet benefit payments "in a timely manner" beginning in late 1982. In the words of David Stockman, "The question before Congress is whether the 36 million Americans who currently depend on Social Security can count on *any check at all* less than 2 years hence."[7]

Congress, ever-inclined to deal with problems only when it must, took action in the fall of 1981 to postpone insolvency of the retirement fund into 1983. By permitting borrowing between the three social security trust funds, the retirement fund—drawing on the reserves of the disability and hospital insurance programs—will be kept afloat beyond the 1982 elections. On net, however, no new revenues were generated. Insolvency of the entire system is therefore likely as early as the end of 1983 or early in 1984.

Though immediately pressing, this problem pales by comparison to the one

Table 9.1. Near-term trust fund operations[a] (dollars in billions)

Year	Revenues	Expenditures	Net increase in funds	Funds at year end	Assets/ expenditures[b]
Old-age and survivors insurance					
1980	$105.8	$107.7	$ −1.8	$22.8	23%
1981	123.3	127.0	−3.7	19.1	18
1982	132.7	144.8	−12.1	7.0	13
1983	146.3	163.3	−17.0	−10.0	4
1984	160.1	183.3	−23.2	−33.2	−5
1985	181.1	203.8	−22.7	−55.9	−16
Disability insurance					
1980	13.9	15.9	−2.0	3.6	35
1981	17.0	18.1	−1.1	2.5	20
1982	23.9	19.6	4.3	6.8	13
1983	27.5	21.0	6.5	13.3	32
1984	31.0	22.8	8.2	21.5	58
1985	39.4	24.6	14.9	36.3	87
Hospital insurance					
1980	26.1	25.6	0.5	13.7	52
1981	35.3	29.6	5.7	19.5	46
1982	40.3	34.2	6.1	25.5	57
1983	45.2	39.8	5.5	31.0	64
1984	50.1	46.1	4.0	35.0	67
1985	56.9	53.5	3.4	38.4	65

Source: 1981 Annual Reports of the Board of Trustees of the Federal Old-Age and Survivors and Disability Insurance Trust Funds, and Federal Hospital Insurance Trust Fund (Washington, D.C.: U.S. Government Printing Offfice, 1981).
a. Intermediate assumptions. Prior to 1981 legislation contained in PL97-35 and PL97-123.
b. Funds at beginning of year as a percentage of expenditures during the year.

posed by the long-run financial condition of Social Security. Illustrated in Figures 1 and 2 are the board's long-run projections of expenditures and taxes for the cash benefit programs, each expressed as a fraction of taxable payroll in the economy.[8] Both their "intermediate" and "pessimistic" economic and demographic assumptions are presented. As illustrated, under intermediate assumptions a continuous increase in taxes during the coming decade ultimately provides a reserve cushion for the system in the mid-to-late 1990s, with surpluses projected to exist through the first decade of the next century. Beginning in 2005, however, a very sharp rise in expenditures is projected to occur, from roughly 10 percent to 16 percent during the following thirty years. By 2015 there would be annual deficits, and by 2025 the combined OASDI funds would be totally depleted and the system insolvent. Under the pessimistic assumptions the Board of Trustees actually projects that expenditures could reach 20 percent before 2030, rising to 28 percent by 2055. Excluding Medicare, this means that in order to finance Social Security cash benefits in 2055 alone, the combined employee-employer tax would have to be increased to 28 percent, or more than 15 percentage points above its scheduled rate of 12.4 percent.[9]

Remarkably, this is all projected to take place despite the fact that everyone faced a Social Security tax increase in five out of ten years during the 1970s, and

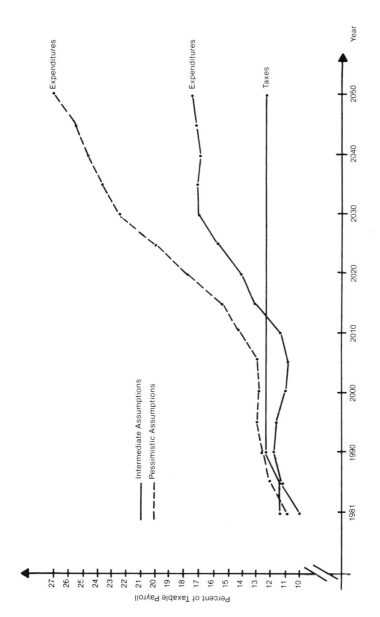

Figure 9.1. OASDI expenditures and taxes as a percent of taxable payroll: long-term projections (excludes Medicare).

Source: 1981 Annual Report of the Board of Trustees of the Federal OASDI Trust Funds, pp. 59–63, and Staff, Committee on Finance, U.S. Senate, *Social Security Financing*, Committee Print 97-98 (Washington, D.C.: U.S. Government Printing Office, 1981), pp. 38–41. These projections do not reflect the impact of the Omnibus Budget Reconciliation Bill of 1981 (P.L. 97-35).

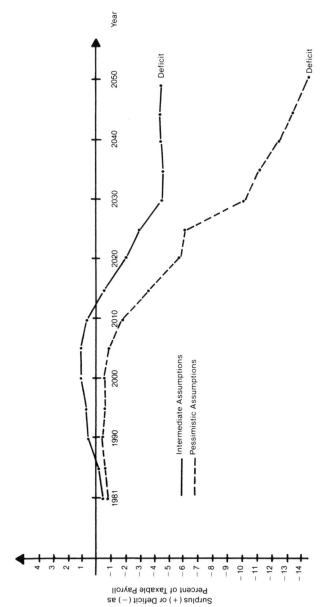

Figure 9.2. Annual OASDI surpluses and deficits as a percent of taxable payroll: long term projections (excludes Medicare).

Source: 1981 Annual Report of the Board of Trustees of the Federal OASDI Trust Funds, pp. 59–63, and, Staff, Committee on Finance, U.S. Senate, *Social Security Financing*, Committee Print 97-98 (Washington, D.C.: U.S. Government Printing Office, 1981), pp. 38–41. These projections do not reflect the impact of the Omnibus Budget Reconciliation Bill of 1981 (P.L. 97-35).

Table 9.2. Social Security taxes, 1979-90

| | | Employee and employer combined | | |
| | Ceiling on taxable earnings | Tax rate | | Anual maximum tax payment |
Year		OASDI	Total[b]	
1979	22,900	10.16%	12.26%	$2,808
1980	25,900	10.16	12.26	3,175
1981	29,700	10.70	13.30	3,950
1982	32,400	10.80	13.40	4,342
1983	35,400[a]	10.80	13.40	4,737
1984	38,700	10.80	13.40	5,186
1985	42,600	11.40	14.10	6,007
1986	46,200	11.40	14.30	6,607
1987	49,800	11.40	14.30	7,124
1988	53,400	11.40	14.30	7,636
1989	57,000	11.40	14.30	8,151
1990	60,600	12.40	15.30	9,272

Source: Social Security Financing, prepared by the Staff of the Committee on Finance, U.S. Senate, 97th Cong., 1st Sess. (Sept. 1981).
a. Beginning in 1982, subject to automatic wage indexing provisions. Projected on the basis of 1981 Board of Trustees' intermediate assumptions.
b. Includes tax rate for hospital insurance.

everyone faces another tax hike again in 1982, 1985, 1986, and 1990. Shown in Table 9.2 are the tax increases scheduled to go into effect under the 1977 amendments, which, it was claimed, would put the financial crisis to rest.

In isolation these deficit figures are staggering; they are even more so however, in relation to their evolution over time.PY As shown in Table 9.3, a long-run deficit was first officially announced by the Board of Trustees, and it was estimated at just one-third of one percent of taxable payroll. At that time expenditures as a fraction of taxable payroll (and thus Social Security taxes) were projected to peak at less than 13 percent. By 1975 the deficit had increased more than ten-fold, and as economic conditions continued to deteriorate, the first short-term deficits were also announced. Expenditures were expected to exceed income in each of the following years, and reserves were expected to be exhausted in the early 1980s. Estimated at over a trillion dollars, nearly half of the long-run deficit in the cash-benefit programs was attributable to the "technically flawed" method of indexing benefits enacted in 1972 that overresponded to inflation. By 1976 Congress had yet to "correct" this flaw, economic and demographic trends continued to deteriorate, the average deficit of the system rose to 8 percent, and it was actually projected that expenditures could reach 28.6 percent of taxable payroll. Together, these figures implied that there was an average shortfall in revenues over the next seventy-five years of more than 40 percent of expenditures!

In December of 1977 Congress finally responded. The automatically adjusted system that overresponded to inflation was "decoupled," and wage indexing of

Table 9.3. The evolution of long-term financial condition of OASDI trust funds, as projected by boards of trustees (as percent of taxable payroll)

Year	Intermediate assumptions						Pessimistic
	1973 Report	1974 Report	1975 Report	1976 Report	1977 Report	1981 Report[d]	1981 Report
Expenditures							
1990	10.0%	11.0%	11.2%	12.1%	12.3%	11.9%	12.7%
2010	10.3	12.7	14.1	16.0	16.6	11.6	14.0
2030	12.5	17.6	21.8	26.0	26.0	16.8	22.7
2050	12.6	17.9	22.4	28.6	26.9	16.7	26.9
Average expenditures[a]							
	11.0%	13.9%	16.3%	18.9%	19.9%	14.1%	18.5%
Average deficit[a]							
	.3%	3.0%	5.3%	8.0%	8.2%	1.8%	6.3%
Average revenue shortfall [c]							
	—[b]	21.6%	32.5%	42.3%	41.2%	13.0%	34.0%

Source: Alicia Munnell, *The Future of Social Security* (Washington, D.C.: The Brookings Institution, 1977), p. 100, and *1981 Annual Report of the Board of Trustees of the Federal OASDI Trust Funds*, pp. 59-63.
a. Over the seventy-five-year planning horizon.
b. Less than 1 percent.
c. The average deficit as a fraction of average expenditures.
d. Prior to 1981 legislation contained in PL97-35 and PL97-123.

earnings histories and the benefit formula was introduced. The long-term cost of the system was thereby reduced. It was reduced substantially less than possible, however, as the new system of indexing would still ensure real growth in initial benefit levels over time. On the tax side Congress legislated the largest peacetime tax increase in United States history—one now expected to generate over $400 billion of additional revenues before 1990.[11]

What was accomplished? The long-run cost of the system is now three percentage points higher—meaning we can now expect Social Security to require 3 percent more of our gross earnings—than anticipated in 1973 before the "crisis," and there is still an average shortfall of revenues estimated to be somewhere between 13 percent and 34 percent of expenditures! If the board's pessimistic assumptions turn out to be correct, the long-run deficit in the cash-benefit programs could be three and a half times higher than now expected, or approximately six times the national debt.

Even without grasping the intricacies of Social Security, these few figures make evident why the program faces a crisis of enormous proportions that has economic, political, and social dimensions that go well beyond actuarial deficits. On the one hand, the ability of the Social Security Administration and its Boards of Trustees to accurately predict the financial condition of the system is in serious doubt. The projections used to expand the program in 1972, for example, which showed the system was overfinanced, were based on a fertility-rate assumption that was already out of date and already 30 percent higher than actual experience.[12] The economic assumptions used throughout most of the 1970s were consistently optimistic and the system became progressively underfinanced. And what about congressional control? To facilitate the enactment of the 1972 amendments, Wilbur Mills, chairman of the Ways and Means Committee, had "assured" members of the House that more money would be taken in than paid out in each of the next seventy-five years. Just months later his statement was shown to be false and the system was reported to be in serious financial shape. It was not until December 1977, however, that legislative action was taken.

On the other hand, how willing and/or able will the people be now and in the future to perpetuate a system whose primary function is thought to be "income security"? Beneficiaries, the elderly and near-elderly, whose life savings decisions have already been made on the basis of a viable, ongoing public retirement system, are increasingly anxious about the continuation of the program and the security of their future incomes. On the other hand, taxpayers and other young people, whose current standards of living and lifetime savings decisions are being vitally determined by the program, now question the type of return they can expect to earn on their tax payments and how they might reasonably hedge against unforseen changes in the program in the years ahead. After all, if workers balked at the one-half percent tax increase that went into effect in January 1981, how might younger workers be expected to respond to a tax rate of 15 or 20 or 25 percent, and what kind of confidence can be had in a system that requires they impose such taxes in order for future retirees to be treated in a way comparable to current beneficiaries? Finally, what are the economic, political, and social ramifications of trying to tax workers at these rates, particularly in a country that is likely to have a considerably higher proportion of old people and beneficiaries than does the state of Florida today?[13]

Illustrated below are certain of the underlying demographic changes to be faced in the decades ahead. Under an intermediate set of assumptions used by Social Security actuaries, the proportion of elderly persons in the overall population is projected to increase by 50 percent in the next forty years, reaching 20 percent by the year 2055. The number of elderly persons per 100 working-age persons, referred to as the "dependency ratio," thus doubles from nineteen to thirty-eight. That is, in the year 2055 it is expected that there will be thirty-eight elderly persons for each one hundred persons between the ages of twenty and sixty-four.

Whereas these trends are a matter of demography (the interaction of declining mortality and fertility rates), it is the current structure of Social Security which pays benefits to retired people, disabled people, and to their dependents and survivors that produces the amplified effects in the last three columns in Table 9.4. As illustrated, the proportion of beneficiaries in the total population is projected to rise from 15 percent to 24 percent, ultimately producing a situation in which two workers would be needed to support each beneficiary. Should the pessimistic assump-

Table 9.4. Demography and Social Security, selected years

Year	Percent of population sixty-five & older	Age sixty-five and older per 100 working age	Percent beneficiaries in total population	Beneficiaries per 100 covered workers	Covered workers per beneficiary
Intermediate assumptions					
1980-81	11.1%	19.5	15.4%	31	3.3
1990	12.6	21.5	16.4	31	3.2
2000	12.2	22.6	16.9	32	3.1
2030	20.4	37.8	24.2	50	2.0
2055	20.4	37.8	24.4	50	2.0
Pessimistic assumptions					
1980-81	11.1%	19.5	15.4%	31	3.3
1990	13.0	22.1	16.8	32	3.1
2000	14.5	24.4	18.1	35	2.9
2030	25.6	47.5	29.7	63	1.6
2055	30.4	59.8	34.4	77	1.3

Source: 1981 Annual Report of the Board of Trustees of the Federal OASDI Trust Funds, pp. 60-61, 74-75.

tions come to bear, the current structure of Social Security implies that 34 percent of the United States population will ultimately be beneficiaries and there will be 1.3 taxpayers supporting each beneficiary!

That we are at a cross-roads with regard to Social Security policy is undeniable. Not surprisingly, therefore, answers are being sought to questions not heretofore posed by the public at large, at least not since the program's stormy beginnings. Every aspect of the program is coming under scrutiny, not the least of which is its possible economic side-effects.[14]

Economic Crisis in Social Security

After nearly a decade of unprecedented inflation, unemployment, and sluggish economic growth, the very high existing and projected Social Security taxes have brought to the foreground a set of economic concerns which to date have been largely ignored. In particular, does the mere existence of Social Security undermine the economic growth upon which its survival depends so critically? That is, by altering the individual's consumption-saving decision, his work-retirement decision, and his work-leisure decision, might the operation of Social Security actually destroy wealth in the United States? While measurement of the aggregate side-effects of Social Security—the costs less visible than rising tax rates—pose large econometric problems, the arguments put forth for their existence are straightforward and the possible welfare losses dramatic.

Social Security and the Retirement Decision of the Elderly

According to a number of recent studies, the effect of Social Security on the retirement decision of the elderly has been to substantially reduce their labor-force participation and to induce a marked trend toward earlier retirement.[15] The adjustments being made to the financial incentives created by the system are, like those for any transfer scheme, the result of efforts by individuals to gain benefit eligibility; their effects are, like those of any other economic distortion, to reduce the total amount of output in the economy. Rather than inducing a reduction in the unemployment rate, the long-run effect of a reduction in labor supply is a reduction in total resources in the economy devoted to market production, and thus a reduction in output per capita.

Social Security affects the work decision of the elderly or, in other words, alters their financial incentive to work in two ways. Most notably, upon reaching age sixty-five, the worker and his dependents are eligible to draw, on a permanent basis, monthly cash benefits. Benefits are also available at reduced rates at age sixty-two. Looking at the benefit side alone, since a higher income can thus be attained from any given amount of work supplied, the individual is motivated to work less in order to consume more leisure.

Given the high and increasing proportion of preretirement earnings replaced by Social Security, this "income effect" can be expected to be quite substantial. As illustrated in Table 9.5, a married worker turning sixty-five in 1981, who retires with average earnings, is eligible for an annual Social Security benefit of $10,218, or 82 percent of his preretirement earnings. The low-income worker with a spouse can actually quit work and receive a benefit equal to his preretirement income. Taking into account that benefits are not taxed while earnings are, that the cost of living typically falls with retirement (approximately 14 percent),[16] and that benefits are also available for dependent children, some workers can evidently improve their financial position by retiring while many others come very close to maintaining it. In a direct financial sense, this benefit effect encourages the elderly to consume more leisure.

The existence of the highly controversial retirement-earnings test, by contrast, discourages the elderly from continuing to work beyond the time of benefit eligibility by placing a high implicit tax on extra hours worked. To be more specific, the individual faces a benefit reduction of $1 for each $2 he or she earns over and above an initial exempt amount, currently $6,000 for those sixty-five and older. Applied to earned income alone, and until the worker attains the age of seventy-two, the earnings test thus implies an implicit marginal tax rate of 50 percent (on earnings in excess of $6,000), which together with the payroll tax and federal income tax, yields a full tax rate considerably higher, possibly in the vicinity of 80 percent.[17]

Considering the implicit tax provisions and the explicit benefit provisions of Social Security, the individual responsive to the financial incentives of the system

Table 9.5. Retirement benefits in relation to previous earnings for representative workers retiring at age sixty-five in 1981

	Prior-year earnings	Benefits		Ratio of benefits to prior-year earnings	
		Single worker	Worker with spouse	Single worker	Worker with spouse
Low	$6,448	$4,420	$6,630	69%	103%
Average	12,454	6,812	10,218	54	82
High	25,900	8,655	12,983	33	50

Source: Office of Actuary, Social Security Administration.

can evidently be expected to either fully retire from gainful activity, to retire at an earlier age, or, to the extent possible, adjust earnings by engaging only in part-time work. Each of these adjustments are observed to have taken place. Between 1954 and 1974, for example, the proportion of elderly men engaged in part-time activity doubled, and in 1974 two-thirds of all women and more than half of all men opted to draw Social Security benefits at age sixty-two rather than at sixty-five.[18] At the time Social Security was enacted, moreover, half of all men over sixty-five were in the labor force; today, with more than 90 percent of the elderly eligible to receive benefits, the proportion has fallen to one in five.[19] This historical decline in labor-force participation by the elderly has tended to be considerably more pronounced during periods of program expansion, with the decline being more significant in 1960 and 1970, for example, than in 1940 and 1950, and across age groups, more pronounced at age sixty-two and sixty-five than at any other ages.[20] Finally, coinciding with a sharp increase in replacement rates under Social Security during the 1970s, the labor-force participation rate among people over sixty actually fell 30 percent for men and 14 percent for women since 1960.[21]

While these trends may seem convincing in and of themselves, there are a number of reasons, such as the fact that the expansion of Social Security coincided with the spread of compulsory retirement rules, that isolating the effect of the system on the retirement decision merited further statistical investigation. In contrast to the early work done within the Social Security Administration, which typically found poor health and involuntary unemployment to be key determinants of the retirement decision,[22] more recent work done by Bowen and Finegan, Boskin, and Viscusi and Zeckhauser has empirically isolated a significant detrimental effect of Social Security on labor-force participation by the elderly.[23] According to Boskin's estimates, for instance, Social Security has actually increased the probability of retirement by as much as 40 percent, and accounted for nearly two-thirds of the decline in participation rates among the elderly.[24] Remarkably, the same people being induced to retire early have never had longer life expectancies, enjoyed better health, or otherwise had better earning capacity. The average sixty- to sixty-five-year-old today can expect to live another seventeen to twenty-two years.[25]

Of what importance is all of this? Distortions in the labor-supply decision of the elderly translate into aggregate welfare losses for society. A reduction in income earned through market transactions, moreover, tends to reduce self-sufficiency among the elderly and negate the attainment of income maintenance goals. That is, by limiting available sources of income and discriminating against those who have invested in human as opposed to nonhuman capital, the income of the elderly is lower than it otherwise would have been, and their welfare, especially that of the elderly poor, is thus reduced.[26] As one critic of the earnings test puts it, "It is a paradox of major proportions why here, as in other "welfare" programs, such high tax rates should strike the poor, whose major asset is their ability to earn in the labor market.[27] Finally, the effect of Social Security on the retirement decision inevitably exacerbates the long-run financial problems of the system. By increasing the proportion of elderly persons choosing retirement over work, the financial burden on workers implied by the sharp increase in the aged population after the turn of the century is made more severe and tax rates made necessarily higher.

Social Security, Capital Accumulation, and Economic Growth

Just as there is a growing consensus about the effects of Social Security on the labor-supply decision of the elderly, there is also a growing consensus among economists that the "pay-as-you-go" method of financing Social Security depresses private saving and capital accumulation. The most forceful statement of this view is provided by Martin Feldstein of Harvard University. Feldstein argues that, from the perspective of an individual contemplating his financial position during retirement, Social Security benefits accumulated through contributions to the payroll tax may be perceived as fully equivalent to the returns from titles to real, private capital. Both involve promises of future income; both, therefore, may be equally good means of transferring income from working years to retirement years. To the extent individuals view the government's promises to provide retirement benefits as a substitute for their own retirement savings, they will reduce private savings. Known as the "asset substitution effect," this reduction in private savings leads to a decline in capital accumulation and eventually to a lower level of real income.[28]

While Feldstein's basic argument is simple, his estimates of the likely effects are considerable—each dollar in taxes contributed to Social Security by the worker or his employer corresponds to an 87-cent reduction in private saving![29] Feldstein estimates that in 1976, for example, Social Security reduced personal saving by as much as $55 billion and thereby depressed total private saving by nearly 60 percent. The resulting decline in national income for that year translated into approximately $1,000 per family.

These possibly dramatic losses of income and consumption are part of the indirect costs of the pay-as-you-go nature of Social Security. They arise not because people are compelled to save for retirement but because under a pay-as-you-go system, current taxes approximate current revenues, and there is no substantial asset accumulation or investment of funds in real capital. These indirect costs thus arise because people are compelled to "invest" in unfunded government debt instead of higher yielding real capital.

Not surprisingly, Feldstein's work set off a major controversy, evoking challenges on both theoretical and empirical grounds. Two other effects of Social Security have thus been suggested as potential offsets for the asset substitution effect he described. The first of these is the "retirement effect." To the extent that Social Security induces earlier retirement among the elderly, it should also increase the rate at which people choose to save privately since they must make financial provision for a longer period of time.

Attempting to determine the importance of this, Alicia Munnell estimated that a substantial portion of the effect of asset substitution on private retirement saving was offset by the retirement effect.[30] Yet, using Munnell's work to estimate the effect on total personal saving (rather than on her concept of retirement saving), Feldstein still found a substantial net negative effect.[31] A series of other more recent studies by Munnell, Feldstein, and Feldstein and Pellechio have also tended to confirm Feldstein's original hypothesis of a depressing effect of Social Security.[32]

The second challenge to Feldstein's argument lies in the "intergenerational transfer effect" advanced by Robert Barro and based on the work of Gary Becker.[33] The underlying logic of their argument is also apparently simple. Social Security benefits increase the wealth of parents while the payroll taxes necessary to finance these benefits reduce the wealth of the parent's offspring. If parents wish their children to have some level of resources and make transfers or bequests in order to bring this about, then they will respond to Social Security by adjusting their private transfers to, in effect, "undo" the compulsory transfer inherent in the system. That is, parents will save the benefits they receive and then bequeath the benefits plus interest to their children so as to enable them to pay off their increased tax liability. This type of adjustment, it is argued, leads to no induced reduction in private savings as a result of the introduction or expansion of a pay-as-you-go system.[34]

While to date there have been no direct empirical tests of this effect, Barro uses tests based on time-series studies to conclude that Social Security does not depress private savings.[35] This finding is corroborated by Louis Esposito, of the Social Security Administration, in a survey of time-series studies dealing with this issue.[36]

These studies questioning the basic empirical findings of Feldstein have not gone unanswered.[37] A recent study by Michael Darby, which allowed for bequest savings as well as retirement savings, corroborated the earlier studies that Social Security greatly reduces private savings. Combining his estimate of the decline in the saving rate with alternative estimates of the program's effect on labor supply, Darby concludes that Social Security has probably reduced the owned capital stock from 5-20 percent and real income from 2-7 percent.[38] In an exhaustive survey of all the major studies dealing with the effects of Social Security on private saving, moreover, Gultekin and Louge conclude that the "weight of the evidence favors the view that the Social Security System depresses personal saving...Social Security contributions may reduce saving by roughly 80 cents per dollar."[39]

A thorough review of this literature and a careful weighing of results brings one full circle to Feldstein's initial position: Social Security adversely affects private savings. As these indirect costs of foregone income and consumption can only become more pronounced over time, with sharp increases in the rate of taxation, they can no longer be ignored in an evaluation of the program or in a consideration of its reform.

Problems of Fairness

Looming as large as issues of efficiency, of course, are the age-old issues of fairness in Social Security, both "intergenerational" and "intragenerational." The very essence of a pay-as-you-go system, constituting as it does a tax-transfer scheme between workers and retirees, is intergenerational transfers of income. Benefits to retirees and other beneficiaries are financed by taxes on workers who, in exchange, hold some expectation that the program will be perpetuated over time. Equity in treatment over time, or intergenerational equity, then refers to the way in which different generations of beneficiaries fare over time.

As discussed in Chapter 6, the implicit return on tax payments is very high for people who retire early in the life of a pay-as-you-go system and tends to decline as the program matures.[40] That is, benefit levels rise with economic growth, but as workers spend an increasing share of their time in covered employment, paying taxes over an increasing proportion of their working lives, the return they earn on taxes declines. Ultimately a "steady state" is reached when workers spend their entire working lives under the system. At this time the return earned falls to its long-run sustainable rate, which is equal to the growth rate of the taxable wage base. Whether or not Social Security provides a reasonable return is therefore determined by: (1) the time of retirement (the earlier in the life of the program, the better); and (2) the rate of growth of the taxable wage base relative to the market return on investments.

The nature and relative magnitude of this form of income redistribution is relatively noncontroversial—at least when discussing the history of the program. According to Robert Myers, for example, individuals retiring in the early decades in the life of Social Security probably paid for no more than 10-20 percent of their benefits, relative to what they might have been able to purchase privately, with the very first married retirees "purchasing" less than 1-2 percent of their expected lifetime benefits.[41] For recent retirees (1975), this "purchased" rate was estimated to have risen to 34 percent. Reporting quite similar results, Colin Campbell estimated that the cost-benefit ratio for married retirees in the 1960s was still in the vicinity of only 15-20 percent.[42] In the most recent such study Freiden, Leimer, and Hoffman utilized actual earnings histories of workers retiring between 1967 and 1970, finding that the average real return still exceeded 14 percent, substantially higher than after-tax real rates available to the typical worker.[43] In the words of Robert Ball, past commissioner of Social Security, the program has been a "tremendous bargain."[44]

But what about the future? How can young workers expect to fare? Given population and labor-force growth rates near zero and near universal coverage, the sustainable rate of return under Social Security is expected to be in the vicinity of only 1-2 percent, the rate of productivity growth.[45] Any further deterioration in economic or demographic trends, of course, would lead to an even lower rate. To the extent this is exceeded by the rate of interest in the economy, as determined by the productivity of investment, young workers are made worse off than if they had invested their tax payments in private capital markets.[46] Only if workers were able to count on an average return at least equivalent to that privately available and count on a continuation of the system, could the system be considered intergenerationally "fair." In this case the high early returns would not have been earned at the expense of later, possibly unborn generations. In Myers' estimate, however, if the employee is assumed to pay the full employer-employee tax, the average young worker today will not get his money's worth from Social Security.[47]

Partly because of this decline in the average return payable, issues of intragenerational fairness have become more significant in recent years. In particular, how have members of a given age-cohort fared relative to one another and how can they expect to fare over time? While the rate of return that a generation can earn is constrained by the rate of growth of the wage base, the individual in any particular income class, marital class, family group, or race faces no such constraint. His return may be positive, negative, or zero. This has nothing intrinsic to do with compulsory insurance, or even with a pay-as-you-go system but is simply a result of the redistributive aspects of the tax and benefit side of the program. On this score, debate has generally centered on the treatment of higher-income workers relative to lower-income workers—although the debate extends to the treatment of women versus men, families versus individuals, and working versus non-working elderly.[48]

According to a growing body of literature, the Social Security system is not neutral in its net redistributive effects, as an insurance program would be, but is highly progressive. In other words, considering both lifetime taxes and benefits, the system redistributes income from higher-income workers to lower-income workers. In the study previously mentioned by Freiden and others the average return to recent retirees with low earnings exceeded the mean return by 70 percent, whereas workers with higher earnings could expect a return 43 percent less than the mean.[49] According to a recent study by the Social Security Administration, moreover, workers just entering the system with very low earnings, regardless of age or family size, can expect a lifetime benefit to cost ratio of two to three times that of workers with maximum taxable earnings.[50] The same holds true for workers, both young and old, already under the system. Whereas the unmarried worker with high earnings entering the system today at age twenty-two to forty-seven is not expected to receive back the value of his tax payments (not even the employee's half of the tax), the same worker with very low earnings may receive benefits of up to two and a half times the value of his combined tax payments. The same holds true for workers who have already been in the system for some time, and the same degree of redistribution tends to hold between single retirees and retirees with dependents. According to another estimate by Myers, the young worker today with relatively high earnings may retire under Social Security having "purchased" up to 218 percent of his expected lifetime benefits.[51]

From an individual equity perspective, Social Security is an inappropriate vehicle for such intragenerational income redistribution and the resulting transfers are widely believed to be inequitable. Viewing the function of Social Security to be like that of a private annuities program that provides retirement income to workers in exchange for their contributions, an equitable system would distribute benefits that were proportional to individual tax payments, and expected returns would be identical for different taxpayers in the same generation. Income transfers to the poor would lie within the realm of an explicit, generally financed, means-tested program.

It is from the "social adequacy" perspective that intragenerational redistribution within the Social Security system has long been defended. One must certainly wonder, however, how a ceiling on taxable earnings which produces a regressive tax structure can be defended on social adequacy grounds, or how the absence of a means-test, or the full payment of benefits to elderly persons as long as they derive their incomes from interest, rents, dividends, and royalties and not from work can be defended. According to a projection by Joseph Pechman, noted tax authority, Social Security would be the highest tax paid by two-thirds of the nation's income recipients in 1977, and $2.5 billion would be collected from people officially classified as living in poverty.[52] That is, even from a social adequacy perspective, as long as the system is basically operated as an earnings-related "insurance" program, Social Security will be an improper vehicle for redistribution.

Evidently, the legislative and bureaucratic effort to maintain the semblance of individual equity and yet attain social adequacy has produced a program that is satisfactory on neither count and that in reality is characterized by a considerable degree of discrimination among participants of all ages. As stated most succinctly many years ago by James Buchanan, the system is "the worst of both worlds," without defense on the basis of individual equity criteria and sorely failing on social adequacy grounds.[53] It truly is a program "in search of an explanation."[54]

The Sources of Conflict

Today, as retired couples can enjoy annual benefits of more than $12,000, the system rapidly approaches a "mature" state—the time when these transitional financial gains have been fully captured by beneficiaries through unsustainable rates of increase in the taxable wage base. With population growth declining, the real return on tax payments then falls, approaching the rate of growth of labor productivity, or only 1 or 2 percent. And, since Social Security possesses no "money machine" capable of producing bargains for everyone,[55] young, higher-income workers face a certain prospect of negative returns.

Without radical reform conflict is clearly in store. And, despite the much-debated question of whether social insurance is or is not like private insurance in terms of contractual obligations and necessary funding requirements, it is on precisely this score that social insurance is identical to an unfunded private insurance program. The simple maturing of the system lowers returns and inevitably produces conflict. This is only made more pronounced by economic and demographic trends that further depress returns. Young participants desire to leave the system in search of more lucrative investments, and older participants, fearing for their benefits, desire to perpetuate the system. Whereas in a private competitive setting such a scheme would tend to terminate with the voluntary exit of the young, a social insurance system can perpetuate itself—but only as long as the majority chooses to use the powers of the state to do so. The relentless truth is that coercion cannot eliminate the desires of participants or the tension created by declining returns. Coercion simply determines in whose favor the conflict is resolved—at least for the time being.

In all, the lessons from history seem abundantly clear: the existing crisis in Social Security is decidedly not financial in nature, it is decidedly not "unexpected," and it rests squarely in the political and economic failures resulting from a loss of individual choice in 1935. The crisis is at base political, lodged in the institutional weaknesses of the program. If nothing else this crucial period in the history of Social Security should foster the development of competing ideas about the crisis, so necessary for rational decision-making in the future.

Toward Meaningful Reform

From a historical perspective, the shortcomings of most current reform proposals can be seen to lie in a misunderstanding of the sources of crisis and thus in the rigid adherence to the present political-monopolistic framework of Social Security. For those who maintain the view that the problem is fundamentally financial, for example, a view typified by Robert Ball, elimination of imbalances in fiscal accounts, possibly coupled with "refinements" in the distribution of benefits, is the solution.[56] The unresolved political problem is then simply which tax shall be utilized to raise revenues and how shall the system's "integrity" be restored. From this camp, which includes lobby groups representing organized labor and the elderly, come the proposals to universalize coverage, increase the ceiling on taxable earnings, increase the "employers' share" of the payroll tax, "borrow" from one of the other trust funds or, more "radically," to supplement Social Security taxes with funds from general revenues or from a value-added tax.[57] For them "reform" involves an expansion of the system, possibly to yet uninsured risks, while maintaining fiscal balance.

At polar extremes politically are those who argue that the key problems in Social Security are the program's size and complexity. Their proposed solutions then lie in such adjustments as reductions in benefit rates or beneficiary categories, or increases in age requirements.[58] For them, "reform" constitutes a shrinking of the program as we know it. Yet a third major camp today holds the view that the problem is basically economic in nature and that the solution lies in eliminating the distortions in labor markets, for example, by using an alternative tax form, or the distortions in capital markets by building up a large Social Security reserve fund. The tax decision or fund decision, for them, is synonymous with a resolution to optimal supply of labor and optimal supply of capital issues.[59]

That none of these constitute "the" problem is suggested not only by the program's history but also by the fact that Social Security represents a world-wide crisis[60] and one that exists despite wide international variation in programs (around the same central monopolistic framework). Everywhere the issue that must be faced in the decades ahead is whether or not social security systems chosen and defined at the turn of the century and the functions they perform are any longer consistent with current aspirations for ourselves and for future generations. Regardless of how taxes and benefits are distributed, do citizens intend to devote an increasing share of economic resources to this particular public activity, and, if so, is Social Security the proper vehicle? Whether or not Social Security has provided income security in the past is undeniable. Whether or not it can continue to do so is the question at hand.

Compulsory insurance, of course, in and of itself, certainly need not be a system in which a growing proportion of people are, or perceive themselves to be, worse off than in its absence. To the contrary, people show a proclivity to voluntarily submit themselves to systems that coerce them to save some minimum amount during their working years to ensure they had accumulated some minimum amount of income at the time of retirement. If one accepts the premise that there is a proper role for the federal government in so compelling people or at the least accepts the political infeasibility of abandoning altogether a system to which there exist roughly $5 trillion of outstanding benefit promises, institutional reform designed to reinstill the elements of a "positive-sum game" into Social Security seems clearly in order. The problem becomes one of designing a system of "income security" without sacrificing economic prosperity and without sacrificing the rights of younger generations. Synonymously, the problem is one of designing a system that protects the rights of individuals of all ages to the fruits of their savings and fosters the economic growth from which all can derive benefits. As forcefully argued by Hayek in the 1950s, Campbell and Buchanan in the 1960s, and Roger Miller in the 1970s, reform, from this perspective, implies the introduction of choice, voluntarism, and competition into the provision of Social Security—the only effective constraints on the future course of the program.[61]

But how can the transition to choice and competition be made without threatening the continuation of outstanding benefit promises? At least conceptually, one possibility is to accumulate a funded system of Social Security so as to place the public supplier on a more equal footing with private insurers.[62] Since, under a funded system, there is no significant relationship between the total number of participants and individual benefit levels, the accumulation of a fund would assure all those who wished to remain under the public system that their benefit payments would be met even if the number of younger workers subject to the tax declined. Once funded, therefore, the need to coerce others to remain in the system simply to protect one's own expected income would be eliminated. Tax payments would truly constitute "contributions" and to the extent that there were efficiency gains to the government producing retirement and survivor income, these gains would be clearly observed through favorable premium-policy conditions, and the government would remain a viable competitor. During the transition period the accumulating fund derived from quite sizable tax increases would require the protection of constitutional amendment and would require investment in either outstanding government debt or private (international or domestic) debt.[63]

Alternatively, the Social Security program could be terminated as of a chosen date, with benefit entitlements earned before that time being honored and no new benefit entitlements being earned.[64] Henceforth, individuals would be required to save a stated percentage of their income each year (possibly an age-graded amount) through private savings and insurance institutions. Based on the view that virtually no one has escaped the benefits of Social Security—either as a direct beneficiary, as a child of a beneficiary, or as a beneficiary of artificially depressed welfare expenditures—the remaining liability would be met by an increase in some general tax levy such as the federal income tax.

Under either scenario the adjustment process would be very long, several decades at least, and the huge unfunded liability of the system would have to be squarely faced as being composed of not just a saving component, the part "earned" in an actuarial sense, but also a welfare component and an unsustainable intergenerational transfer component. Because of the latter two components, the size of the liability would undoubtedly warrant a reduction in scheduled benefits—whether uniformly and across-the-board, or inversely related to age, or borne entirely by secondary beneficiary groups.

In the new environment private institutions would assume the saving-insurance function of Social Security, and public institutions would be expanded to assume its welfare function. The role of the federal government vis-à-vis insurance could then be altered dramatically toward the fostering of improvements in private markets, for instance, by issuing a price-indexed bond which would enable private insurers to index annuity payments, or by assuming a role in educating the public on alternative policies offered, or possibly by removing existing regulations that mandate redistribution in favor of directly subsidizing such activities.[65] To deal with the ex-ante problem of inadequate savings among poor workers, some type of subsidy scheme could be introduced whereby the worker's savings would be matched by a government contribution, and to deal with the ex-post problem of poverty in old age, the federal Supplemental Security Income program would guarantee a basic level of support for the elderly poor—a level that could certainly be increased. In any event, all such redistributive or welfare activities would be made explicit and financed by general government revenues.

While the problems of transition would evidently be significant, the various means that might be chosen to "privatize" Social Security seem to be considerably less important, as a first step, than understanding the likely consequences of doing so. Not the least important, real capital accumulation would replace the accumulation of an "implicit and covert national debt."[66] Free choice for participants would then eliminate the potential for discriminatory and involuntary income redistribution. A lower bound on returns would thereby be introduced which, being determined by the productivity of investment in the economy, would certainly exceed the return ultimately payable under the current system. Voluntary customer flows and differential profit-and-loss positions of firms would provide highly visible signs of performance and serve as effective means of monitoring both private and public suppliers. Competition for customers within a flexible system of nongovernmental organizations, moreover, would foster experimentation which, in turn, would foster yet unanticipated innovations in financial markets.[67] In short, in an institutional environment in which people were permitted free choice between competing private and possibly public suppliers of retirement income, everyone could be assured of "income security."

That the suggestion to introduce competition into the provision of Social Security constitutes a truly radical reform proposal today only attests to the extent to which Social Security has been redirected since its inception in 1935, and the extent to which the initial choice of bureaucratic supply has tended to put, in the words of Hayek, a "strait jacket on evolution."[68] When the Clark amendment was offered in 1935 to permit individuals free choice between the new public program and private suppliers, the private pension industry was in its infancy, doing something less than a tenth of the business it does today.[69] The amendment nevertheless won majority approval in the Senate and went on to stalemate congressional conferees. Failure to reconsider such "radical" reform today, when alongside the compulsory system there stands a private system of pension plans covering more than thirty million employees, may well mean the acceptance of the "ineluctable lesson of recent events that Social Security can no longer be a positive sum game where everybody wins and nobody loses."[70]

Notes

Chapter 1. The Political Economy of Government Growth

1. "Big Government," *Newsweek*, 15, Dec. 1975, p. 37.

2. On the magnitude and meaning of these deficits, see, for example, *1975 Annual Report of the Board of Trustees of the Federal Old-Age and Survivors Insurance and Disability Insurance Trust Funds*, House Doc. No. 94-135 (Washington, D.C.: U.S. Government Printing Office, 6 May, 1975); and A. Haeworth Robertson, "OASDI: Fiscal Basis and Long-Run Cost Projections," *Social Security Bulletin*, vol. 40, no. 1 (Jan. 1977): 25.

3. William Simon, "How to Rescue Social Security," *Wall Street Journal*, 3 Nov. 1976.

4. Don Wortman, cited in "Social Security Amendments of 1977: Legislative History and Summary of Provisions," *Social Security Bulletin*, vol. 41, no. 3 (March 1978): 4.

5. Cited in ibid., p. 3.

6. *1982 Annual Report of the Board of Trustees of the Federal Old-Age and Survivors Insurance and Disability Insurance Trust Funds* (transmitted to Congress 1 April, 1982); *1982 Annual Report of the Board of Trustees of the Federal Hospital Insurance Trust Fund* (transmitted to Congress 1 April, 1982); and *Staff Data and Materials Related to Social Security Financing*, CP97-8, prepared by Staff for the Committee on Finance (Washington, D.C.: U.S. Government Printing Office, Sept. 1981).

7. *Social Security Financing*.

8. F. A. Hayek, "History and Politics," in *Capitalism and the Historians*, ed. F. A. Hayek (Chicago: Univ. of Chicago Press, 1954), pp. 1-2.

9. Martha Derthick, *Policymaking for Social Security* (Washington, D.C.: The Brookings Institution, 1979), is an excellent and comprehensive book on the history and politics of Social Security. It differs from the present study by focusing on the more recent history, on the people and personalities, and on the politics of Social Security as unique from other government programs. Endeavoring to provide insight into the general process of government growth, this study, by contrast, focuses on the political and fiscal institutions that conditioned outcomes, especially at such key times as emergence in 1935 and reform in 1939.

10. For several informative sources on the growth of government and nonmarket controls in the United States, see Thomas E. Borcherding, "One Hundred Years of Public Spending, 1870-1970," in *Budgets and Bureaucrats: The Sources of Government Growth*, ed. Thomas E. Borcherding (Durham, N.C.: Duke Univ. Press, 1977), pp. 19-44; Roger A. Freeman, *The Growth of American Government: A Morphology of the Welfare State* (Stanford, Calif.: Hoover Institution Press, 1975); and Jonathan R. T. Hughes, *The Governmental Habit: Economic Controls from Colonial Times to the Present* (New York: Basic Books, 1977).

11. For a general discussion of these two views and the need for integration, see James M. Buchanan, "Why Does Government Grow?" in *Budgets and Bureaucrats*, ed. Borcherding, pp. 3-18, and "Public Finance and Public Choice," *National Tax Journal* 28 (Dec. 1975): 383-94; Peter Aranson and Peter Ordeshook, "Alternative Theories of the Growth of Government and Their Implications for Constitutional Tax and Spending Limits," in *Tax and Expenditure Limitations*, ed. Helen F. Ladd and T. Nicholas Tideman (Washington, D.C.: The Urban Institute Press, 1981), pp. 143-72, and Richard Musgrave, "Leviathan Cometh—or Does He?" in *Tax and Expenditure Limitations*, ed. Ladd and Tideman pp. 77-117. See also Thomas E. Borcherding, "The Sources of Growth of Public Expenditures in the United States: 1902-1970," in *Budgets and Bureaucrats*, ed. Borcherding, pp. 45-70.

12. For a selection of papers that view political outcomes as being determined simply by the aggregation of citizen-voter demands through majority voting processes, see Thomas E. Borcherding and Robert T. Deacon, "The Demand for the Services of Non-Federal Governments," *American Economic Review* 62 (Dec. 1972): 891-901; Theodore C. Bergstrom and Robert P. Goodman, "Private Demands for Public Goods," *American Economic Review* 63 (June 1973): 280-96; William J. Baumol, "Macroeconomics of Unbalanced Growth: The Anatomy of the Urban Crisis," *American Economic Review* 57 (May 1967): 415-26; and Winston C. Bush and Robert J. Mackay, "Private Versus Public Sector Growth: A Collective Choice Approach," in *Budgets and Bureaucrats*, ed. Borcherding, pp. 188-210; the former two being empirical studies of the demand for various public services, the latter two being theoretical models of the growth of government.

13. See James M. Buchanan, *The Demand and Supply of Public Goods* (Chicago: Rand McNally 1968), and *The Limits to Liberty: Between Anarchy and Leviathan* (Chicago: The Univ. of Chicago Press, 1974), pp. 17-52; James M. Buchanan and Gordon Tullock, *The Calculus of Consent: The Logical Foundation of Constitutional Democracy* (Ann Arbor: Univ. of Mich. Press, 1962); and Lance E. Davis and Douglass C. North, *Institutional Change and American Economic Growth* (Cambridge: Cambridge Univ. Press, 1971).

14. For a statement of the view that politicians and bureaucrats are perfectly constrained by political competition, see George Stigler, "Economic Competition and Political Competition," *Public Choice* 13 (Fall 1972): 91-106.

15. For an alternative view from a constitutional perspective, see Buchanan and Tullock, *The Calculus of Consent*, pp. 189-99. An extreme myopia-view of the function of Social Security was expressed by Paul Webb, regional commissioner for the Social Security Administration, when he said "Critics make the unlikely assumption that we humans, if we did not pay into Social Security, would wisely save our money or buy a private insurance policy of high value." Cited by Warren Shore in *Social Security: The Fraud in Your Future* (New York: Macmillan Publishing Co., 1975), p. 97. See also, Paul A. Samuelson, "Optimum Social Security in a Life-Cycle Growth Model," *International Economic Review* 16 (Oct. 1975): 539-44.

16. For example, Abraham Epstein, an early social insurance advocate, cited the failure of private insurance markets as one of several key reasons for enacting compulsory old-age insurance in *Insecurity— A Challenge to America: A Study of Social Insurance in the United States and Abroad* (New York: Harrison Smith and Robert Haas, 1933), pp. 116-40. Two other rationalizations for Social Security are the potential gains from a pay-as-you-go system, and the social gains from an income redistribution program. The former rationalization is not discussed here partly because the system was not designed to be pay-as-you-go in 1935, and partly because it is only under a specific and unlikely set of economic circumstances that society can be made better off under a pay-as-you-go system than a funded system. The latter is not a reason for creating a compulsory "insurance" program. These arguments are examined in some detail in Chapters 3-5.

17. Even taking into account such factors as income, scheme of financing, political system, and proportion of elderly population, empirical studies of the determinants of Social Security expenditures cannot fully account for the variation among countries. Age of the system invariably enters the equations significantly and positively. See Joseph A. Pechman, Henry Aaron, and Michael Taussig, *Social Security: Perspectives for Reform* (Washington, D.C.: The Brookings Institution, 1968), pp. 300-304; and Harold L. Wilensky, *The Welfare State and Equality: Structural and Ideological Roots of Public Expenditures* (Berkeley: Univ. of Calif. Press, 1975), pp. 135-39.

18. The seminal works applying economic theory to bureaucracy are Gordon Tullock, *The Politics of Bureaucracy* (Washington, D.C.: Public Affairs Press, 1965); Anthony Downs, *Inside Bureaucracy*, Rand Corporation Research Study (Boston: Little, Brown, 1967); William A. Niskanen, *Bureaucracy and Representative Government* (New York: Aldine Atherton, 1971); and Ludwig von Mises, *Bureaucracy* (New Rochelle, N.Y.: Arlington House, 1969). For a survey of more recent models, see Robert J. Mackay and Carolyn L. Weaver, "Monopoly Bureaus and Fiscal Outcomes: Deductive Models and Implications for Reform," in *Policy Analysis and Deductive Reasoning*, ed. G. Tullock and R. Wagner (Lexington, Mass.: D. C. Heath, 1978).

19. Herbert Kaufman, *Are Government Organizations Immortal?* (Washington, D.C.: The Brookings Institute, 1976), p. 81.

20. See Niskanen, *Bureaucracy and Representative Government*; Richard E. Wagner, "Supply Side Aspects of the Theory of Local Government: Owners, Managers, and Take-Over Bids" (mimeographed, Va. Polytechnic Institute and State Univ., 1975); and Jack A. Stockfish, "Analysis of Bureaucratic Behavior: The Ill-Defined Production Process" (Working Paper, The Rand Corporation, Santa Monica, Calif., 1975).

21. On political ignorance as a rational response to costly and imperfect information, see Downs, *An Economic Theory of Democracy*, pp. 207-59; and Gordon Tullock, *Toward a Mathematics of Politics* (Ann Arbor: Univ. of Mich. Press, 1967), pp. 100-114. For a discussion of the different incentives to utilize and accumulate information in the private and public sector, see Robert Staaf, "Limits to Rational Ignorance: Private vs. Collective Markets" (mimeographed, Va. Polytechnic Institute and State Univ., 1976). On the impact of uncertainty on information manipulation by public suppliers, see Tullock, *Toward a Mathematics of Politics*, pp. 100-132; and Randall Bartlett, *Economic Foundations of Political Power* (New York: The Free Press, 1973), pp. 70-75.

22. For discussions of monitoring or agent-principal problems in the private sector directly applicable

to an analysis of these problems in the public sector, see Armen Alchian and Harold Demsetz, "Production, Information Costs, and Economic Organization," *American Economic Review* 62 (Dec. 1972): 777-95; Henry Manne, "Some Theoretical Aspects of Share Voting," *Columbia Law Review* 64 (1964); Armen Alchian, "Corporate Management and Property Rights" in *Economic Policy and the Regulation of Corporate Securities*, ed. H. Manne (Washington, D.C.: American Enterprise Institute 1969), and Michael Jensen and William Meckling, "Theory of the Firm: Managerial Behavior, Agency Costs and Ownership Structure," *Journal of Financial Economics* 3 (Oct. 1976): 305-60. For application of these types of arguments to the public sector and the control of bureaucracy, see Roland McKean, "Divergences Between Individual and Total Costs Within Government," *American Economic Review* 54 (May 1964): 243-49, and "Property Rights within Government, and Devices to Increase Governmental Efficiency," *Southern Economic Journal* 34 (Oct. 1972): 177-86; and Wagner, "Supply Side Aspects of the Theory of Local Government."

23. See, for instance, William A. Niskanen, "Bureaucrats and Politicians," *Journal of Law and Economics* 17 (Dec. 1975): 617-43; and Niskanen, *Bureaucracy and Representative Government*.

24. Niskanen presents the first analytical model of the monopoly practices of bureaus in *Bureaucracy and Representative Government*, and this model is extended and tested in Thomas Romer and Howard Rosenthal, "Political Resource Allocation, Controlled Agendas and the Status Quo," *Public Choice* 33 (Winter 1978): 27-43; "Bureaucrats vs. Voters: On the Political Economy of Resource Allocation by Direct Democracy," *Quarterly Journal of Economics* 93 (Nov. 1979): 563-87. For models of other monopoly practices by bureaus, see Arthur Denzau and Robert J. Mackay, "A Model of Benefit and Tax Share Discrimination by a Monopoly Bureau," *Journal of Public Economics* 13 (1980): 341-68; Robert J. Mackay and Carolyn L. Weaver, "On the Mutuality of Interests Between Bureaus and High Demand Review Committees: A Perverse Result," *Public Choice* 34 (1979): 481-91; Mackay and Weaver, "Agenda Control by Budget Maximizers in a Multi-Bureau Setting," *Public Choice* 36, no. 4 (Winter 1981): 325-52; Mackay and Weaver, "Commodity Bundling and Agenda Control in the Public Sector" *Quarterly Journal of Economics* (forthcoming); and Richard E. Wagner and Warren E. Weber, "Competition, Monopoly, and the Organization of Government in Metropolitan Areas," *Journal of Law and Economics* 18 (Dec. 1975): 661-89.

25. For two case studies of the impact of bureaucracy on the growth of public education, see Robert J. Staaf, "The Growth of the Educational Bureaucracy: Do Teachers Make a Difference?" in *Budgets and Bureaucrats*, ed. Borcherding, pp. 148-68; E. G. West, "The Political Economy of American Public School Legislation," *Journal of Law and Economics* 10 (Oct. 1967): 101-28. See Robert Mackay and Joseph Reid, "On Understanding the Birth and Evolution of the SEC," *Regulatory Reform in an Atmosphere of Crisis: Current-Day Implications of the Roosevelt Years*, ed. G. Walton (New York: Academic Press, 1979), for an application of this perspective to the history of the Securities and Exchange Commission.

26. For such a view see F. A. Hayek, *The Constitution of Liberty* (Chicago: Univ. of Chicago Press, 1960), pp. 285-305.

27. These differences are discussed more fully in Buchanan, *The Limits to Liberty.*

28. On this transformation of government, see Douglass C. North, "Structure and Performance: The Task of Economic History," *Journal of Economic Literature* 16 (Sept. 1978): 968-69.

29. Peter H. Aranson and Peter C. Ordeshook, "A Prolegomenon to a Theory of the Failure of Representative Democracy," in *American Re-evolution*, ed. R. D. Auster and B. Sears (Tucson: Univ. of Ariz., Department of Economics, 1977); Kenneth Goldin, "Price Externalities Influence Public Policy," *Public Choice* 20 (Fall 1975): 1-10; Richard Auster, "The GPITPC and Institutional Entropy," *Public Choice* 19 (Fall 1974): 77-83; and Gordon Tullock, "The Paradox of Revolution," *Public Choice* 11 (Fall 1971): 89-99.

30. See George Stigler, "The Theory of Economic Regulation," *The Bell Journal of Economics and Management Science* 2 (Spring 1971): 3-21; Richard Posner, "Theories of Economic Regulation," *The Bell Journal* 2 (Autumn 1974): 335-58; Sam Peltzman, "Toward a More General Theory of Regulation," *Journal of Law and Economics* 19 (Aug. 1976): 211-40; and Robert McCormick and Robert Tollison, *Politicians, Legislation, and the Economy: An Inquiry into the Interest-Group Theory of Government* (The Hague: Martinus Nijhoff, 1981).

31. See, for instance, Posner, "Theories of Economic Regulation," p. 337; Isaac Ehrlich and Richard Posner, "An Economic Analysis of Legal Rule Making," *Journal of Legal Studies* 111 (Jan. 1974): 257-86; and Peltzman, "Toward a More General Theory of Regulation."

32. See Posner, "Theories of Economic Regulation," pp. 338-39.

33. Hayek, *The Constitution of Liberty*, p. 296. Other attempts to integrate the demand and supply side include Douglas C. Hartle, *A Theory of the Expenditure Budgetary Process*, Ontario Economic Council

Research Studies (Toronto: Univ. of Toronto Press, 1976); Bartlett, *The Economic Foundations of Political Power*; and Albert Breton, *The Economic Theory of Representative Government* (Chicago: Aldine, 1974).

34. Buchanan, *Limits to Liberty*, p. x.

35. For alternative views of institutional change, see Davis and North, *Institutional Change and American Economic Growth*; Downs, *Inside Bureaucracy*; Jonathan R. T. Hughes, "Transference and Development of Institutional Constraints Upon Economic Activity" (mimeographed, Northwestern Univ., 1976); R. M. Hartwell, "The Social Inquiry Trap" (presented at Liberty Fund Seminar in Modern Economic History, July 1979), and Joseph Reid, "Understanding Political Events in the New Economic History," *Journal of Economic History* (June 1977). Whereas Downs examines bureau growth from the supply side, North and Davis and Hughes examine the emergence and growth of government institutions and nonmarket controls almost exclusively from the demand side. Hartwell presents an interesting mix in which government evolves out of social inquiry by proponents of government action, and Reid presents a preliminary discussion of the importance of attitudes and institutions on political outcomes. For a retrospective evaluation of these views, see North, "Structure and Performance."

36. For elaboration and a discussion of the importance of the reformer's focus on the ills of society, see Hartwell, "The Social Inquiry Trap."

37. Works stressing economic crises on government intervention include James M. Buchanan and T. N. Tideman, "Gasoline Rationing and Market Pricing: Public Choice in Political Democracy" (mimeograph, Va. Polytechnic Institute and State Univ., 1974); Hughes, *The Governmental Habit*; and Jonathan R. T. Hughes, "American Capitalism and Social Control" (mimeograph, Northwestern Univ., 1977).

38. See Downs, *Inside Bureaucracy*; Ehrlich and Posner, "An Economic Analysis of Legal Rule Making"; and Posner, "Theories of Economic Regulation," pp. 339-40.

39. Although their demand-side explanation is quite different, Davis and North make this point in *Institutional Change and American Economic Growth*, p. 44.

40. Hughes, *The Governmental Habit*, p. 8.

41. See James M. Buchanan, "Individual Choice in Voting and the Market," *Journal of Political Economy* 62 (Aug. 1954): 334-43; Downs, *An Economic Theory of Democracy*, pp. 36-50, 82-95; Tullock, *The Mathematics of Politics*, pp. 100-114; and Staaf, "Limits to Rational Ignorance," for discussions of the logic of rational ignorance in political settings.

42. For an early discussion of "political entrepreneurship," see Downs, *An Economic Theory of Democracy*, pp. 164-206. See also, Richard E. Wagner, "Pressure Groups and Political Entrepreneurs: A Review Article," *Papers on Non-Market Decision-Making* 1 (1966): 161-70; and Norman Frohlich, Joe A. Oppenheimer, and Oran R. Young, *Political Leadership and Collective Goods* (Princeton, N.J.: Univ. Princeton Press, 1971).

43. Statement by Senator Clark (R.-Mo.), *Cong. Rec.* 9627 (1935).

44. For a clear statement of the importance of "marketing," "packaging," and "labeling" legislation, see Michael Pertschuk, "A Law to Call Your Own" (portion of a proposed manual for freshman Senators, prepared for the Commission on the Operation of the Senate, 1975).

45. See Tullock, "The Paradox of Revolution"; Auster, "The GPITPC and Institutional Entropy," pp. 77-83; and Aranson and Ordeshook, "A Prolegonemon to a Theory of the Failure of Representative Democracy."

46. Douglas C. Hartle, *A Theory of the Expenditure Budgetary Process*, Ontario Economic Council Research Studies (Toronto: Univ. of Toronto Press, 1976), p. 82. See also Bartlett, *The Economic Foundations of Political Power*, and Tullock, *The Mathematics of Politics*, pp. 115-32, on the gains from information control.

47. See Niskanen, *Bureaucracy and Representative Government*; Wagner, "Supply Side Aspects of the Theory of Local Government"; and McKean, "The Unseen Hand in Government," for more general statements of this problem. For empirical studies which show a significant cost differential attributable to public provision, see Robert M. Spann, "Public versus Private Provision of Government Services," in *Budgets and Bureaucrats*, ed. Borcherding, pp. 71-89; Roger Albrandt, "Efficiency in the Provision of Fire Services," *Public Choice* 13 (Fall 1973); and David G. Davies, "The Efficiency of Public versus Private Firms: The Case of Australia's Two Airlines," *Journal of Law and Economics* 14 (April 1971).

48. Downs refers to an "initial survival threshold" that the bureau must surpass to attain autonomy in *Inside Bureaucracy*, pp. 7-10.

49. For an empirical study of the impact of complex revenue structures on public sector outcomes, see Richard E. Wagner, "Revenue Structure, Fiscal Illusion, and Budgetary Choice," *Public Choice* 25 (Spring 1976): 45-65.

50. This is central in Niskanen, *Bureaucracy and Representative Government*; and Kenneth Shepsle, *The Giant Jigsaw Puzzle: Democratic Committee Assignments in the House of Representatives* (Chicago: Univ. of Chicago Press, 1978).

51. Alexis de Tocqueville, concerned about the redistributive potential of majority rule, wrote: "A democratic government is the only one in which those who vote for a tax can escape the obligation altogether," in *Democracy in America*, ed. J. P. Mayer, trans. George Lawrence (Garden City, N.J.: Doubleday, 1969), p. 210. See also Hayek, *The Constitution of Liberty*, pp. 103-17.

52. Another way of stating the thrust of these arguments is that by either controlling the information with which choices are made or by directly controlling the choices presented the legislature or the electorate, the bureaucracy may powerfully influence legislative outcomes. In recent years economists and political scientists have begun to develop theoretical models which embody this latter point. In these models political outcomes are viewed as resulting from the manipulation of the democratic process by strategically placed agents—agenda setters. For models of agenda control, see Richard McKelvey, "Intransitivities in Multi-dimensional Voting Models and Some Implications for Agenda Control," *Journal of Economic Theory* 12 (1976): 472-82; Charles Plott and Michael Levine, "A Model of Agenda Influence on Committee Decisions," *American Economic Review* (March 1978): 146-60; Denzau and Mackay, "A Model of Benefit and Tax Share Discrimination by a Monopoly Bureau"; Mackay and Weaver, "Commodity Bundling and Agenda Control in the Public Sector," and "Agenda Control by Budget Maximizers in a Multi-Bureau Setting"; and Romer and Rosenthal, "Political Resource Allocation," and "Bureaucrats vs. Voters." See Kenneth Shepsle, "The Role of Institutional Structure in the Creation of Policy Equilibrium," in *Sage Yearbook in Politics and Public Policy*, ed. D. Rae (Sage, 1979), for a survey of this literature and its relationship to actual legislature processes.

53. Rather than suggesting that citizens fail to learn and are therefore irrational to permit the creation of such institutions, this view makes it all the more likely that citizens will participate actively at the time of emergence to institutionalize constraints on the new program.

Chapter 2. Poverty Relief Before 1900: A Brief Historical Overview

1. Roy Lubove, *The Professional Altruist: The Emergence of Socal Work as a Career, 1880-1930* (New York: Atheneum, 1969), p. 54.

2. Institutions for the sick, needy, and aged, financed wholly or in part by public funds, private endowments, subscriptions, donations, or gifts. Excludes public and private institutions for care of insane, schools for feeble-minded, and almshouses. See Bureau of Census, *Benevolent Institutions: 1904*, Special Report (Washington, D. C.: U.S. Government Printing Office, 1905), pp. 12, 16.

3. Before 1929 the federal government made grants in local emergency cases of fire, flood, and other disasters, the first being made in 1803. See Edith Abbott, *Public Assistance: American Principles and Policies* (1940; reissued in 2 vols., New York: Russell and Russell, 1966), 2: 645-55, 691; and Bureau of Census, *Historical Statistics of the United States: Colonial Times to 1970*, Bicentennial Edition (2 vols.; Washington, D.C.: U.S. Government Printing Office, 1975), 1: 359 and 2: 1120, 1125, 1128.

4. Between 1902 and 1927, in fact, a declining proportion of government expenditures was devoted to public welfare (institutional or noninstitutional aid to the needy). Bureau of Census, *Historical Statistics*, 2: 1120. See also "Cost and Conduct of American Almshouses," *Bulletin of the U.S. Bureau of Labor Statistics*, No. 439 (June 1927): 445-54, and "Cost of American Almshouses," *Bulletin of the U.S. Bureau of Labor Statistics*, No. 386 (June 1925): 1-55.

5. As of 1928. Bureau of Census, *Historical Statistics*, 2: 1058.

6. Ibid., 2: 1119-20.

7. National Industrial Conference Board, *Support of the Aged: A Review of Conditions and Proposals* (New York: National Industrial Conference Board, 1931), p. 25.

8. Institutional responses to the financial problems of people of all ages indicated that, unlike today, there was a very clear distinction between the ex-post problem of poverty and its alleviation and the ex-ante problem of financial insecurity and its prevention. The problem of poverty was perceived as a social problem to be dealt with by collective action of some sort—whether mutual and voluntary or mutual and coercive. In a growing economy, however, it was a problem likely to affect only a small portion of the population. The problem of financial insecurity, by contrast, was considered to be a private or individual problem likely to affect most individuals of all ages. As an individual problem the prevention of future poverty was expected to be solved by continued employment, the accumulation of private savings and insurance, and financial planning, not by direct government intervention. Unattractive methods of relief,

strict conditions on eligibility, and provisions placing the primary burden of support on immediate families limited the state's role to the creation of incentives for thrift and for the teaching of thrift.

9. Bureau of Census, *Historical Statistics*, 2: 1120, 1125.

10. Social Security Administration, *Social Security Bulletin: Annual Statistical Supplement, 1975*, pp. 72, 88.

11. On the origins of public poverty relief in the United States, see Blanche D. Coll, "Public Assistance in the United States: Colonial Times to 1860," in *Comparative Development in Social Welfare* ed. E. W. Martin (London: George Allen and Unwin, 1972), pp. 128-57; Helen I. Clarke, *Social Legislation: American Laws Dealing with Family, Child, and Dependent*, The Century Social Science Series (New York: D. Appleton-Century 1940), pp. 417-31; Walter Trattner, *From Poor Laws to Welfare State: A History of Social Welfare in America* (New York: The Free Press, 1974), pp. 16-31; Hace Tishler, *Self-Reliance and Social Security: 1870-1917* (Port Washington, N.Y.: Kennikat Press, 1971), pp. 1-11; and Lawrence Friedman, *A History of American Law* (New York: Simon and Schuster, 1973), pp. 77-78, 187-91, 428-34.

12. For an informative account of social welfare legislation in Massachusetts, colonial times through 1940, see Clarke, *Social Legislation* pp. 417-44.

13. Compulsory taxation for the support of the poor was first legislated in Plymouth in 1642. See Coll, "Public Assistance in the United States," pp. 128-31; and Trattner, *From Poor Law to Welfare State*, pp. 16-18.

14. In order to control the social difficulties and financial obligations implied by the transient poor the customs of "passing on" and "warning off" developed and were utilized in some cases into the twentieth century. A town that warned off an individual disclaimed financial responsibility for him and placed responsibility on the town in which he had last been. In some cases transportation and lodging in the direction of that town were also provided. See Abbott, *Public Assistance*, 1: 150-55; Friedman, *A History of American Law*, pp. 77-78; Coll, "Public Assistance in the United States," pp. 131-32; and Trattner, *From Poor Law to Welfare State*, pp. 19-20. As pointed out in David J. Rothman's and Sheila M. Rothman's "The Experience of Poverty in America," in *The Poor in Modern America: On Their Own* ed. David J. Rothman and Sheila M. Rothman (Reading, Mass.: Addison-Wesley, 1972), pp. v-xxv, there was, for reasons of religion and survival, a high degree of tolerance for the poor in colonial days, but this was a tolerance fostered by settlement laws and the like that limited care to community residents. For an excellent discussion of the poor-law statutes, especially the essential features remaining in the 1930s and court enforcement of these statutes, see Abbott, *Public Assistance*, 1: 126-79.

15. In Massachusetts, for example, the decision to grant aid to the needy was made by the citizenry in town meetings. All care was in kind, provided in the home of the needy or in the home of his overseer. Clarke, *Social Legislation*, p. 420. "Outdoor relief" referred to any relief provided to a needy individual outside of an institution. This could be, say, coal, wood, medical supplies, groceries, or cash. By the 1900s outdoor relief generally referred to the cash component. Indoor relief referred to relief granted in an institution whether that was an almshouse, reformatory, asylum, hospital, school for the deaf and blind, or the like. Charity and relief were used interchangeably.

16. Ibid., p. 420; and Trattner, *From Poor Law to Welfare State*, pp. 18-23.

17. Caring for the poor who were not from the community, whether by migration or immigration, was a key factor in the drive for public provision and for higher level financing. The first exception to local financing in Massachusetts, for example, was the by-product of a mass influx of destitute refugees into Boston in 1675, driven from their homes by Indians in King Phillip's War. The reimbursal of local expenditures was expanded in 1701 to cover expenditures for the diseased poor and, in 1720, the poor who had not gained settlement. See Clarke, *Social Legislation*, pp. 418-22.

18. Public almshouses, the first erected in Boston in 1660, came into general use after 1700 and, during the 1800s, became a key method for dealing with the poor. The development of the almshouse tended to replace the public auction, although the practice of "letting out" the poor for a fixed sum continued into this century. See ibid., pp. 420-21; Edward T. Devine, *The Principles of Relief* (1904; reprinted, New York: Arno Press and The New York Times, 1971), pp. 284-88; Coll, "Public Assistance in the United States," pp. 133-39; and "The Cost and Conduct of American Almshouses" and "The Cost of American Almshouses," *Bulletin of the U.S. Bureau of Labor Statistics*.

19. The distinction between worthy and unworthy poor is emphasized in, for example, Josiah Quincy, *Report of the Committee on the Pauper Laws of this Commonwealth* (1821), p. 4, and J. N. Yates, *Report of the Secretary of State in 1824 on the Relief and Settlement of the Poor* (1824), pp.

1137-38, both reprinted in *The Almshouse Experience* (New York: Arno Press and New York Times, 1971); Frank Watson, *The Charity Organization Movement in the United States: A Study in American Philanthropy* (1922; reprinted, New York: Arno Press and The New York Times, 1971), pp. 180-81; Tishler, *Self-Reliance*, pp. 8-10; Friedman, *A History of American Law*, pp. 191, 432-33; and Coll, "Public Assistance in the United States," pp. 146-48, 152-55. On the legal distinction between pauper and poor, see Abbott, *Public Assistance*, 1: 97-102. This is not to say that the attitude toward the poor was without change. In the aftermath of the American Revolution and with the opening of the west, attitudes toward the public care of the poor became more negative, as the view that poverty was an individual fault became prevalent.

20. Tishler, *Self-Reliance*, pp. 9-10.

21. The work exacted, if any, was typically modest since inmates were often ill or disabled and because of a lack of monitoring almshouse care. By the late 1800s, moreover, public institutions were pressured not to produce goods with cheap labor that competed in outside markets. Amos G. Warner, *American Charities* (New York: Thomas Y. Crowell, 1908), pp. 220-23, 410; and Coll, "Public Assistance in the United States," p. 137.

22. As late as 1883 the Kansas Supreme Court upheld the action of an almshouse that bound out the son of an inmate until the age of eighteen without parental knowledge or consent. As of 1890, moreover, more than a quarter of the states retained the constitutional authority to deny recipients their civil rights, and as late as 1940 the constitutions in such states as Delaware, Rhode Island, New Jersey and South Carolina still denied recipients the right to register and vote. See Abbott, *Public Assistance*, 1: 127-29; and Tishler, *Self-Reliance*, pp. 9, 81.

23. In 1836 all of the north and middle Atlantic seaboard states, excluding New York, required the mutual support of the needy by his grandparents, parents, children, and grandchildren. By 1870 every state placed legal responsibility on family members, if only the adult family members. These requirements, constitutionally upheld and still enforced in some counties in the 1930s, were not frequently litigated, at least in part because poor people without family support tended to have poor relatives. See Abbott, *Public Assistance*, 1: 155-76; Tishler, *Self-Reliance*, pp. 5-7; Coll, "Public Assistance in the United States," pp. 132-33. See also Bureau of Census, *Summary of State Laws Relating to the Dependent Classes: 1913* (Washington, D.C.: U.S. Government Printing Office, 1914).

24. Poor relief accounted for 10-35 percent of outlays in both northern and southern municipalities. Trattner, *From Poor Law to Welfare State*, p. 30. See ibid., pp. 29-43, on poverty relief during and after the Revolution. Among other things the creation of a federal system of government during this period enhanced principles of local control, and the formal separation of church and state led to the development of new religious sects and a concomitant widening of private sources of relief.

25. On outdoor relief, institutional care, and subsidies during the 1800s, see Warner, *American Charities*, pp. 104-12, 195-225, 226-43, 399-419; Amos G. Warner, Stuart A. Queen, and Ernest B. Harper, *American Charities and Social Work* (New York: Thomas Y. Crowell, 1930) pp. 90-112, 181-95; Devine, *The Principles of Relief*, pp. 127-34, 278-313; Clarke, *Social Legislation*, pp. 420-21, 429-31; Trattner, *From Poor Law to Welfare State*, pp. 44-74; *The Almshouse Experience*, and Coll, "Public Assistance in the United States," pp. 141-45.

As of 1901 there were nineteen states in which subsidies were granted to private charitable institutions, mostly in the northeastern states with older poor relief laws. See Warner, *American Charities*, pp. 339-419; Warner, Queen, and Harper, *American Charities and Social Work*, pp. 181-95; and Clarke, *Social Legislation*, pp. 429-30, for more on this.

In historical order, there emerged educational institutions for the deaf and blind, asylums for the insane, orphanages for dependent children, hospitals for the ill, and villages for the epileptic. See Bureau of Census, *Benevolent Institutions: 1904*, for a detailed account of the number, distribution and size of these institutions. See also Warner, *American Charities*, pp. 198-209; Trattner, *From Poor Law to Welfare State*, p. 57; Clarke, *Social Legislation*, pp. 421, 431; and David Rothman, *The Discovery of the Asylum* (Boston: Little Brown, 1971).

26. Two frequently cited examples of abuse were relief in Brooklyn and Indiana. In Brooklyn, for example, between 1872 and 1877, the number of recipients of outdoor relief increased 100 percent and by 1877 one out of sixteen persons in the city were receiving relief. In Indiana the total cost of outdoor relief averaged $550,000 a year between 1890 and 1895, and in 1894 one in every thirty-one of the state's inhabitants were receiving relief. In some of the richest counties the proportions were as high as one in thirteen. Warner, *American Charities*, pp. 230-34. These problems were certainly influenced by severe recessions in the 1870s and 1890s and the dislocations created by the Civil War. On the perceived abuses

and disadvantages of the prevailing systems, see ibid., pp. 228-42, 412-19; Devine, *The Principles of Relief*, pp. 308-13; Warner, Queen, and Harper, *American Charities and Social Work*, pp. 106-10, 190-95; and Trattner, *From Poor Law to Welfare State*, pp. 44-74; Abbott, *Public Assistance*, 2: 514-22; three original reports by Quincy, Yates, and the Philadelphia Board of Guardians, reprinted in *The Almshouse Experience*; and Josephine S. Lowell, *Public Relief and Private Charity* (1884; reprinted, New York: Arno Press and The New York Times, 1971), pp. 54-69.

27. Warner, *American Charities*, pp. 399-405.

28. According to the general secretary of the New York City Charity Organization Society, "There has been no period within the century when the system of public outdoor relief has gone unchallenged." Devine, *Principles of Relief*, p. 282. Two early critical examinations of prevailing systems of care were the 1821 report to the General Court of Massachusetts by Josiah Quincy, president of Harvard University, and the 1824 report to the New York Legislature by J. N. Yates, secretary of state. In the words of Quincy, "Of all the modes of providing for the poor, the most wasteful, the most expensive, and most injurious to their morals and destructive to their industrious habits is that of supply in their own families." See Quincy, *Report of the Committee on Pauper Laws*, p. 9 and Yates, *Relief and Settlement of the Poor*, reprinted in *The Almshouse Experience*. See also Devine, *Principles of Relief*, pp. 282-89; Clarke, *Social Legislation*, pp. 423-25; and Coll, "Public Assistance in the United States," pp. 133-35.

29. In 1879, for example, Brooklyn terminated outdoor relief altogether; and in Indiana a law was passed in 1899 requiring investigation of all overseers of the poor, the financial aid of friends and relatives, the compelling of the able-bodied poor to work, and the limiting of outdoor relief to the temporarily needy, with specified maximum amounts. The per capita cost of relief in Indiana fell 65 percent between 1895 and 1905. In Buffalo, moreover, the substitution of investigated for uninvestigated city aid, and the substitution of work for outright relief was believed to be responsible for cutting the proportion of the population receiving outdoor relief from 10 percent in 1875 to 1 percent in 1907. See Warner, *American Charities*, pp. 231-32; Devine, *The Principles of Relief*, pp. 307-09; Abbott, *Public Assistance*, 2: 521. The New York Commission on Old-Age Security, *Old-Age Security*, Leg. Doc. No. 67 (Albany, N.Y.: J. B. Lyons, 1930), p. 21, and Calif. State Department of Social Welfare, *Old-Age Dependency: A Study of the Care Given the Needy Aged in California* (Sacramento: Calif. Printing Office, 1929), p. 8.

30. Warner, *American Charities*, pp. 399-419; and Clarke, *Social Legislation*, pp. 429-30.

31. In England as well the seeds of reform had been sewn. The mercantilism, paternalism, and government intervention that provided a climate for the English Poor Law were criticized as both morally and economically flawed. As a result of both economic and social changes during the post-Revolutionary era, the English Poor Law was thus reformed in 1834 to emphasize deterrence rather than alleviation. The Reform Bill set the precedent of providing relief only to those able-bodied poor who showed themselves "worthy" by meeting a work-test. See Hanson, "Welfare Before the Welfare State," pp. 114-16; Rhodes, *Public Sector Pensions*, p. 187-91; Trattner, *From Poor Laws to Welfare State*, pp. 46-55; Clarke, *Social Legislation*, pp. 405-07; and Watson, "From Parish to Union," pp. 38-56.

32. According to Frank Watson, professor of sociology and social work, in 1922, the movement for organization resulted from the rapid growth of public relief and the expenditure of vast sums of private money: "without wisdom or caution. An age in which the two richest nations of the world (England and the U.S.) were doubling their accumulating wealth every twenty years had become lavish of alms, and in this soil had sprung up a race of charity-mongers with canvassing books, most of whom were free to apply their easily-gotten subscriptions according to their own judgment or caprice." Watson, *The Charity Organization Movement in the United States*, pp. 53-54. For three quite thorough examinations of this movement to organize relief and charity monies, see ibid., Warner, Queen, and Harper, *American Charities and Social Work*, pp. 425-56; and Lowell, *Public Relief and Private Charity*.

33. On the emergence, function, and staffing of these boards, predecessors to state welfare departments, see Warner, *American Charities*, pp. 425-36; Warner, Queen, and Harper, *American Charities and Social Work*, pp. 196-202. See also Tishler, *Self-Reliance*, p. 25; and Clarke, *Social Legislation*, p. 432.

34. London's society was established in 1869 with the sharp rise in relief expenditures in the aftermath of the American Civil War. Between 1860 and 1869 the number of recipients in London rose from 85,000 to 120,000 and expenditures rose from $4 million to $70 million. See Watson, *The Charity Organization Movement*, pp. 49-63; and Hanson, "Welfare Before the Welfare State," pp. 117-18.

On the American charity organization movement, see in particular Watson, *The Charity Organization Movement*, pp. 11-121; Warner, *American Charities*, pp. 437-56; Warner, Queen, and Harper, *American Charities and Social Work*, pp. 203-14; Lubove, *Professional Altruists*, pp. 1-21.

35. New York Directory of Charities (1892), cited in Warner, *American Charities*, p. 443.

36. For clear statements of this view, written by leading figures in the charity organization movement, see Lowell, *Public Relief and Private Charity*, pp. 54-69, and Warner, *American Charities*, pp. 195-224, 228-43, and 366-76.

Reflecting the opposition to relief of the able-bodied in 1882, Reverend Gurteen, founder of the first American charity organization society said, "There is no room in this busy world of ours for those social drones who prey upon the industry of others, and prefer to beg rather than to work. . . . Look abroad over our own city, over every large city of the country, and is there not a "wound" (and oh! how deep and ghastly) visible on every hand. There is the wound of idleness and improvidence." Cited in Lubove, *Professional Altruist*, pp. 5, 8.

37. See ibid., p. 5, for more on this.

38. Trattner, *From Poor Law to Welfare State*, p. 83.

39. In Boston, for example, there were more than fourteen hundred charitable organizations by the turn of the century ("concisely described in a volume of 500 pages"), each providing specialized services to particular classes of "dependents." A certain amount of coordination had naturally evolved for religious and nationality groups, as in Baltimore or New York where a German, Scotsman, or Jew could turn to a benevolent society providing all forms of aid. But there were also specialized donor groups that provided only, say, coal and groceries, only medical supplies, or only clothing. The process of matching the poor with the proper agency was thus an important concern. Warner, *American Charities*, pp. 437-42; and Watson, *The Charity Organization Movement*, pp. 64-93.

40. See Warner, *American Charities*, pp. 228-35, and Tishler, *Self-Reliance*, pp. 31-43. According to the Wisconsin State Board of Charities and Reform in 1883, "A large amount of poor relief does not indicate a large amount of suffering which needs to be relieved, but a large amount of laxity or corruption on the part of officers and a large amount of willingness by able-bodied idlers to be fed at the public expense." Cited in Lowell, *Public Relief and Private Charity*, p. 57.

41. Cited in Warner, *American Charities*, p. 231.

42. Tishler, *Self-Reliance*, p. 19. While military pensions had a long history dating to the American Revolution, the Civil War led to an expansion of the program "unequalled in the history of the world." In 1862 monthly benefits were made payable for wounds and diseases attributable to military service, equal benefits were made payable to widows and children and, for the first time in history, mothers of soldiers and dependent orphaned sisters as well. Benefit provisions were then liberalized in 1864, 1865, 1866 (when benefits were made payable to fathers and dependent brothers of soldiers), 1868, 1870, and 1873. The Arrears Act, making pensions retroactive, was passed in 1879. By 1900 the cost of military pensions since the close of the Civil War totaled $2.5 billion, there were one million names on the pension rolls, and the annual cost of the program exceeded $140 million. According to one student of military pensions, the Arrears Act, "instead of satisfying the pension attorneys and claimants, resulted in a demand for further legislation. Adapting to his purpose a phrase from classical English, one of the speakers in the Congressional debates remarked that 'this appetite for pensions both increase by what it feeds on.' The voting strength of the veterans of the Civil War was so great that both political parties feared to oppose pension measures." President Cleveland actually vetoed 228 pension bills during his first term of office. For a lively and quite informative legislative history of the military pensions, see William H. Glasson, *History of Military Pension Legislation in the United States* (1909; reprinted, New York: AMS Press, 1968), pp. 9, 71-86, 108-14.

43. Trattner, *From Poor Law to Welfare State*, pp. 81-84. See, for example, William Graham Sumner, *What Social Classes Owe to Each Other* (reprinted, Caldwell, Idaho: The Caston Printers, 1974).

44. See Devine, for example, on "The Immigrant and the Colonist," *The Principles of Relief*, pp. 162-70. Between 1860 and 1900 the proportion of the population in cities doubled, from one-sixth to one-third, and fourteen million persons immigrated to this country. During the same period Chicago's population increased by twenty-fold, and by 1900 three-fourths of the city's population were foreign born. Trattner, *From Poor Law to Welfare State*, pp. 137-38.

45. Lubove, *Professional Altruist*, p. 23. For several other informative discussions of the changes in social work, see Warner, Queen, and Harper, *American Charities and Social Work*, pp. 25-39, 554-72; and Frank J. Bruno, *Trends in Social Work: 1874-1956, A History Based on the Proceedings of the National Conference of Social Work* (New York: Columbia Univ. Press, 1957) pp. 134-50. See also Trattner, *From Poor Law to Welfare State*, pp. 193-211.

Accompanying these changes affecting social work was a change in attitudes toward the poor during the Progressive era. The causes of, and responsibility for, poverty were seen to be more complex, deriving from imperfections in the industrial economy and society—unemployment, accident, disease, slums, alienation—not only from personal fault. It was in the interests of social workers endeavoring to professionalize, of course, to foster the view of complex causation. See Trattner, *From Poor Law to Welfare State*, pp. 179-92; Tishler, *Self-Reliance*, pp. 80-107; and Rothman and Rothman, "The Experience of Poverty in America," pp. xi-xii.

46. This is clear in Warner, Queen, and Harper, *American Charities and Social Work*, pp. 25-39, 554-72, and is a central theme in Lubove, *Professional Altruist*.

47. Fostering a new alliance between the social worker and the social scientist, there were forty professional schools in the United States and Canada by 1928. The merging of "theory and practice" added legitimacy to social work and created mutual employment opportunities as well as political force. In 1921 the first national organization was created, the American Association of Social Work. Being primarily concerned with employment opportunities, the association restricted membership to social workers who had a period of service in an approved agency, or else a professional education in a school accredited by the Association of Professional Schools of Social Work. The effort to restrict the supply of individuals into social work was carried on at lower levels of association as well. The New York Charity Organization Society, for example, decided in 1919 to recruit and train volunteers, requiring their satisfactory performance on a course and in field work. The first year in effect certification was denied to two-thirds of the volunteers. "Increasingly, the professional welcomed the volunteer only to the degree that she submitted to agency supervision and accepted a supporting role under the paid worker's leadership." Lubove, *Professional Altruist*, p. 52.)

The elevation of the social sciences along with developments in medicine and psychiatry in the early 1900s led to changes in public hospitals, public mental health care, and public schools that broadened the market for social workers and hastened the formation of the professional. By the 1920s there were whole new categories of social work in existence: hospital, psychiatric, visiting teacher, vocational guidance, and community organization. See ibid., pp. 55-156; Bruno, *Trends in Social Work*, pp. 134-51; Warner, *American Charities*, pp. 461-65; and Warner, Queen, and Harper, *American Charities and Social Work*, pp. 30-31, 37-39, 563-69.

48. Lubove, *Professional Altruist*, p. 18.

49. For more on the relationship between social workers and the universities, see Bruno, *Trends in Social Work*, pp. 134-44; Warner, Queen, and Harper, *American Charities and Social Work*, p. 38; and Warner, *American Charities*, pp. 461-65. The policies endorsed by organized social workers in the second and third decades of the twentieth century—minimum wages, child labor laws, eight-hour days, industrial accident and hygiene laws, and compulsory social insurance—were very similar to those of the Progressives and the Socialists of the day. Bruno, *Trends in Social Work*, pp. 220-29.

50. The Federal Emergency Relief Act, for example, was passed in 1933, making $500 million in federal funds available to states and localities. With hardly inconsequential effects on the employment of social workers, the act stipulated that every local relief administrator had to employ at least one experienced social worker on his staff and one qualified supervisor per twenty employees. By directive of Harry Hopkins, moreover, federal funds could only be distributed by a public agency. Trattner, *From Poor Law to Welfare State*, pp. 236-37. For more on the impact of the depression on the demand for the services of social workers, see Bruno, *Trends in Social Work*, pp. 318-21.

51. On the trend toward state participation, see Abbott, *Public Assistance*, 2: 509-32.

52. Real outdoor poor relief at the state and city level increased at twice the rate of total governmental expenditures between 1915 and 1928, rising more than 250 percent in states and 150 percent in cities. Reflecting the pronounced reallocation of the mix of charity expenditures during the 1920s, the proportion of outdoor poor relief to total charity expenditures in cities rose from 19 percent in 1919 to 34 percent in 1928; and in states, from 2 percent to 9 percent. See Bureau of Census, *Financial Statistics of States* (Washington, D.C.: U.S. Government Printing Office, 1917-30), and Bureau of Census, *Financial Statistics of Cities Having a Population of Over 30,000* (Washington, D.C.: U.S. Government Printing Office, 1917-30).

53. Lubove, *Professional Altruist*, p. 52.

54. Bureau of Census, *Financial Statistics of States* and *Financial Statistics of Cities*.

55. Mabel Newcomer, "Fifty Years of Public Support of Welfare Functions in the United States," *Social Sciences Review* 15 (1941), cited in Lubove, *Professional Altruist*, p. 53.

56. For more on "voluntarism" and "individualism" and their role in limiting government in the realm of social welfare, see, for example, Roy Lubove, *The Struggle for Social Security: 1900-1935* (Cambridge, Mass.: Harvard Univ. Press, 1968), pp. 1-24, and forward by Oscar Handlin.

Chapter 3. The Elderly and the State: 1900–1929

1. Samuel Gompers, "Not Even Compulsory Benevolence Will Do," *The American Federationist* 24 (Jan. 1917): 48.

2. See Bureau of Census, *Paupers in Almshouses: 1923* (Washington, D.C.: U.S. Government Printing Office, 1925), pp 2-3, 9-10; "Cost and Conduct of American Almshouses," *Bulletin of the U.S. Bureau of Labor Statistics*, no. 439 (June 1927): 445; "The Cost of American Almshouses," *Bulletin of the U. S. Bureau of Labor Statistics*, no. 386 (June 1925): 1-51; Barbara N. Armstrong, *Insuring the Essentials: Minimum Wage Plus Social Insurance—A Living Wage Program* (New York: Macmillan, 1932), pp. 394-97; and U.S. Committee on Economic Security, *Social Security in America*, cited in *Statutory History of the United States: Income Security* ed. Robert B. Stevens (New York: Chelsea House, 1970), p. 20.

3. In 1932 total government expenditures for public welfare amounted to $445 million, whereas in 1940 expenditures on old-age assistance alone amounted to $473 million. See Bureau of Census, *Historical Statistics of the United States: Colonial Times to 1970*, Bicentennial Edition (2 vols.; Washington, D.C.: U.S. Government Printing Office, 1975), 2:1120; and Social Security Administration, *Social Security Bulletin: Annual Statistical Supplement, 1973* (Washington, D.C.: U.S. Government Printing Office, 1974), p. 157.

4. A notable exception was the care of veterans and their families, discussed below. According to one estimate, Civil War pensions provided aid to two-thirds of the aged native white population in the northern states in 1910. Hace Tishler, *Self-Reliance and Social Security: 1870-1917* (Port Washington, N.Y.: Kennikat, 1971), p. 89.

5. U.S. Committee on Economic Security, *Social Security in America*, cited in Stevens, *Statutory History of the United States*, ed. Stevens, p. 20; and Armstrong, *Insuring the Essentials*, pp. 394-97.

6. For detailed analyses of the nature, use, and condition of almshouses, see Bureau of Census, *Paupers in Almshouses: 1904, Special Report* (Washington, D.C.: U.S. Government Printing Office, 1906) and *Paupers in Almshouses: 1923*; "The Cost of American Almshouses," *Bulletin of the U.S. Bureau of Labor Statistics*, no. 386 (June 1925): 1-51; "Cost and Conduct of American Almshouses," *Bulletin of the U.S. Bureau of Labor Statistics*, no. 439 (June 1927): 445-54; Bureau of Census, *Summary of State Laws Relating to the Dependent Classes: 1913* (Washington, D.C.: U.S. Government Printing Office, 1914); Armstrong, *Insuring the Essentials*, pp. 394-97; U.S. Committee on Economic Security, *Social Security in America*, cited in *Statutory History of the United States*, ed. Stevens, p. 20; Amos Warner, *American Charities* (New York: Thomas Y. Crowell, 1908), pp. 195-225; New York Commission on Old-Age Security, *Old-Age Security: Report of the New York State Commission*, Leg, Doc. No. 67 (Albany, N.Y.: J. B. Lyons, 1930), pp. 397-403; and Calif. State Department of Social Welfare, *Old-Age Dependency: A Study of the Care Given to Needy Aged in California* (Sacramento: Calif. Printing Office, 1929), pp. 20-28.

7. "Care of the Aged in the United States," *Monthly Labor Review* 28 (March 1929): 419-58. See also "Administration and Conditions of Old People's Homes," *Monthly Labor Review* 29 (July 1929): 1-21; and "Care of Aged Persons in the United States," *Bulletin of the U.S. Bureau of Labor Statistics*, no. 489 (Oct. 1929): 3-193.

8. Fraternal homes normally made provisions for widows, wives, and orphans of members. By contrast, there were many states with an administrative rule requiring separate housing of the sexes in public institutions that forced the separation of elderly poor couples, in some cases, to different geographic locations. See "The Care of the Aged in the U.S.," *Monthly Labor Review* 28 (March 1929): 424; and Armstrong, *Insuring the Essentials*, p. 396.

9. For an excellent early history, see William H. Glasson, *History of Military Pension Legislation in the United States* (New York: Columbia Univ. Press, 1900); reprinted, New York: AMS Press, 1968. See also Paul Studensky, *The Pension Problem and the Philosophy of Contributions* (New York: Pension Publishing, 1917); "Public Service Retirement Systems: U.S., Canada, and Europe," *Bulletin of the U.S. Bureau of Labor Statistics*, no. 477 (Jan. 1929): 1-170, and no. 491 (Aug. 1929): 542-47; "Care of the Aged by the Federal Government," *Bulletin of the U.S. Bureau of Labor Statistics*, no. 489 (Oct. 1929): 63-64; "The Cost of Existing Retirement Systems," *The Congressional Digest* 14 (March 1935): 73; Abraham Epstein, *Insecurity*, pp. 520-30; and Bureau of Census, *Summary of State Laws Relating to Dependent Classes: 1913*.

10. For purposes of comparison, figures calculated in 1980 dollars are given in parentheses here and elsewhere in this chapter.

11. For data on state and local expenditures, see Bureau of Census, *Financial Statistics of Cities Having a Population Over 30,000* (Washington, D.C.: U.S. Government Printing Office), and *Financial Statistics of States: 1925* (Washington, D.C.: U.S. Government Printing Office, 1926).

12. In 1927 a study of states and cities (with populations over 400,000) found that public retirement systems for police and firemen existed in almost every city, and were very common for teachers. There were statewide systems for all public employees in six states, city-wide systems in nine large cities, and twenty-one states had systems covering all teachers. See in particular, "Public Service Retirement Systems: U.S., Canada, and Europe," *Bulletin of the U.S. Bureau of Labor Statistics* no. 477 (Jan. 1929): 1–170; and "Public Service Retirement Systems in the United States," *Bulletin of the U.S. Bureau of Labor Statistics* no. 491 (Aug. 1929), 542–49.

13. The most frequent annuity payment was actually the maximum payable of $1,000. On the basis of past service credits alone 6,400 employees had been immediately eligible to draw federal civil-service retirement annuities. "Public Service Retirement Systems," *Bulletin of the U.S. Bureau of Labor Statistics* no. 477 (Jan. 1929): 23–24.

14. This was particularly true as the systems ran into financial difficulties. As vividly illustrated in the following two cases, the government's share of the cost tended to rise over time as the systems' expenditures rose "unexpectedly" rapidly, and system members failed to raise revenues accordingly. The New York Police Pension Fund, for example, was organized in 1857 with revenues to be derived from the income from rewards and the sale of unclaimed property. New sources of income were added over time and in 1892 a law was passed compelling the government to cover any deficits that might result. A deficit amounting to $200,000 first appeared in 1904, rising within the next eleven years to $1.5 million—nearly 60 percent of annual benefit payments.

In 1887, moreover, a group of teachers in New York City established a voluntary mutual benefit association to which they contributed 1 percent of their salaries in exchange for the right to receive a $600 pension at retirement. Over time, deficits developed, younger workers opted out of the system, and the pension fell to $75. As the system was failing, a group of industrious teachers won support for a system that compelled participation. With income that was still insufficient, a city contribution of 5 percent of excise tax revenues was secured just two years later and by 1901 teachers were sitting on the board that supervised the disbursement of funds. By 1910, with compulsory participation and government contributions, benefit payments once again exceeded income. Paul Studensky, *The Pension Problem*, pp. 4, 19. For more on the nature and fiscal-political difficulties of many of the early public pension schemes, particularly those resulting from the choice of a "cash disbursement" over an "actuarial reserve" system (a pay-as-you-go over a funded system), see ibid., "Public Service Retirement Systems in the United States," *Bulletin of the U.S. Bureau of Labor Statistics* no. 491 (Aug. 1929): 542–47. See "Public Service Retirement Systems: United States, Canada, and Europe," *Bulletin of the U.S. Bureau of Labor Statistics* no. 447 (Jan. 1929): 1–170, for an in-depth account of the nature and status of municipal, state, federal, and other retirement programs for public employees in the 1920s.

15. Between 1900 and 1930 life expectancy at birth rose from 47.3 years to 59.7 years. Bureau of Census, *Statistical History*, p. 55.

16. For several informative early histories, see William Willoughby, *Workingmen's Insurance* (New York: Thomas Y. Crowell, 1898), Charles R. Henderson, *Industrial Insurance in the United States* (Chicago: Univ. of Chicago Press, 1909); Isaac M. Rubinow, *Social Insurance: With Special Reference to American Conditions* (New York: Henry Holt, 1916), pp. 345-88. See also Armstrong, *Insuring the Essentials*, pp. 398-431; "Old-Age Pension and Insurance Systems in Foreign Countries," *Bulletin of the U.S. Bureau of Labor Statistics* 30 (April 1930): 5-8; U.S. Committee on Economic Security, *Report to the President* (Washington, D.C.: U.S. Government Printing Office, 1935), pp. 69-70; and Epstein, *Insecurity*, pp. 551-65.

17. In Belgium, for example, subsidies were first paid to mutual aid societies whose members purchased voluntary annuities from the public system. By 1900 allowances were made directly to individuals who purchased these annuities. The effect was dramatic for in the following eight years the number of participants tripled. As the subsidies were not directed to lower income workers alone, however, opponents argued that industrial workers were not the primary beneficiaries and the program was therefore too expensive for results obtained. Armstrong, *Insuring the Essentials*, pp. 407-08. See also Rubinow, *Social Insurance*, pp. 329-44, for a discussion of the early voluntary subsidized schemes in Europe, particularly the French system, which was in existence for over sixty years by 1916.

18. With the exception of unemployment insurance, which first emerged in England in 1911, each form of compulsory insurance was introduced in Germany in the 1880s. For surveys of European developments, see Roy Lubove, *The Struggle for Social Security: 1900-1935* (Cambridge: Harvard Univ.

Press, 1968), pp. 28-34; and Armstrong, *Insuring the Essentials*, pp. 232-50, 303-62, and 446-60. For partial listings of the early works on social insurance, see Rubinow, *Social Insurance*, pp. 503-06; and Tishler, *Self-Reliance*, pp. 202-14.

19. On the relationship between social workers, the universities, and the Progressives, see Bruno, *Trends in Social Work*, pp. 134-44, 220-29; Warner, *American Charities*, pp. 461-65; Warner, Queen, and Harper, *American Charities and Social Work*, p. 38. See also Trattner, *From Poor Law to Welfare State*, pp. 150-51; and Tishler, *Self Reliance*, pp. 80-104.

20. For more on the AALL, see Lubove, *The Struggle for Social Security*, pp. 29-44.

21. Early efforts were concentrated on public policies for accident compensation, industrial safety and hygiene, and employment, as well as social insurance of various types. Ibid., pp. 30-34.

22. This view is central in Armstrong, *Insuring the Essentials: Minimum Wage Plus Social Insurance—A Living Wage Program*; Rubinow, *Social Insurance*; and *The Quest for Security* (New York: Henry Holt, 1934); Epstein, *Insecurity*, and *Facing Old-Age*.

23. In 1929 Governor Franklin Roosevelt said, "I am appalled every day by the number of people writing to protest that they hope that the United States will no longer remain in the class with Mexico and China as the only two countries which have made no provision for the care of the aged." Cited in "Three States Adopt Old-Age Pensions," *Bulletin of the American Association for Old-Age Security* 3 (April 1929): 1.

24. Cited in Lubove, *The Struggle for Social Security*, pp. 42-43.

25. Rubinow received his medical degree from New York University in the 1890s. Two years later he began taking courses in political science at Columbia University, shortly thereafter abandoning his medical practice and going into government employment. While working with the federal government, he directed a major study of social insurance in Europe, on the basis of which he was awarded a Ph.D. from Columbia. Becoming chief actuary and statistician for the Ocean Accident and Guarantee Company, 1911-16, publishing a leading book on social insurance in 1913, and founding the Casualty Actuarial and Statistical Society of America in 1914, he thus established his reputation as a leading scholar of private and social insurance. See Lubove, *The Struggle for Social Security*, pp. 34-44, for more on the life and views of Rubinow.

26. Epstein, *Insecurity*, p. 3. Epstein emigrated to the United States from Russia in 1910, received his undergraduate degree from the University of Pittsburgh in 1917, and studied economics in graduate school. He was appointed the research director of the Pennsylvania Commission on Old-Age Pensions in 1917, retaining his position through 1927. In 1933 he established the American Association for Old-Age Security. See Lubove, *The Struggle for Social Security*, pp. 138-40, and Rubinow, *The Quest for Security*, p. 279.

27. Epstein, *Insecurity*, p. 6.

28. Ibid., p. 23.

29. Rubinow, *The Quest for Security*, p. 508.

30. "But," he continued, "social insurance might almost be defined as a form of insurance which cannot live up to the exacting laws of insurance science. Then again it may and has been decried as rank paternalism, and this indictment must be readily admitted." Rubinow, *Social Insurance*, p. 11.

31. Cited in Lubove, *The Struggle for Social Security*, p. 38.

32. This view of the problem and its solution is explicit in Rubinow, *Social Insurance*, pp. 28-45, 301-17, 345-88, and *The Quest for Security*, pp. 19-38, 219-74, 288-302; Epstein, *Insecurity*, pp. 81-188, 491-531, 551-65; and Armstrong, *Insuring the Essentials*, pp. 376-97. The influence of this view is clear, for example, in Kansas Legislative Council, *Old-Age Pensions: Analysis of Existing Laws and the Experience of Other States* (Kan. Legislative Council, 1934). See F. A. Hayek, "History and Politics," in *Capitalism and the Historians*, ed. F. A. Hayek (Chicago: Univ. of Chicago Press, 1974), pp. 3-29, for a discussion of how this basically socialist view of captialism and industrialization permeated the interpretation of history.

33. Unlike today, there was a focus on the problem of "dependency" in addition to poverty. The distinction, if properly made, is very important. Whereas a poor person has little wealth and income, a dependent person, strictly speaking, is one whose income or wealth derives from another individual or organization, presumably in a noncontractual way, whether private or public. This person may or may not be poor and the other source may or may not be relief or charity. In most then-current studies, for example, elderly wives were counted as dependent (on their husbands), as were the elderly who were supported in the homes of their families. Unfortunately, the words were often used either interchangeably or in a causal relation to one another, and their meaning consequently obscured. A high degree of "dependency," as we would expect to see during times and in places characterized by extended families and limited government, was often mistakenly taken to imply widespread poverty.

34. Armstrong, *Insuring the Essentials*, p. 381.

35. Ibid., pp. 381-84; Rubinow, *Social Insurance*, p. 9, and *The Quest for Security*, p. 250; and Epstein, *Insecurity*, p. 23.

36. Armstrong, *Insuring the Essentials*, p. 381. Armstrong was a member of the law school at the University of California and was selected in 1934 to be a member of the staff of the Committee on Economic Security—the presidential committee that formulated the Social Security program—to head the studies on old-age insurance. She was also influential in the formation of unemployment insurance policy. See Edwin Witte, *The Development of the Social Security Act* (Madison: Univ. of Wis. Press, 1963), pp. 30, 33, 55-56, 116, 122). According to Welling Squier, in *Old-Age Dependency in the United States*, death was "a final and welcome end to it all." Cited in Rubinow, *Social Insurance*, p. 306.

37. Rubinow, *Social Insurance*, p. 306.

38. That social insurance at this early stage represented a fundamental attack on the profit motive, the market system, and on the distribution of income so produced is expressed most aptly by Epstein when he said, "Social insurance . . . bars all profit. It seeks no private gain at the expense of the poor and unfortunate; it reaps no advantage from human misery and insecurity. Since protection against social misfortune has become absolutely essential to workers, even as water, light and sanitation, no institution should be permitted to grow rich out of this vital need." Epstein, *Insecurity*, p. 35.

39. Since the time of the Great Depression and the enactment of Social Security, a set of rationalizations for the program have emerged. For example, it is said that lower income workers are myopic, tending to save too little, and must be compelled to save in order to prevent them from becoming charges of the state; and/or lower paid workers will rationally choose not to save adequately because of the existence of public poverty relief programs and the disincentives so generated. It is extremely important to note, first, that the role for government in these arguments derives from the prior role of government. Second, these are not the thrust of arguments actually advanced by proponents (although in 700 pages of text, both sides of issues were often argued). After all, advocates sought the favorable treatment of wage-earners who, they believed, were unjustly treated in a capitalistic society. Even their attacks on private insurance markets were little more than easily disputed attacks on the "failure" of any market in the presence of profits, rather than being attacks on failures deriving from problems of risk-pooling, adverse selection, or the like. Third, even if accepted, neither argument calls for public production of insurance, only compulsory purchase, as discussed below.

40. The fact that the first social insurance schemes had been created by Otto von Bismarck, that the AALL had its origins in the International Association for Labor Legislation, and that many of the progressive intellectuals of the period were trained in or influenced by the German school of thought all fostered this view. The social insurance movement was associated with German impetus as early as 1904. In that year the St. Louis Exposition contained elaborate exhibits prepared by the German government lauding the merits of compulsory insurance. See Lubove, *The Struggle for Social Security*, p. 7.

Interestingly, one of Rubinow's early articles on unemployment insurance was rejected in 1903 by one of his former professors at Columbia University as "too un-American and revolutionary" for the *Political Science Quarterly*. Lubove, *The Struggle for Social Security*, p. 34. According to Frederick Hoffman of the Prudential Life Insurance Company, moreover, social insurance was a "propaganda for paternalism and coercion," and "the duty of every American to resist unnecessary coercion or compulsion, but especially in a field of effort and enterprise which has heretofore been chiefly, if not exclusively, a matter of personal concern." Frederick Hoffman, *Facts and Fallacies of Compulsory Health Insurance* (Newark: Prudential Insurance, 1917), p. 6. See also Frederick Hoffman, "Autocracy and Paternalism vs. Democracy and Liberty," an address before the International Association of Casualty and Surety Underwriters on 14 Dec. 1918 (New York: International Association of Casualty and Surety Underwriters, 1919), and *More Facts and Fallacies of Compulsory Health Insurance* (Newark: Prudential Press, 1919), and P. Techumseh Sherman, "Dangerous Tendencies in the American Social Insurance Movement," an address before the Insurance Society of New York on 21 Nov. 1916 (New York: Insurance Society of New York, 1917).

41. Cited in Lubove, *The Struggle for Social Security*, p. 139.

42. Samuel Gompers, "Not Even Compulsory Benevolence Will Do," *The American Federationist* 24 (Jan. 1917): p. 48.

43. Ibid., p. 48. See also Samuel Gompers, "Intellectuals,' Please Note," *The American Federationist* 23 (March 1916): 198, in which he continues, "All these solutions are formulated along lines that necessitate governmental machinery and the employment of experts—the "intellectuals." The conclusion is inevitable that there is a very close connection between *employment* as experts and the enthusiasm for human welfare."

44. Cited in Lubove, *The Struggle for Social Security*, p. 16. On the opposition of organized labor, see Daniel S. Sanders, *The Impact of Reform Movements on Social Policy Change: The Case of Social Insurance* (Fairlawn, N.J.: R. E. Burdick, 1973), pp. 131-41.

45. John F. Dryden, *Addresses and Papers on Life Insurance and Other Subjects* (1909), cited in Lubove, *The Struggle for Social Security*, p. 23.

46. For an indication of the level of interest in old-age dependency and government policy, see Julia Johnson, *The Reference Shelf: Old-Age Pensions* (New York: H. W. Wilson, 1935), 10: 39-74, in which she provides an extensive listing of articles, books, government bulletins and statements. The study and presentation of these issues became a prominent part of both the *Monthly Labor Review* and the *Bulletin of the U.S. Bureau of Labor Statistics* in the middle to late 1920s and were the focus of The American Association for Old-Age Security, *Bulletin* 1-9 (1927-35).

47. Studies were conducted in Massachusetts (1910, 1914, 1917, 1925), Wisconsin (1915), California (1917, 1928), New Jersey (1917, 1928, 1929), Pennsylvania (1919, 1925, 1926, 1927), Connecticut and Ohio (1919), Nevada and Indiana (1925), Virginia (1926), and Minnesota and Maine (1929). See New York Commission, *Old-Age Security*, pp. 48-49, 312-24.

48. Lubove, *The Struggle for Social Security*, pp. 118-19; New York Commission, *Old-Age Security*, pp. 48, 312-13; and Tishler, *Self-Reliance*, p. 88.

49. On the admitted failure of the movement, see Epstein, *Insecurity*, pp. ix-x, and 62-78; Rubinow, "The Collapse of a Movement," *The Quest for Security*, pp. iv, 207-17, and 600-616; and Armstrong, *Insuring the Essentials*, pp. 370-75. For a critical reexamination of the view that ideology was the key deterrent to social insurance in the 1920s, see Carolyn L. Weaver, "On the Lack of a Political Market for Compulsory Old-Age Insurance Prior to the Great Depression: Insights from Economic Theories of Government" (mimeographed, Va. Polytechnic Institute and State Univ., 1981).

50. Cited in Lubove, *The Struggle for Social Security*, p. 113. On the ebb and flow of the movement, see Armstrong, *Insuring the Essentials*, pp. 370-75; Lubove, *The Struggle for Social Security*; Epstein, *Insecurity*, pp. ix-x, 62-78; Rubinow, *The Quest for Security*, pp. iv, 207-27, 606-16. See also Witte, *The Development of Social Security*, pp. 173-89; Theodore Marmor, *The Politics of Medicare* (Chicago: Aldine, 1970); and Odin Anderson, "Compulsory Medical Care Insurance, 1910-1950," in *Medicare Policy and Politics*, ed. Eugene Feingold (San Francisco: Chandler, 1966), pp. 86-95.

51. New York Commission, *Old-Age Security*, p. 48-49, 312-24.

52. Lubove, *The Struggle for Social Security*, p. 118.

53. See ibid., pp. 118-19; New York Commission, *Old-Age Security*, pp. 312-13.

Echoing what would be the consensus of the New York Commission twenty years later, the commission remarked on the wide differences in the European and American responses to problems, saying, "It is of striking interest that, at a time when European governments are instituting systems of state insurance and pensions . . . the American railroad and industrial corporations are attempting to solve this problem on their own initiative, through private systems."

54. Evidence on the conditions of the elderly is taken from the state commission reports which, being the first investigations of their kind, were plagued with problems. (There were, at that time, no federal surveys available since, beginning in 1902, the federal government prohibited the Bureau of Census from enumerating and investigating the poor residing outside almshouses.) Among the more important problems with the state surveys was their use of very small samples. In Ohio, for example, 1,858 residents in two cities were surveyed; in Wisconsin, the number was 1,395. The most extensive studies were conducted in Massachusetts with a sample of 21,000 elderly persons, and by the National Civic Federation with 15,000 aged. Also, the samples were often poor representations of the states' overall elderly populations.

Other important problems involved the treatment of individuals in couples, the treatment of individuals without their own sources of income or wealth, and the measurement of income. In some studies the total income of an elderly couple was counted as the income of two individuals in the same income class. In others, it was counted as if one had the full income and the other had no income at all. The latter aggregation technique then raised the problem of interpreting "dependency" and its relationship to poverty, referred to below. Some of the major studies of the period, including the one cited by the Supreme Court in upholding the constitutionality of Social Security, used this technique, thereby counting all wives as dependent on their husbands, and then using these figures to indicate a social problem of poverty. By both aggregation techniques both members of an elderly couple were counted as poor and dependent, regardless of their standard of living, if they lived with their families.

Finally, the measurement of income was imperfect since the elderly had been raised before the day of the federal income tax and before payment in wages was the rule. In California, for example, three-fourths of the aged sampled could not say what their incomes had been during working years as they had done seasonal or piecework, had been self-employed as farmers, miners, or lumbermen without accounts of earnings, or were simply employed with payment in the form of room and board.

Despite each of these problems these census results were nevertheless influential to policy-makers, being the first of their type, and can still be useful today with a recognition of the limits of the data. See "Care of the Aged," *Monthly Labor Review* 30 (April 1930): 11-13; New York Commission, *Old-Age Security*, pp. 48-76; and Calif. State Department of Social Welfare, *Old-Age Dependency: A Study of the Care Given to the Needy Aged in California* (Sacramento: Calif. State Printing Office, 1929), p. 37. On the Supreme Court decision, see F. A. Hayek, *The Constitution of Liberty (Chicago: Univ. of Chicago Press, 1960), pp. 296-97.*

55. Using this method of counting wives, the study cited by the Supreme Court, *supra*, n. 54, estimated that three-quarters of the elderly were "dependent." Hayek, *Constitution of Liberty*, pp. 296-97.

The New York Study of 1929 is especially useful because it was the last major study conducted prior to the onset of the depression. Amounting to more than 700 pages, it also provides a detailed examination of conditions that were prevailing in New York. The conclusions of the commission were based on a series of separate studies, each canvassing a small number of elderly persons, but benefiting from either being inclusive door-to-door surveys or from sampling rural communities, representative towns and blocks of cities, as well as the poor in New York City. New York Commission on Old-Age Security, *Old-Age Security: Report of the New York State Commission*, Leg. Doc. No. 67 (Albany, N.Y.: J. B. Lyon, 1930).

56. Of those persons surveyed, age seventy and older, the two studies found 19-21 percent supported by public funds or organized private charity, 11-12 percent of whom were receiving public pensions.

The study of the 1925 Massachusetts Commission on Pensions was the most extensive to date, surveying more than 21,000 elderly persons in ten towns and twenty-three cities. Along with the studies made by the National Civic Federation, the Massachusetts study was judged by the Bureau of Labor Statistics as having samples large enough and sufficiently representative to have findings of use in evaluating old-age dependency in other areas. New York Commission, *Old-Age Security*, pp. 40, 47-48; and "Care of the Aged," *Monthly Labor Review* 30 (April 1930): 11-13.

57. According to one critic, "Superannuation is an increasing cause of pauperism. This is strikingly shown by the U.S. Census figures. In 1880 only 25.6 percent of the almshouse population had passed their sixty-fifth year. This percentage rose steadily to . . . 53.8 percent in 1923." Abraham Epstein: *Insecurity: A Challenge to America, A Study of Social Insurance in the United States and Abroad* (New York: Random House, 1938), p. 501. For statistics see Bureau of Census, *Paupers in Almshouses: 1923*, pp. 9-10, 50; and Bureau of Census, *Statistical History of the United States from Colonial Times to the Present* (New York: Basic Books, 1976), p. 15.

58. The cut-off was generally $3,000 for "adequate" property holdings and this was the figure most often used in the forthcoming state laws.

59. Kansas estimated—on the basis of actual experience in states with laws in operation in 1933 corrected for full participation—that 11 percent of the aged would be eligible for poverty assistance. Contrast this with the fact that in 1913-14, 31 percent of the elderly in New Zealand were receiving pensions, 41 percent in Australia, and 64 percent in Great Britain. By 1930 the figure had risen to 80 percent in Great Britain. Kansas Legislative Council, *Old-Age Pensions*, pp. 10-13; Rubinow, *The Quest for Security*, p. 281; and Armstrong, *Insuring the Essentials*, p. 405.

60. Extremely important for the failure of federal social insurance legislation and even the failure to amass significant support for state-financed pensions was the lack of a common poverty problem. The number and characteristics of the elderly poor, the causes of their poverty, as well as the institutional responses to poverty varied widely between states and, in a system of local control, widely within states. In the northeastern states, for example, 48 percent of the elderly in almshouses were foreign born; in the south, 30 percent were black. In the South the proportion of elderly males gainfully occupied in 1930 was as high as 72-75 percent; in the Midwest, as low as 47-49 percent. Even the importance of the elderly in the overall population varied widely from 2-3 percent in many states to more than 8 percent in certain New England states. While some states in the West sought in-migration with very lenient residency requirements in their poor laws, others in New England had the opposite goal. While many of the elderly in the northern states were supported by federal Civil War pensions, the elderly in the South were more frequently cared for in homes and institutions. New states in the West, moreover, with sparse populations and without already existing public institutions, faced quite different decisions as to the future provision for the poor than did states in the North with extensive systems of very old public institutions. In short, the heterogeneity in problems, responses, and attitudes was an important constraint on the expansion of the public sector at a centralized level. For statistics, see "Care of the Aged," *Monthly Labor Review* 30 (April

1930): 9-11; "Extent and Distribution of Old-Age Dependency in the United States," *Monthly Labor Review* 38 (Jan. 1934), 1-7; and Bureau of Census, *Paupers in Almshouses: 1923*, p. 420.

61. The characteristics of the almshouse poor typically differed, sometimes markedly, from the poor residing with their families or receiving outdoor relief. See, for example, New York Commission, *Old Age Security*, pp. 409-25. See also Calif. State Department of Social Welfare, *Old-Age Dependency*, pp. 34-38.

62. In a survey of eight thousand lower-income elderly persons, the Massachusetts Commission found that 63.5 percent were partially or totally impaired from earnings, with 45 percent of the males totally impaired. The proportion of the elderly experiencing impairment, moreover, was shown to rise with age from 57 percent in the age group sixty-five to sixty-nine, to 88 percent in the age group of seventy-five and older. The New York Commission found that two-thirds of the aged inmates were unable to work, and more than one-half had been admitted because of physical handicaps or illness. Finally, of the elderly filing for assistance in Pennsylvania in 1924, one-third were disabled by infirmities peculiar to old-age, and one-half were additionally handicapped by ill health or some definite physical disability. See "Care of the Aged," *Monthly Labor Review* 30 (April 1930): 11-16, and New York Commission, *Old-Age Security*, pp. 82, 421.

63. Analytical meaning for the notion of "family solidarity" and the importance of the extended family in the care of the elderly can be found in Laurence Kotlikoff and Avia Spivak, "The Family as an Incomplete Annuities Market," Unpublished working paper no. 362 (Cambridge, Mass.: National Bureau of Economic Research, 1979). Simply put, the extended family is comparable to an "annuities market" in which family members are able to hedge against various risks. As families become smaller and individual members more mobile, this source of insurance becomes less viable.

64. The New York Commission was thus prompted to say, "Your Commission is unable to state authoritatively that insecurity and need in old-age is increasing or decreasing in the State of New York.... There is a great deal of evidence which indicates that the people of this State are from generation to generation in a better economic situation ... also that provision for the future is being made through the accumulation by individuals of large economic resources." New York Commission, *Old-Age Security*, p. 21.

65. Relatively high unemployment rates and declining labor-force participation rates among the elderly were claimed by social insurance advocates to be evidence of the animosity between industry and the elderly and the introduction of mandatory retirement rules. Interestingly, as late as the 1960s, or some twenty years after the widespread adoption of formal pension plans, mandatory retirement ages were found "vastly more frequently" in industries with pension or profit-sharing arrangements and thus in unionized sectors. The vast majority of firms without pensions had completely flexible retirement ages. And the declining labor-force participation rates certainly were influenced by the rising standard of living and the expansion of pension schemes. Not all unemployment was involuntary and not all went uncompensated. See Fred Slavick, *Compulsory and Flexible Retirement in the American Economy* (Binghamton, N.Y.: Hall Printing, 1966).

66. See Raymond Goldsmith, *A Study of Saving in the United States* (2 vols.; New York: Greenwood Press, 1969), 1: 6-8; Michael R. Darby, *The Effects of Social Security on Income and the Capital Stock*, American Enterprise Institute Study in Social Security and Retirement Policy, no. 227 (Washington, D.C.: American Enterprise Institute, 1979), pp. 23-26; and Alicia H. Munnell, *The Effect of Social Security on Personal Saving* (Cambridge, Mass.: Ballinger Publishing Co., 1974), pp. 110-11.

67. Together with consumer durables, these saving forms rose in importance from 20.3 percent of total personal saving in 1900-08, to 31.4 percent in 1922-29. Goldsmith, *A Study of Saving*, 1: 6-10; and Munnell, *The Effect of Social Security*, pp. 38-49, 107, 110-11. See also Bureau of Census, *Historical Statistics*, 1: 253.

68. To appreciate how recent the development was, in the mid-1800s life-insurance policies were typically high-cost term insurance, containing no periods of grace for late payment, no provisions for surrender value, loans, changes of beneficiaries, or settlement in other than lump sum, and there was no scientific grading of premiums. Travel was restricted without consent of the insuring company, policies were issued to men alone, and policy-holders had to warrant the truth of all statements. There were yet no adding machines, few actuarial officers, and mortality tables were still based on English experience. On the nature and early history of life insurance, see Joseph B. MacLean, *Life Insurance* (New York: McGraw-Hill, 1935); Mildred Stone, *A History of the Mutual Benefit Life Insurance Company: Since 1854* (New York: Book Craftsmen Associates, 1957); Malvin E. Davis, *Industrial Life Insurance in the United States* (New York: McGraw-Hill, 1944); and Robert I. Mehr and Emerson Cammack, *Principles of Insurance*, Irwin Series in Insurance and Economic Security (Homewood, Ill: Richard D. Irwin, 1976), pp. 396-97. See also Charles R. Henderson, *Industrial Insurance in the United States* (Chicago: Univ. of Chicago

Press, 1909); J. Owen Stalson, *Marketing Life Insurance: Its History in America* (Cambridge, Mass.: Harvard Univ. Press, 1942); and Morton Keller, *The Life Insurance Enterprise, 1885-1910* (Cambridge, Mass.: Harvard Univ. Press, 1963).

69. Ramond W. Goldsmith, *Financial Institutions* (New York: Random House, 1968), pp. 163-64.

70. For more on regulation and the legal aspects of insurance, see MacLean, *Life Insurance*, pp. 155-89, 450-70.

71. Unlike English fraternals which placed emphasis on their social function, American fraternals placed emphasis on their insurance function and operated more or less as mutual life-insurance companies. In both countries sickness insurance was broadly defined to cover all types of incapacity including old-age. For an interesting early history of fraternal societies, see Walter Nichols, "Fraternal Insurance in the United States: Its Origin, Development, Character, and Existing Status," *Annals of the American Academy of Political and Social Science* 70 (March 1917): 109-22. See also Abb Landis, "Life Insurance by Fraternal Orders," *Annals of the American Academy of Political and Social Science* 24 (July-Dec., 1904): 475-88; National Fraternal Congress, *Fraternal Life Insurance*; Lubove, *The Struggle for Social Security*, pp. 19-22; and Tishler, *Self-Reliance*, p. 23. It was estimated in 1904 that the management costs for private companies were approximately $8–$9 per $1,000 worth of insurance in force compared to fraternals whose costs were less than $1 per $1,000 worth of insurance in force. Landis, "Life Insurance by Fraternal Orders," *Annals of American Academy of Political and Social Science*, p. 482.

72. Tishler, *Self-Reliance*, p. 69.

73. The financial difficulties of fraternals and their need for regulation were prone to exaggeration, especially by competing commercial companies, because of their quite radically different actuarial and contractual nature. Fraternal insurance did not generally involve individual policies; instead, the details of plans were a part of the by-laws of each society. Moreover, fraternals invariably had the right of unlimited assessment of each of its members so that their contractual and actuarial conditions were quite radically different from their commercial counterparts. Partly because of their rapid growth in the late 1800s, fraternals were then sharply attacked by insurance companies already subject to legal restrictions on solvency and management. A number of the most important actuarial changes to result in the first decades of the 1900s were the product of efforts of the National Fraternal Congress and the Associated Fraternals of America who accumulated and published their own mortality statistics and set standards of solvency. See MacLean, *Life Insurance*, pp. 402-05; and Nichols, "Fraternal Insurance in the United States," *Annals of American Academy of Political and Social Science*, pp. 113-16.

74. As of 1923. See Goldsmith, *A Study of Saving*, p. 462; and MacLean, *Life Insurance*, p. 357.

75. For several informative sources on industrial life insurance, see Stalson, *Marketing Life Insurance*, pp. 462-81; Davis, *Industrial Life Insurance*; and MacLean, *Life Insurance*, pp. 385-400.

76. MacLean, *Life Insurance*, pp. 385-86, 399-400; and Davis, *Industrial Life Insurance*, pp. 1-11.

77. MacLean, *Life Insurance*, p. 400. Two other developments were "intermediate" life insurance (a type of ordinary insurance), introduced in the 1890s with policies as low as $500 and quarterly premium payments, and in the 1920s, monthly premium insurance.

78. Ibid., pp. 357-59; Mehr and Cammack, *Principles of Insurance*, p. 459; and Davis, *Industrial Life Insurance*, p. 13.

79. MacLean, *Life Insurance*, p. 497. See also Davis, *Industrial Life Insurance*.

80. MacLean, *Life Insurance*, pp. 495-99; and Bureau of Census, *Historical Statistics*, 2: 1056-60.

81. Eight-hundred million dollars was paid on death benefits, and $130 million on matured endowments and annuities.

82. Bureau of Census, *The Statistical History*, p. 1058.

83. Goldsmith, *A Study of Saving*, p. 468.

84. See Murray Latimer, *Industrial Pension Systems in the United States and Canada* (2 vols.; New York: Industrial Relations Counselors, 1932); National Industrial Conference Board, *Elements of Industrial Pension Plans* (New York: National Industrial Conference Board, 1931); Charles Dearing, *Industrial Pensions* (Washington, D.C.: The Brookings Institution, 1954); Rainard Robbins, *Impact of Taxes on Industrial Pension Plans* (New York: Industrial Relations Counselors, 1949); "Industrial Old-Age Pension Plans," *Bulletin of the U.S. Bureau of Labor Statistics*, no. 439 (June 1927): 329-33, 436-45.

85. "Industrial Old-Age Pension Plans," *Bulletin of the U.S. Bureau of Labor Statistics*, p. 438.

86. Latimer, *Industrial Pension Plans*, 2: 843.

87. As also illustrated in Table 3.8, there were not even 150,000 beneficiaries of private pension plans in 1928, and just over a half million beneficiaries of public pension systems. Rather than reflecting any necessary failure on the part of private markets, this low number of beneficiaries reflected the lag characterizing the start-up of any pension program in which benefits are earned. Given this situation, there

may well have been a period during which the need for poverty relief for the elderly was temporarily more acute, as the same factors which increased the demand for retirement income among workers—demographic and family changes, periodically severe recessions, and increased industrial employment—also created, in some respects unexpectedly, a group of elderly persons with less than their desired level of financial protection. On the tax and legal status of private pensions, see Dan M. McGill, *Fundamentals of Private Pensions* (Homewood, Ill.: Richard D. Irwin, 1964), pp. 24-31; Robbins, *The Impact of Taxes on Industrial Pension Plans*; and Latimer, "Legal Aspects," *Industrial Pension Systems*, 2: 643-748.

88. In Samuel Gomper's words, "This fundamental fact stands out paramount, that social insurance cannot remove or prevent poverty." Cited in Hoffman, *Facts and Fallacies of Compulsory Health Insurance*, p. 62.

89. In the long run, a pay-as-you-go system offers a sustainable return for a generation of only the rate of growth of the taxable wage base, which is unlikely to exceed the pretax return to private capital. For the two most informative discussions of the operation and politics of a pay-as-you-go system, see Edgar Browning, "Social Insurance and Intergenerational Transfers," *Journal of Law and Economics* 16 (Oct. 1973): 215-73, and "Why the Social Insurance Budget Is Too Large in a Democracy," *Economic Inquiry* 13 (Sept., 1975): 373-88. Regarding political aspects, Browning focuses on the politics of growth and on the effects of an aging population and other factors on the size of an existing program. He does not examine questions regarding political and economic risk, those that are crucial to the collective decision to create a pay-as-you-go system at all.

90. For more on the nature and fiscal-political difficulties of many of the early public pension schemes, particularly those resulting from the choice of a pay-as-you-go over a funded system, see "Public Service Retirement Systems in the United States," *Bulletin of the U.S. Bureau of Labor Statistics*, no. 491 (Aug. 1929): 542-47, "Public Service Retirement Systems: United States, Canada, and Europe"; *Bulletin of the U.S. Bureau of Labor Statistics*, no. 447 (Jan. 1929): 1-170; Paul Studensky, *The Pension Problem and the Philosophy of Contributions* (New York: Pension Publishing, 1917). See also Edwin Witte, "Old-Age Security in the Social Security Act," *Journal of Political Economy* (Feb. 1937): 1-44; and Latimer, *Trade Union Pensions*.

91. For a union-by-union account of the operation of trade union pensions before and during the depression, see Latimer, *Trade Union Pensions*.

92. Twenty-eight percent were covered by pensions as opposed to one of the other of several forms of benefits for the elderly. Ibid., pp. 113-16. See also William Greenough and Francis King, *Pension Plans and Public Policy* (New York: Columbia Univ. Press, 1976), pp. 40-42.

Also, with labor union membership declining throughout the period—membership in the AFL, for example, declined from 4 million workers in 1920 to 2.9 million in 1929—and with limited time and resources labor leaders naturally directed their efforts toward more immediate problems such as limiting the use of court injunctions against striking workers, eliminating "yellow-dog" contracts, and restricting the influx of immigrant workers. That is, with important advances to be made for their own members in terms of raising wages, cutting hours of work, and improving working conditions, social legislation such as old-age insurance, with any benefits widely dispersed and extending to union and nonunion members alike, must have had low priority.

93. See Roy Lubove, *The Professional Altruist: Emergence of Social Work as a Career* (New York: Atheneum, 1969); and Amos Warner, Stuart Queen, and Ernest Harper, *American Charities and Social Work* (New York: Thomas Y. Crowell, 1930), pp. 25-39, 554-72; and Trattner, *From Poor Law to Welfare State*, pp. 193-211.

94. The Federal Emergency Relief Act, for example, passed in 1933, made available $500 million in federal funds to states and localities. With hardly inconsequential effects on the employment of social workers, the act stipulated that every local relief administrator had to employ at least one experienced social worker on his staff, and one qualified supervisor per twenty employees. By directive of Harry Hopkins, moreover, federal funds could only be distributed to a public agency. Between 1930 and 1940, the depression decade, the number of social workers doubled. See Trattner, *From Poor Law to Welfare State*, pp. 236-37 and 243.

95. On the American old-age pension movement—early history, politics, and legislative developments—see Paul H. Douglas, *Social Security in the United States: An Analysis and Appraisal of the Federal Social Security Act* (New York: McGraw-Hill, 1939), pp. 5-10; Epstein, *Insecurity*, pp. 532-50; and National Industrial Conference Board, *The Support of the Aged: A Review of Conditions and Proposals* (New York: National Industrial Conference Board, 1931), pp. 44-65. See also "Old-Age Pensions and Relief," *Bulletin of the U.S. Bureau of Labor Statistics*, no. 439 (June 1927): 431-36, and no. 491 (Aug. 1929): 529-32; New York Commission, *Old-Age Security*, pp. 220-70; U.S. Committee on

Economic Security, *Report to the President*, p. 13; "Status of Old-Age Pension Legislation in the United States," *Monthly Labor Review* 29 (July 1929): 21-28; Florence Parker, "Experience Under State Old-Age Pension Acts," *Monthly Labor Review* 29 (Aug. 1934): 255-72, and 34 (Oct. 1936): 811-37.

96. New York Commission, *Old-Age Security*, pp. 312-24.

97. A resolution to put the AFL on record as supporting public old-age pensions failed in 1905 but was passed in 1907. Tishler, *Self-Reliance*, p. 88. In mid-1921 the Indiana State Aerie of the Fraternal Order of Eagles (FOE) adopted a resolution in support of state pension legislation. Symbolizing a break with a long tradition of voluntary mutual assistance, the Eagles' endorsement of old-age pensions and their cooperation with organized labor represented a significant addition ot the strength of the pension movement. The publicity and legislative campaigns they helped carry out hastened the process of familiarizing the public with issues that had heretofore been argued by intellectuals. See Lubove, *The Struggle for Social Security*, pp. 137-43.

98. It was apparently during the first decade of the 1900s that the first piece of federal pension legislation was introduced into Congress by William Wilson of Pennsylvania, who later became the secretary of labor. Believing that legislation to provide pensions to civilians would be found unconstitutional, he proposed an "Old Age Home Guard," a pseudomilitary corps within the United States Army. The elderly would have been enlisted to report annually on patriotic sentiments in their communities, and then be eligible for federal pensions. The bill, of course, died in committee. In 1911 another federal pension bill was introduced into Congress by Victor Berger of Wisconsin, the first socialist representative. The plan was designed to provide pensions of up to $4 a week to all persons over the age of sixty who had weekly incomes less than $10. The bill died in committee. Bills of this sort were regularly introduced thereafter, but it was not until 1927 that more moderate proposals involving only partial federal financing were introduced, and it was not until the 1930s that such a bill was reported out of committee. Abraham Epstein, *Insecurity*, pp. 532-33, and *The Challenge of the Aged*, pp. 260-61; and "Efforts Seeking Federal Action on Old-Age Pensions: 1909-1935;" *The Congressional Digest* 14 (March 1935): 76.

99. In 1929, the average yearly pension was $204 ($981). "Old-Age Pension Laws in Operation," *Bulletin of the U.S. Bureau of Labor Statistics*, no. 491 (Aug. 1929): 531-32.

100. See "Efforts Seeking Federal Action on Old-Age Pensions," *The Congressional Digest*, p. 72; and the U.S. Committee on Economic Security, *Report to the President*, pp. 68-69.

101. In some states opposition to old-age pensions remained primarily among business interests such as the Chamber of Commerce or associations of manufacturers. In 1924, for example, the Pennsylvania Chamber of Commerce remarked that pensions were an "insidious experiment in paternalistic government." Lubove, *The Struggle for Social Security*, pp. 139-40. In other states there was opposition even among the public officials designated to implement laws already in existence, and in some states (such as in the South), the opposition was still broadly based. Opponents typically argued that pensions reduced self-reliance as well as the responsibility of children to support their parents, and like all previous experiments of this sort would have a "disposition to make pensions increasingly large and the conditions of granting them increasingly easy." "Care of the Aged in the United States," *Monthly Labor Review* 28 (March 1929): 35. Opponents argued that they were of no significant improvement over almshouses or payments from ordinary poor funds and were undesirably costly. In the long run some argued, the cost of old-age pensions might serve as an "entering wedge" for social insurance. And yet to some the question of public relief remained unresolved. According to President Herbert Hoover, who rejected proposals for federal aid even after the onset of the Great Depression, "You cannot extend the mastery of government over the daily lives of the people . . . without at the same time making it the master of their souls and thoughts." Cited in Trattner, *From Poor Law to Welfare State*, p. 231. Arguments against old-age pensions are presented in Johnson, *The Reference Shelf: Old-Age Pensions*; National Industrial Conference Board, *The Support of the Aged;* "Care of the Aged in the United States," *Monthly Labor Review* 28 (March 1929): 35-40; and "Old-Age Pensions and Relief," *Bulletin of the U.S. Bureau of Labor Statistics*, no. 491 (Aug. 1929): 532-33. The latter two contain responses of states already having laws in existence.

In England Alfred Marshall had opposed state pension schemes, saying in 1893, "My objections to them are that their educational effect, though a true one, would be indirect; that they would be expensive; and that they do not contain, in themselves, the seeds of their own disappearance. I am afraid that, if started, they would tend to become perpetual. I regard all this problem of poverty as a mere passing evil in the progress of man upwards; and I should not like any institution started which did not contain in itself the causes which would make it shrivel up, as the causes of poverty itself shrivelled up." *Official Papers by Alfred Marshall*, ed. J. M. Keynes (London, 1926), p. 244, cited in Hayek, *The Constitution of Liberty*, p. 509.

102. There were no counties participating in providing old-age pensions in Maryland, for example, by

the close of the decade, one out of 63 counties participating in Colorado, and just 3 out of 120 counties participating in Kentucky. The highest rate of participation was in Montana, with 42 out of 56 counties providing pensions. In Montana, however, the state with the oldest and most extensively operating system, the number of pensioners peaked in 1927 at 884, or less than 6 percent of the state's elderly population. New York Commission, *Old-Age Security*, pp. 248-59; "Care of the Aged in the United States," *Monthly Labor Review* 28 (March 1929): 34; and "Care of Aged in the United States," *Bulletin of the U.S. Bureau of Labor Statistics*, no. 491 (Aug. 1929): 529-32.

103. As discussed earlier, the make-up of the poor varied markedly across states, particularly with respect to race and nationality. (New England states had elderly almshouse populations of almost 50 percent foreign-born, for example, and in the southern states almost a third were black.) To the extent that the electorate's willingness to provide welfare was directly related to the similarity of the poor population to the overall taxpaying population, a liberalization of the northeastern laws was a predictable outcome of the curtailment of immigration into the United States. Also, laws would be likely to emerge sooner in the North, because heterogeneity in northern almshouses derived from place of birth, not race, and this was easily dealt with by very long residency requirements. Evidently, the "technologies of discrimination" were quite different in the various regions of the country and thus the willingness to adopt outdoor relief policies.

104. With the possibility of higher level financing, the benefits of a locally controlled relief system would in certain localities be well outweighted by the benefits to be derived from the geographical redistribution of tax costs made possible by more centralized schemes of finance. This would be especially true in the older, more industrialized cities and states with more extensive poverty problems.

105. Epstein, *Insecurity*, p. vii.

106. Social insurance advocates were highly critical of the voluntary nature of the early old-age pension laws. According to Rubinow, they threatened to convert the "entire movement into a snare and delusion." See ibid., pp. 141-42, and Rubinow, *The Quest for Security*, pp. 278-79.

Chapter 4. Preludes to Social Security: The Great Depression, President Roosevelt, and the Report of the CES

1. The number of persons receiving aid from public assistance and federal work programs in 1933 actually reached 25.5 million. See U.S. Committee on Economic Security, *Supplement to the Report of the Committee on Economic Security*, Hearings before the Committee on Finance on S. 1130, U.S. Senate 74th Cong., 1st Sess., p. 40; and U.S. Social Security Board, Bureau of Research and Statistics, *Trends in Public Assistance: 1933-1939*, Bureau Report No. 8 (Washington, D.C.: Government Printing Office, 1940), p. 6.

2. For more on the "Great Contraction," see Milton Friedman and Anna J. Schwartz, *A Monetary History of the United States: 1867-1960* (Princeton, N.J.: Princeton Univ. Press, 1963), pp. 299-419. One of the few surveys of the unemployed in 1934 showed that the average duration of unemployment rose with age. Ranking the unemployed according to the length of time they had been out of work and seeking employment, the survey found that for those individuals 25-44 years of age, the most frequent duration of unemployment was 12-23 months; for those 45-54, it was 24-35 months; for those 55-64, 24-35 months; and for those at least 65 years of age, the most frequent duration exceeded 48 months. "Survey of Occupational Characteristics of Persons Receiving Relief" (May 1934), prepared by Federal Emergency Relief Administration and reprinted in *The Statutory History of the United States: Income Security*, ed. Robert Stevens (New York: Chelsea House, 1970), p. 68.

3. Department of Commerce, *Survey of Current Business* 8 (Jan. 1933): 105 and *Survey of Current Business: Annual Supplement, 1932*, p. 33; U.S. Bureau of Census, *Historical Statistics of the United States* (1976), p. 266.

4. U.S. Committee on Economic Security, *Supplement to the Report of the Committee on Economic Security*, p. 40. The number of recipients of public assistance and federal work programs at that time was 23 million, having peaked in January 1934 at 28.2 million. The number of such recipients did not fall below 20 million until May of 1936. U.S. Social Security Board, *Trends in Public Assistance: 1933-1939*, p. 6. By the end of 1934, moreover, perhaps as many as three-quarters of a million elderly persons were receiving direct relief from the federal government. Paul Douglas, *Social Security in the United States*, p. 6.

5. Frederick Allen, "Economic Security," in *Social Security: Policies, Problems, and Prospects*, ed. Wilbur J. Cohen, p. 30.

6. Speech delivered 5 March 1934 to a meeting of the National Recovery Administration; cited in

Cong. Rec (22 June 1935), p. 9906. For two primary works with this viewpoint published after the onset of the depression, see Abraham Epstein, *Insecurity: A Challenge to America* (1933), and Isaac Rubinow, *The Quest for Security* (1934).

7. For a sampling of discussions and debates on the old-age pension issue during the depression, see National Industrial Conference Board, *The Support of the Aged: A Review of Conditions and Proposals* (New York: National Industrial Conference Board, 1931), pp. 44-55; Abraham Epstein, *Insecurity* pp. 532-50: Douglas, *Social Security in the United States*, pp. 7-11; "Congress Faces the Question of Old-Age Pensions," *The Congressional Digest* 14 (March 1935), pp. 69-72, and Johnsen, "Old-Age Pensions," *The Reference Shelf.*

8. Administrative authorities in New York and Massachusetts, the two largest pensioning states, estimated that from 30 to 35 percent of the increase in the number of their pensioners between 1930 and 1931 was due to the depression alone as it affected unemployment among the elderly and among children who would typically have helped support them. (There was a seven-fold increase in the number of pensioners in the United States between 1930 and 1931.) "Operation of Public Old-Age Pension Systems in the United States in 1931," *Monthly Labor Review* (June 1932): 1260.

For a series of informative sources on the operation of old-age pension laws — funding, administration, and new developments—see ibid., pp. 1259-68; "Experience Under State Old-Age Pension Acts in 1933," *Monthly Labor Review* 39 (Aug. 1934): 255-72; "Experience Under State Old-Age Pension Acts in 1935," *Monthly Labor Review* 34 (Oct. 1936): 811-37; U.S. Committee on Economic Security, *Supplement to the Report of the Committee on Economic Security*, Hearings before the Committee on Finance on S. 1130, pp. 50-51; and "Congress Faces the Question of Old-Age Pensions," *The Congressional Digest* 14 (March 1935): 69-72.

9. For purposes of comparison, figures calculated in 1980 dollars are given in parentheses.

10. See "Experience Under State Old-Age Pension Acts in 1935," *Monthly Labor Review*, p. 832.

11. "Experience Under State Old-Age Pension Acts in 1933," *Monthly Labor Review* 39 (Aug. 1934): 255-57.

12. "Experience Under State Old-Age Pension Acts in 1935," *Monthly Labor Review*, p. 832, and "Experience Under State Old-Age Pension Acts in 1933," *Monthly Labor Review*, p. 257.

13. An often-repeated argument for federal participation was that the "less progressive" states (i.e., in the South and West) were failing to take initiative to create their own programs. This passiveness concerned advocates of "social justice" and also, because of the mobility of the poor, was said to place the more progressive states in the position of having prohibitively costly programs or else restrictive eligibility requirements. As proponents of equalizing differences in state programs argued for federal funding as opposed to simple federal standards, doubt is cast on the view that their demands emerged out of these concerns alone. States such as New York and California, for example, which together accounted for nearly 90 percent of all expenditures on old-age pensions and housed nearly 75 percent of all pensioners in 1931, had a great deal to gain from federal financing and a geographic redistribution of tax costs — regardless of their impact on the laws of other states.

14. On the renewed interest after the onset of the depression, see Douglas, "The Tide Turns," *Social Security in the United States*, pp. 3-27; Epstein, *Insecurity*, pp. vii-viii; and Rubinow, *The Quest for Security*, pp. iii-v.

15. For a careful examination, see Lubove, *The Struggle for Social Security*, pp. 113-14, 135-43. For a sampling of the works on social insurance (old-age and unemployment) during the depression, see Armstrong, *Insuring the Essentials*; Eveline Burns, *Toward Social Security* (New York: McGraw Hill, 1936); Paul Douglas, *Standards of Unemployment Insurance* (Chicago: Univ. of Chicago Press, 1933); Epstein, *Insecurity*; and Issac Rubinow, ed., *The Care of the Aged* (Chicago: Univ. of Chicago Press, 1931); and Rubinow, *The Quest for Security*. Also, see American Association for Old-Age Security, *Bulletin* 1-9, an informative monthly newsletter put out by the AAOAS between June 1927 and December 1935.

16. Rubinow, *The Quest for Security*, p. 278. Epstein established the American Association for Old-Age Security in 1927, independent of the fraternals that had led the pension movement and AALL. The AAOAS took an active role in drafting models for mandatory pension laws, in disseminating information on the advantages of abandoning the almshouse, and in supporting the Administration's forthcoming Social Security bill. See American Association for Old-Age Security, *Bulletin*, Vols. 1-9 (June 1927-Dec. 1935), and for more on this subject, see Lubove, *The Struggle for Social Security*, pp. 141-43.

17. For more information, see Lubove, "Health Insurance: Made in Germany," *The Struggle for Social Security*, pp. 66-90, 114.

18. Murray W. Latimer, *Industrial Pension Systems in the United States and Canada* (New York:

Industrial Relations Counselors, 1933), 2: 893. This publication is a thorough treatment of new developments in industrial insurance during the depression.

19. See, for example, Epstein, "The Inadequacy of Private Insurance," in *Insecurity*, pp. 116-61.

20. See Douglas,*Social Security in the United States*, p. 246-48, and Latimer, *Industrial Pension Systems*, pp. 681-706, 846-49.

21. Latimer, *Industrial Pension Systems in the United States*, p. 843.

22. Ibid., pp. 842-44, and Douglas, *Social Security in the U.S.*, p. 250.

23. Latimer, *Industrial Pension Systems*, p. 841-49.

24. According to Latimer, for example, "Railroad pensioners as a group are thus seen to have ... fared exceedingly well, despite the absence of anything which might be construed by the courts as a legal contract between themselves and the roads paying pensions." Ibid., p. 653.

25. Since trade-union pension schemes were typically unfunded, the depression led to the bankruptcy of most such plans, drying up union coffers while increasing demands thereon. This certainly worked to reduce the opposition of organized labor to compulsory old-age insurance. See Latimer, *Trade Union Pension Systems*.

26. Latimer, *Industrial Pension Systems*, p. 850-86.

27. The average annuity was twice this value in the banking and insurance industries. Douglas, *Social Security in the United States*, p. 252, and Latimer, *Industrial Pension Systems*, p. 869.

28. Rubinow, *The Quest for Security*, pp. iv, 605-6. The author went on to ask, "Will it be Bismarck, Lloyd George and—Franklin D. Roosevelt?" Ibid., p. 606.

29. For more on the Dill-Connery bill (H R. 8461), a proposal for the federal government to match 30 percent of state expenditures on old-age pensions, see Epstein, *Insecurity*, pp. 533, 546; Douglas, *Social Security in the United States*, pp. 10-11; and Witte, *The Development of the Social Security Act*, pp. 5, 7. See also American Association for Old-Age Security, *Bulletin* 8 (June-July 1934): 1, 5-6.

30. American Association for Old-Age Security, "Both Major Parties Promise Social Legislation," *Bulletin* 8 (June-July 1934): 5-6.

31. Douglas, *Social Security in the United States*, pp. 11, 26. According to Witte, who would come to play a key role in the enactment of Social Security, proponents of the Dill-Connery bill were advised by the President that he had in mind to "delay action on these bills, prepare a more comprehensive program in the interim before the next congress convened, and then to push this program promptly to enactment in the early weeks of the first session of the next congress." Witte, *The Development of the Social Security Act*, p. 5.

32. Text of speech in *Cong. Rec.* (8 June 1934), pp. 10769-71.

33. Ibid., p. 10771.

34. The executive order is duplicated in Witte, *The Development of the Social Security Act*, pp. 201-02, which is perhaps the most informative account of the creation, staffing, and activities of the CES. See also, Charles McKinley and Robert Frase, *Launching Social Security — A Capture-and-Record Account: 1935-1937* (Madison: Univ. of Wisc. Press, 1970), pp. 9-10; Douglas, *Social Security in the United States*, pp. 27-28; Altmeyer, *The Formative Years*, pp. 7-29; and Frances Perkins, *The Roosevelt I Knew* (New York: Harper and Row, 1946), pp. 278-301. For a comprehensive legislative account, see *The Statutory History of the United States: Income Security*, ed. Robert Stevens, pp. 59-88.

35. The basic research and preparation of preliminary reports were all done under Witte's supervision by a staff he personally selected. This work was then presented to the technical board for discussion and modification before reaching the CES. Witte, *The Development of the Social Security Act*, pp. 22-40.

36. The twenty-three representatives of the "public" were carefully selected by the President along with Perkins, Altmeyer, and Witte. According to Witte, Chairman Graham, for example, was selected because the South housed the greatest opposition to social security and he was a "genuine progressive." All employer members except one "were connected with firms which had experimented with voluntary unemployment insurance plans." The representatives of "labor" were three members of the executive council of the AFL, and two representatives of state federations. Representatives of the "public" at large included, most notably, well-known participants in the social insurance movement and friends of the committee, and representatives of the pension movement charities, and settlement houses. The final report of the advisory council then endorsed a program with considerably more federal control than contained in the CES's proposals. Ibid, pp. 51-64.

37. Franklin D. Roosevelt, *Message from the President Transmitting A Recommendation for Legislation on the Subject of Economic Security*, Hearings before the Committee on Finance on S. 1130, U.S. Senate, 74th Cong., 1st Sess. (17 Jan. 1935), p. 1307.

38. *Message from the President*, Hearings before the Committee on Finance on S. 1130, p. 1307.

39. For the details of the three plans for the elderly, presented in only nine pages, see U.S. Committee on Economic Security, *Report of the Committee on Economic Security*, Hearings before the Committee on Finance on S. 1130, pp. 1330-39. For discussion see Douglas, *Social Security in the United States*, pp. 151-84.

40. U.S. Committee of Economic Security, *Report of the Committee on Economic Security*, Hearings before the Committee on Finance on S. 1130, p. 1334

41. Ibid., p. 1336.

42. Both benefit formulas were to be applied to the worker's average wages in covered employment, either weekly (AWW) or monthly (AMW), counting only the first $150 per month in covered employment. For early entrants retiring in 1942, the monthly annuity would be 15 percent of AWW. For early entrants retiring between 1943 and 1947, this basic benefit would be increased 1 percent for each 40 weeks of contributions but by no more than 1 percent for each year covered by the system. For those retiring between 1948 and 1957, the increment to the basic benefit would be 2 percent of AWW for each 40 weeks of contributions but no more than 2 percent per year. The maximum annuity payable thereafter would be 40 percent of AMW. For late entrants the monthly benefit would be 10 percent of AMW plus 1 percent for each 40 weeks of contributions in excess of a 200-week minimum. Ibid., pp. 1335-36.

43. Ibid., p. 1336.

44. A not-too-careful examination of Table 4.3 reveals that any worker who would earn the actuarial equivalent of his tax payments had not yet been born. All workers—young and old—were scheduled to receive "unearned benefits." According to Director Witte, neither the CES nor the President realized that the CES staff had designed the formulas to grant unearned benefits to everyone alive. See Witte, *The Development of the Social Security Act*, pp. 148-49. Furthermore, given the progressive benefit formula, what held true for actuarial fairness of benefits pertained to benefits for a generation, not for particular individuals in that generation.

45. U.S. Committee on Economic Security, *Report of the Committee on Economic Security*, pp. 1337-38. It is interesting to note that expenditures on Social Security exceeded $75 billion in 1975.

46. U.S. Committee on Economic Security, *Report of the Committee on Economic Security*, p. 1337.

47. Ibid., p. 1338.

48. Ibid., p. 1339.

49. *Message From the President*, Hearings before the Committee on Finance on S. 1130, p. 1307. Also, the CES said, "The CES in its recommendations places first the matter of employment assurance . . . the stimulation of private employment and the provision of public employment." Hearings before the Senate Finance Committee on S. 1130, 74th Cong., 1st Sess., p. 32.

50. The Lundeen bill provided the radical alternative to the Administration's unemployment compensation program. Introduced into Congress by Farmer-Laborer Rep. Ernest Lundeen of Minnesota in 1934, and, again in 1935, the bill proposed the creation of a commission staffed by ordinary laborers and farmers that would administer unemployment compensation. Anyone out of work through no fault of his own was to be paid a benefit equivalent to the average local wage for the entire duration of unemployment. See *The Congressional Digest* 14 (March 1935): 79, and Douglas, *Social Security in the United States*, pp. 74-83.

51. *Cong. Rec.* (22 June 1935), p. 9908. For more on Long and the "Share-Our-Wealth" Society, see *The Congressional Digest* 14 (March 1935): 79; Schlesinger, *The New Deal in Action*, pp. 36-37, and *Cong. Rec.* (22 June 1935), pp. 9906-11, and (24 June 1934), p. 9928.

52. Speech delivered 5 March 1934 at a meeting of the National Recovery Administration, cited in *Cong. Rec.* (22 June 1935), p. 9906.

53. In a New York Times article, for example, it was said that "he [President Roosevelt] hopes to cut into the political forces behind Huey Long and Dr. Townsend by means of his own more rational proposals. They may not be financially sound, or capable of realization, but politically they ought to serve very well in 1936." Cited in *Cong. Rec.* (22 June 1935), p. 9907.

54. Average monthly earnings in 1933 were only $83. U.S. Bureau of Census, *Statistical History of the United States* (1976), p. 164. For more on the Townsend Plan, see, in particular, the Committee on Old-Age Security, *The Townsend Crusade* (Washington, D.C.: Twentieth Century Fund, 1936); "Is the Townsend Plan for 'Old-Age Revolving Pensions' Sound?" *The Congressional Digest* 14 (March 1935): 92-94, 79; Douglas, *Social Security in the U.S.*, pp. 69-74, and Schlesinger, *New Deal in Action*, pp. 36-37.

55. Committee on Old-Age Security, *The Townsend Crusade*, p. 5.

56. Ibid., pp. 7-10. In response to questions raised concerning why the pensions were so large, Townsend responded: "Because to cut it in two would be to cut its economic benefits in two. Please understand this; the persons more than sixty who receive pensions *will be performing a task and a duty*

when they spend their pensions. The chief purpose is to get someone to spend money, to increase the buying power of the nation. The more that is put into circulation, the better off we will be as a nation." "Is the Townsend Plan Sound?" *The Congressional Digest* 14 (March 1935): 93. Critics of the Townsend plan, including most prominently members and allies of the CES, estimated that the plan would have made benefits payable to 85 percent of the persons over sixty, or nearly two million people, at a cost of $24-$25 billion annually. This figure represented one-half of national income in 1934 and nearly two times the total tax revenues of all levels of government in 1932. See statements by Edwin Witte and Walter Lippmann in *The Congressional Digest* 14 (March 1935): 92, 94.

57. This question is the focus of investigation in Weaver, "On the Lack of a Political Market for Compulsory Old-Age Insurance Prior to the Great Depression."

58. Thomas Elliot (principal draftsman of the Social Security Act), "The Story of the Social Security Act," seminar presented at Tulane University (19 March 1977).

59. When the compulsory old-age insurance titles of the Social Security program were coming under attack in the Senate Finance Committee, Witte said that he used the most effective argument he could for the program by placing "emphasis upon the fact that the probable alternative was a modified Townsend plan." Witte, *The Development of the Social Security Act*, p. 103. At the same time, of course, conservatives who opposed compulsory old-age insurance were motivated to form a coalition with Townsendites in an effort to increase the perceived opposition to the Administration's bill.

60. An elaboration on the notion of political failure in the agenda formation process resulting in restrictions on scope or access is contained in Mackay and Weaver, "Monopoly Bureaus and Fiscal Outcomes: Deductive Models and Implications for Reform," *Policy Analysis and Deductive Reasoning.* For two earlier discussions of the failure of political competition as well as a discussion of the incentive to overcome these failures through constitutional initiatives see, respectively, Tullock, "Entry Barriers in Politics," *American Economic Review* 55 (May 1965): 458-66; "Public Decisions as Public Goods," *Journal of Political Economy,* 79 (July/Aug. 1971): 913-18; and Arthur Denzau, Robert Mackay, and Carolyn Weaver, "Spending Limitations, Agenda Control, and Voters' Expectations," *National Tax Journal* (June 1979): 189-200.

61. The impact of uncertainty on information manipulation by public suppliers is examined in more detail in Tullock, *Toward a Mathematics of Politics*, pp. 100-132, and Bartlett, *Economic Foundations of Political Power*, pp. 70-75. For a discussion of the calculus of lobbying, see Aranson and Ordeshook, "A Prolegomenon to the Theory of the Failure of Representative Democracy," and for a similar model of participation, see Tullock, "The Paradox of Revolution," *Public Choice,* and Auster, "The GPITPC and Institutional Entropy," *Public Choice.*

62. According to Arthur Altmeyer, who would become the Social Security Board's first chairman and maintain the top appointed position for eighteen years, "There is no question, of course, that sooner or later the same world-wide economic, social, and political forces responsible for the emergence of social security programs in 125 nations would have resulted in the development of a social security program in the United States. But . . . if Franklin D. Roosevelt had not been President and if the nation had not been plunged into the Great Depression of the 1930's, action might not have been taken at that time or might have taken a different form. As it was, the President believed strongly that, besides taking the emergency measures necessary to relieve the human distress caused by the Great Depression, it was essential to develop a long-range program to protect the American people from the ill effects of unemployment and other personal economic hazards. The President was fortunate in having at his right hand two persons [Frances Perkins, secretary of labor, and Harry Hopkins, federal emergency relief administrator] who not only shared his convictions but also had the knowledge, experience, and skill necessary to develop such a program." See Altmeyer, *The Formative Years in Social Security,* pp. 6-7.

63. For models of the practice of tie-in sales by private sector monopolists, see Martin Burstein, "The Economics of Tie-In Sales," *Review of Economics and Statistics* 42 (Feb. 1960): 68-73; and William Adams and Janet Yellen, "Commodity Bundling and the Burden of Monopoly," *Quarterly Journal of Economics* 90 (Aug. 1976): 475-98. For the case of public-sector monopolists, see James Buchanan, "The Economics of Earmarked Taxes," *The Journal of Political Economy* 71 (Oct. 1963): 457-69; Richard Wagner and Warren Weber, "Competition, Monopoly, and the Organization of Government in Metropolitan Areas," *Journal of Law and Economics* 22 (Dec. 1975): 661-84; and Robert Mackay and Carolyn Weaver, "Commodity Bundling and Agenda Control in the Public Sector," *Quarterly Journal of Economics* (forthcoming).

64. Thomas Eliot, principal draftsman of the Social Security Act, said that his greatest contribution was making Title I of the act old-age assistance (welfare), and "burying" old-age insurance in Titles II and VIII. He admitted that old-age insurance was so unpopular that if it were not drafted that way, "no one

would have kept on reading." Thomas Eliot, "The Coming of the Social Security Act," seminar presented at Tulane Univ. (17 March 1977).

65. The practice and consequences of all-or-none offers by public suppliers are examined in Thomas Romer and Howard Rosenthal, "Bureaucrats vs. Voters," *Quarterly Journal of Economics* 93 (1979): 563-87 and "Political Resource Allocation, Controlled Agenda, and the Status Quo," *Public Choice* (Winter, 1978); Niskanen, *Bureaucracy and Representative Government*; Denzau and Mackay, "A Model of Benefit and Tax Share Discrimination by a Monopoly Bureau," *Journal of Public Economics* 13 (1980): 341-68; and Mackay and Weaver, n. 63 above.

66. See, for example, Altmeyer, *The Formative Years in Social Security*, pp. 12 and 34; and Witte, *The Development of the Social Security Act*, pp. 78-79.

67. American Association for Old-Age Security, "Social Security Bill Impractical," *Bulletin* 9 (June-July 1935): 11.

Chapter 5. The Journey of Compulsory Old-Age Insurance Through Congress

1. Witte, *The Development of the Social Security Act*, pp. 78-79.

2. For two especially informative accounts of the legislative history of the Social Security Act from 1934 to 1935, written by two people who were integrally involved with the legislation, see Paul Douglas, *Social Security in the United States*, and Edwin Witte, *Development of the Social Security Act*. See also, Arthur Altmeyer, *The Formative Years in Social Security* (Madison: Univ. of Wisc. Press, 1968), and Frances Perkins, *The Roosevelt I Knew* (New York: Harper and Row, 1946).

3. See U.S. Congressional Hearings before the Committee on Finance, U.S. Senate, 74th Cong., 1st Sess., on S. 1130 (22 Jan.-20 Feb. 1935), and Hearings before the Committee on Ways and Means, House of Representatives, 74th Cong., 1st Sess., on HR. 4120 (21 Jan.-12 Feb. 1935). According to Witte, employer groups simply knew too little about the legislation to take any active role at this early date. See Witte, *The Development of the Social Security Act*, p. 90.

4. See, for example, Douglas, *Social Security in the United States*, pp. 5-12.

5. Several popular level debates on these issues are contained in "Is the Administration's Program for Old-Age Pensions Sound?" *The Congressional Digest* 14 (1935): 80-91. See also Johnson, *The Reference Shelf*, for a quite thorough list of publications for and against federal old-age pensions and insurance.

6. See exchange between Senators Couzens, Hastings, and Wagner, in Hearings before the Committee on Finance on S. 1130, p. 21.

7. Douglas, *Social Security in the United States*, p. 99.

8. According to Altmeyer, Social Security was viewed by Roosevelt as the "cornerstone" of his Administration, and compulsory old-age insurance a vital aspect. Since the time Roosevelt was Governor of New York he had argued that social insurance was the only solution to the dependency problem among the elderly. See Altmeyer, *The Formative Years*, pp. 12, 34, and Witte, *The Development of the Social Security Act*, pp. 18, 78-79. This view is expressed again in the *Report of the Committee on Economic Security*, Hearings before the Committee on Finance on S. 1130, U.S. Senate, 74th Cong., 1st Sess., p. 1334.

9. Said Roosevelt, "It is childish to speak of recovery first and reconstruction later." Cited in American Association for Social Security, "Roosevelt Pledges Administration to Social Insurance," *Social Security* 8 (June-July 1934): 5.

10. Statement by Senator Hastings in "Is the Administration's Program for Old-Age Pensions Sound?" *The Congressional Digest*, pp. 81-83.

11. Statement by Senator Gore in "Is the Administration's Program for Old-Age Pensions Sound?" *The Congressional Digest*, pp. 83-85.

12. See exchange between Senators Hastings and Wagner over the problems encountered with the civil service annuity program in Hearings before the Committee on Finance on S. 1130, p. 16, in which Hastings states that by 1935 the federal civil-service employees retirement program had already accrued a deficit of $100 ($511) million.

13. See, in particular, statements by Senator Clark and Senator Tydings, *Cong. Rec.* (19 June 1935), pp. 9510-35, and (19 June 1935), pp. 9635-31.

14. See *Report of the Committee on Economic Security*, Hearings before the Committee on Finance on S. 1130, pp. 1334, 1337, and statements by Sen. Wagner (D.-N.Y.) and J. Douglas Brown in "Is the Administration's Program for Old-Age Pensions Sound?" *The Congressional Digest*, pp. 70, 80, 82, and 84.

15. A frequently cited study by the Brookings Institution indicated that in 1929 there were 24,000 families with incomes over $100,000 enjoying a total income three times that earned by the 6 million families earning less than $1,000 a year. See *The Congressional Digest* 14 (March 1935): 80. Rubinow, moreover, argued that nearly half the population was living in "poverty," where a reasonable standard of living was defined as the "opportunity to enjoy life." Rubinow, *The Quest for Security*, pp. 8-11. See also Epstein, *Insecurity: A Challenge to America*, Eveline Burns, *Toward Social Security*, and statements by Rep. Benjamen Focht (R.-Pa.) and Rubinow in "Is the Administration's Program for Old-Age Pensions Sound?" *The Congressional Digest*, pp. 86, 88, and 90.

16. Robert J. Myers, *Expansionism in Social Insurance* (London: Institute of Economic Affairs, 1970), p. 17.

17. Statement by J. Douglas Brown in "Is the Administration's Program for Old-Age Pensions Sound?" *The Congressional Digest*, p. 84. See also *Report of the Committee on Economic Security*, Hearings before Committee on Finance on S. 1130, p. 1338, and Douglas, *Social Security in the U.S.*, pp. 62-68.

18. By increasing costs, the employers' tax tends to reduce the demand for labor, leading to temporary layoffs and shifts of labor among industries until nominal wages fall by the value of the tax. This backward shifting of the tax depends upon labor supply being relatively wage inelastic, an assumption which is substantiated by most empirical studies of labor supply. For a thorough discussion of the incidence of the payroll tax and a survey of empirical work, see Joh Brittain, *The Payroll Tax for Social Security*, Study of Government Finance (Washington, D.C.: The Brookings Institute, 1972).

19. During Senate hearings Sen. Hastings remarked to Sen. Wagner, the bill's sponsor, "It would be a little easier for this man to pay that [the payroll tax] if he knew that that contributed by his employer at the same time constituted part of the fund. . . . In other words, instead of returning to him 50 percent of that which has been accumulated for his benefit, why don't you return all of it to him?" Sen. Wagner responded, incorrectly, "It is all returned." Hearings before the Committee on Finance, on S. 1130, p. 29.

20. Cited in Michael Schiltz, *Public Attitudes Toward Social Security*, p. 30.

21. It remains an empirical issue whether earmarked taxes enhance bureaucratic control, but when compounded with an employer's tax that is generally not perceived as part of the worker's cost, the likelihood of enhanced bureaucratic control is certainly increased. International studies of the determinants of social security expenditures indicate that earmarking leads to higher per capita expenditures than general funding. See Joseph Pechman, Henry Aaron, and Michael Taussig, *Social Security: Perspective for Reform* (Washington, D.C.: The Brookings Institute, 1968), pp. 294-304.

22. See, for example, the statement by Abraham Epstein, Hearings before the House Committee on Ways and Means, House of Representatives on the HR. 4120, 74th Cong., 1st Sess., p. 558; a clear statement by the CES in *Report of the Committee on Economic Security*, Hearings before the Committee on Finance on S. 1130, pp. 1336-7; and statement by Brown in "Is the Administration's Program for Old-Age Pensions Sound?" *The Congressional Digest*, pp. 82-84.

23. Morgenthau clearly stated this position in Hearings before the Committee on Ways and Means on HR. 4120, U.S. House of Representatives, 74th Cong., 1st Sess., pp. 898-99. See also, statement by Noel Sargent in "Is the Administration's Program for Old-Age Pensions Sound?" *The Congressional Digest*, pp. 87, 89. According to Witte, when the CES presented its report to Roosevelt, he noticed the deficits and the need for federal contributions, and, just one day before presenting the legislation to Congress, insisted that if they were not mistakes, the compulsory old-age insurance would have to be modified so as to put it on a self-supporting basis. Without time to make these major changes, he suggested that the CES's benefit and tax schedules be presented to Congress as just one of several possibilities. The CES consented. See Witte, *The Development of the Social Security Act*, pp. 74-75.

24. Douglas, *Social Security in the U.S.*, pp. 56-58.

25. Brown, "Is the Administration's Program for Old-Age Pensions Sound?" *The Congressional Digest*, p. 86.

26. See statement by Morgenthau in Hearings before the Committee on Ways and Means on HR. 4120, pp. 898-905.

27. Witte, *The Development of the Social Security Act*, p. 90.

28. Ibid., p. 93.

29. Altmeyer, *The Formative Years*, pp. 12, 34. Altmeyer would be appointed the first chairman of the Social Security Board.

30. Hearings before the Committee on Ways and Means on HR. 4120, pp. 898-905.

31. As a point of reference, Social Security benefit payments exceeded $50 billion in 1973, and today, trust-fund assets are less than one-fourth of annual benefit payments.

32. Hearings before the Committee on Ways and Means on HR. 4120, p. 899.

33. According to Witte, Morgenthau was the last member of the CES to sign the CES Report, having hesitated because he believed the financing of the compulsory old-age insurance program was unsound. After receiving a "personal appeal" by Labor Secretary Perkins, who sought unanimous support for the Report from CES members, Morgenthau signed the Report without attaching a qualifying statement. See Witte, *The Development of the Social Security Act*, pp. 72-73. That the program was not self-supporting was said to have come as a surprise to Roosevelt. See 23 above.

34. *Report of the Committee on Ways and Means on the Social Security Bill*, House of Representatives, 74th Cong., 1st Sess., Report No. 615, HR. 7260.

35. According to Ways and Means Committee estimates, this would leave approximately 26 million out of 49 million gainfully employed covered by the system. *Report of the Committee on Ways and Means on HR. 4120*, pp. 14, 37. See Douglas, *Social Security in the United States*, pp. 101-02; and Witte, *The Development of the Social Security Act*, pp. 153-57. According to Witte, the Ways and Means Committee was probably responding to the fact that farmers would "object" to being taxed! See ibid., p. 153.

36. Witte, *The Development of the Social Security Act*, p. 157.

37. Douglas, *Social Security in the United States*, pp. 105-06. See also *Report of the Committee on Ways and Means*, HR. 7260, p. 29.

38. *Report of the Committee on Ways and Means*, HR. 7260, pp. 43-44.

39. Douglas, *Social Security in the United States*, pp. 109-10.

40. Witte went on to say that if it had not been for the fortuitous timing of the vote on the compulsory old-age insurance program, held immediately after he made a statement of how the Townsend plan was the "probable alternative," he felt "quite sure that Title II (compulsory old-age insurance) would have gone out of the bill." Witte, *The Development of Social Security*, pp. 102-03.

41. See *Report of the Senate Finance Committee*, 74th Cong., 1st Sess., Report No. 628, Senate Calendar, No. 661.

42. Ibid., p. 3. Were the program truly designed as an annuity program, of course, the work status of the elderly would have been immaterial. According to Witte, the prior omission of this requirement had been due to an inability of the Ways and Means Committee to define employment, not realizing that actuarial calculations for the program had been based on the assumption that the elderly would, in fact, be required to retire in order to draw the old-age benefits. Witte, *The Development of the Social Security Act*, p. 159.

43. For some of the key debates on the Senate floor, see *Cong. Rec.* (15 June 1935), pp. 9354-62, 9366-68, (17 June 1935), pp. 9418-21, (18 June 1935), pp. 9510-38, and (19 June 1935), pp. 9625-45.

44. *Cong. Rec.* (19 June 1935), pp. 9640-41.

45. *Cong. Rec.* (19 June 1935), pp. 9634-35.

46. Ibid., p. 9635.

47. Ibid., p. 9635.

48. See *Cong. Rec.* (18 June 1935), p. 9520-21, (19 June 1935), pp. 9630-31, and Witte, *The Development of the Social Security Act*, pp. 102-08.

49. *Cong. Rec.* (17 June 1935), p. 9442 and (18 June 1935), p. 9510.

50. For more of his arguments, as well as the ensuing debates, see *Cong. Rec.* (17 June 1935), p. 9442 (18 June 1935), pp. 9510-36, and (19 June 1935), pp. 9625-31. Remarkably, according to Director Witte, the interrelationship between private insurance and the public program was not seriously considered by the CES. Witte, *The Development of the Social Security Act*, p. 157.

51. See Douglas, *Social Security in the United States*, pp. 120-25, 252-65, for a summary and evaluation of these arguments.

Interestingly, this is basically the same argument advanced today for extending coverage to government employees. The redistributive benefit formula pays a higher rate of return on the workers' first block of income so that there is, in effect, an optimal number of years to be covered (a number of years to maximize the rate of return). Then, should the worker opt for private coverage he can gain a potentially higher market rate of return on larger accumulated earnings. It is, of course, the benefit formula that creates the "inequity," not the private alternative. Opponents of the alternative, however, argue that the government plan must be expanded to eliminate this anomaly, rather than deal with it directly by changing the benefit formula.

52. Immediately before the vote was taken on the Clark Amendment, a letter from William Green, president of the AFL, was read in which he expressed strong opposition to the amendment. In part, he argued that industries with private pension plans had instituted them to inhibit unionization and that pension plans gave industries "complete control over their employees." See *Cong. Rec.* (19 June 1935), p. 9630. According to Witte, moreover, organized labor had been relatively disinterested in Social Security

initially, having other more important policies to pursue. Later, though, the AFL used votes on the Clark amendment and the entire bill as a test of congressmen's attitudes toward organized labor. Witte, *The Development of the Social Security Act*, p. 88.

53. *Cong. Rec.* (18 June 1935), p. 9525.

54. *Cong. Rec.* (18 June 1935), pp. 9532-33.

55. Thomas Eliot (principal draftsman of Social Security Act), "The Coming of the Social Security Act," seminar presented to Tulane Univ. (17 March 1977). Eliot went on to say that the "White House assigned three experts to each of twelve Senators to change the vote."

56. Witte, *The Development of the Social Security Act*, p. 161. Senator Clark was prompted to say, "No careful and intelligent observer in these unhappy times . . . can have failed to observe that this has ceased to be a government in which legislation is by congressional consideration and vote, but has become a government by experts." See *Cong. Rec.* (19 June 1935), p. 9627.

57. Douglas, *Social Security in the United States*, p. 257.

58. See *House Conference Report*, U.S. House of Representatives, 74th Cong., 1st Sess., Report No. 1540. For further discussion, see Witte, *The Development of the Social Security Act*, pp. 159-62.

59. *Cong. Rec.* (9 Aug. 1935), pp. 12793-94.

60. This was purportedly because the private insurance industry thrived in 1935-36, a phenomenon that those most intensely interested in the Clark Amendment believed was a result of the publicized need for insurance surrounding the enactment of Social Security. Thomas Eliot (principle draftsman of the Social Security Act), "The Coming of the Social Security Act," seminar presented to Tulane University (17 March 1977). According to Altmeyer, once the act was passed, employers "lost interest" as they came to recognize the extensive federal regulation of private plans that would likely result if the exemption were granted. Arthur Altmeyer, *The Formative Years*, p. 42.

61. The Social Security Act, Public No. 271, 74th Cong. [HR. 7260]; Approved 14 Aug. 1935. The terms "annuity," "insurance," and "pension" were not used in the original act because of the desire to avoid constitutional problems. They are used here for simplicity, having been used by the President in the CES Report and in congressional hearings, and again after the Supreme Court ruling in 1937.

62. During deliberations on the 1977 amendments, it was argued that the original program established a ceiling on taxable earnings that exceeded the incomes of approximately 90 percent of the covered population and that the current ceiling should be increased to restore this relationship. This suggestion, advanced to increase the redistributive impact of the program, ignores the fact that coverage was limited to lower-paid occupations in the 1930s. The redistributive impact of the program was necessarily limited since higher-income workers were not generally covered. (Average earnings for covered workers in 1937 were \$900, whereas the average earnings for all workers were 30 percent higher, or \$1,258.)

63. Referring to the redistributive potential of the new program that was disguised as "insurance," Friedrick Hayek said that it was ". . . all a part of the endeavor to persuade public opinion, through concealment, to accept a new method of income distribution, which the managers of the new machine seem to have regarded from the beginning as a merely transitional half measure which must be developed into an apparatus expressly aimed at redistribution." Hayek, *The Constitution of Liberty*, p. 293.

64. L. Meriam and K. Schlotterbeck, *The Cost of Financing Social Security* (Washington, D.C.: The Brookings Institute, 1950), p. 8.

65. Hayek, *The Constitution of Liberty*, p. 293.

66. Hearings before the Committee on Ways and Means on HR. 4120, p. 552.

67. Schlesinger, *The New Deal in Action*, p. 31.

68. Lubove, *The Struggle for Social Security*, pp. 175-78. See also the foreward by Frances Perkins in Witte, *The Development of Social Security*, p. vii; Frances Perkins, *The Roosevelt I Knew*, pp. 278-301; and Arthur Altmeyer, *The Formative Years*, pp. 4-5, 12, on the importance to Roosevelt of "cradle-to-grave" social insurance.

69. In March of 1934 Rubinow, a long-time advocate of social insurance, described a "fundamental difference in the history of social legislation in Europe and in the United States. With us such legislation usually starts as a 'reform movement' initiated by private individuals and groups. Not only the government but even the social group directly concerned often remains indifferent or even antagonistic to the proposal for a long time. It takes an American Association for Labor Legislation, an American Association for Old Age Security, or a Child Labor Committee or a Consumers League, through education, propaganda, wire-pulling and sometimes unesthetic lobbying, to pass an act; sometimes jam it down unwilling throats, not only of unwilling legislators and protesting chambers of commerce, but even of labor itself." *The Quest for Security*, p. 604.

70. The benefit formula was 1/2 percent of the first \$3,000 of total covered wages (TCW), plus 1/12 percent of the next \$42,000 of TCW, plus 1/24 percent of TCW exceeding \$45,000.

Chapter 6. The Institutionalization of Expansionary Forces and Program Redirection: 1935-39

1. Arthur J. Altmeyer, "Progress and Prospects under the Social Security Act" (address before the National Conference of Social Workers, 25 May 1937, unpublished, U.S. Department of Health, Education and Welfare). Altmeyer was the chairman of the Social Security Board from 1936 to 1946. After the Federal Reorganization Act of 1946 dissolved the Social Security Board, he was designated the commissioner of social security, and maintained that position until he resigned in 1953.

2. The top executive for Social Security was the chairman of the Social Security Board until 1946 when the board was abolished and the commissioner of Social Security took over. In 1939 the board was made subordinate to the Federal Security Agency, along with five other agencies. See Charles McKinley and Robert W. Frase, *Launching Social Security: A Capture-and-Record Account, 1935-1937* (Madison: Univ. of Wisc. Press, 1970), for a fascinating and detailed account of the financial and organizational aspects of the Social Security Board in its early years. For a less detailed discussion of staffing and administration during the early years, by perhaps the most important person to influence them, see Altmeyer, *The Formative Years*, pp. 47-73.

3. McKinley and Frase, *Launching Social Security*, pp. 382-91, 407-24.

4. Ibid, p. 18.

5. Ibid., p. 417.

6. "Altmeyer insisted that the Bureau of Old-Age Benefits was in reality administering a labor law and, therefore, experience in labor relations work ought to qualify, but the Civil Service Commission staff held the view that insurance was the essential background." Ibid., pp. 417-18. See also pp. 407-24.

7. Ibid., pp. 423-24.

8. As noted by the past deputy commissioner of social security, appointment of upper-level staff members via the Civil Service (or other nonpolitical means) produces a situation in which the bureaucracy can take on a momemtum of its own in policy planning, independent of the desires of the administration. In his words, "How can he (a high-ranking civil-service technical employee) be expected to produce a vigorous, airtight rebuttal for his political superior to an attack on administration proposals" if it is inconsistent with his own desires as a "public advocate." See Robert J. Myers, *Expansionism in Social Insurance* (Westminster: The Institute of Economic Affairs, 1970), pp. 29-30.

9. According to Altmeyer, a contributing factor to the "continued improvement in the provisions of the act itself, was the establishment of an adequate research unit at the very beginning. This unit had the largest technical staff of any federal agency carrying on economic and social research." Altmeyer, *The Formative Years*, p. 55.

For a more thorough discussion of the problems of bureaucracy and information control, see von Mises, *Bureaucracy*; Tullock, *The Mathematics of Politics*, pp. 100-132; and Bartlett, *The Economic Foundations of Political Power*.

10. Myers, *Social Insurance Expansionism*, p. 29. In the early years this may have been influenced by "the immediate establishment of an intensive training program for all administrative and professional personnel . . . covering the historical background of the Social Security Act, as well as the economic and social considerations which created a need for this legislation. Pervading all of this training has been the effort to imbue each employee with his affirmative responsibility for carrying out the provisions of the Social Security Act." Altmeyer, *The Formative Years*, p. 53.

11. Holding administrative costs constant, a reduction in the size of the firm may necessitate larger reserves (higher premiums) to offset the risk of accidental or random fluctuations in benefit claims. See Robert J. Myers, *Social Insurance and Allied Government Programs*, Irwin Series in Risk and Insurance (Homewood, Ill.: Richard D. Irwin, 1965), p. 7.

12. McKinley and Frase, *Launching Social Security*, p. 18.

13. The Board's appropriations were held up, again, for five months in fiscal year 1938, while Senator Glass got passed an amendment to require Senate confirmation of all of the board's high-paid (above $5,000) expert appointments. Ibid., pp. 29, 423.

14. Cited in John Corson and John McConnell, *Economic Needs of Older People* (New York: Twentieth Century Fund, 1956), pp. 133-34.

15. Text of address by Governor Landon, *The New York Times*, 27 Sept. 1936, pp. 1-2, cited by Daniel S. Sanders in *The Impact of Reform Movements on Social Policy Change: The Case of Social Insurance* (Fair Lawn, N.J.: R. E. Burdick, 1973), p. 89. See also Schlesinger, *The New Deal in Action*, pp. 39-41.

16. McKinley and Frase, *Launching Social Security*, pp. 29-30. The AAA Supreme Court decision generated a great deal of concern over the constitutionality of the Social Security Act, discussed below.

17. Ibid., pp. 356-61. For more on Winant's resignation and the board's flooding of the country with counterinformation, see Altmeyer, *The Formative Years*, pp. 68-69.

18. Schlesinger, *The New Deal in Action*, p. 41.

19. McKinley and Frase, *Launching Social Security*, p. 359.

20. Cited in McKinley and Frase, *Launching Social Security*, p. 11, n. 14.

21. Sanders, *The Impact of Reform Movements*, p. 140.

22. Ibid. As an indication of the extent to which the Townsend Plan gained national attention, a Gallup poll in 1939 indicated that, out of the persons surveyed, 95 percent knew of the plan, 40 percent favored it, and 49 percent knew the exact amount of the proposed transfers. This finding was contrasted with a general lack of understanding of the Social Security program—even the Gallup poll questions were incorrectly stated. See Schiltz, *Public Attitudes Toward Social Security*, pp. 34, 42.

23. Schlesinger, *New Deal in Action*, p. 37.

24. Charles Denby, "The Case Against the Constitutionality of the Social Security Act," *Law and Contemporary Problems* 3 (1936): 328-30.

25. Edwin Witte, "The AAA Decision and the Constitutionality of the Social Security Act," address presented 20 Jan. 1936 (Library, U.S. Department of Health, Education and Welfare).

26. Harry Shulman, "The Case for the Constitutionality of the Social Security Act," *Law and Contemporary Problems* (1936): 306. On the constitutionality of the act, pro and con, see also Barbara Armstrong, "The Federal Social Security Act in Its Constitutional Perspective," *California Law Review* 24 (1936): 247-74; Douglas, *Social Security in the United States*, pp. 349-57, and Edwin Witte, "Old-Age Security in the Social Security Act," *Journal of Political Economy* 45 (Feb. 1937), pp. 1-44.

27. Charles Denby, "The Case Against the Constitutionality of the Social Security Act," *Law and Contemporary Problems* 3 (1936): 325-29.

28. Witte, "The AAA Decision and the Constitutionality of the Social Security Act," p. 8.

29. McKinley and Frase, *Launching Social Security*, p. 453. Constitutional doubts also played a role in slowing the early organizational growth of the Social Security bureaucracy. By 15 March 1936 the BOAB, for example, had only three employees in addition to the director and his associate. Ibid., p. 28.

30. Schlesinger, *The New Deal in Action*, p. 48. Between 1790 and 1937, 40,000 cases were tried by the Supreme Court, out of which seventy-six acts were found unconstitutional. Between March 1933 and March 1934 twelve New Deal acts were found unconstitutional. See "The Supreme Court Controversy," *The Congressional Digest* 16 (1937): 75-76.

31. For an interesting debate on President Roosevelt's reorganization plan, see "The Supreme Court Controversy," *The Congressional Digest*, pp. 65-76.

32. Schlesinger, *New Deal in Action*, pp. 49-50. In Altmeyer's words, "This decision of the United States Supreme Court was, of course, epoch-making and represented a complete reversal of the trend of previous decisions.... It came after the President had recommended that the court membership be increased in the hope of obtaining a majority on the court who would uphold New Deal legislation." The concern that had existed over the constitutionality of the act, he said, could not be exaggerated. Arthur Altmeyer, *The Formative Years*, pp. 20-21, 56.

33. (Helvering vs. Davis), see U.S. Congress, 75th Cong., 1st Sess., Senate Doc. No. 74 (24 May 1937), pp. 29-35. Opinion delivered by Mr. Justice Cordoza, Senate Doc. No. 74, 75th Cong., 1st Sess., p. 30.

34. Ibid., pp. 33-34. In line with the gratuitous transfer interpretation, old-age retirement benefits have never been taxable.

In Altmeyer's view this decision demonstrated the "value" of the Bureau of Research and Statistics in a "rather dramatic fashion," since Cordoza was quoting from a study they had undertaken, entitled "Economic Insecurity in Old Age," which was filed with the case's legal brief. Altmeyer, *The Formative Years*, p. 56.

35. During an investigation into Social Security in 1954 Altmeyer was questioned about his use of the term "insurance" beginning immediately after the Supreme Court decision. Remarkably enough, Altmeyer responded by saying that in his "humble judgment," the Supreme Court validation of the compulsory old-age insurance titles of the act revealed that "Titles II and VIII were inseparable and formed a single plan ... clearly established that in the opinion of the Court both the contributions and the benefit titles made a single whole which ... can be properly described as an insurance system." Altmeyer, *The Formative Years*, p. 226.

36. U.S. Bureau of Census, *The Statistical History of the United States* (1976), p. 1083.

37. Arthur J. Altmeyer, "Progress and Prospects Under the Social Security Act," address before the

National Conference of Social Workers, 25 May 1937 (unpublished addresses by A. J. Altmeyer, Library, U.S. Department of Health, Education and Welfare), p. 4.

38. *Cong. Rec.* (17 March 1937), p. 2324.

39. *Cong. Rec.* (10 May 1937), pp. 4262-63.

40. See U.S. Social Security Board, *Annual Report: 1935-1936* (Washington, D.C.: The Social Security Board, 1937), p. 17. For an overview of these initiatives to the 1939 amendments, see "Congress Looks at Social Security," *The Congressional Digest* 18 (May 1939): 133-60; Altmeyer, *The Formative Years*, pp. 88-99; and *The Statutory History of the United States: Income Security*, ed. Robert Stevens, pp. 214-24.

41. Cited in "Congress Looks at Social Security," Ibid., pp. 140-41.

42. "Congress Looks at Social Security," *The Congressional Digest*, pp. 141-44. *Final Report of the Advisory Council on Social Security*. Senate Doc. No. 4, 76th Cong., 1st Sess. (10 Dec. 1938).

43. For an alternative view for why benefits were paid out early, the 1938 advisory council argued that this would have the "social advantage in enhancing public understanding of the method of contributory social insurance." U.S. Advisory Council on Social Security, *Final Report* (10 Dec. 1938), p. 37.

44. *Cong. Rec.* (10 May 1937), pp. 4262-63.

45. See U.S. Advisory Council on Social Security, *Final Report*, 10 Dec. 1938 (Washington, D.C.; The Social Security Board, 1938). For more on their backgrounds, see Witte, *The Development of the Social Security Act*, and McKinley and Frase, *Launching Social Security*.

46. Advisory councils were appointed by the Senate Committee on Finance in 1947, and by the Department of Health, Education, and Welfare (HEW) in 1953. The amendments of 1956 contained a provision for the periodic appointment of an advisory council to study financing. Under this provision, the secretary of HEW appointed a council in 1957 and 1963. Since 1966 advisory councils have been appointed each four years. See Myers, *Social Insurance and Allied Government Programs*, pp. 58-59. On the politics of advisory councils, see Derthick, *Policymaking for Social Security*, pp. 89-109.

47. Sanders, *The Impact of Reform Movements*, p. 91.

48. Excerpts from the hearings and floor debates are contained in *The Statutory History of the United States: Income Security*, ed. Robert Stevens, pp. 223-45; and are discussed along with the reports of the two committees in Altmeyer, *The Formative Years*, pp. 100-113. For a sampling of the floor debates, see *Cong. Rec.* (6 June 1939), pp. 6849-83; (9 June 1939), pp. 6889-6942; (10 June 1939), pp. 6951-70; (11 July 1939), pp. 8826-54; (12 July 1939), pp. 8913-25; and (13 July 1939), pp. 8995-9031. See also "Congress Looks at Social Security," *The Congressional Digest*, and Sanders, *The Impact of Reform Movements*, pp. 82-97.

49. Statement by Abraham Epstein, 10 Dec. 1937, cited in Sanders, *The Impact of Reform Movements*, pp. 91-92.

50. Statement by Francis Townsend in "Congress Looks at Social Security," *Congressional Digest*, p. 158.

51. See, in particular, exchanges between Senators Vandenberg, Schwellenbach, and Norris, *Cong. Rec.* (17 March 1937), pp. 2324-30. During this exchange, Vandenberg presented a list of the sixty largest insurance companies in the country who agreed that a social insurance system did not need a full reserve "to accomplish the result which we [Congress] desire."

52. A number of critics likened the pay-as-you-go system to mutual assessment plans or life-insurance plans, which typically had very low initial premiums, then steadily rising premiums. As the systems "matured," the eventual premiums were, in some cases, too high to interest participants and thus too high to pay promised benefits. See statement by Senator Schwellenbach, *Cong. Rec.* (17 March 1937), pp. 2327-28; and Edwin Witte, "Old-Age Security in the Social Security Act," *Journal of Political Economy* 45 (Feb. 1937), pp. 1-44.

53. *Cong. Rec.* (17 March, 1937), p. 2330.

54. U.S. Social Security Board, *Annual Report, 1936-1937*, p. 23. See also *Annual Report, 1935-1936*, p. 14; and *Annual Report, 1937-1938*, pp. 36-38. At that time the board recognized only one alternative to the reserve principle—current financing out of general revenues. For that reason, it concluded that "the question of whether we should have a reserve system or a pay-as-you-go system cannot be decided without considering the whole theory of the present plan, particularly as it concerns the interrelationship between earnings and benefits." U.S. Social Security Board, *Annual Report, 1935-1936*, p. 14.

55. U.S. Social Security Board, *Annual Report, 1937-1938*, p. 37.

56. Arthur J. Altmeyer, "Future of Social Security in America" (Address before the Institute of Public Affairs, Univ. of Va., 17 July 1937), p. 8; and "Progress and Prospects under the Social Security Act" (address before the National Conference of Social Workers, 25 May 1936), pp. 9-10.

57. Recommendations detailed in U.S. Social Security Board, *4th Annual Report* (Washington, D.C.: Federal Security Administration, 1940). A contingency fund, the alternative to an actuarial reserve fund,

was one large enough to cover current expenditures with allowance for unexpected changes in cash flow.

58. "Social Security Act Amendments of 1939," *U.S. Statutes at Large,* 76th Cong., 1st Sess., Vol. 53, Part 2, pp. 1360-1402. For a detailed description of the amendments, see John D. Corson, "Explanation of Federal OASI Under the Social Security Act Amendments of 1939," Bulletin No. 17, 26 Aug. 1939, in *Director's Bulletin of Progress: 1938-1940* (unpublished memos by director of Bureau of OASI, Library, U.S. Department of Health, Education, and Welfare). See also, U.S. Social Security Board, *5th Annual Report, 1939-1940,* and *Statutory History of the United States: Income Security,* ed. Robert Stevens, pp. 246-53.

59. For more on the political difficulties associated with constraining a social insurance program designed to provide "adequate" incomes for the elderly, see F. A. Hayek, *The Constitution of Liberty,* pp. 285-305.

60. According to Altmeyer, minority members of the Ways and Means Committee considered the elimination of the refund provisions as "confiscatory." Altmeyer, *The Formative Years,* p. 106. During fiscal year 1938-39 there were 93,000 claims for refunds at age sixty-five, totaling $6.5 ($39) million, and 119,000 claims for death benefits, totaling $7.9 ($47) million. The cumulative total of these benefits was $20.2 ($120) million. U.S. Social Security Board, *4th Annual Report, 1938-1939,* p. 29.

61. If a person pays taxes periodically over his working life but does not accumulate enough covered quarters or have high enough wages, he may receive no benefits from Social Security.

Also, while the 1939 amendments provided refunds to workers who had paid more than the maximum tax payment because of having more than one job, there was no such provision for the employer's share of the tax. As is the case today, there is no refund of the employers' share of taxes paid on workers' earnings above the taxable ceiling, accrued on second jobs. There is, therefore, no true maximum tax payment. Moreover, the income earned above the ceiling and the excess taxes paid as a result of second jobs are not credited toward future benefit eligibility.

62. Regardless of income class, the married worker who would retire with only three to five years of coverage had benefit increases scheduled to exceed 100 percent. Benefit increases then scaled down reaching less than 5 percent for married workers retiring forty years hence. The largest gains were made by persons with average monthly earnings less than $100 (median covered monthly earnings in 1940 were only $62). The pay-as-you-go nature of the system permitted a postponement of these costs well into the future. Discrimination against married women eligible for benefits as retired workers has existed since the 1939 amendments introduced wives' benefits.

63. Cited in "Congress Looks at Social Security," *The Congressional Digest,* p. 144.

64. For an interesting discussion of the continuous increase in tax rates necessary to finance a hypothetical old-age pension program on a current-cost basis (from .03 percent of taxable payroll in the first year, to a long-run rate of 14.54 percent), see Robert Myers, "Application of the Concept of Individual Equity for Young New Entrants under a National Pension System." None of this increase in rates is due to program expansion or economic and demographic change.

65. Edwin Witte, "Old-Age Security in the Social Security Act," in *Social Security Perspectives: Essays by Edwin Witte,* ed. Robert Lampman (Madison: Univ. of Wisc. Press, 1962), p. 130.

66. Ibid., p. 130. For two other clear statements of the political consequences of moving from a reserve system to a pay-as-you-go public retirement system, based on a great deal of experience with such programs at the state, city, and local level, see "Public Service Retirement Systems in the U.S.," *Bulletin of the U.S. Bureau of Labor Statistics,* no. 491 (Aug. 1929), pp. 542-44, and no. 477 (Jan. 1929), pp. 2-3; and Paul Studensky, *The Pension Problem and the Philosophy of Contributions* (New York: Pension Publishing, 1917).

67. For an interesting discussion of the political incentives of taxpayers and beneficiaries, and the effect of the program and its administrators in creating a constituency for expansion, see William Mitchell, *The Popularity of Social Security* (Washington, D.C.: American Enterprise Institute, 1977).

68. The argument advanced here that the introduction of a pay-as-you-go system would adversely affect voting decisions on the size and nature of the compulsory insurance program is based on the differential information requirements and political power of voter coalitions that characterize the two fiscal systems. Even with a passive bureaucracy and a relatively well-informed electorate, and without differential political power of voter coalitions, majority voting can be expected to generate "too large" social insurance budgets—larger budgets than a funded system. The extent to which the funded and pay-as-you-go budgets diverge is then enhanced by the presence of costly information and differential voter participation rates.

For an elaboration on the operation of a pay-as-you-go system, see Edgar Browning, "Social Insurance and Intergenerational Transfers," *Journal of Law and Economics* 16 (Oct. 1973): 215-73, and "Why the Social Insurance Budget is Too Large in a Democracy," *Economic Inquiry* 13 (Sept. 1975): 373-88.

69. According to the 1935 act, the fund was intended to grow to the point that by 1980, interest alone would have produced 40 percent of the revenues needed for benefit payments. Current tax receipts would have met the balance. By that time expenditures were projected to have stabilized at 10 percent of taxable payroll. A switch to a pay-as-you-go system, with no change in benefit expenditures, thus implied an eventual 10 percent tax rate as opposed to the maximum scheduled rate of 6 percent. According to the 1939 amendments, the existing tax rate of 2 percent (1937-39) was "frozen" at that rate for three more years, without provision for offsetting increases later. Rather than adopting a pay-as-you-go or "contingency" reserve system, they more accurately simply abandoned the objective of accumulating a fund. The war years, for example, led to a sizable build-up of revenues in excess of current benefits. See Edwin Witte, "Old-Age Security in the Social Security Act," in *Social Security Perspectives: Essays by Edwin E. Witte*, ed. Robert Lampman, (Madison: Univ. of Wisc. Press, 1962), pp. 128-29; and Robert Myers, *Social Security* (Homewood, Ill.: Richard D. Irwin, 1975), pp. 135-65.

70. A "level premium" assumption is made here for simplicity, although there are any number of other ways to finance a funded system. See Myers, *Social Security*, pp. 135-56. See also his discussion of the various definitions of "actuarial soundness."

71. This assumes, of course, the government fund is invested in private securities.

One cannot ignore the costs imposed on the individual by coercing him to adjust to a collectively determined compulsory program. For those who wished to save more than federally mandated each year, however, the program would be completely neutral in its impact on individual choice. (This last statement does assume that there are no problems associated with the asymmetrical taxation of capital income and earnings under Social Security and problems of the risk composition of alternative portfolios.)

72. Specifically, the constraint would be that the market rate of interest equal a weighted average of the rates of return paid under Social Security, where the weights are equal to the proportion of covered workers earning that return.

73. It is also possible that the choice of a funded program, with the private insurance comparison, would condition some notions of equity that would limit the extent of intragenerational transfers.

74. Milton Friedman used the "chain-letter" analogy in Wilbur Cohen and Milton Friedman, *Social Security: Universal or Selective?* Rational Debate Seminars, no. 5 (Washington, D.C.: American Enterprise Institute, 1972), p. 24. Assuming individuals have independent utility functions, the pay-as-you-go system will generate overlarge budgets, where the funded system is taken as benchmark.

75. Even under the 1935 act, all or virtually all workers alive were expected to get unearned benefits on their combined tax payments. This was because the tax rate rose slowly to its maximum, but benefit schedules were designed to yield actuarially fair benefits on the assumption that workers had paid, on average, a 5 percent tax during their entire working lives. For more on this subject, see Witte, "Old-Age Security in the Social Security Act," reprinted in *Social Security Perspectives*, pp. 122, 133-36.

A second conceptual advantage of this sort of program is that the return payable on tax payments may possibly exceed that attainable with the fund if the growth rate of the wage base exceeds the market rate of interest. However, the average rate of return payable to a generation, the real rate of growth of wages, averaged only 3.2 percent from 1956 to 1976, as compared to a real pretax return on capital investment of 9 to 16 percent. (During periods of rapid coverage expansion, of course, the rate of growth of the taxable wage base is considerably higher than overall wages.) See Alicia Munnell, *The Future of Social Security*, Brookings Studies in Social Economics (Washington, D.C.: The Brookings Institute, 1977), p. 128.

76. For a similar argument relating to the burden of the public debt, see J. M. Buchanan, *Public Principles of Public Debt* (Homewood, Ill.: Richard D. Irwin, 1958), and Buchanan and Wagner, *Democracy in Deficit: The Legacy of Lord Keynes* (New York: Academic Press, 1977).

77. This prediction follows directly from the intergenerational models of growth and capital accumulation applied to Social Security. See, for example, Martin Feldstein, "Social Security, Induced Retirement, and Aggregate Capital Accumulation," *Journal of Political Economy* 72 (Sept. 1974), pp. 905-25. This issue is discussed in detail in Chapter 9.

78. Likewise, to the extent voters believe incorrectly that Social Security is funded, their opposition to current period expansion (tax increases) may be further reduced as this would simply reflect a collective decision to "save" more federally.

79. Text of President Franklin D. Roosevelt's Message to Congress, 16 Jan. 1939, in "Congress Looks at Social Security," *Congressional Digest*, pp. 140-41. Bismarck (who advocated the use of the split payroll tax for social insurance in Germany) utilized the insurance terminology as well. In his words, "Our lack of experience in these matters [taxing employees and employers] has induced us to be very careful about the necessary *contributions* . . . the present bill is intended to keep the sense of human dignity alive . . . [the worker] should feel that he is no mere eleemosynary, but that he possesses a fund which is his very own."

"Speech on Practical Christianity" (1914), cited in Marjorie Shearon, *Wilbur Cohen: The Pursuit of Power* (Washington, D.C.: Gray Printing, 1967), p. 4.

80. The Supreme Court declared that covered employees had a "noncontractual interest that cannot be soundly analogized to that of a holder of an annuity, whose rights to benefits are bottomed on his contractual premium payments." Flemming vs. Nestor, 363 U.S. 603, 1960.

81. See Eveline M. Burns, "Private and Social Insurance and the Problem of Social Security," in *Analysis of the Social Security System: Hearings before a Subcommittee on Ways and Means*, House of Representatives, 83rd Cong., 1st Sess., No. 38458 (Washington, D.C.: Government Printing Office, 1954), p. 1475. For more on the differences between private and social insurance, see Joseph Pechman, Henry Aaron and Michael Taussig, *Social Security: Perspectives for Reform* (Washington, D.C.: The Brookings Institute, 1968), pp. 69-77, and Myers, *Social Insurance and Allied Government Programs*, pp. 8-10.

82. It seems evident that the private insurance analogy, which accounts for the program's sustained popularity, has created enough confusion over the impact of the program that rationalizations for changes based on social adequacy arguments have been integrated into defenses of the system on equity grounds. The program, however, has shown these two goals to be inconsistent.

Chapter 7. Coverage Expansion and Program Proliferation: 1940-60

1. Ellen Woodward, "Social Security Today and Tomorrow," address before the Mississippi Conference of Social Workers, 29 April 1943 (unpublished addresses by members of the Social Security Boards, Library, U.S. Department of Health, Education, and Welfare), p. 2.

For a book of great value on this period see Altmeyer, *The Formative Years in Social Security*. Altmeyer (who retained the top appointed position in Social Security for eighteen years, 1936-53) chronicles, from his own perspective, the legislative and political history and administration of social security from its inception in 1934 through 1954. Although perhaps influenced by his resignation in 1953 and the incoming Republican Administration, Altmeyer singles out the period 1934-54 as defining the "formative" years in Social Security. In his view, "The events of those years determined the major characteristics of our social security system as it exists today (1965)." Ibid., p. 256.

2. Sanders, *Impact of Reform Movements*, p. 101. Beginning in 1940, the Social Security Board was no longer an independent agency. The Federal Reorganization Act of 1939 created the Federal Security Agency to administer the Board, the U.S. Public Health Service, the Office of Education, the Civilian Conservation Corps, and the National Youth Administration.

3. *Report of the Social Security Board for 1943: Social Security During and After the War*, reprinted in *Statutory History of the United States: Income Security*, ed. Robert B. Stevens, pp. 267-68.

4. *Annual Report of the Federal Security Agency, 1945*, reprinted in ibid., pp. 300-302.

5. For historical statistics, see Social Security Administration, *Social Security Bulletin: Annual Statistical Supplement, 1977-79* (Washington, D.C.: Government Printing Office, 1980), pp. 101, 104-05.

6. Ibid., pp. 80-81. See also Table 7.3 below.

7. Congressional Quarterly Service, *Congressional Quarterly Almanac* 6 (1950): 140, and 10 (1954): 188.

8. The three major objectives of the original act (limited coverage, benefits closely related to earnings, and a program financed on a funded basis) are stated in U.S. Social Security Board, *Annual Report: 1935-1936*, p. 14.

9. Myers, *Social Security and Allied Government Programs*, p. 140-41. For the individual with average earnings retiring in 1940, combined employee-employer tax payments would have purchased a private annuity yielding $6.50 per year. The annual benefit for a sixty-five-year-old male retiring under Social Security was $271. See Donald Parsons and Douglas Munro, "Intergenerational Transfers in Social Security," in *The Crisis in Social Security: Problems and Prospects*, ed. Michael Boskin (San Francisco: Institute for Contemporary Studies, 1978), pp. 74-75. These issues are discussed more fully in Chapter 9.

10. In 1955 average annual earnings in covered employment were 31 percent lower than average annual earnings in all employment. See Social Security Administration, *Social Security Bulletin: Annual Statistical Supplement, 1973*, p. 66, and U.S. Department of Commerce, *Statistical History of the U.S.*, p. 164.

11. U.S. Advisory Council on Social Security, *Final Report of the Advisory Council on Social Security: 1948* (Washington, D.C.: Federal Security Administration, 1948), p. 6.

12. A more sophisticated argument used today is that the reduction in poverty due to Social Security (and the resulting reduction in general revenue expenditures) is a public good for which all workers ought to contribute. This argument makes very clear the redistributive nature of the program. In either case, it would

appear to be the case that "bureaucrats see in the failure of their preceding measures a proof that further inroads into the market system are necessary." Ludwig von Mises, *Bureaucracy* (New Rochelle, N.Y.: Arlington House, 1939), p. 31.

13. See, for example, the Republican Party Platform in 1936, 1944, and 1952, in John Corson and John McConnell, *Economic Needs of Older People* (New York: Twentieth-Century Fund, 1956), pp. 133-36. See also Altmeyer, *Formative Years of Social Security*, pp. 209-55.

14. Newspaper and magazine vendors were excluded from coverage and a narrower definition of "employee" was introduced. See *The Statutory History of the U.S.: Income Security*, ed. Robert Stevens, pp. 318-19, and Altmeyer, *The Formative Years*, pp. 152-68.

The appointment of the Advisory Council on Social Security by Senate resolution in 1947 confronted expansionists with concern because they believed employer interests were too strongly represented. Six of the seventeen appointed members were, in fact, from private industry, but represented varying degrees of "employer interests." Folsom, who later became the secretary of HEW, was on the committee representing employers, as he had done in 1934 and 1938. In addition, the "citizens advisory committee" included Douglas Brown, a consultant to the Social Security Board and member of the 1934 and 1938 advisory councils, as well as Frank Bane, former executive director of the Social Security Board.

15. See, for example, Edwin Witte, "Social Security and Free Enterprise," an address at the Kansas State Teachers' College, 13 April 1950 (unpublished addresses, Library, U.S. Department of Health, Education and Welfare), and Altmeyer, *The Formative Years*, pp. 169-70. In his address Witte said that during the past two years a "great outcry has been raised that the quest for social security is undermining our economy of free enterprise and threatens freedom itself." This complaint, he said, had never been more strongly advanced. Ibid., p. 1.

16. Altmeyer, *The Formative Years*, pp. 169-70.

17. Daniel Holland, *Private Pension Funds: Projected Growth* (New York: National Bureau of Economic Research, 1966), p. 19.

18. Witte, "Social Security and Free Enterprise," p. 8. In the words of Arthur Altmeyer, commissioner of social security, "to me it seemed that the events of 1949 would be decisive as to whether the old-age and survivors' insurance system would survive as a contributory, wage-related system." Altmeyer, *The Formative Years*, p. 169.

19. *Fourth Annual Message to Congress* (5 Jan. 1949), reprinted in *Statutory History of the U.S.: Income Maintenance*, ed. Robert Stevens, p. 350.

20. *Annual Budget Message of the President* (10 Jan. 1949), reprinted in ibid., pp. 350-51.

21. The 1948 Advisory Council recommended liberalizing the determination of insurance and benefit eligibility status, liberalizing benefit formulas, increasing benefits, postponing scheduled tax-rate increases, and raising the tax ceiling. Also, the council recommended extending coverage to farm workers, household workers, and employees of nonprofit organizations excluding churches, federal civil service, armed forces, and state and local governments. The advisory council added that voluntary coverage was only "defensible" if the federal government was constitutionally unable to compel certain groups of workers to pay taxes, i.e., state and local governments. See U.S. Advisory Council on Social Security, *Final Report: 1948*, p. 8.

22. For a general discussion of the amendments and the debates surrounding their enactment, see Sanders, *Impact of Reform Movements*, pp. 103-07. Also see *Congressional Quarterly Almanac* 5 (1949): 288-92 and 6 (1950): 165-77.

23. *Congressional Quarterly Almanac* 5 (1949): 288-92; and 6 (1950): 165-77. See also Lewis Meriam, Karl T. Schlotterbeck, and Mildred Maroney, *The Cost of Financing Social Security* (Washington, D.C.: The Brookings Institute, 1950). The House Ways and Means Committee and the Senate Finance Committee together produced five thousand pages of hearings.

24. *Congressional Quarterly Almanac* 5 (1949): 289.

25. For purposes of comparison, figures calculated in 1980 dollars are given in parentheses.

26. Federal Security Administration, *Annual Report: 1951* (Washington, D.C.: The Federal Security Administration, 1952), and *Congressional Quarterly Almanac* 6 (1950): 166. The benefit increase exceeded the rate of inflation by 1.5 percent. The tax ceiling was not, in real terms, raised above its 1935 level until 1967.

Expenditures financed by increases in the tax ceiling (rather than tax increases) impose no additional cost on covered workers with earnings less than the ceiling. Instead, the full cost of additional expenditures, which are distributed more heavily toward low-average earners, is shifted to the minority of workers who earn more than the previously existing tax ceiling. As such, ceiling hikes, as regularly endorsed by congressional liberals and lobbies such as AFL-CIO, transferred the burden of expenditures onto those persons who could have best employed private savings institutions and generated windfall gains to current beneficiaries, the near-elderly, and most workers.

27. Whereas the number of elderly persons receiving old-age assistance doubled from 1.1 million to 2.8 million between 1936 and 1950, the continued liberalization of eligibility requirements and the increase in minimum benefits payable under the OASI program led to a steady decline in the absolute number of old-age assistance recipients after 1950. *Annual Report of the Federal Security Administration: 1951*, p. 4, 23; and Social Security Administration, *Social Security Bulletin: Annual Statistical Supplement, 1973*, p. 157.

28. *Annual Report of the Federal Security Administration: 1950*, p. 17, and *Annual Report of the Federal Security Administration: 1951*, pp. 11-13. The Federal Reorganization Plan of 1946 abolished the Social Security Board within the FSA. Arthur Altmeyer, former chairman of the Social Security Board, became the commissioner of social security.

29. The benefit increase outpaced the rate of inflation by 3 percent. In instances where this was not the case, previous benefit increases typically more than offset forthcoming price increases. See Table 8.1. For a discussion of congressional legislation and debates surrounding the 1952 amendments, see *Congressional Quarterly Almanac* 8 (1952): 140-42; and Altmeyer, *The Formative Years*, pp. 195-208.

30. For example, there were no major bills before the Ways and Means Committee, and extensive hearings on social security had already been held. Also, R. L. Doughton, chairman of the Ways and Means Committee, who sponsored the original social security bill in 1935 and also the pending bill, was due for retirement at the end of the session. It was deemed appropriate by some congressmen, therefore, to enact some final legislation in his honor. See Sanders, *The Impact of Reform Movements*, pp. 107-09.

31. The following year Altmeyer prepared a memorandum for the incoming federal security administrator in which he informed her that one matter that had to be considered by the newly appointed Advisory Council was the disability freeze which—having never been instituted—he said, was nearing expiration! Altmeyer, *The Formative Years*, p. 213.

32. *Congressional Quarterly Almanac* 9 (1953): 199-200.

33. Ibid., p. 199.

34. U.S. Congress, House Ways and Means Committee, Subcommittee on Social Security, Staff, *Social Security After 18 Years*, A Staff Report to Honorable Carl T. Curtis, chairman of the subcommittee, 83rd Cong., 2nd Sess. (1954).

35. *Congressional Quarterly Almanac* 9 (1953): 200.

36. Ibid., For a lengthy and personal discussion of this exchange, see Altmeyer, *The Formative Years*, p. 221-37.

37. *Congressional Quarterly Almanac* 9 (1953): 200.

38. Ibid.

39. Arthur Altmeyer, *The Formative Years*, p. 234.

40. *Social Security Bulletin: Annual Statistical Supplement, 1975*, pp. 57, 69.

41. The Administration's proposals are described in more detail in the *Congressional Almanac* 9 (1954): 189-90. See also ibid., pp. 190-94, and Altmeyer, *The Formative Years*, pp. 239-55, for an account of the hearings, lobby stands, and the various drafts of the bill.

42. In Altmeyer's view, the inclusion of farm operators was vitally important in the history of the program by securing its future. Altmeyer said, "The farm group exercises political power far in excess of its number and . . . when its attitude coincides with the attitude of organized labor, the combined effect is decisive." He went on to say that this probably made the eventual creation of medical insurance much more certain as well. See *The Formative Years*, p. 248.

43. The President had recommended instituting a permanent public assistance formula as a means of protecting states' rights and reducing congressional discretion in increasing the matching rate. To make their feelings on this proposal clear, all Democratic senators sponsored a bill to extend the existing public assistance formula for another two years. *Congressional Quarterly Almanac* 9 (1954): 188-90.

44. For a summary of the debates and congressional action on the 1956 amendments, see *Congressional Quarterly Almanac* 12 (1956): 392-97.

45. See Myers, *Social Insurance Expansionism*, on incrementalism as a key method used by the bureaucracy to expand the basic program.

46. Meriam, Schlotterbeck, and Maroney, *The Cost and Financing of Social Security*, pp. 19-20.

47. Ibid., p. 22.

48. *Congressional Quarterly Almanac* 12 (1956): 392-95. HEW was created in 1953. Secretaries during the Eisenhower Administration included Oveta Culp Hobby, Marion Folsom, and Arthur Flemming.

49. *Congressional Quarterly Almanac* 12 (1956): 392-93, *Social Security Bulletin: Annual Statistical Supplement, 1975*, pp. 15-31, and Charles Schottland, "Social Security Amendments of 1956: A Legislative History," *Social Security Bulletin* 19 (Sept. 1956): 3-15.

50. For more on this, see U.S. Congress, Committee on Finance, *Issues Related to Social Security Act*

Disability Programs, 96th Cong., 1st Sess. (1979). Interestingly, Social Security actuaries predicted that by 1970 DI benefit payments would run between their low- and high-cost estimates of $572 million and $1.1 billion. Actual DI benefit payments exceeded $1.1 billion in the program's sixth year, and by 1970, the program was spending more than $3 billion in benefits. See Robert Myers, "OASI: Financing Basis and Policy under the 1956 Amendments," *Social Security Bulletin* 19 (Sept. 1956), p. 17; and *Social Security Bulletin: Annual Statistical Supplement, 1975*, p. 6.

51. U.S. Advisory Council on Financing, *Financing OASDI* (Washington, D.C.: U.S. Department of Health, Education and Welfare, 1959). For more on the 1958 amendments, see *Congressional Quarterly Almanac* 14 (1958): 156-59.

52. Ibid.

53. Ibid.

54. According to the 1935 act, benefits were to be calculated on the basis of covered earnings accrued from 1937 until the time of retirement. In 1950 benefits were to be calculated on the basis of average covered earnings from 1950 until retirement. In 1954 workers were allowed to ignore four years of low earnings in their calculations, and in 1956 they were permitted to ignore five years. Social Security Administration, *History of the Provisions of OASDHI: 1935-1973*, p. 3.

Concerning the "retirement" or "earnings" test, under the original act, no earnings were permitted without precluding the entire monthly benefit. An exempt amount of earnings was introduced in 1939, and raised in 1950, 1952, and 1954. In 1950 age seventy-five was introduced as the age at which the test would no longer be applied, and this age was lowered to seventy-two in 1954. It was not until 1960 that a benefit-reduction rate was introduced to determine the rate at which monthly benefits would be cut as earnings exceeded the exempt amount. *Social Security Bulletin: Annual Statistical Supplement, 1975*, p. 29. A liberalization of the retirement test was a means to induce groups with late retirement ages to accept compulsory coverage. Altmeyer, for example, encouraged a member and former chairman of the Senate Finance Committee in 1954 to reduce the age limitation and introduce a benefit increment for late retirement to induce farm operators to accept coverage. Altmeyer, *The Formative Years*, p. 246.

55. An increase in the rate of federal sharing or in the reimbursable limit was enacted in 1946, 1948, 1952, and 1958. In 1950 new assistance programs were introduced for the permanently and totally disabled and for the reimbursement of medical payments. See *Welfare Reform Proposals*, Legislative Analysis No. 4 (Washington, D.C.: American Enterprise Institute, 17 May 1971), pp. 3-9, for a summary of this expansion in the federal role.

56. *Social Security Bulletin: Annual Statistical Supplement, 1975*, p. 57.

57. The nonlegislative revenue sources were wage and employment growth, and interest income on assets. Legislative sources were coverage expansion, tax increases, and tax-ceiling increases.

Chapter 8. The Realization of Social Security's Redistributive Potential: 1960-73

1. *Congressional Quarterly Weekly Report* (30 July 1965): 1493.

2. Social Security Administration, *Social Security Bulletin: Annual Statistical Supplement, 1975*, p. 65.

3. Social Security Administration, *Social Security Bulletin: Annual Statistical Supplement, 1977-79*, p. 87.

4. U.S. Bureau of the Census, *The Statistical History of the United States* (1976): 10.

5. Social Security Administration, *Social Security Bulletin* 40 (May 1977): 46.

6. "Social Welfare Expenditures, 1976," *Social Security Bulletin* 40 (Jan. 1977): 5-7, and Social and Rehabilitation Service, *Trend Report: Graphic Presentation of Public Assistance and Related Data, 1966* (Washington, D.C.: Department of Health, Education, and Welfare, 1967), p. 11.

7. For example, Russell Long (D.-La.), chairman of the Senate Finance Committee, was an ardent supporter of increasing the minimum OASDI benefit and liberalizing eligibility, policies which tended to transfer costly state-welfare responsibilities to the federal insurance titles of the Social Security program. His stands are not surprising given that in 1973, Louisiana ranked second in the country for the number of elderly receiving old-age assistance and fifty-first in the country for the number receiving OASDHI benefits. Per 1,000 elderly people in Louisiana 328 were receiving old-age assistance in 1973, compared to the national average of 89 out of 1,000. See Social Security Administration, *Social Security Bulletin: Annual Statistical Supplement, 1973*, p. 50.

8. In 1940, 21.7 percent of the elderly were receiving old-age assistance. This proportion fell steadily, reaching 8.9 percent in 1973. Social Security Administration, *Social Security Bulletin: Annual Statistical Supplement, 1975*, p. 57.

9. For several informative sources on the history of the health-insurance movement, see Lubove, *The Struggle for Social Security*, pp. 66-90; Witte, *The Development of the Social Security Act*, pp. 173-89; Theodore Marmor, *The Politics of Medicare* (Chicago: Aldine, 1970); Eugene Feingold, *Medicare: Policy and Politics* (San Francisco: Chandler, 1966); Odin Anderson, "Compulsory Medical Care Insurance, 1910-1950," in *Medicare Policy and Politics*, pp. 86-95; and *Statutory History of the U.S.: Income Security*, Robert Stevens, ed.

10. Lubove, *The Struggle for Social Security*, pp. 65-71.

11. For a statement of this view, see Frederick von Hoffman, *More Facts and Fallacies on Compulsory Health Insurance* (Newark: Prudential Press, 1919).

12. Cited in Marmor, *The Politics of Medicare*, p. 7.

13. Organized labor's early opposition to compulsory insurance is discussed by Sanders, *The Impact of Reform Movements on Social Policy Change: The Case of Social Insurance*, pp. 131-34; Lubove, *The Struggle for Social Security*, pp. 15-18; Irving Bernstein, *A History of the American Worker: 1920-1933, The Lean Years* (Boston: Houghton Mifflin, 1960), pp. 237-38; and Louis Reed, *The Labor Philosophy of Samuel Gompers* (Port Washington, N.Y.: Kennikat Press, 1966), pp. 115-17, 178, 180.

14. Witte, *The Development of the Social Security Act*, pp. 173-89.

15. Marmor, *The Politics of Medicare*, p. 30.

16. For a discussion of the legislative developments preceding the 1960 amendments, see *Congressional Quarterly Almanac* 16 (1960): 148-65. From a broader historical perspective, the developments from 1960-65 are discussed in Feingold, *Medicare: Policy and Politics*, pp. 101-55.

17. *Congressional Quarterly Almanac* 16 (1960): 152.

18. Ibid., p. 153.

19. Ibid., p. 153.

20. Ibid., p. 148. On the metamorphosis of Eisenhower's and Flemming's views, see Feingold, *Medicare: Policy and Politics*, pp. 104-07.

21. For more on the 1960 amendments, see *Congressional Quarterly Almanac* 16 (1960): 148-50; Wilbur Cohen and William Habar, "The Social Security Act Amendments of 1960: An Analysis of the Provisions of the Legislation and Its Potentialities," in *Social Security: Programs, Policies, and Problems*, ed. William Habar and Wilbur Cohen, pp. 579-91.

22. *Congressional Quarterly Almanac* 17 (1961): 258.

23. For purposes of comparison, figures calculated in 1980 dollars are given in parentheses. For more on the 1961 amendments, see ibid., pp. 257-61; and Wilbur Cohen, "Summary of the 1961 Amendments to the Social Security Act," in *Social Security: Programs, Problems, and Policies*, pp. 593-95.

In 1962 no changes were made in the OASDI program, but a fairly extensive welfare program was enacted that incorporated changes in the public assistance titles of the Social Security Act. The Public Welfare Amendments of 1962 (HR 10606) called for an increase in aid to the needy as well as the introduction of rehabilitation programs designed to reduce future public assistance costs. Passed by Congress with little serious debate, the federal matching rate for public assistance was increased for the tenth time. See *Congressional Quarterly Almanac* 18 (1962): 212-18.

24. Feingold, *Medicare: Policy and Politics*, pp. 101-55. In the words of President Kennedy, the proposal was based on the "fundamental premise that contributions during the working years, matched by employers' contributions, should enable people to prepay and build earned rights and benefits to safeguard them in their old age." *Congressional Quarterly Almanac* 19 (1963): 234.

25. *Congressional Quarterly Almanac* 20 (1964): 231-32.

26. The Administration's cost estimates were based on the erroneous assumption that hospital costs would increase at the same rate as earnings; see ibid., pp. 231-32. This assumption was still used in the 1970s. See "Report by the Panel of Actuaries to the Subcommittee on Cost Estimates and Financial Policy," in the *Report of the 1971 Advisory Council on Social Security* (Washington, D.C.: U.S. Department of Health, Education, and Welfare, 1971), p. 124.

27. *Congressional Quarterly Almanac* 20 (1964): 232-37.

28. *Congressional Quarterly Almanac* 21 (1965): 54.

29. Ibid., pp. 66, 340. See also Feingold, *Medicare: Policy and Politics*, pp. 139-42.

30. The conference report was supported by House Republicans by a narrow margin (70-68), and opposed by Senate Republicans (13-17). *Congressional Quarterly Weekly Report* (30 July 1965), p. 1493. The 1965 Advisory Council on Social Security recommended instituting hospital insurance, increasing the number of years during which children would be eligible for benefits, increasing the tax ceiling, weighting the benefit formula toward lower-income persons, and expanding coverage to doctors. All of these recommendations were enacted in 1965. See U.S. Advisory Council on Social Security, *Status of the*

Social Security Program and Recommendations for Its Improvement (Washington, D.C.: U.S. Department of Health, Education, and Welfare, 1965).

31. Marmor, *Medicare: Policy and Politics*, pp. 5, 28-32. Every aspect of the elderly's income, wealth, and health were the subject of a vast number of controversial studies at this time, most of which relied on quite speculative survey data. For a sampling of study findings and the resulting controversies, see ibid., pp. 24-63.

32. The National Council of Senior Citizens, an active lobby group for Social Security which numbered two million in 1965, was already demanding an elimination of deductibles and coinsurance terms, the extension of the program to cover prescription drugs, and the extension of Medicare benefits to the disabled. See *Congressional Quarterly Almanac* 22 (1966): 1300.

33. Judith M. Feder, *Medicare: The Politics of Federal Hospital Insurance* (Lexington, Mass.: Lexington Books, 1977), p. 111.

34. For more on this subject, see *Medicare and Medicaid: Problems, Issues, and Alternatives*, Report of the Staff to the Committee on Finance, U.S. Senate, 91st Cong., 1st Sess. (9 Feb. 1970).

35. *Congressional Quarterly Weekly Report* (1966); p. 633; and *Congressional Quarterly Almanac* 22 (1966); 547-89.

36. *Congressional Quarterly Weekly Report* (27 Jan. 1967), pp. 124-25. By the time the 1967 benefit increase became effective in February 1968, prices had risen 9.2 percent since the last benefit increase.

37. For more on lobby stands, see *Congressional Quarterly Weekly Report* (1967), pp. 340-41, 497-98, and 590-91.

38. See Committee on Ways and Means, U.S. House of Representatives, *Summary of Provisions of HR 12080: The "Social Security Amendments of 1967,"* 90th Cong. (7 Aug. 1967), and *Congressional Quarterly Weekly Report* (22 Dec. 1967); pp. 2598-2601.

39. In constant (1980) dollars, this was an increase from $16,296 in 1967 to $18,483 in 1968, relative to the real ceiling in 1935 of $17,964.

40. Coverage was extended in 1954 to the self-employed except professional doctors, lawyers, dentists, and other medical groups. In 1956 compulsory coverage was extended to the professional self-employed except doctors. Doctors were not covered until 1965. See Social Security Administration, *Social Security Bulletin: Annual Statistical Supplement, 1973*, p. 15. Moreover, in 1965 average annual earnings for covered wage and salary workers were two-thirds the average for covered self-employed. See ibid., p. 66.

41. Social Security Administration, *Social Security Bulletin: Annual Statistical Supplement, 1975*, p. 88; and U.S. Bureau of Census, *Statistical History of the U.S.* (1976), p. 10.

42. American Enterprise Institute, *Social Security Amendments*, Reprint of Legislative Analysis no. 14, p. 21.

43. Ibid., p. 22. Under the proposal for indexing Social Security, if prices increased at least 3 percent over the course of the year, an equivalent increase in Social Security benefits was to be reflected in checks mailed out the following year. The ceiling on taxable earnings, beginning with a base of $9,000, was to be indexed to increases in average earnings. There was no symmetrical provision for benefit reductions if prices fell, and no provision for tax rate adjustments.

44. *Congressional Record* (21 May 1970): 4669.

45. What had been the case historically was that larger than cost-of-living benefit increases, which were legislated one year to offset some expected future inflation, were met the following year by cries of an "erosion of purchasing power for persons on fixed incomes" as prices began to rise. This naturally led to an increase in real benefits over time. Although indexing would make this process more apparent, it could not eliminate this course of events. As the "crisis" in Social Security was announced shortly after the enactment of indexing, this did not prove to be a problem.

46. For a discussion of the double-indexing, see Colin D. Campbell, *Over-Indexed Benefits: The Decoupling Proposals for Social Security*, Domestic Affairs Study No. 46 (Washington, D.C.: American Enterprise Institute (May 1976), pp. 5-6; "Propping Up Social Security," *Business Week*, 19 July 1976, p. 36; Alicia H. Munnell, *The Future of Social Security*, Brookings Studies in Social Economics (Washington, D.C.: The Brookings Institution, 1977), pp. 32-40; and Robert Kaplan, *Indexing Social Security* (Washington, D.C.: American Enterprise Institute, 1977).

47. See "Social Welfare Expenditures, Fiscal Year 1976," *Social Security Bulletin* 40 (Jan. 1977): 5-7; and Social and Rehabilitative Service, *Trend Report: Graphic Presentation of Public Assistance and Related Data*, p. 11.

48. See *Congressional Quarterly Almanac* 25 (1969): 814-40; American Enterprise Institute, *The Pending Social Security Amendments of 1970*, Legislative Analysis No. 14 (Washington, D.C.: American Enterprise Institute, 7 Oct. 1970); and American Enterprise Institute, *Welfare Reform Proposals*, Legislative Analysis No. 4; for detailed examinations of the legislative developments in 1969-70.

49. *Congressional Quarterly Almanac* 25 (1969): 840.

50. See American Enterprise Institute, *The Pending Social Security Amendments of 1970*, Legislative Analysis No. 14; and *Social Security Amendments of 1970*, Legislative Analysis No. 5 (19, May 1971); and *Congressional Quarterly Weekly Report* (1971), p. 1367. The 1970 Amendments (HR 17750) were reported out of the Ways and Means Committee in 1970 without provision for automatic adjustments. It was not until Jackson Betts (R.-Ohio) moved to recommit the bill to the committee for inclusion of such a provision that the Ways and Means Committee took positive action.

51. See *Congressional Quarterly Almanac* 27 (1971): 421-25. Since January 1970, the time of the last benefit increase (15 percent), prices had only increased 5.9 percent.

52. For the details of the bill, see *Congressional Quarterly Weekly Report* (1971), pp. 1367, 1449; and *Congressional Quarterly Almanac*, 27, pp. 519-25.

53. *Congressional Quarterly Almanac* 27 (1971): 525, and *Congressional Quarterly Weekly Report* (17 June 1972), pp. 1495-99.

54. *Congressional Quarterly Weekly Report* (17 June 1972), pp. 1495-99.

55. Ibid. (17 June 1972), p. 1495; and (8 July 1972), pp. 1702-03.

56. *Congressional Quarterly Weekly Report* (1972), p. 1630; and *Congressional Quarterly Almanac* 28 (1972): 399-403.

57. *Congressional Quarterly Almanac* 28 (1972): 402. The Advisory Council recommended benefit increases, particularly for the minimum benefit, to insure that no recipient was below the poverty line, larger widow(er) benefits, liberalized eligibility requirements for disability insurance, a liberalized earnings test, extended Medicare coverage to include the disabled, and more services to be covered by Medicare. To finance the changes and to put the system on a pay-as-you-go basis, the council recommended increasing the ceiling on taxable earnings and reducing future tax rates. That is, it proposed a tax-rate schedule that actually declined through the twenty-first century, then rose rapidly. A pay-as-you-go system, the council said, allowed the postponement "well into the next century, [of] any increases in the contribution rates for a cash benefit program with benefits adjusted to price changes." 1971 Advisory Council on Social Security, *Reports on Old-Age, Survivors, and Disability Insurance, and Medicare Programs* (Washington, D.C.: U.S. Department of Health, Education and Welfare, 1971), p. 90.

58. *Congressional Quarterly Weekly Report* (1972): 1752, and *Congressional Quarterly Almanac* 28 (1972): 399. This constituted a 14 percent increase in real benefit levels since the last benefit increase a year earlier.

59. In Rep. Byrne's words: "If you insist on voting a 20 percent Social Security benefit increase without any study by the Ways and Means Committee of the soundness of the fundamental concepts involved in the financing provided, it may well mark a turning point in the capacity of the Social Security system to respond with equity to the needs of our older people." Ibid., pp. 402-03.

60. *Congressional Quarterly Weekly Report* (7 Oct. 1972), pp. 2628-29, (28 Oct. 1972), p. 2804, and *Congressional Quarterly Almanac* 28 (1972): 899-914.

61. The increment provision was an attempt to mitigate demands for eliminating the retirement test. Officials recognized that the complete elimination of the test, as demanded by the elderly and income redistributionists, would have been quite costly.

62. As Senator Gerry of Rhode Island remarked in April 1939, "When Uncle Sam offers the helping right hand of financial assistance to a state, he extends at the same time a grasping left hand toward the administrative jurisdiction of the sovereign beneficiary." Cited in "Should the Powers of the Federal Government be Increased?" *The Congressional Digest* 19 (1939): 221.

63. *Congressional Quarterly Almanac* 29 (1973): 543, 550, 570-80.

64. Ibid.

65. For a summary of the amendments, see ibid., pp. 570-80.

66. Ibid. By the time the 11 percent increase went into effect prices had increased 16.4 percent since the last benefit increase.

67. *Cong. Rec.* (14 Nov. 1973), pp. 9988-89.

68. Ibid., p. 9995.

69. On the problems with the 1972 adjustment mechanism, see *Social Security Financing*, prepared by the Staff, Committee on Finance, U.S. Senate, 95th Cong., 1st Sess. (June 1977); Colin D. Campbell, *Over-Indexed Benefits: The Decoupling Proposals for Social Security* (Washington, D.C.: American Enterprise Institute, 1977); Robert J. Kaplan, *Indexing Social Security: An Analysis of the Issues* (Washington, D.C.: American Enterprise Institute, 1977); "Propping Up Social Security," *Business Week*, 19 July 1976, pp. 34-43, and Robert J. Kaplan, *Financial Crisis in the Social Security System* (Washington, D.C.: American Enterprise Institute, 1977).

70. The 1971 Advisory Council on Social Security actually reported that the Social Security program

was overfinanced and would eventually have accumulated reserves near $1 trillion (by the year 2025). They recommended, therefore, financing the program so that trust fund reserves would be kept to approximately one year's expenditures in order to alleviate this "unnecessary and undesirable" accumulation. It was this information that, in part, contributed to the significant liberalization of the program in 1972. See 1971 Advisory Council on Social Security, *Reports on OASDI and Medicare* (Washington, D.C.: 1971), pp. 91-92, 124-33. The Subcommittee on Cost Estimates and Financial Policy of the Advisory Council included Otto Eckstein, Arnold Harberger, Murray Latimer, Wendell Milliman, and Nancy Teeters.

Chapter 9. The Nature and Dimensions of Crisis

1. Hearings before the Committee on Ways and Means on HR4120, U.S. House of Representatives, 74th Cong., 1st Sess., p. 899.

2. William Simon, "How to Rescue Social Security," *Wall Street Journal*, 3 Nov. 1976, p. 20.

3. Hearings before the Subcommittee on Social Security, U.S. House of Representatives, 97th Cong., 1st Sess. (28 May 1981).

4. Sections of this chapter are published in Carolyn L. Weaver, *Understanding the Sources and Dimensions of Crisis in Social Security: A First Step Toward Meaningful Reform* (Washington, D.C.: Fiscal Policy Council, 1981).

5. On an "open-group basis." See A. Haeworth Robertson, *The Coming Revolution in Social Security* (McLean, Va.: Security Press, 1981), pp. 86-90, 98-100; and *Social Security Financing*, prepared by the Staff of the Committee on Finance, U.S. Senate, 97th Cong., 1st Sess. (Sept. 1981), p. 26.

The actuarial deficit is quite distinct from the system's accrued liability, which measures the present value of benefits that are owed—that is, all benefits that have been earned by the act of paying taxes but have not yet been paid. Estimated at approximately $4-5 trillion, the unfunded accrued liability for OASDHI is the amount of money that would have to be combined with existing trust-fund balances and invested today in order to pay off, as they come due, all the benefits that have already been earned by beneficiaries and taxpayers and to which they are yet entitled. The unfunded liability conveys information on the difference between social insurance and private insurance, and the inability of the pay-as-you-go system to operate like a funded system. On the differences between actuarial deficits, accrued liabilities, and unfunded liabilities, see A. Haeworth Robertson, "OASDI: Fiscal Basis and Long-Run Cost Projections," *Social Security Bulletin* vol. 40, no. 1 (Jan. 1977): 25, and Robert Myers, *Social Security* (Homewood, Ill.: Richard D. Irwin, 1975), Chapter 4.

6. *1979 Annual Report of the Board of Trustees of the Federal OASDI Trust Funds*, p. 31.

7. Hearings before the Subcommittee on Social Security, U.S. House of Representatives, 97th Cong., 1st Sess. (28 May 1981).

8. Taxable payroll is an adjusted figure so that, for example, if expenditures are anticipated to be 10 percent of taxable payroll, then 10 percent is roughly the combined employee-employer tax necessary to finance those expenditures. A deficit of 2 percent of taxable payroll, moreover, can be eliminated by increasing the combined tax rate by two percentage points. For comparison purposes taxable payroll in the economy in 1981 is $1.3 trillion or 40 percent of GNP.

9. None of the long-run cost projections take account of the trend toward withdrawal from Social Security by state and local government employees. The trend has accelerated in recent years, with the number of employees giving notice of intention to withdraw exceeding the number becoming newly covered for the first time in 1977 and 1978. See Rita R. Campbell, *Social Security: Promise and Reality* (Stanford, Calif.: Hoover Institution Press, 1977), p. 289, and *1979 Annual Report of the Board of Trustees of the Federal OASDI Trust Funds*, p. 41.

10. For several informative sources on the development of the financial crisis in Social Security, see Robert S. Kaplan, *Financial Crisis in the Social Security System* (Washington, D.C.: American Enterprise Institute, 1976); J. W. Van Gorkom, *Social Security—The Long-Term Deficit* (Washington, D.C.: American Interprise Institute, 1976); Edward Cowan, "Background and History: The Crisis in Public Finance and Social Security," in *The Crisis in Social Security: Problems and Prospects*, ed. Michael Boskin (San Francisco: Institute for Contemporary Studies, 1977), pp. 1-15; and Alicia H. Munnell, *The Future of Social Security* (Washington, D.C.: The Brookings Institution, 1977).

11. Also enacted was a liberalization of the retirement-earnings test and benefit eligibility conditions for widow(er)s and divorcees, along with a freezing of the minimum benefit. For more on the 1977 amendments, see *Social Security Amendments of 1977, Public Law 216, 95th Congress*, prepared by the Staff of the Subcommittee on Social Security, U.S. House of Representatives, 95th Cong., 1st Sess. (3

April 1978); *Social Security Financing*, prepared by the Staff of the Committee on Finance, U.S. Senate, 96th Cong., 1st Sess. (Feb. 1980); John Snee and Mary Ross, "Social Security Amendments of 1977: Legislative History and Summary of Provisions," *Social Security Bulletin* 41 (March 1978): 3-20; A. Haeworth Robertson, "Financial Status of Social Security Program After the Social Security Amendments of 1977," *Social Security Bulletin* 41 (March 1978): 21-30; and Colin D. Campbell, *The 1977 Amendments to the Social Security Act* (Washington, D.C.: American Enterprise Institute, 1978).

Additional amendments were enacted in 1980 that reduced projected expenditures, especially in disability insurance, and realigned revenues into the three trust funds. See *Legislative Review Activity*, Report of the Committee on Finance, U.S. Senate, 97th Cong., 1st Sess. (19 Jan. 1981), Senate Report No. 97-1.

12. Kaplan, *Financial Crisis in the Social Security System*, pp. 5-7.

13. According to A. H. Robertson, Chief Actuary of the SSA from 1975 to 1978, the "steadily growing cost" of Social Security and other employee benefit programs, "may well be developing into an unsustainable burden. . . . It seems highly unlikely that the active working population, already chafing under the yoke of today's burden, will be able and willing to assume the heavier burden tomorrow." Echoing a similar theme, recently resigned commissioner of social security, Stanford Ross argued the need for recognizing "the limits of Social Security" and the need for stimulating the spread of private pensions. See A. Haeworth Robertson, "Providing for Social Security," *Wall Street Journal*, 6 Sept. 1978, p. 22; and "Social Security Commissioner Departs with Strong Views of System's Future," *Wall Street Journal* 31 Dec. 1979, p. 8.

14. For two informative books of readings on the economic aspects of the crisis in Social Security, see *Social Security versus Private Saving*, ed. George M. von Furstenberg (Cambridge, Mass.: Ballinger Publishing Co., 1979), and *The Crisis in Social Security*, ed. Boskin.

15. For surveys of these studies and discussions of the economic problems at hand, see Colin D. Campbell and Rosemary G. Campbell, "Conflicting Views on the Effect of Old-Age and Survivors Insurance on Retirement," *Economic Inquiry*, 14 (Sept. 1976): 369-88; Michael J. Boskin, "Social Security and Retirement Decisions," *Economic Inquiry* 15 (Jan. 1977): 1-6; and Munnel, *The Future of Social Security*, pp. 62-83.

16. Munnell, *The Future of Social Security*, pp. 63-64.

17. W. Kip Viscusi and Richard J. Zeckhauser, "The Role of Social Security in Income Maintenance," in *The Crisis in Social Security*, ed. Boskin, p. 56.

18. Campbell and Campbell, "Conflicting Views," pp. 379-80.

19. Michael Boskin, "Social Security: The Alternatives Before Us," in *The Crisis in Social Security*, ed. Boskin, p. 175; and Munnell, *The Future of Social Security*, p. 62.

20. Based on statistics compiled by Bureau of Census and reviewed by Campbell and Campbell in "Conflicting Views," pp. 374-77. See also Munnell, *The Future of Social Security*, pp. 69-71 and Colberg, *The Retirement Test*, pp. 43-46.

21. U.S. Advisory Council on Social Security, 1978-1979, "Normal Retirement Age," *Report on Public Hearings: Background Papers* (Department of Health, Education, and Welfare, Sept. 1978), p. 3.

22. Even the findings of the SSA, however, showed a marked increase in voluntary retirement since the 1960s. The first survey, conducted in 1941-42, concluded that only 3-6 percent of the Social Security beneficiaries retired voluntarily in order to enjoy leisure. Similar results were reported for a 1940-47 and 1951 survey. By 1963 findings were considerably different, with 19 percent of the men retiring at sixty-five having done so voluntarily. Preliminary findings from a survey in the early 1970s indicate that 52 percent of the men who retired at sixty-four or sixty-five did so voluntarily. For a discussion of these findings and also a skeptical view of the relatively small effect of Social Security on the retirement decision implied by the SSA surveys, see Campbell and Campbell, "Conflicting Views," pp. 372-73. See also, Munnell, *The Future of Social Security*, pp. 68-69.

23. William G. Bowen and T. Aldrich Finegan, *The Economics of Labor Force Participation* (Princeton, N.J.: Princeton Univ. Press, 1969); Boskin, "Social Security and Retirement Decisions"; and Viscusi and Zeckhauser, "Social Security in Income Maintenance," pp. 56-59. See Richard E. Barfield and James N. Morgan, *Early Retirement: The Decision and the Experience and a Second Look* (Ann Arbor: Univ. of Mich., Survey Research Center, 1974); and Joseph F. Quinn, "The Microeconomics of Early Retirement" (Ph.D. dissertation, MIT, 1975), for two studies which find health and retirement benefits to be mutually important.

24. Boskin, "Social Security and Retirement Decisions," p. 19, and Boskin, "Social Security: The Alternatives Before Us," p. 176.

25. Campbell, *Social Security: Promise and Reality*, p. 203.

26. Sherwin Rosen, "Social Security in the Economy," in *The Crisis in Social Security*, ed. Boskin, pp. 100-103; and Viscusi and Zeckhauser, "Social Security in Income Maintenance," pp. 56-60, stress this point.

27. Rosen, "Social Security in the Economy," p. 101. On the history and politics of the earnings test, see Marshall Colberg, *The Social Security Retirement Test: Right or Wrong?* (Washington, D.C.: American Enterprise Institute, 1978), and Rita R. Campbell, *Social Security: Promise and Reality* (Stanford, Calif.: Hoover Institution Press, 1977), pp. 199-224.

28. See Martin Feldstein, "Social Security, Induced Retirement, and Aggregate Capital Accumulation," *Journal of Political Economy* 82 (Sept./Oct. 1974): 905-26, for the initial statement of this view. See also Rosen, "Social Security and the Economy," pp. 93-95.

29. Martin Feldstein, "Social Security, Induced Retirement and Aggregate Capital Accumulation: A Correction and Update," National Bureau of Economic Research, Working Paper No. 579 (Nov. 1980), pp. 10-11.

30. Although the retirement effect was initially discussed by Feldstein, it has been the focus of Munnell's work. See, in particular, Alicia Munnell, "The Impact of Social Security on Personal Savings," *National Tax Journal* 27 (Dec. 1974): 553-57, and *The Effect of Social Security on Personal Savings* (Cambridge, Mass.: Ballinger Publishing, 1974).

31. Martin Feldstein, "The Social Security Fund and National Capital Accumulation," in *Funding Pensions: Issues and Implications for Financial Markets*, Conference Series No. 16 (Boston: Federal Reserve Bank of Boston, 1976), p. 37.

32. See Alicia Munnell, "Private Pensions and Savings: New Evidence," *Journal of Political Economy* 84 (Oct. 1976): 1013-32; Martin Feldstein, "Social Security and Private Savings: International Evidence in an Extended Life Cycle Model," in *The Economics of Public Services*, an International Economics Association Conference Volume, ed. M. Feldstein and R. Inman; (London: The Macmillan Press Ltd. 1977); and Feldstein and Anthony Pellechio, "Social Security and Household Wealth Accumulation: New Microeconometric Evidence," Harvard Institute of Economic Research, Discussion Paper Number 530 (Jan. 1977).

33. See Robert Barro, "Are Government Bonds Net Wealth?" *Journal of Political Economy* 82 (Nov./Dec. 1974): 1095-1117, and Gary Becker, "A Theory of Social Interaction," *Journal of Political Economy* 82 (Nov./Dec. 1974): 1063-93.

34. See Rosen, "Social Security and the Economy," pp. 95-97, for an intuitive and more detailed discussion and critique of this effect. Barro's argument has been challenged on theoretical grounds by William Buiter, "Government Finance in an Overlapping Generations Model with Gifts and Bequests," in *Social Security versus Private Savings*, ed. George von Furstenberg (Cambridge, Mass.: Ballinger, 1979), pp. 395-425.

35. Robert Barro, *Social Security and Private Saving—Evidence from the U.S. Time Series* (Washington, D.C.: American Enterprise Institute, 1978). In addition, the empirical work testing the hypothesis that government deficits are equivalent to current taxes by Levis Kochin is also offered in support of Barro's theoretical argument. See Levis Kochin, "Are Future Taxes Anticipated by Consumers?" *Journal of Money Credit and Banking* 6 (Aug. 1974): 385-94.

36. Louis Esposito, "Effect of Social Security on Saving: Review of Studies Using U.S. Time Series Data," *Social Security Bulletin* 41 (May 1978): 9-17.

37. For responses to the Esposito article by Barro, Darby, Feldstein, and Munnell, see "Social Security and Private Saving: Another Look," *Social Security Bulletin* 42 (May 1979): 33-40. For a critical reevaluation of the empirical work by Kochin on debt neutrality, see William Buiter and James Tobin, "Debt Neutrality: A Brief Review of Doctrine and Evidence," in *Social Security versus Private Saving*, pp. 39-63.

38. Michael Darby, *The Effects of Social Security on Income and the Capital Stock* (Washington, D.C.: American Enterprise Institute, 1979), p. 79.

39. N. Bulent Gultekin and Dennis Logue, "Social Security and Personal Saving: Survey and New Evidence," in *Social Security versus Private Saving*, p. 97.

40. See Robert Myers, "Application of the Concept of Individual Equity for Young New Entrants Under a National Pension System Financed on a Current-Cost Basis," *Proceedings*, 21st International Congress of Actuaries, Zurich (June 1980).

41. Refers to OASDI and combined taxes of employers and employees. Robert J. Myers, *Social Security and Allied Government Programs* (Homewood, Ill.: Richard D. Irwin, 1975), pp. 140-42, and *Social Security*, pp. 212-26.

42. Refers to OAI. Colin D. Campbell, "Social Insurance in the United States: A Program In Search of an Explanation," *Journal of Law and Economics* 12 (Oct. 1969): 252-54.

43. Refers to expected returns at retirement to worker-only beneficiaries under OAI. Alan Frieden, Dean Leimer, and Ronald Hoffman, "Internal Rates of Return to Retired Worker-Only Beneficiaries under Social Security, 1967-1970," *Studies in Income Distribution*, HEW Publication No. (SSA) 77-11776 (Washington, D.C.: Department of Health, Education and Welfare, 1977), pp. 16-20.

44. Ball, *Social Security: Today and Tomorrow*, p. 333.

45. Feldstein, "The Social Security Fund," p. 43.

46. It is Feldstein's central thesis that by perpetuating the pay-as-you-go system, society foregoes the opportunity to invest at substantially higher returns. Additional investment in the corporate sector capital stock, he argues, would yield a real pre-tax return of about 12 percent. Feldstein, ibid., pp. 46-47.

47. Myers, *Social Security*, p. 210.

48. On the treatment of women relative to men, see Campbell, *Social Security: Promise and Reality*, pp. 83-124; Marilyn R. Flowers, *Women and Social Security: An Institutional Dilemma* (Washington, D.C.: American Enterprise Institute, 1977); and "History and Development of Dependents' and Survivors' Benefits," *Background Materials for the National Commission on Social Security* (Washington, D.C.: Library, Social Security Administration, 1979).

49. See Freiden, Leimer, and Hoffman, "Internal Rates of Return," pp. 16-20.

50. Orlo R. Nichols and Richard G. Schreitmueller, "Some Comparisons of the Value of a Worker's Social Security Taxes and Benefits," Actuarial Note No. 95, HEW Pub. No. (SSA) 78-11500 (April 1978). The latter study refers to OASDI.

51. Myers, *Social Security*, p. 216. The very poor expected returns for young higher paid workers actually prompted Robert Ball to propose that general revenues be used to improve returns! Ball, *Social Security: Today and Tomorrow*, pp. 333-34.

52. Joseph A. Pechman, "The Social Security System: An Overview," in *The Crisis in Social Security*, p. 33. The heavy burden of the payroll tax on the poor has been partially offset by the refundable income credit enacted in 1975. For more on this subject, see Colin D. Campbell and William D. Peirce, *The Earned Income Credit* (Washington, D.C.: American Enterprise Institute, 1980).

53. James M. Buchanan, "Social Insurance in a Growing Economy: A Proposal for Radical Reform," *National Tax Journal* 21 (Dec. 1968): p. 386.

54. Campbell, "Social Insurance in the U.S.: A Program in Search of an Explanation."

55. Robert Myers, *Social Security*, p. 210.

56. See Robert Ball, *Social Security: Today and Tomorrow*, pp. 421-47, 456-87.

57. See Statement by Betty Duskin, National Council of Senior Citizens, "Social Security Issues," Hearings before the Committee on Ways and Means, U.S. House of Representatives (21 July 1977); and Larry Smedly (AFL-CIO), "Maintaining the Balance in Social Security," *American Federationist* (Feb. 1979), pp. 20-25, and "Sound Financing for Social Security," *American Federationist* (June 1977): 15-17. For a survey of proposals for general revenue financing, see, for example, Louis Esposito and David Podoff, *General Revenue Financing*, Staff Paper No. 33 (Washington, D.C.: Department of HEW, 1978).

58. See Campbell, *Social Security: Promise and Reality*; Rita R. Campbell, "Is Social Security's Future Secure?" Reprint Series No. 10 (Stanford, Calif.: Hoover Institution); and Simon, "How to Rescue Social Security," p. 20.

Among this group there would also be proponents of price indexing. Correctly designed, price indexing would lead to a slower rate of growth of the program than wage indexing and to gradually declining replacement rates over time. See Robert Kaplan, *Indexing Social Security: An Analysis of the Issues* (Washington, D.C.: American Enterprise Institute, 1977).

59. See Martin Feldstein, "The Optimal Financing of Social Security," Discussion Paper No. 338 (Harvard University, 1974); Martin Feldstein, "Toward Reform of Social Security," *Public Interest* (Summer 1975), pp. 75-95; Brittain, *The Payroll Tax for Social Security*; Munnell, *The Future of Social Security*, pp. 127-33; and Charles McLure, "Financing Social Security: VAT vs. the Payroll Taxes," prepared for the Conference on Social Security Financing, SSA, Washington, D.C. (21-22 April 1980).

The rarely argued position of maintaining the status quo is presented in Robert Myers, "Expansion or Contraction: Serious Side Effects," *Annals, AAPSS*, no. 433 (May 1979): pp. 63-71.

60. For more on this, see Stanford Ross, "Social Security: A Worldwide Issue," *Social Security Bulletin* 42 (Aug. 1979), pp. 3-10.

61. See Hayek, "Social Security;" James Buchanan and Colin Campbell, "Voluntary Social Security," *Wall Street Journal* (20 Dec. 1966), p. 14; Buchanan, "Social Insurance in a Growing Economy"; and

Roger L. Miller, "Social Security: The Cruelest Tax," *Harpers* (June 1974), pp. 22-27. See also Dan Orr, "Social Security's Problems," *Wall Street Journal* (9 July 1979), p. 17; and Charles Hobbs and Stephen Powlesland, *Retirement Security Reform* (Concord, Vt.: Institute for Liberty and Community, 1975).

62. Funding is endorsed in Feldstein, "The Social Security Fund and National Capital Accumulation"; Boskin, "The Alternatives Before Us"; and Daniel Orr, "Toward Necessary Reform of Social Security," *Policy Review* (Fall 1977), pp. 47-65. Boskin goes on to argue that there would then be no sound reason for preventing individuals from purchasing their insurance privately.

63. To build up a fund that is invested in new government bonds does not deal with the capital accumulation problem. Instead, it would involve an increase in revenues to the federal government which might then be utilized in any number of ways inconsistent with Social Security.

Once funded, moreover, it is certainly not a matter of indifference whether or not there is public or private supply. Private supply by a large number of competing firms has the clear advantage of decentralizing the investment decision.

64. In content, this proposal is like that of Buchanan and Campbell, and Miller whereby the federal government issues bonds to the SSA for the full amount of the system's outstanding debt, and then individuals are offered the right to leave the system, taking with them claims to future income. In both cases, the debt becomes a general obligation of the government, rather than one that is focused on young covered workers.

65. For an informative discussion of pension-fund legislation and its effect on industry performance, see Dennis Logue, *Legislative Influence on Corporate Pension Plans* (Washington, D.C.: American Enterprise Institute, 1979).

66. Buchanan and Campbell, "Voluntary Social Security."

67. On the flexibility and adaptability inherent to private provision which produced continuous historic improvement in the pension field, see Peter Drucker, *The Unseen Revolution: How Pension Fund Socialism Came to America* (New York: Harper and Row, 1976), pp. 167-70.

68. Hayek, *The Constitution of Liberty*, p. 304.

69. On the history and development of private pensions, see for example, William Greenough and Francis King, *Pension Plans and Public Policy* (New York: Columbia University Press, 1976); and Norman Ture, *The Future of Private Pension Plans* (Washington, D.C.: American Enterprise Institute, 1976). A modified form of "contracting out" has been adopted in the United Kingdom, and mandatory private pension systems, in addition to a basic level of Social Security protection, have been adopted in the Netherlands, Switzerland, and Sweden. See Max Horlick and Alfred Skolnik, *Mandating Private Pensions: A Study of European Experience*, Research Report No. 51 (Washington, D.C.: Department of HEW, 1978).

70. Gene Koretz, "The Social Security Bomb Is Still Ticking," *Business Week* (9 Jan. 1978).

Index

Dr. Carolyn Weaver is a professional staff member with the U.S. Senate Finance Committee, working in the areas of social security, welfare and unemployment compensation, and is senior advisor to the National Commission on Social Security Reform. She is on leave from Virginia Polytechnic Institute and State University where she is a member of the economics department and has been a research associate of the Center for Study of Public Choice. Prior to assuming her position at Virginia Tech, Dr. Weaver taught at Tulane University. She received her Ph.D. in Economics from Virginia Tech in 1977 and her B.A. from Mary Washington College in 1973.

Dr. Weaver has authored and coauthored a series of papers in professional journals dealing with the economics of bureaucracy and the economics and politics of social security. She is the author of *Understanding the Sources and Dimensions of Crisis in Social Security: A First Step Toward Meaningful Reform.*